D1713983

Middle Grades Education

A REFERENCE HANDBOOK

CONTEMPORARY EDUCATION ISSUES

Middle Grades Education

 A REFERENCE HANDBOOK

edited by

Pat Williams-Boyd

A B C ☰ C L I O

Santa Barbara, California • Denver, Colorado • Oxford, England

Copyright © 2003 by Pat Williams-Boyd

Library of Congress Cataloging-in-Publication Data
Williams-Boyd, Pat.
   Middle grades education : a reference handbook / Pat Williams-Boyd, editor.
      p.   cm — (Contemporary education issues)
Includes bibliographical references and index.
ISBN 1-85109-510-1 (hardcover : alk. paper)
   1. Middle school education—Handbooks, manuals, etc.   I. Title. II. Series.
LB1623.W55 2003
373.236—dc22   2003019563

06   05   04   03   02   10   9   8   7   6   5   4   3   2   1

This book is also available on the World Wide Web as an e-book. Visit abc-clio.com for details.

ABC-CLIO, Inc.
130 Cremona Drive, P.O. Box 1911
Santa Barbara, California 93116-1911
This book is printed on acid-free paper ∞.
Manufactured in the United States of America

*To Blanche and Dell Williams,
who unconditionally supported, guided, and
believed in their children and who by virtue of
their own lives taught us the greater lessons of
wisdom and of persistent strength, of purpose,
and of our Higher Power. It has been a long journey
from the back hills of Tennessee and from
the long-ago villages of our once-proud people,
and yet it was perhaps only just over the next rise.*

❧ Contents

⚫⊸ Series Editor's Preface

The Contemporary Education Issues series is dedicated to providing readers with an up-to-date exploration of the central issues in education today. Books in the series will examine such controversial topics as home schooling, charter schools, privatization of public schools, Native American education, African American education, literacy, curriculum development, and many others. The series is national in scope and is intended to encourage research by anyone interested in the field.

Because education is undergoing radical if not revolutionary change, the series is particularly concerned with how contemporary controversies in education affect both the organization of schools and the content and delivery of curriculum. Authors will endeavor to provide a balanced understanding of the issues and their effects on teachers, students, parents, administrators, and policymakers. The aim of the Contemporary Education Issues series is to publish excellent research on today's educational concerns by some of the finest scholar/practitioners in the field while pointing to new directions. The series promises to offer important analyses of some of the most controversial issues facing society today.

Danny Weil
Series Editor

⚫➤ Preface and Acknowledgments

The notion of an educational organization based primarily on human development is unique in the grand scope of American education. Although some ideas are borrowed from other historical and educational programs, middle grades schools reflect in philosophy, organization, program implementation, and instructional practice the only authentically student-centered schooling American students experience.

As knowledge of the development of young adolescents, or transescents, has evolved, so too has middle grades education. Based on the understanding of transescents' cognitive, social, emotional, physical, and moral growth, middle grades schools have responded with teaching and instructional practices, classroom and school environments, and student-teacher relationships that are quite different from their elementary and secondary counterparts.

No longer is this time frame looked at as a phase to simply endure or, as some have written, a time period during which little learning takes place, but rather it is considered an exciting and stimulating period in young lives, a time during which kids are making important life decisions. Young adolescents are at once capricious children and mature adults, fluctuating between the two from moment to moment. They are vibrant, talented, curious, and compassionate people who need only the opportunity to demonstrate the good they can do in the world.

Although we recognize that schooling prepares the student for the next level, we look at middle grades education not only as preparation for high school but as a collection of dynamic learning experiences that challenge all students to realize their hopes, to reach for their dreams, to fulfill both the moment and their futures. And for the professional called to be a middle grades teacher, there could be no greater gift than to participate in the lives of so many youngsters, to help all students succeed.

This text is written by teachers who have dedicated their professional careers to middle grades kids. Together, we examine the differences between traditional junior high schools and high-performing middle grades schools; seminal studies that describe quality learning environments for transescents; the developmental characteristics of ten to fourteen year olds and the implications for practice; the defining characteristics of middle grades schools as organizations; the role of the family, of the trained middle grades teacher, and of the community; the education of adolescents as young citizens; and particular research-based best instructional practice and curriculum. We conclude with an annotated bibliography of organizations, conferences, researchers, and print and nonprint resources.

This book has been forged in the lives of many people—students, teachers, parents. Each author stands on someone else's shoulders as he or she advocates on behalf of middle grades students and their families.

- To all of our students, thank you for sharing your lives, your joy, your curiosity, your struggle, and your willing-ness to believe that we really care about you.
- To our colleagues who support us and believe in the power of learning to change lives
- To Dr. Valerie Janesick, scholar, mentor, educator, col-league, student of the world, and friend, for your selfless encouragement and abiding guidance.

Pat Williams-Boyd

Chapter One

⚬⟶ **Overview**

Pat Williams-Boyd

Jason, an eighth-grade student wearing baggy ragged jeans, a dirty T-shirt, and a purple porcupine haircut, grudgingly sits slumped in a chair outside the principal's junior high school office. He has skipped school for three days and, now back, finds himself being punished with a three-day suspension. Jason will have lost six irretrievable days of education. Questions such as Why did he skip? What is going on at home? What is getting in the way of his learning? How can the school help? are never asked. Rather, because of an undiagnosed learning problem, school absences, and his appearance, he is seen as a problem student, one with whom the school must particularly work to "get him to conform," to follow the rules, to fit in along with 600 other young adolescents, most of whom feel anonymous, part of a crowd. Often they are even disrespectfully spoken of as existing in the magnified hormonal phase of life, one their parents and teachers hope to survive.

For Jason, who struggles to read and who enjoys little if any success, school is anathema. His father—just released from jail and in a drunken state—had beat his wife into unconsciousness in front of Jason and his younger siblings. After taking all the family's money, the father left, leaving Jason to care for his three younger brothers and nurse his mother back to health. That was what Jason was doing for the three days he was out of school.

Jason's story is not unusual in today's social milieu. Those of us who have spent over thirty years in public education have seen too many similar situations. The names change and particular events are a bit different, but the results in the lives of children are the same, just as are the challenges they pose to the neighborhood school. The wide variance of student social and human service needs, abilities and disabilities, experiences and deprivations, possibilities and disenfranchisements, family support and isolation, and hope and despair poses little less than a daunting task to the nation's schools. Yet, public schools throw open their arms to all students and their families and say "come."

Are there schools that meet students' basic needs and then succeed in capturing and maximizing their talents? Are there schools that have helped young people like Jason begin to dream again and to realize their dreams? Are there schools where the worth of young adolescents is measured simply by the integrity of the individual human personality, schools where who students are and what they need in order to succeed academically and socioemotionally are the factors that drive what schools do and how they function?

Are there schools where the family is embraced as a viable and intrinsically important part of a student's education? Are there schools where every young adolescent's culture, beliefs, perceptions, heritage, and orientations are celebrated? Are there schools where adults function not only as teachers but also as mentors, role models, and advocates for their students and families, schools where the health needs of a student must be met before the academic needs can be addressed? Simply put, yes. And they are most often called middle schools.

JUNIOR HIGHS AND MIDDLE SCHOOLS

Even though middle schools usually include the same age group (usually ten to fourteen year olds) as their junior high school counterparts, the similarities end there. To critically understand middle schools in theory, in program structure, and in instructional practice, a comparative analysis between the junior high and the middle school is useful.

Junior high schools contend that their primary purpose is to prepare students for high school. Some researchers believe students do not learn or retain much knowledge during this period of explosive growth. They would argue that junior high schools are little more than holding areas intended to maintain adolescents and mold their behavior in preparation for the "real" academic learning that awaits them. They frequently see young adolescents as existing in the period of *sturm und drang,* or storm and stress, a season to be weathered. Middle schools, however, celebrate this period, when adolescents are a wonderful blend of capricious children and mature young adults, as a time of natural development.

Each structure looks at the individual student differently; each has its own scaffold of understanding. Although the junior high builds its work around content-specific information, the middle school constructs everything it does and the ways in which it does it around the rigorous developmental understanding of the child or transescent. In other words, the middle school grounds its instructional practice, its interrelationships, its expectations, its programs, and its purposes in how middle grades students think and learn most effectively, how they make sense of the world around them, and how they see themselves. All learning is then connected to these understandings. In both settings the same information is learned, but in the middle school it is understood more personally and more deeply because of its relevance to the student's life (Table 1.1).

Eighth-grade students study symmetry in transformational geometry. Rather than listening while the junior high teacher lectures about mirror images, middle schoolers find examples of symmetry in different areas. The student who loves nature finds images of butterflies and seashells. Another enjoys cultural artifacts and finds a variety of symmetrical masks from around the world. Yet another student is interested in heraldry and examines flags and family crests while car buffs take pictures of different kinds of hubcaps. Have all students learned about symmetry? Yes. But some will retain knowledge longer than others. On the one hand, a single teaching strategy—primarily lecture. On the other, teachers connecting subject content to their students' experiences and using a variety of instructional formats, including inquiry-based cooperative learning, action research, critical questioning, concept-based learning, and differentiated instruction.

Junior highs are content driven and teacher directed, whereas middle schools are developmentally organized and student centered. Where junior highs construct artificial barriers between learning segments by scheduling separate fifty-five-minute classes in various subjects, in which teachers alone make decisions about their classrooms, middle schools believe that knowledge and learning are both integrative and exploratory. They contend that deep understanding is constructed through active, hands-on student learning. They provide flexible chunks of time about which an interdisciplinary team of teachers, who share the same students, make decisions according to the requirements of specific tasks. With the support of the principal, who serves as

4

Table 1.1

Junior High–Middle School Comparison

Junior High School	Middle School
1. Focus is on preparation for high school	1. Focus is on developmentally appropriate practice
2. Little real learning occurs	2. Real learning is driven by curiosity and connections
3. Sees students as developmentally conflicted	3. Sees students as experiencing a normal developmental period
4. Pre-adolescence is to be endured	4. Pre-adolescence is seen as transescence—a transitional time to be celebrated
5. Subject centered	5. Student centered
6. Emphasizes the students' responsibility to learn	6. Emphasizes the teacher's responsibility to create relevant connections between the students' world and the content
7. Teacher directed	7. Teacher and students are collaborators in learning
8. Lecture method is predominant	8. Varied instructional practices are common
9. Emphasis on cognitive development	9. Emphasis on cognitive and affective development
10. Primary mode of instruction is lecture	10. Primary mode of instruction is constructivist discovery using multiple tools
11. Focus is on mastery of basic knowledge	11. Focus is on exploration and creative experimentation on the factual level on the conceptual level across content areas
12. Class work and school activities emphasize competition	12. Class work and school activities emphasize cooperation and collaborative participation
13. School day consists of fifty-five-minute single-subject periods	13. School day consists of flexible chunks of time used to integrate conceptual understanding and experiences
14. Teachers' rooms are organized and grouped by content area	14. Teachers' rooms are organized by interdisciplinary teams within a grade-level house
15. Teachers have little to no common planning time	15. Interdisciplinary teams share a common planning time
16. Each discipline relies on a single textbook	16. Interdisciplinary study relies on a variety of sources

(continues)

Table 1.1 (continued)

Junior High School	Middle School
17. Learning is assessed primarily through periodic written tests and quizzes	17. Learning is measured through ongoing authentic assessments
18. Assessments are used to demonstrate success or failure to the student	18. Assessments are used to inform teaching
19. Instruction is designed for the average learner	19. Instruction is differentiated for all learners
20. Students are frequently tracked or grouped	20. Students are grouped heterogeneously by ability
21. Subjects are usually offered for one semester or one year	21. Length of courses varies to facilitate more exploration
22. Guidance counselor meets with problem students and is primarily responsible for the master schedule	22. All school personnel are advocates and counselors for students
23. Emphasis is on organized interscholastic sports for chosen athletes	23. Emphasis is on intramural sports in which all students may participate
24. The family's role is to be supportive	24. The family's role is to be actively involved
25. Teacher-student relationship is random	25. Teacher-student relationship is advisory and cultivated
26. Student groupings are by grade level	26. Student groupings are developmental and multiage
27. Teacher preparation is content driven	27. Teacher preparation is both in content and in appropriate developmental practice
28. Teacher is a content expert	28. Teacher is a flexible resource

facilitator, teachers design the school day around student learning rather than around a bell or a bus schedule.

Junior high schools pose students as "empty vessels" into which teachers as experts place their knowledge; they believe knowledge is transmitted. Middle school teachers are facilitators of student-constructed understanding and are student advocates. Middle school students' voices are both respected and nurtured, as the students are seen as active learners rather than passive receivers of information. Junior highs deliver information in an artificial context of fact-based learning, but middle schools create and exchange information in an authentic, real-world connected arena where students construct their own understandings through critical thinking and exploratory activities. Junior highs tend to stress the acquisition of facts and knowledge through a one-dimensional presentation with little emphasis on meaning; middle schools, in contrast, emphasize the conceptual application and implementation of knowledge through multisensory, multimedia stimulation.

Whereas junior highs emphasize recitation and repetition and frequently present only one avenue to knowledge, middle schools present multiple avenues, with divergent active construction of meaning and personal understanding. Assessment of learning in middle schools assumes varied but authentic forms as opposed to the junior high school final exams executed with paper and pencil. A seventh-grade middle school social studies class concluding a unit on the Civil War may engage in a weekend battle reenactment during which the students sleep in tents, prepare and eat food, and live in the ways in which their 1860s counterparts did. As a final assessment, students are required to write a letter to their families as if they were yet on the Gettysburg battlefield. The letters are assessed for authenticity, for capturing the spirit of the time, and for the details specific to the battle.

When an eighth-grade middle school math class concludes a unit on angles, the students are divided into construction teams and given a specific budget. With the help of adult volunteers, often family and retired community residents, students build a playground for their neighboring elementary school. They must design the playground equipment, call the lumber yard and hardware stores for prices, engage the elementary students in the project, and secure donations and contributions for the project construction. The students are assessed on their critical thinking and problem-solving skills, on their interpersonal skills of interviewing the younger students and of working with the adults and with their team, and on their utilization and implementation of the unit concepts.

This is learning that has no walls or barriers; learning that is active and democratically responsible; learning that is cooperative, collaborative, and community oriented. Although junior high learning focuses on cognitive or intellectual development alone, middle schools focus on the development of the whole child. Therefore, instead of targeting standardized tests as the primary measure of progress, middle schools use multifaceted assessments to measure individual student's progress.

Whereas the junior high teaches as if all students were variants of the same model or "track" students (a process in which the higher-ability students are placed in a separate group, leaving at-grade-level and below-grade-level students together and therefore limiting expectations and possibilities for all students), middle schools group students heterogeneously and differentiate their instruction (see Chapter 5). These schools challenge and motivate all levels of students with respectful, exciting work. Throughout the school year they flexibly group and regroup students on the basis of a variety of individual student characteristics. Middle schools maximize the "differences" in students and see them as strengths, whereas junior highs focus time and attention on the sameness of all students. And although junior high schools have historically been institutions that socialize all cultures and differences in students into the mainstream culture primarily for economic purposes, middle schools are multicultural institutions that incorporate experiences, skills, and understandings of all peoples.

Given this comparative background, let's examine what high-performing middle schools really are and the impetus that has propelled current practice.

INFLUENTIAL DOCUMENTS

Three critically important studies that have helped shape and describe effective middle schools came from three various sectors of the community: *An Agenda for Excellence at the Middle Level,* written by the National Association of Secondary School Principals (NASSP) (1985); *This We Believe,* the benchmark publication of the National Middle School Association (NMSA) (1995); and *Turning Points: Preparing American Youth for the 21st Century,* drafted by Carnegie Corporation's Council on Adolescent Development (1989). These publications became the foundation upon which middle schools crafted programs, philosophies, policies, and practices.

An Agenda for Excellence

The NASSP seminal study entitled *An Agenda for Excellence at the Middle Level* recognized the need for a different form of schooling for students between the ages of ten and fourteen. NASSP's Council on Middle Level Education, composed of established leaders in the middle grades movement, stated positions quite reflective of NMSA's and Carnegie's. They offered the following programmatic recommendations:

- *Core values* guide institutional policies and practices as well as individual behavior, and they must address personal responsibility.
- *Culture and climate.* Effective school improvement depends on systemic reform rather than on add-on programs.
- *Study development.* The school's focus should be on the mastery and practice of those skills necessary for successful participation in the adult world.
- *Curriculum.* There must be a balance between intellectual skill development, problem solving, and lifelong learning.
- *Learning and instruction.* Middle grades teachers should be caring, enthusiastic, optimistic, patient, skilled in the craft and art of teaching, content-area experts, people who hold high expectations for all students and who should be swift to acknowledge student performance.
- *School organization.* The culture of the school should promote a sense of belonging, a smooth functioning of daily operation, and a sense of grounded communication. The provision of small learning communities and site-based decisionmaking creates ownership and security.
- *Technology.* The use of technology should be thoughtfully integrated both in content-specific situations and in problem solving.
- *Teachers.* Middle grades professionals are specially prepared in both content and in the understanding of students' developmental characteristics. They model intellectual growth and enthusiasm for learning.
- *Principals.* Administrative leadership should be visionary and confident.
- *Connections.* The school must initiate and maintain substantive ties to and with the community.
- *Client centeredness.* Teachers should be versed in the development of young adolescents to the extent that they do not create instances in which students will fail owing to lack of growth.

Since this study there has been considerable research to support not only the above recommendations but also the necessity for administrators to be particularly trained to work in the middle grades in addition to having the particular skills necessary for classroom teachers. Administrative expertise in appropriate developmental practice and preparation, and in how to support a staff that can effectively implement the above recommendations, may well be the key to the success or failure of middle grades reform.

This We Believe

The second seminal study, *This We Believe* from the National Middle School Association, stated that effective, developmentally responsive middle schools share the following major characteristics: a shared vision, educators who are committed to young adolescents, a positive school climate, adult advocates for every student, family and community partnerships, and high expectations for all.

As adult-student relationships develop, young adolescents begin to feel the sense of security and community necessary to academic risk taking. They feel the sense of advocacy that allows them the space to curiously explore and examine the world around them. In company with family and community stakeholders, middle schools hold up students to a populace who usually sees them only as saggy-pants, tight-clothes, noisy young people who "hang out" in the mall. Middle school students, when held to high expectations and when given the opportunity, adopt an acre in the rain forest, clean up a mile of Interstate 70, initiate a SADD (Students Against Drunk Driving) chapter in their school, adopt twenty senior citizens every year and raise enough money to spend $100 on each, lobby for clean water in a town downriver from Detroit, and initiate a fingerprinting program because one of their friends had been kidnapped. This is more than expectations; it is the enablement that actively provided an opportunity for them to exercise their own resiliency, their developing sense of moral justice and ethical responsibility.

NMSA concluded that high-performing schools provide the following:

- Challenging, integrative, exploratory curriculum
- Varied instruction practices and learning approaches
- Assessment and evaluation that promote learning
- Flexible organizational structures
- Health, wellness, and safety policies and programs
- Comprehensive guidance and support services

Effective middle schools are academically rigorous. They use ongoing assessments to inform their teaching as well as to guide the work of the classroom. Looking at the student holistically, the school attends to health, wellness, and safety so that they do not impinge on or obstruct the learning that could take place. When the school joins the family and the community in substantive ways, students realize they are surrounded by caring adults whose intent is to guide them in the realization of their aspirations.

Turning Points

The third study, from the Carnegie Corporation (1989), similarly stated that middle grades schools should:

- create small, caring communities for learning
- teach a core academic program that is rigorous
- ensure success for all students through effective instructional strategies and program components
- empower teachers and administrators through site-based decisionmaking
- use teachers who are experts at teaching adolescents
- improve academic performance through fostering health, fitness, creativity, and the development of character
- reengage families in adolescents' education
- connect schools with communities

This single document has had more widespread effect on middle grades education than any other source, perhaps because it was prepared by noneducational people—political leaders, policy specialists, researchers, and lay leaders—whose vested interest represented the corporate world.

A decade after the publication of *Turning Points: Preparing American Youth for the 21st Century,* the Carnegie Corporation's second report, *Turning Points 2000: Educating Adolescents in the 21st Century* (Jackson and Davis 2000), offered the following reflections on the above eight principles and suggested that middle schools should:

- *Teach a rigorous standards-based curriculum.* This curriculum should be relevant to the concerns of adolescents and based on how students learn best.

- *Use instructional methods designed to prepare all students to achieve higher standards and become lifelong learners.* They further suggest that instruction should be integrated with assessments and that instructional practices should be multiple and varied to meet students where they are in their learning.
- *Employ only professionals trained to teach in the middle grades and offer them ongoing staff development.*
- *Create a caring learning culture built on organized relationships that promote intellectual development and shared educational purpose.* This reflects their former recommendation of small communities or interdisciplinary teams of students and teachers who work closely together. It also includes the development of teachers' capacity for leadership and nurture of a collaborative and collegial professional culture
- *Govern democratically and proactively ensure success for every student.*
- *Provide a safe and healthy school environment that nurtures improved academic success and the growth of ethical, caring citizens.* Not only do schools provide physical education opportunities, but in many schools where the lack of access to health care intrudes on a student's learning, schools have initiated collaborative partnerships with mental health and other health care and human and social agencies to provide services on the school site (see Williams-Boyd 1996).
- *Involve parents and the community in the support of student learning and development.* Connections or networks with schools that share both this philosophy and practice and that promote a district atmosphere that supports data-based change should be initiated. (Jackson and Davis 2000, 23, 24)

In comparing the two Carnegie documents, we see noticeable differences.

1. In the second report, the panel recognized that ensuring the success of every student is the overall goal of every effective middle school and of the *Turning Points 2000* de-

sign as explained above; it is not simply one goal among the other recommendations as earlier listed. Each of the subsequent recommendations is a means to achieving this end, or they can be seen as the objectives that accomplish the goal.

2. The second report also posed teaching and learning as the central driving force that ensures student success, a point easily recognized from the classroom perspective. The emphasis on teaching and learning, however, should guide all other decisions, including teacher preparation, organization, governance, bridges to the family and to the community, culture, environment, and ongoing professional development.

3. The second report moved away from describing a core of knowledge that all students should know. Instead it reflected the expanding nature of knowledge, addressed the skills and habits of mind transescents should acquire, accounted for the changing concerns of transescents, and incorporated the expanding body of knowledge regarding how young adolescents learn (Jackson and Davis 2000).

4. The second report added to the teacher's curriculum knowledge an instructional piece that calls for the use of varied teaching techniques to help all students succeed.

5. And finally the second report has merged the family and community connections into one recommendation to reflect the inseparable and reciprocal relationship between both.

Tom Erb, editor of *This We Believe . . . and Now We Must Act* (2001), noted the obvious parallels or interweaving between *Turning Points 2000* and NMSA's document *This We Believe*. Where *Turning Points* called for a standards-based curriculum relevant to adolescents' world of experience and the use of varied assessments, *This We Believe* suggested using assessment and evaluation to promote learning and curriculum that are challenging, respectful, exploratory, and integrative. Both documents called for the use of varied instructional and learning strategies, the importance of educators particularly trained to work with young adolescents, the engagement of families and communities in the work of the school, and the importance of programs that provide a safe and healthy environment for transescents. Where *Turning Points* noted the necessity of organized relationships to successful learning, *This We Believe* pointed to flexible organizational structures, the importance of an adult advocate for every student, and the use of comprehensive guidance and support services. Where *Turning Points* called for schools to be democratically governed by all school personnel, *This We Believe* noted the importance of a shared vision, high expectations for all students, and a positive school climate (Erb 2001, 3).

All three of these documents contended that the more extensive the attention to or inclusive the implementation of the recommendations in creating more effective middle schools—that is, reforms such as advisories, interdisciplinary teaming, and curriculum integration—the higher the students' achievement and the lower the number of student behavior and truancy problems (Erb 2001). Likewise, the longer the support for the implementation of these recommendations, the more apparent student successes become.

Yet in the face of such well-founded research, too many school districts and middle schools still make piecemeal changes, add programs to an existing dysfunctional school, or examine only one aspect of the recommendations. In these cases, the "reform" measures are not surprisingly seen as faddish, weak attempts to jump on the current bandwagon. They are programs both short-lived and of little consequence.

Effective middle schools do not see these organizations' recommendations as items on a checklist that add up to high-performing schools but rather as an interconnected design. Each of the recommendations exists within a rich environment where social as well as curricular interrelationships create a culture of community, a habit of mind and of place (Williams-Boyd 2002). An effective middle school is more than the sum of its dynamic elements. Schwab (1973) saw these elements as the subject matter, the student, the teacher, and the milieu itself. I would suggest pedagogy as the fifth element, for the art and the craft of teaching play a particular role in the combination of each of the other four elements.

As Schwab and Erb contended, schools, and in particular learning, cannot be reduced to a one-test, external accountability system based on establishing and assessing adherence to standards. Where outside systems may believe that all children should and can learn the same things, in the same ways, at the same time, middle grades educators hold fast to the belief that responsive schools must flexibly provide varied avenues and pathways to learning in order that all children may grow and succeed.

A TURNING POINTS SCHOOL

The New American Schools (NAS), a private nonprofit corporation that supports systemic or whole-school reform initiatives, has adopted *Turning Points* as its first middle grades design model. NAS's fifty-school network, coordinated by the Center for Collaborative Education in Boston, supports the change process through technical assistance and professional development through the guidance of leadership teams. A self-study provides baseline data that inform and shape all individual school reform decisions (Gallagher-Polite et al. 1996).

Amherst Regional Middle School in Amherst, Massachusetts, is a Turning Points school in the NAS network. Seven hundred and thirty seventh and eighth graders, one-third of whom qualify for free or reduced-priced lunches and whose families speak a total of twenty-seven different languages, experience rigorous academic classes, choose from a variety of foreign language and music classes, and participate in a rich menu of after-school activities. Guided by the school's self-study, the leadership team makes all decisions on the basis of meeting the students' academic, social, emotional, and physical needs.

Yet despite careful planning and rigorous quality teaching, characteristically one-fifth of the school's eighth graders fail the state test every year. In 1990 the National Association for the Advancement of Colored People (NAACP) filed suit against the Massachusetts department of education for its disproportionate assignment of minority students to low-level classes. Amherst had six academic tracks at that time, in which students were grouped by academic ability. As a result of the suit and as a Turning Points school, this school has eliminated ability grouping with the exception of mathematics classes—not all students take algebra (Bradley 2000).

Amherst instituted block scheduling, sectioning a chunk or block of time for academic work. An interdisciplinary team of teachers who share the same students decides how to flexibly use this time. Advisory periods provide specific time during which teachers function as advocates for a small group of students; unlike homerooms, during which school business is addressed or announcements are made, advisories focus on supporting students and helping them through developmental struggles, both academic and socioemotional. Teacher-based guidance is a characteristic of Turning Points and NMSA effective schools. In addition to an individual planning time for each teacher, the interdisciplinary team has two planning times, one team plan and one individual plan. The prime goal of teaching and learning shapes the work of the team. Through shared instructional strategies, content areas are bridged and vital student learning information is more complete. Such cooperative and coordinated efforts have improved and strengthened families' involvement in their child's learning.

Teachers share and examine the work of their students in order to continually inform instructional decisions. Amherst has adopted a school-wide reading comprehension program selected by the teachers, who enjoy a depth in decisionmaking that is based on their self-study. The school offers a selection of music, art, and foreign language classes. And teachers talk of projects, exhibitions, and demonstrations rather than of tests and quizzes. These are all distinctive characteristics of both the middle school movement and of a Turning Points school. But the faculty would hasten to point out that all of the school's structural aspects are a means to an end, rather than an end in themselves. For too often junior high schools will move to engage all of the middle school program components without realizing that the structure is a scaffold for effective developmental teaching and rigorous academic learning.

Turning Points schools offer a smorgasbord of after-school activities. Amherst Regional provides a federally funded program called Savuka, a Zulu word for "awakening," that is open to all students. Many of the latch-key students who were going home to empty houses now participate in Savuka. And their grades have improved. As well, teachers are collegial, caring, and compassionate, and they enjoy teaching at Amherst. This alone can make a striking difference in student achievement.

THE NATIONAL FORUM AND
HIGH-PERFORMING MIDDLE SCHOOLS

In 1997 a group of educators, researchers, state and regional school leaders, and representatives of national education associations and foundations formed the National Forum to Accelerate Middle-Grades Reform. With support from the W. K. Kellogg, the John S. and James L. Knight, and the Edna McConnell Clark Foundations, the National Forum began to fashion its vision of effective schools for young adolescents. Through regional forums, public engagement and communication, national meetings, and ongoing networking, the National Forum began its dissemination of best practice in middle grades education.

The National Forum contends that high-performing middle grades schools are socially equitable, developmentally appropriate, and academically rigorous. These schools are typified by a nonnegotiable commitment to intellectual growth, to a rigorous academic regime, and to the healthy development of all students. Such schools are keenly aware of and diligently and deliberately work to diminish the disparities in educational opportunities and in academic achievement among all students. According to the 2002 policy statement of the National Forum, part of the school's mission is to equip students with the skills and perspectives necessary to successfully participate in and contribute to their schools and to a democratic society.

Because tracking denies a particular population equitable opportunities for success, National Forum schools group and regroup students heterogeneously based on student interests, needs, talents, learning profiles, and readiness for a particular task rather than on a single achievement inventory. Teachers continually assess student achievement and skillfully adapt instruction to meet the student at particular learning entry points and move the student forward. Deliberate attention to issues of class, race, ethnicity, gender, language, and needs further shapes instruction. The family contributes valuable information about the student and becomes involved in the work of the school in very visible ways.

Because the National Forum's model for effective school reform will have an abiding effect on the nation's middle schools, it is worthwhile to examine more closely what is meant by each of the three broad characteristics—academic excellence, developmental responsiveness, and social equity.

Academic Excellence

The National Forum offers the following characteristics of high-performing middle schools:

1. All students are expected to meet high academic standards. Through the use of sample exemplary work, students are supported in their learning until they have

reached concept and/or skill mastery or have exceeded the performance standards.

2. Curriculum, instruction, and assessment are dovetailed to coherently provide a forward-moving academic plan based on high academic standards for all students.

3. The curriculum is concept based and emphasizes both deep understanding as well as content-area connections to students' lives in a noncompetitive environment.

4. Varied instructional strategies provide a challenging and hands-on relationship with the concepts and skills being taught.

5. Teachers and students use a variety of collected assessments to chart growth and progress and to inform ongoing teaching and learning.

6. Flexible scheduling provides students with varying amounts of time necessary to the successful learning of concepts and skills. Class time is spent in inquiry-based, concept-based, active learning.

7. School personnel are afforded quality staff development aligned with the National Council for Staff Development standards. Faculty and staff work collegially to edify their own practice and to improve teaching and learning for students (Education Development Center 2000).

The National Forum has launched a "Schools to Watch" initiative that recognizes those middle schools that practice all three of its guiding principles. There are large numbers of schools that excel in one or two of the National Forum's principled areas, but four schools excelled in all three: Thurgood Marshall Middle School (3900 Lawndale, Chicago, Illinois 60618); Barren County Middle School (555 Trojan Trail, Glasgow, Kentucky 42141); Freeport Intermediate School (1815 West 4th Street, Freeport, Texas 77541); and Jefferson Middle School (1115 Crescent Drive, Champaign, Illinois 61821). Because a tour of each of the four designated schools may be accessed via the Internet, we will examine them here as practical exemplars of the above theories and beliefs.

Thurgood Marshall Middle School (whose principal is José Barillas) offers a full exploratory program that helps students define career goals in addition to being academically prepared. Students shadow businesspeople and conduct interviews in areas of career interest. They then develop "living situations" or patterns of earning money and paying bills that will correspond to that profession. Their experiences in fiscal responsibility, including balancing a checkbook, draw the "real-world" connections so necessary to motivating middle grades students. Interdisciplinary and integrated units assist students in seeing patterns across disciplines and compel a deeper understanding of the cyclical nature of learning and of knowledge.

Marshall Middle School offers students a spectrum of ways to demonstrate their learning. Projects, performance demonstrations, choice in selecting a particular topic within a conceptual study, all motivate and engage students as active participants in their own learning. During an art project students photographed Chicago's public art. The students researched acquisition information, cataloged their photographs with appropriate dialogue, gave an oral PowerPoint presentation of their work, and noted trends in public art after 1967. The students' active research about the city in which they lived drew acclaim from the city and from the school district.

The level of academic excellence that Marshall students have achieved is due in part to the staff's creative use of scarce resources. The district provides a counselor, a gym teacher, and a music teacher. With the discretionary funds the staff hires a drama teacher, two reading teachers, a bilingual education teacher, a curriculum support administrator, a case manager, a half-time social worker, a security officer, and a second office person. These particular positions were created in order to buttress the academic work of the teams, to encourage enrichment experiences, and to efficiently provide a safe and socially supportive environment. For students who struggle below grade level in reading and math, the Lighthouse program provides remedial instruction while during the same period those students who are advanced in math and reading participate in the Bull Scholars, named after the National Basketball Association Chicago Bulls, who fund the program. Taking classes on Saturdays, the highly motivated Bull Scholars may take content-area state tests to receive high school credit for many of these courses.

Marshall's Social Center houses a computer lab, woodshop, music studies area, basketball court, open library, art club, and space to play chess and Frisbee. Student council, yearbook, cheerleading, the computer lab, and academic tutoring are available to youth before and after school.

The individual student's academic needs and accomplishments are the focal point of the school. The interdisciplinary teacher teams meet to discuss the students for whom they are responsible, sending some to Lighthouse, others to Bull Scholars, and still others to exploratory courses. The teams examine student work and bases instructional and learning decisions on the disaggregated data regarding student progress in math and reading. Additionally, students receive tutoring from a federally funded GEAR UP (Gaining Early Awareness and Readiness for Undergraduate Programs) college orientation and preparation program, from their teachers (all of whom hold office hours), and from other volunteers. The general message sent to students and to their families is that all students can become successful with necessary support and assistance.

Summary: Academic Rigor

In National Forum terms then, a high-performing middle school that has a strong academic program engages the family in the students' learning goals and progress. Everyone understands what students are learning and why. The school demonstrates product expectations through examples of high-quality work that is nonrepetitious, creative, and demanding. It is work that matches the student's prior knowledge with an appropriate entry point that moves learning forward. Students are critically engaged in problem solving, in analysis, and in application of knowledge to their own experience of the world. Students have choices regarding how they demonstrate their learning. They can articulate the quality of their work against content standards through various venues, for example, community presentations, special evenings for the family to come to the school, student-led conferences, and other performances.

Teachers have an intimate understanding of content standards and therefore clearly know what concepts, skills, and dispositions students should acquire. They use a variety of instructional strategies that motivate and actively engage all students, not only in the core academic subjects but also in the fine arts and in technology. Teachers know and understand the developmental characteristics of young adolescents and gear their teaching accordingly. They also know how students learn both individually and as a class, how they make sense of the world, and what their prior learning experiences have been, and they build on this knowledge in a resilient and positive fashion. Teachers work together on behalf of every student on their team.

Developmental Responsiveness

High-performing middle schools challenge and draw upon the unique developmental characteristics of young adolescents. In particular the National Forum lists the following criteria:

1. The school is grouped into small, stable, caring learning communities that support students' ethical, physical, social, intellectual, and moral development and that are characterized by supportive relationships.
2. The school provides access to coordinated and comprehensive services that address students' healthy physical, social, emotional, and intellectual development.
3. Teachers engage students' natural sense of curiosity, exploration, and creativity and help develop social skills through the use of varying instructional strategies.
4. The curriculum is made socially and personally relevant to students' lives.
5. Teachers draw conceptual connections across disciplines and examine real-world problems.
6. Schools provide multiple opportunities in a rich variety of topics and interests through which young adolescents develop their own sense of identity, discover and demonstrate their competence, and plan for their futures.
7. Students are active participants in their own learning through making decisions, reflecting on learning experiences, constructing rubrics, and posing questions.
8. The school sees families as partners in students' education and involves them in the work of the school.
9. The school helps develop students' citizenship skills by providing a communal learning environment both in the classroom and through connections to the neighborhood community. (Education Development Center 2000)

Barren County Middle School has been recognized by the National Forum as a "School to Watch" because of its outstanding achievement in all three key areas—developmental appropriateness, academic rigor, and social equity. The National Forum cites the relationship among parents, teachers, students, and administrators as one of the more visible witnesses to excellence. This facilitates an environment of caring necessary for young adolescent achievement. The culture of teamwork, of shared vision, and of shared purpose—that of academic achievement and social support—permeates all interactions in the school. The staff talks about caring about the students' family experiences, about the youths' friends, and about the students as human beings first and as students second.

These relationships and behavioral perspectives may well exist in other schools that are not as successful as Barren County Middle School. Part of the school's success is due to the principal, Michelle Pedigo, who has facilitated this culture of caring through organizational structures. Grouping the students and teachers into four small teams, two seventh-grade teams of 135 students and six teachers each (representing math, social studies, science, and two language arts) and two eighth-grade teams of 150 students and six teachers each (math, science, social studies, language arts, and one interdisciplinary teacher), she created smaller communities characterized by personal interaction. Each team, in addition to the content-area teachers, also has an exceptional education teacher who collaborates with science and social studies teachers. All students stay within their teams with the exception of related arts classes. They are more personally known by their team teachers. Each team has a designated space within the building in which the students move between classrooms and to their lockers. Often each grade's teams are together called a house, and activities occur not only in the team but across teams within the house; that is, two seventh-grade teams would constitute the seventh-grade house. Students take more responsibility for each other just as a small community would. And although learning experiences and social activities occur within the team—creating a sense of team cohesiveness—they also occur across each house, allowing students to interact with other friends and peers not on their teams. Additionally, activities occur on a third level, as indicated in Figure 1.1, that of the school.

When schools move to interdisciplinary teaming, often a great deal of energy and time is put into helping students on individual teams feel that sense of unity, camaraderie, and belonging necessary to the establishment of a community culture. Students may be separated from elementary school friends, however, with whom they feel safe and comfortable. Therefore, it is helpful for the faculty and staff to be mindful of the necessity for activities on all levels of organization—team, house and school.

Returning to Barren County Middle School, we easily find that most of the students are engaged in small teams or in group projects. From statistics and stock market probability projects in eighth grade to groupings according to students' multiple intelligences in an integrated curriculum class, students work in different settings and assume different roles. In cooperative groups each student has a specific task neces-

Figure 1.1
Organizational Structure that Fosters
Small Communities

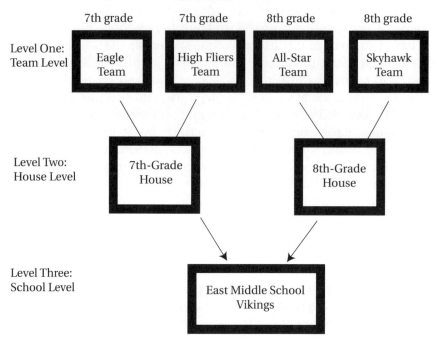

sary to the completion of the team's whole project. Learning activities are active, engaging, critical in their challenge of students' thinking, collaborative, and interdependent. Not only does this hands-on learning motivate middle grades students, who tend to need physical activity and manipulation of tasks to create meaning, it also increases academic performance (Education Development Center 2000).

    There is another dimension to Barren County Middle School's response to students' developmental needs. The school's Youth Service Center (YSC) serves the emotional, social, and psychological needs of students, thereby reducing the barriers to learning. The YSC serves as a liaison to community social services for both the student and the family. The center facilitates drug and alcohol awareness programs, takes students to and from physician's appointments, and has established student support groups, peer mediation, and a teen pregnancy awareness program. It also conducts a special counseling program for students who get easily lost in the system. The program, called Junior Guard, matches students with local armory guardsmen who help the students with issues of maturity and self-esteem while providing a more private, nonacademic venue in which students may demonstrate their strengths and talents. The program has reaped the benefits of fewer class disruptions and behavioral problems and of higher attendance in school.

As transescents begin thinking of life beyond high school, Barren County Middle School has created a range of technology programs that assist the students in thoughtful exploration of career possibilities. Along with CyberPublishing Company's work with students in developing their own web pages, the school's technology class focuses on using technology to solve real-world problems.

The principal actively values and supports working with the community. She builds teacher morale, creates a welcoming school, engages a professional staff in school-based decisions, and provides opportunities and support for all students to succeed. Twelve formal business partners provide students connections to life beyond the school as teachers take learning into the community. Students experience the value of participatory democracy early on as the school engages in more than 5,000 hours a year of formal volunteer work in addition to hours donated for community social events. It is no wonder Barren County Middle has received the Kentucky Middle School Volunteer of the Year Award from 2000 to 2003.

Meeting students' needs on multiple levels, removing obstacles to learning, providing opportunities for students to exercise in the community what they learn in the classroom, and making ties among the community, businesses, families, and the school are dynamic.

Summary: Developmental Responsiveness

High-performing middle schools, according to the National Forum, understand what it is to be a transescent or middle schooler. These schools create an atmosphere of advocacy through sharing a small number of students whom the team supports, respects, and guides throughout the school year. A cadre of support personnel—such as the school nurse, guidance counselor, social worker, and school psychologist, as well as paraprofessionals, the community, and the family—also provide individual contact and undergirding necessary for young adolescent learning. Teachers work together across content areas to motivate students with hands-on projects connected to their world of understanding. Students' viewpoints on issues and their perceptions of their place in the world are valued and nurtured. Their talents, their interests, their sense of healthy curiosity, their fears of the future, and their hopes for them-selves are all embraced as part of the natural process of growing up. Through a rich smorgasbord of school-day and after-school activities— created by the students and the faculty— students explore areas of interest in a safe environment, free of failure.

Social Equity

High-performing middle schools are democratic, socially equitable, and fair. All students have high-quality teachers, resources, and learning opportunities and experiences, and the necessary support to be successful. The National Forum further notes:

1. All school personnel are committed to expecting high performance from all students and assisting them in that accomplishment through tutoring, mentoring, adaptations, and varied support.
2. Students use a menu of approaches to learning and the demonstration of their mastery of content standards.
3. Curriculum, instruction, assessment, and scheduling are flexibly adapted to the changing needs of young adolescents.
4. In all classes and activities, all students have equal access to the same conceptual, valued knowledge.
5. The school experience is infused with ongoing opportunities for students to value their own culture and that of their peers. The students' and the nation's diverse cultures are experientially valued by the school.
6. Every student's voice is heard, respected, and valued.
7. Families are welcome participants in the life of the school.
8. The school's reward system or policy bears witness to the school's value of diversity, civility, service, and democratic citizenship.
9. The faculty is culturally and linguistically diverse.
10. The school's suspension rate is low and is in proportion to the disaggregated student population. (Education Development Center 2000)

Freeport Intermediate School provides every student with the resources, learning experiences, support, and quality instruction necessary for academic achievement. Full inclusion is the norm at Freeport. With all staff trained in full inclusion and with the support of trained teacher aides, those students who need modified learning experiences receive the necessary help. As well, the gifted and talented students, who by state mandate are placed on SEARCH teams, one team per grade taught by a certified gifted and talented teacher, move more quickly and more deeply through their learning. But because the principal, Clara Sale-Davis, and the school are committed to social equity, the principal facilitates gifted and talented certification for all the school's teachers, who in turn offer an enriched curriculum and more advanced classes and learning experiences for non-SEARCH students. At Freeport all students have access to valued learning in every class and in all activities.

Freeport views parents as partners in their children's education. As the faculty and staff engage both the parent and the student in the amelioration of impediments to learning, parents in turn feel valued and authentically involved in the work of the school. Where many schools experience a dramatic drop in parent involvement as students move from elementary to middle school, Freeport's Parent-Teacher Association routinely has 145 active family members, and the numbers continue to rise. Communication between the home and the school is reciprocal and respected. Where families have computers, teachers daily contact the home regarding a student's progress, just as a family may query the teacher regarding the child's progress. With other homes, telephone calls are personally made or in some instances letters are sent.

The sense of family and community assumes other shapes. The local Youth Home, which houses several Freeport students who have been abused, abandoned, or deemed unmanageable by the family, has worked in consort with the school to minimize destructive student behavior and maximize communication and academic achievement. Because the school treats the staff of the Youth Home as the students' family, work relationships are sensed to be very different by and for the students. Respect and social equity are the key words for Freeport Intermediate School, which embraces all students and their families as valued human beings who represent a variety of experiences.

Jefferson Middle School has also taken a firm stand for full inclusion. It was not an easy task when first implemented, but now all students benefit, those in regular education as well as special education students. Students with learning disabilities and behavior disorders are team taught by the regular classroom teacher and a special educator.

Teachers think of individual students and their learning needs and make the necessary modifications to the curriculum or the learning experiences as a matter of course. They believe that all students are held to a higher standard of learning while the special education students also learn necessary survival skills.

Jefferson's principal, Dr. Carol Stack, addresses equity in another organizational way—through scheduling. The eighth-grade unified arts schedule drew a majority of the students into band and foreign languages, leaving a racially identifiable group in performing arts, vocal music, and industrial technology. In examining the options, Jefferson has moved to a unified-arts block of study where students move to different classes on alternate days. What is important to note is not the particular proposed alternative, but that, because of a commitment to social equity, the school identified the problem, initiated an attempt to rectify the disproportionate class populations, and will evaluate the plan.

Part of the support structure that allows for such kinds of problem solving as the example of the alternating-day unified-arts block is due to grade-level team meetings and their focus. Daily meetings include the classroom, the unified arts, and the special education teachers as well as the counselor and a reading teacher. Unlike many team or grade-level meetings that are devoted to the discussion of organizational or bureaucratic issues, Jefferson's grade-level meetings focus on the students—on their needs and on their work in the classroom. Do students need tutors? Is this student a good candidate for mentorship in the Big Brothers/Big Sisters program? Who needs help with particular concepts? These are the kinds of questions that shape the team's positive look at their students. Jefferson is quick to point out that parents are frequently invited to these meetings in order to involve another knowledgeable agent on behalf of the student.

Barren County Middle School uses data regarding student achievement to guide thoughtful changes in school support services and in programs. Barren has initiated an Academic Connections after-school program to help students in taking the Kentucky state standards-based test. Using a variety of remediation tools that include Stanford Reading Assessment reading materials, "Corrective Math," Extended School Services to students who need one-on-one tutoring, and what Barren calls the Club House, which offers academic classes such as the Reading Club, Museum of the Barrens, After-School Homework Help and Tutoring, and Hands-on Science Projects, Barren offers all of its students, not only the large number of high-poverty youngsters, extended learning opportunities and support (Education Development Center 2000).

Summary: Social Equity

In high-performing middle schools students' needs, ranging from health to academic, are addressed in a range of creative ways. From wellness centers to after-school tutoring programs, from differentiated instruction to multicultural thinking that undergirds all decisions made in the school, the schools' features challenge students to reach high standards by removing obstacles to learning and by adapting and creating new atmospheres for nontracked success. Students are recognized not only for academic excellence or for excelling in sports but also through a variety of recognition programs—for example, Inkspots (the all-school literary anthology) Outstanding Author Award; Journalist of the Year; Citizens of the Year; art, technology, drama, and chess club, Native American club; Excaliber's Honor Choir Musicians of the Year awards; and the 100 percent club for students who complete and submit 100 percent of assigned work; to name a few. When the family is engaged, when the school provides opportunities for all students to find their niche and then recognizes the diverse panoply of accomplishment, and when students sense they are valued, academic achievement soars, the number of behavioral problems drops, absences decline, and the amount of completed homework increases.

Common Characteristics

There are qualities common to all the schools that the National Forum has cited as "Schools to Watch." Some of them are:

- Sense of community shared by all school participants
- Sense of family—created both within the school in small teams and with the students' families
- Active engagement of the family as a valued partner in the child's education
- Active engagement of the community as partners and instructional liaisons
- Sincere belief that all students can learn and achieve high academic standards
- Recognition of the necessity for resources and support to help all students succeed

- Commitment to and celebration of all students
- Commitment to full inclusion
- Recognition that the arts are important to the full learning experience of students
- Provision of ongoing professional development
- Use of data for continuous self-assessment and self-improvement
- Ownership by the staff of high standards for all students
- Provision of multiple layers of services for the student and for the family
- Shared decisionmaking on-site
- Orientation of the school to small teams/small communities
- Principalship that facilitates a vision shared by the entire faculty and staff
- Teacher teams that are autonomous and actively supported by the principal
- Instruction that is flexible, active, engaging, motivational, and hands-on
- Teachers who can modify and adapt their curriculum based on their professional expertise
- Creation and maintenance of a warm, caring, welcoming environment
- Organization that is action oriented in its problem solving
- Identification of clear academic outcomes and objectives to reach the outcomes
- Focus of the entire staff on strategic goals that help students achieve high academic success.
- Leadership that is visionary, distributed, and modeled by the principal

One of the organizational hallmarks of middle schools that incorporates many of the above qualities is effective small learning communities. Working on an early draft version of a Middle Start school—a systemic reform model based on social equity, developmental responsiveness, and academic rigor—the Working Middle Start Model Development Committee (consisting of K. Skaggs, P. Benson, N. Fenton, S. Hoelscher, T. West, and P. Williams-Boyd) constructed the rubric in Table 1.2 to assist schools as they examine themselves. Critical areas include teaming, communication with the family, and small learning communities that help foster the healthy development of transescents while maintaining a caring atmosphere.

As a school moves from beginning to use the middle grades philosophy to substantially reflecting middle grades practice, there is a more conscious effort to respect teachers' professional tasks and time. Team planning centers more around issues of student learning as teams share effective practices and flexibly group heterogeneous teams of students. Likewise, schools move from being a closed environment to actively engaging the family and the community in the work of the school.

Organizational Structure

High-performing middle schools are themselves learning organizations. Schools establish norms and common values and put in place organizational structures that support and sustain teaching and learning. The National Forum lists the following as criteria for outstanding schools. They:

1. Share a vision of what high-performing means and looks like and then work to implement that vision. Distributed leadership protects institutional purpose and preserves the school's history.
2. Designate a person or group of people who hold the authority for and are responsible for the continuity of the school improvement strategic plan.
3. Are active, healthy learning communities in which all members are engaged in continuous improvement strategies. These schools support the work of teachers through the provision of necessary resources.
4. Commit resources to ongoing, sustained, high-quality professional development geared to accomplishing the school's vision.
5. Develop partnerships and networks with the community and draw on other resources, on research, and on other's experiences.
6. Use data to analyze school performance and make wise decisions. They hold themselves accountable for the academic performance of their students.
7. Overcome barriers to learning while the collective commitment to achievement is continually nurtured.

Table 1.2
Middle Start Working Rubric for Effective Small Communities

Practice	1=Beginning	2=Developing	3=Substantial
• School teams use common planning time to coordinate the curriculum, instruction, and assessment for all students and to identify an instructional focus that crosses all content areas. • Teams regularly review student work to assess progress toward their teaching and learning goals and to set future directions.	• The school has a plan for providing for at least 4 periods per week of Common Planning Time (CPT) for all teams and teaching staff (including elective teachers), in addition to regular prep time. • The school has planned for teachers who need it to receive professional development in using CPT to coordinate curriculum, instruction, and assessment and in reviewing student work. (Need is determined by data collection and analysis.) • Teachers have discussed an instructional focus that crosses all content areas.	• All teams meet at least 2 periods per week for common planning time. • All teachers and school administrators who need it have participated in professional development in using CPT to coordinate curriculum, instruction, and assessment and in reviewing student work. (Need is determined by data collection, review, and analysis.) • All teams have identified and are beginning to implement an instructional focus that crosses all content areas. • 50% of the teams use CPT to look at student work at least once a week and are using CPT to coordinate curriculum, instruction, and assessment.	• All teams meet at least 4 periods per week for common planning time, in addition to individual prep time. • New teachers are trained by fellow team members in reviewing student work and coordinating curriculum, instruction, and assessment. • All teams have identified and fully implemented an instructional focus that crosses all content areas. • All teams use CPT to look at student work at least once a week and are using CPT to coordinate curriculum, instruction, and assessment.

- School teams are involved in making decisions about school policies, practices, and procedures in collaboration with the school leadership team.
- School teams cultivate meaningful, two-way, and regular communication between home and school that builds families' understandings of the academic and developmental needs of young adolescents.
- Teams also involve families and community agencies in classroom and school activities and invite their perspectives on future directions for the school.

- The school has a plan to ensure that all teams are involved in the decision-making process.
- The school has a plan for communicating between teaching teams and the school leadership team.
- The school has a plan for developing a communication strategy with families that is two-way and meaningful and builds families' understandings of the needs of young adolescents.
- The school has a plan for involving families and community agencies in teaching and learning activities.

- 50% of the teams are involved in making decisions about school policies, practices, and procedures.
- There is an informal process in place for communication between the school leadership team and teaching teams.
- 50% of the teams communicate with the school leadership team on school policies, practices, and procedures.
- The school has begun to implement a strategy for communicating with families that is two-way and meaningful, and builds families' understandings of needs of young adolescents.
- The school has also begun to involve families and community agencies in teaching and learning activities.

- 100% of the teams are involved in making decisions about school policy, practices, and procedures.
- There is a formal process in place for communication between the school leadership team and teaching teams.
- 100% of the teams communicate with the school leadership team on school policies, practices, and procedures.
- The school has fully implemented a strategy for communicating with families that is two-way and meaningful, and builds families' understandings of the needs of young adolescents.
- Families and community agencies are formally and fully engaged in teaching and learning activities.

(continues)

Table 1.2 *(continued)*

Practice	1=Beginning	2=Developing	3=Substantial
• School teams promote the intellectual, physical, emotional, moral, and social development of every student. • Students are flexibly grouped within small learning communities so that every child has access to rigorous curriculum, effective instruction, and an appropriate level of support.	• The school has a plan for providing professional development to teams on promoting the needs of young adolescents. Such professional development is based on a data collection, review, and analysis. • The school has a plan for grouping students in heterogeneous flexible groups that allows for all children to have access to rigorous curriculum, effective instruction, and an appropriate level of support.	• The school has provided professional development on how to promote the needs of young adolescents to teachers and administrators. Participation in such professional development is based on a data collection, review, and analysis. • 50% of students are in heterogeneous flexible groups that allow for all children to have access to rigorous curriculum, effective instruction, and an appropriate level of support.	• All teams formally share strategies, practices, and approaches to promoting the healthy development of students. • The school communicates and shares these practices and strategies with families and community partners. • ≈90% of the students are in heterogeneous flexible groups that allow for all children to have access to rigorous curriculum, effective instruction, and an appropriate level of support.

Source: K. Skaggs, P. Benson, N. Fenton, S. Hoelscher, T. West, and P. Williams-Boyd (2001). Working Middle Start Model Development Committee.

8. Collaborate with colleges and universities to help recruit, prepare, and mentor novice teachers. They hire professionals who have special preparation in teaching and working with young adolescents and who are culturally and linguistically diverse.
9. Engage multiple stakeholders in setting and attaining high standards. The family and the community are thoughtfully engaged in ongoing dialogue, in decision-making, and in the support of the school's commitment to high academic standards. (Education Development Center 2000)

Thurgood Marshall Middle School provides robust, ongoing professional development for all of its teachers as they focus on working with students. But it is the staff who decide on their own professional development, both motivational and informational in nature. With the support of the Carnegie Corporation, the school joined the Accelerated Schools Network. The network is guided by the following principles: united purpose, empowerment or enablement joined to responsibility, and resilience or building on the school's strengths (Education Development Center 2000). Marshall recognizes the power of collaboration and collegial work with like-minded reform professionals. It is a member of the Association of Illinois Middle Level Schools Network. As well, with other Chicago schools, Marshall receives funding to study ways to effectively integrate technology into its curriculum.

At Freeport Intermediate School the staff is divided into six groups: planning, curriculum and instruction, communication, school climate, technology, and staff development. Each team has two leaders who together make up the Campus Advisory Team, the shared decisionmaking and leadership team for the school. They are seen as the spokes of the school's wheel. Department chairs make up another wheel, and the school is divided into four small tribes or houses, each with its own leader. Initially the leaders were chosen by the principal; however, now the teams choose their own leaders by consensus. Additionally, the principal has invited both the feeder elementary school and the high school to which her students will go to be a part of the math department's vertical team. Consequently, when the high school students achieved exemplary Texas Assessment of Academic Skills status, they came to Freeport and praised the teachers for their work.

Like Marshall, Freeport's teams have implemented an A/B block schedule that allows them to alternate interdisciplinary team planning on A day and department planning on B days. Each teacher also has a daily ninety-minute individual planning time. The special education teachers are a part of the tribe meetings as are the arts or encore teachers. Each team keeps a written agenda that is vigilantly read by the principal. She facilitates the work of the teams, but when there is an open position on the team, the team interviews and hires someone who will fit the character and personality of the group. If there is a lack of consensus, then the principal intervenes but only when asked to do so. Similar support comes from the central office. When administrators at both the building and district levels facilitate and support the work of teachers, the self-efficacy and professionalism of the staff in turn benefit students.

Jefferson Middle School also exercises site-based management. The eighteen-person Building Council represents a variety of community stakeholders who make decisions regarding improved student achievement. Their focus is clear. Their work is not about minor issues of management, but about helping students succeed academically. They considered whether or not they should hire another teacher in order to reduce class size. Instead, the Building Council hired another counselor so each grade or house had its own counselor who followed students through their three years at Jefferson. Acknowledged by the union as the group that influences the students' environment and helps affect their achievement, the Building Council is a testimony to the power a community can bring to bear on its local school.

Summary: Organizational Structure

Trust, action, resourcefulness, and student centeredness characterize all four of these schools. The support structures, organizational plans, professional development of staff, facilitative leadership from the principal, community engagement, family investment, and site-based decisions answer one question: How can we help our students succeed? For each school, the dynamic effects of their work happen in relationships, in the power of people to touch each others' lives in positive ways, to believe in families as partners, to engage the community as collaborators, and to enable students to empower themselves to take risks, to step out apart from their peer group, and to chance success.

Effective middle schools have a strategic plan of action to achieve their shared vision, a plan constructed by a variety of stakeholders who assume ownership for student learning. The family and the business community are held in high regard by the school, which sees them as partners in student learning. Leadership in these schools is facilitative and shared. A school improvement team that meets frequently and regularly is charged with the coordination and communication of the goals, the objectives, and the business of the school. Ongoing assessment of student learning drives school decisions and instructional practice. And effective schools provide ongoing high-quality, teacher-identified staff development that nourishes a healthy culture of learning and leading by all constituents.

The Middle Start model of systemic middle grades reform set forth in Table 1.2 adds another layer of support structure to the school, that of regional networks. Middle Start contends that regional networks:

- Provide access to resources, best-practice research, and data regarding middle grades education
- Encourage data-based inquiry, assessment, and the development of knowledge, skills, and dispositions
- Forge regional networks of schools and related organizations that serve young adolescents and the people who work with them
- Support leadership development
- Recommend policy and practices at all levels—local, regional, state, national
- Conduct research and evaluation that inform teaching and learning practices (Academy for Educational Development 2001)

Regional networks are teacher based and school based in that educators conduct their own learning experiences and guide their own growth. Professional development is then more consonant with their daily educational needs.

BEYOND STRUCTURE

A recent Eastern Michigan University graduate class of middle school educators listed program components unique to the middle school. Their list included teaming, sharing of students, interdisciplinary thinking and curricula, supportive and flexible grouping, diverse instruction, active learning, advocacy and advisory teacher-based guidance, site-based decisionmaking, exploration, family and community engagement, and support of curiosity and creativity. They noted that every student should know and be known by an adult in the school who accepts the responsibility for that student's guidance. Recognizing the importance of an accepted body of knowledge as iterated by each state's content standards and benchmarks, these teachers emphasized the necessity of providing multiple ways in which students could create their own meaning and understanding of concept-based knowledge and various ways in which they could demonstrate what they had learned. The teachers commented on the important shift in their classroom role from being a lecturer to being a facilitator, one who creates learning opportunities in which transescents actively connect new experiences to previous ones.

Listing the importance of higher-order thinking skills, of application of knowledge to student-world experiences, of scaffolding success for students, and of creating an atmosphere that encourages risk taking and honors curiosity, the teachers then asked, "Of all the program components, which is the most critical to the success of high-performing middle schools?" Arguably their final decision was having educators who are specifically trained, or grounded, in the developmental literature of middle grades students and well versed in attendant implications for their own practice.

TEACHERS AS EXPERT PEDAGOGUES

In a recent poll commissioned by the Public Education Network and *Education Week,* Americans indicated the number one way to improve schools was to raise teacher quality (Deily 2002).

To begin to accomplish the criteria set forth by the National Forum, *Turning Points, This We Believe,* or the *Agenda for Excellence,* middle schools would agree that raising teacher quality is essential. Every middle grades school needs skilled pedagogues, teachers well versed in their content areas and in the development of young adolescents. In essence the key to the success of a middle school is the middle grades teacher who is both prepared and skilled but who also has that particular personality and sense of self that is flexible, adaptable, and compatible to the ever-changing worlds and experiences of middle grades students.

Personal Characteristics

The following traits could easily characterize all effective teachers; however, they are especially important at the middle level given the special needs of young adolescents. Teachers:

- Enjoy young adolescents and create a special bond with them. They don't just tolerate adolescents' moodiness, their unpredictability, their noise, and their confusion, they embrace it as a normal part of growing up.
- Are caring and compassionate, willing to give of themselves.
- Enjoy life, are intellectually curious, are active and positive in their outlook and in their relationships.
- Are enthusiastic. They model the behaviors and the practices they expect of their students.
- Are secure in themselves and self-confident. They can then withstand criticism expressed against them, which in many instances represents the student's powerlessness to control a given situation or reflects the angst of the developmental stage.
- Approach all students and interactions with an attitude of trust and belief.
- Trust each other and value collaboration.
- Honor the student's family and the varied contributions that can be made.
- Are not afraid to laugh at themselves and with their students.
- Nurture the social, moral, emotional, spiritual, and physical aspects of themselves.
- Are flexible, open to change and innovation. They are problem solvers, critical thinkers, people who see opportunity in challenging situations.
- Possess a depth of content knowledge that allows them to flexibly adapt content to the needs of their students and to draw connections to the students' world of experiences.
- Possess a wealth of the talent, creative ability, and skills necessary to help all students succeed.
- Are resilient and ever hopeful. Even in the most limiting circumstances, teachers believe that motivation, will, and the human mind can triumph over deprivation.
- Believe in the power of the moment as a function of learning. They express their understanding that the purpose of middle schools is not to prepare students for high school but to maximize the creative potential for learning in the present.

- Believe in the worth and the abilities of every student. They do not see students from a deficit perspective—as problems that need to be fixed. Rather they skillfully discover the strengths and talents of each student and match learning to those entry points.
- Believe in active advocacy. They are willing to stand in the gap for students and their families by accessing needed services, by connecting families to resources, and by serving as a liaison between the student-family and the community.
- Are comfortable with ambiguity and constant fluctuation.
- Can multitask in a noisy and yet productive environment.

Undoubtedly the single most important trait of effective middle grades teachers, beyond their academic preparation, is their honest desire to work with young adolescents. At a time when students are pressured by the family, by peers, by teachers, and by themselves, the teacher who exudes enthusiasm, humor, caring, and competence acts as an important safety valve for young adolescents.

Middle grades students are quick to detect people whom they can trust. Their astute powers of observation and analysis, although sometimes flawed, more often cut through masks that the adult world tends to wear. All interactions, all relationships, and the degree to which students are able to learn in a given classroom are based on one trait—trust. A well-meaning principal of a middle grades, Title I school wanted to instill pride in his student body. So at the beginning of the school year, he had the year's slogan "Be Proud" printed on faculty shirts, painted on hallway banners, and explained to the student body as an acrostic. Just as pride cannot be taught to someone, so it is with trust. These immeasurable dimensions of the human spirit must be experienced internally. Young people trust adults as they watch and weigh what they see. They have pride in themselves when they succeed in ways other students and schools experience as success. As middle grades youth are developing their own sense of right and wrong, as they test that which their families have taught them, they watch their teachers, whom they see as transitional authority figures. That teacher whom the students trust becomes a counselor, a role model, an advocate, and a protector.

Professional Competencies

Wiles and Bondi (1993) listed a number of teacher competencies essential to an effective middle school. Some of the following are adapted from their list. Effective teachers:

- Are knowledgeable about the physical development of young adolescents and their attendant needs for activity
- Possess knowledge about transescent intellectual development and the needs presented in the shift from concrete to abstract formal thinking
- Use their knowledge of developmental and personality theory to implement appropriate instructional strategies
- Use their understanding of transescent socioemotional development to assist students as they adjust to their changing bodies
- Exercise their management skills to allow students to work both independently and in groups and to match learning experiences to students' varying knowledge levels
- Examine and understand cultural and social forces of the neighborhood that affect the school
- Understand the transitional nature of young adolescents as they move from children in the elementary school to young adults in the high school
- Exercise collaborative skills in teaming with colleagues
- Create interdisciplinary and integrative units of students and can teach them with their team teachers or by themselves
- Continue to augment the depth of their content knowledge in at least two subject areas and expand the breadth of their knowledge across content areas
- Demonstrate expected learning and use a variety of media to motivate students
- Develop and implement learning situations that promote independent student learning, that maximize choice, and that stimulate students' responsibility for their own learning
- Possess and exercise the skills that assist middle grades students in organizing their work, in setting priorities, and in budgeting time

- Teach high-order thinking, critical thinking, and inquiry-based lessons
- Use direct and inductive lessons to help students discover learning and create their own understanding of content knowledge
- Expand the students' affective domain through cooperative learning lessons, gaming and simulations, role playing and creative dramatics
- Assist students in developing their own value systems through affective learning experiences and in tandem with their familial and cultural teachings
- Model verbal skills and behaviors that challenge students in a variety of group settings
- Exercise diagnostic skills to assess students' strengths and weaknesses, learning entry points, and abilities and disabilities and can create appropriate learning experiences, assess their success, and adapt their teaching
- Are innovative and unafraid to experiment with various teaching techniques that may be better suited to a student's learning needs
- Possess the skills and can teach students to communicate effectively in written, spoken, and oral fashion
- Are fluent readers and help all students progress in their reading skills in all content areas
- Assist students by promoting positive self-concepts, self-reliance, and resilience
- Display a strong sense of group dynamics and exercise the ability to organize groups that will make interdependent decisions while developing their own sense of leadership
- Possess the skills that facilitate active multitasking, working simultaneously with varied groups engaged in different learning experiences
- Have a working knowledge of various careers and help students explore options
- Distinguish between students' emotional and physical difficulties and can assist them in building a foundation of problem-solving experiences
- Work with students in other venues such as extracurricular activities and/or community-based youth activities

- Are willing to thoughtfully gather and analyze as much information regarding the student as possible (using, for example, learning inventories, interest inventories, questionnaires, learning logs, interviews, critical case studies, and observations)
- Provide frequent, varied, and timely feedback to students regarding their learning progress
- Help students analyze their own learning in self-reliant and responsible ways
- Function calmly and creatively in high-activity, high-noise environments
- Handle disruptive behavior in respectful, positive, and creative ways that allow the students involved to assume ownership for the behavior and for the solution to the problem while maintaining their dignity before their peers
- Work cooperatively and collaboratively with colleagues, resource people, families, and the community
- Actively listen to and empathize with students—assisting them in solving their problems rather than "rescuing" them from their problems
- Create a classroom culture of community, of caring, of flexibility, of learning, and of leadership
- Design curriculum and learning experiences, both cooperatively and singularly, that are standards based, connected to the students' current experiences, actively engaging, and motivating
- Persist in their search for and creation of more effective learning experiences for their students and frequently use the textbook as only one source of information and augment it with ancillary resources
- Create varied learning and social experiences in which all students will succeed
- Assess a lesson in progress and can quickly adapt it or change it given the students' level of engagement
- Are constantly observing and evaluating their students' cognitive and affective investment in their learning

In a survey by Arth et al. (1995) that examined the qualities of excellent teachers, it was curious to note that although teachers and principals agreed on most of the above characteristics, principals felt the most significant characteristics of the effective middle grades teacher were that the teacher displays "sensitivity to the individual differences, cultural backgrounds, and exceptionalities of young adolescents, treats them with respect, and celebrates their special nature" (14). Teachers, on the other hand, ranked "establishes and maintains a disciplined learning environment that is safe and respects the dignity of young adolescents" (17) as their most important traits. Common to all principals who responded were four main themes that portrayed outstanding middle grades teachers: a belief that all youth could learn, a flexibility in quickly modifying or adapting curriculum to meet all students' needs, an acceptance and embrace of middle grades youth and their behavior, and a willing collaboration with colleagues (18).

Middle grades teachers are the transitional people who help students move from the one-primary-adult relationship in grade school to multiple adults in the high school. Young adolescents are no longer challenged by the self-contained classroom of their early years, nor are they ready for the complete freedom of movement in the high school. Effective middle schools draw the best from both ends of the learning experience; that is, they provide multiple, meaningful adult interactions for the students while at the same time making sure each student has a close relationship with one particular adult, most often the advisor. In what is often a conflicted time of development, students are drawn to teachers who they feel can be trusted, who are competent, caring, dependable, and positively enthusiastic.

Academic Preparation

Historically, teachers have come out of undergraduate programs with either an elementary education degree that usually extends from kindergarten through eighth grade (K–8) or a secondary education degree with a major or minors in particular content areas that, upon successful completion of state licensure exams, will enable them to become certified to teach specified subjects in seventh through twelfth grades (7–12). Junior high schools were not established for any sound educational reasons but were a temporary solution to the overcrowding of elementary and secondary schools in local neighborhoods and were intended to respond to contextual issues of desegregation. Elementary teachers were then asked to "move up" to the junior high school and secondary teachers at the high school were asked to "move down" to the junior high. With no professional training in working with transescents and for negative professional reasons, many of these teachers floun-dered, resorting to direct lessons or straightforward, nonengaging lec-tures. They were creating their own discipline problems.

Joan Lipsitz, a career middle grades reformer, noted of the junior high school: "The kids' physical energies were overwhelming, and our attempts to keep them quiet and still were draining them of their moti-vation. We were creating discipline problems by not appealing to their interests, by trying to keep them physically confined, and by ignoring what we saw as static in their head, but was real life for them" (Bradley and Manzo 2000, 9).

The same comments could be made about the unprepared teachers who found themselves in the middle school. In the mania of the current standards movement there is a disturbing tendency to re-vert to the junior high school model. Rather than seeing a pendulum swing to more appropriately conceived high academic expectations based on sound developmental practice, once again we are seeing a bustle of activity to convert buildings and programs in order to save money. Does the construction of a new school building or the reassign-ment of faculty or the redistricting of students fundamentally affect stu-dents' achievements? Or should we spend more time with the internal interactions between students and teachers and leave cosmetic changes to other institutions?

Or could there be something more basic that underlies the per-sistent artificial shifting that goes on with middle grades education? Most Americans have little understanding, much less appreciation, for young adolescents. What contact they have is distant, impersonal. Groups of young teens are banned from the malls, they block busy street intersections, and they are looked at askance for their sloppy dress and unruly haircuts. In tight economic times those who make de-cisions about middle grades education based on cost effectiveness rather than on sound educational theory often see transescence as a pe-riod in students' lives that adults outside of the school endure rather than treasure.

Teachers as well as administrators who are specifically trained to work in middle grades see a far different version of transescents than does the general public. A variety of studies conducted by such groups as the National Commission on Teaching and America's Future (Dar-ling-Hammond 1996) and by the University of Tennessee Value-Added Research and Assessment Center (Sanders and Rivers 1996) contend that of all factors, quality middle grades teachers have the single great-est effect on student academic success. There are several states—North

Carolina, Georgia, Ohio—and several national organizations—the National Board for Professional Teaching Standards, the National Association of State Directors of Teacher Education and Certification, and the National Middle School Association—that have adopted specialized standards and performance assessments for middle grades teacher preparation and licensure. Other states, such as Michigan, have made strides toward the licensure process by adopting endorsement standards for middle level teachers. Some forty-three states have some form of middle grades teaching credential. Yet nationwide the majority of current middle grades teachers are untrained for middle grades or they are teaching out of their content field of preparation (McEwin, Dickinson, and Jenkins 1996; Scales and McEwin 1994). Only 20 percent of the teachers nationwide are prepared to teach in the middle grades, and over 30 percent of the teachers who teach in grades seven and eight lack the proper content area background (Education Development Center 2000). It is even worse in urban areas. "Poor students, minority students, and lower achieving students of all races are far more likely than other students to be taught by undereducated teachers" (Haycock and Ames 2000, 14).

In most states any type of teaching credential is accepted for teaching in the middle grades. Where there are specific standards, endorsements and licenses are too often overlapping; for example, elementary certification is usually K–8 whereas secondary certification is 7–12. The current move by 86 percent of the states to adopt some form of specialized middle grades training holds promise for the future.

Summary: Preparation

The need for teachers well grounded in the knowledge of their content areas, of the pedagogy of teaching, and of transescent learning appears obvious. The commitment required of middle grades teachers is significant, both in its breadth and in its depth. It is a commitment that respects, supports, and celebrates young adolescents as they struggle to find their way. It is a commitment born of an impassioned belief in the integrity of the individual human personality, in the dignity of the spirit, and in the beauty of curiosity so particular to the middle grades age group. It is a commitment that simultaneously requires one to be an artist, a craftsperson, a collaborator, an advocate, a perpetual learner, a leader, a protector, a mentor, a role model, and a cheerleader, as well as a quarterback for justice and opportunity for all students and their families, a counselor, a friend, a colleague, and a true believer in one's power to create a more just and caring world. This is no small order. Highly effective middle grades teachers seldom pause to hear their own voices for they continually seek to learn and incorporate better ways of teaching. They do reflectively examine their practice and assess student learning to inform their teaching and take stock of themselves and of their own needs. Effective middle school teachers know what to teach, know how to teach, and know the students they are teaching.

CHAPTER SUMMARY

Just as there are common threads woven through all of the Schools to Watch, Table 1.3 notes the critical characteristics of effective middle schools cited in the three hallmark documents that have helped shape responsive middle schools.

Although variance is one of the most striking characteristics of young adolescents, effective middle schools consciously and strategically work to reduce the disparities in learning achievement as well as in access to the resources necessary for success. Educators base their teaching on the ongoing assessment of student interest, learning profile, and readiness for a given segment of study or attainment of a particular skill level. Students are provided both the culture of initiative and the opportunity for taking ownership of their learning in a safe, respectful, and stable environment.

George and Alexander (1993), noted middle school reformers, contended that there are three overall goals of middle school education: academic learning, group citizenship, and personal development. They would further say the two operative words that characterize all the seminal documents, all effective middle schools, and all young adolescents would be *unique* and *transitional.*

Middle grades program components are thoughtfully constructed to meet and to build on the unique characteristics of transescents as they move from the elementary school to the high school. Middle grades are not merely downward preparatory extensions of the high school organized by subjects, neither are they upward continuations of the elementary school organized by grade level.

Middle schools are themselves unique in that they are the only institutions of learning built and designed solely upon the identity and needs of the learners whom they serve. The aggressive understanding of the intellectual, physical, social, emotional, psychological, and moral

Table 1.3

Critical Characteristics of Effective Middle Schools

---

1. A philosophy based on the unique needs of early adolescents
2. Educators knowledgeable about and dedicated to working with young adolescents
3. Educators who have depth of content knowledge, who use varied instructional and assessment strategies, and who provide learning experiences that reflect respect for students' cultural heritage as well as their skill and learning differences
4. Educators who hold high expectations for all students in the heterogeneously grouped classroom
5. A curriculum balanced between the cognitive and affective needs of young adolescents and that presents a rigorous core of knowledge
6. A full exploratory program
7. Interdisciplinary team organization for all grades
8. Team planning and personal planning time for all teachers
9. A flexible block/chunk master schedule
10. A comprehensive advisor/advisee program in which each child has an adult advocate
11. A positive school culture
12. Site-based shared decisionmaking where the people closest to the students are involved in the process of making school decisions
13. Principals who are knowledgeable about and committed to the middle grades philosophy, programs, and practices
14. A smooth transition process from elementary to middle school and from middle to high school
15. A strong co-curricular program including intramurals, interest-based minicourses, clubs, and periodic social events
16. A physical plant in which teams can be housed together for core classes and in which there are large areas for full teams to meet
17. A commitment to the importance of health and physical fitness for all students and provision of opportunities for development on a regular basis
18. An acknowledgement of the value of the family to the student's success and a commitment to reengage families in the education of young adolescents by keeping them informed of student progress and school programs and by providing meaningful roles for them in the schooling process
19. A cooperative connection between school and the community through student service projects, business partnerships, and the use of community resources within the school
20. An emphasis on developing higher-order thinking skills, problem solving, lifelong learning skills, and hands-on, active learning
21. Learning activities that are connected to the students' experiences and to their perception of the "real world"

Sources: Carnegie Council on Adolescent Development (1989), *Turning Points: Preparing American Youth for the 21st Century*. National Middle School Association (1995), *This We Believe*. National Association of Secondary School Principals (1985), *An Agenda for Excellence at the Middle Level*.

development of young adolescents positions the ways in which learning experiences are constructed and assessed. Middle schools are not small high schools; they are not holding tanks where little if any learning occurs; nor are they places where only social needs are addressed in less than substantive ways. Middle grades education is demanding, rigorous, creative, motivating, challenging, and wonderfully rewarding. Middle grades teachers are unique, specially prepared to work with young adolescents, and committed to the highest principles of learning, teaching, and personal interaction. They have chosen to work with what middle grades theorist James Beane (1990) called the age group most misunderstood and most disliked. To middle grades teachers, young adolescents are creative, energetic, thoughtful, caring people who are creating their own pasts in their teacher's present. We would say with Stanford emeritus professor and Eastern Michigan University Porter Chair in Urban Education Nel Noddings that the "student is infinitely more important than the subject matter" (1984, 176). "The special gift of the teacher, then, is to receive the student, to look at the subject matter with him. Her commitment is to him, the cared-for, and he is—through that commitment—set free to pursue his legitimate projects" (177). This is not an idealistic, fanciful notion. It is the world of the practical, the effective, that to which all outstanding teachers and middle grades schools strive. Just as Jason in our opening vignette struggled for competence, so too do all young adolescents. They need a caring adult guide who models competence, who lives a caring life, who connects with them through trusted, stable relationships. Caring is a spiritual ethic of belief, but it is also a moral ethic of action.

In the objectified world of standardized tests, when those who know little of young adolescents would cast them all in one mold, we are aware with theorist Madeline Grumet that "because schools are ritual centers cut off from the real living places where we love and labor we burden them with all the ornate aspirations our love and labor are too meager and narrow to bear" (1981, 292).

Today's best-practice middle school is thoughtfully and responsively designed as a caring community dedicated to the success of every young person. It is a place of learning guided by people who have chosen to work with young adolescents and who are especially prepared to help them develop positive attitudes about lifelong learning, to help them forge their own identities, to help them succeed academically and socially, and to help them find their place in a world that neither cherishes them nor protects them.

What are middle schools? They are places where administrators nurture the leadership capacity of their staff, places where teachers stand as sentinels on behalf of young adolescents, places where the family is valued for its role in the learning process of its children, and places where the community joins hands in supporting its young people. Middle schools are places where all adolescents are celebrated, where they dance their math and sing their science and sniff the winds of history, and where the joy of learning is bounded only by the human imagination. These are places of hope and of promise. These are places limited only by our meagerness and hesitation to dream.

REFERENCES

Academy for Educational Development. 2001. *Middle Start: Partners for Student Success in the Middle Grades.* New York: Author.

Arth, A., J. Lounsbury, C. K. McEwin, and J. Swaim. 1995. *Middle Level Teachers: Portraits of Excellence.* Columbus, OH: National Middle School Association and National Association of Secondary School Principals.

Beane, J. 1990. *A Middle School Curriculum: From Rhetoric to Reality.* Columbus, OH: National Middle School Association.

Bradley, A. 2000. "A Feast of Offerings." *Education Week, Special Edition: Middle Grades: Feeling the Squeeze* (October 4): 10–14.

Bradley, A., and K. Manzo. 2000. "The Weak Link." *Education Week, Special Edition: Middle Grades: Feeling the Squeeze* (October 4): 6–9.

Carnegie Council on Adolescent Development. 1989. *Turning Points: Preparing American Youth for the 21st Century.* New York: The Carnegie Corporation.

Darling-Hammond, L. 1996. *What Matters Most: Teaching for America's Future.* New York: National Commission on Teaching and America's Future.

Deily, M. E. P. 2002. "Topping the Charts." *Education Week* 26, no. 6 (July): 12–16.

Education Development Center. 2000. *National Forum on Accelerated Middle-Grades Reform.* Newton, MA: Author.

Erb, T., ed. 2001. *This We Believe . . . and Now We Must Act.* Westerville, OH: National Middle School Association.

Gallagher-Polite, M., L. DeToye, J. Fritsche, N. Grandone, C. Keefe, J. Kuffel, and J. Parker-Hughey. 1996. *Turning Points in Middle Schools: Strategic Transitions for Educators.* Thousand Oaks, CA: Corwin Press.

George, P., and W. Alexander. 1993. *The Exemplary Middle School.* New York: Holt, Rinehart, and Winston.

Grumet, M. 1981. "Conception, Contradiction, and Curriculum." *Journal of Curriculum Theorizing* 3: 292.

Haycock, K., and N. Ames. 2000. "Where Are We Now: What Is the Challenge for Middle-Grades Education?" In *U.S. Department of Education National Conference on Curriculum, Instruction, and Assessment in the Middle Grades: Linking Research and Practice.* Washington, DC: National Educational Research Policy and Priorities Board.

Jackson, A. W., and G. A. Davis. 2000. *Turning Points 2000: Educating Adolescents in the 21st Century.* New York: Teachers College, Columbia University.

McEwin, C., T. Dickinson, and D. Jenkins. 1996. *America's Middle Schools: Practices and Progress: A 25-Year Perspective.* Columbus, OH: National Middle School Association.

National Association of Secondary School Principals. 1985. *An Agenda for Excellence at the Middle Level.* Reston, VA: Author.

National Middle School Association. 1995. *This We Believe.* Columbus, OH: Author.

Noddings, N. 1984. *Caring: A Feminine Approach to Ethics and Moral Education.* Berkeley: University of California Press.

Riley, R. 2002. "The Push/Pull of Growing Up." *Middle Ground* 6 (2): 55–56.

Sanders, W. L., and J. C. Rivers. 1996. *Cumulative and Residual Effects of Teachers on Future Student Achievement.* Knoxville: University of Tennessee Value-Added Research and Assessment Center.

Scales, P., and C. McEwin. 1994. *Growing Pains: The Making of America's Middle School Teachers.* Columbus, OH: National Middle School Association and the Center for Early Adolescence.

Schwab, J. J. 1973. "The Practical 3: Translation into Curriculum." *School Review* 81: 501–522.

Wiles, J., and J. Bondi. 1993. *An Exemplary Middle School.* Upper Saddle River, NJ: Merrill–Prentice Hall.

Williams-Boyd, P. 2002. *Educational Leadership: A Reference Handbook.* Santa Barbara, CA: ABC-CLIO.

———. 1996. "A Case Study of a Full Service School: A Transformational Dialectic of Empowerment, Collaboration, and Communitarism." Ph.D. diss., University of Kansas.

Chapter Two

❧ Chronology

Matthew J. Harbron and
Pat Williams-Boyd

Most contemporary educational programs, policies, and perspectives are adaptations of other historic ideas and concepts. The education of students who range from ten to fourteen years of age, however, is unique in its development and in the influence the developmental characteristics of the population served have enjoyed. Centering educational practice solidly around the students and their needs and abilities had been previously unheard until the middle grades movement. Middle grades education and schools tout very clear objectives, philosophies, ideologies, programs, practices, and pedagogy. And although some would see middle schools as merely "holding tanks" for pre-adults, maintaining children until they are prepared for high school, middle grades professionals see their schools as challenging, relevant, connected to the real world in motivating and exciting ways.

Many aspects of the student centeredness and active learning indicative of middle grades education trace their intellectual impetus to eighteenth- and nineteenth-century European philsophers and educators Jean Jacques Rousseau, Johann Heinrich Pestalozzi, and Friedrich Froebel, who suggested that learning was a personal and active endeavor (Wiles and Bondi 1993).

1872   Harvard president Charles Eliot expresses concern that the average age of entering freshmen is too old and calls for an examination of the ways in which elementary and secondary education can be reduced in duration.

1880s   During the centennial celebration in Philadelphia, many of the concepts of learning espoused by Pestalozzi, Froebel, and Rousseau are examined with great interest.

51

1890s   The Committee of Ten of the National Education Associa-
          tion (NEA), comprising secondary teachers and university
          professors, recommends the standardization of credits for
          graduation, courses necessary for adequate preparation,
          and the proper time for college application (Wiles and
          Bondi 1993).

1893   The NEA's Committee of Fifteen on Elementary Education
          recommends that the secondary program should begin
          two years earlier, that is, there should be six years of ele-
          mentary and six years of secondary schooling.

          NEA's Committee of Fifteen radically recommends that
          the center of study in secondary schools is the child rather
          than the subject matter.

1904   Psychologist G. Stanley Hall's book *Adolescence* argues for
          education based on adolescent cognitive development.

1905   With the explosion in numbers of secondary students—
          from 200,000 in the mid-1890s to approximately five mil-
          lion by 1925—the secondary schools are coming under se-
          vere criticism given the high number of drop-outs and
          inordinate discipline problems.

1909   Columbus, Ohio, institutes the first junior high school.

1910   Berkeley, California, follows Ohio's lead and creates its first
          junior high school.

1913   The Committee on the Economy of Time in Education
          makes the first specific reference to a separate junior divi-
          sion of secondary education (Gruhn 1970). This school is
          to be based on adolescent characteristics, with particular
          attention to learning skills, and is to offer greater depth in
          academic studies. Additionally, this new junior high
          school will offer more independence, student responsibil-
          ity, vocational training, and guidance and exploration. The
          junior high school should prepare adolescents for a
          smooth transition into high school (Tye and Tye 1984).

1913–1918   The Committee on the Reorganization of Secondary Education suggests a broader, more utilitarian purpose for secondary education (Wiles and Bondi 1993).

1918   Following World War I the overcrowding of elementary and secondary schools additionally prompts the emergence of a new facility called the junior high school.

1919   The accrediting body the North Central Association of Colleges and Secondary Schools offers a general definition for a junior high school: "one in which grades seven through nine are placed in a building of their own with a special teaching staff and administrators" (Wiles and Bondi 1993, 5).

1920   Meetings of committees similar to the above three, which met between 1890 and 1920, lead indirectly if not directly to the establishment of junior high schools; it is not until after 1920, however, that junior high schools begin to flourish. By 1925 approximately 400 junior high schools are in operation.

    In less populated states, junior high schools replace high schools if there are insufficient numbers of students. High school students then attend larger-populated county seat secondary schools (George et al. 1992).

    The junior high school curriculum, after its high school model, is compartmentalized, and less attention is paid to the student's needs than to the importance of subject knowledge.

1930–1960   The implementation of many new instructional strategies expands in direct proportion to the vigor of child-development research: for example, cooperative learning, team teaching, open space education, outdoors education.

1940s   Progressive educators such as John Dewey help shape curriculum to reflect such phrases as "experiential learning," "life education," "problem solving," "community," and "student-centered learning." This thinking lays the groundwork for the emergence of the middle school.

The distinctions between the functions of junior high schools and middle schools are poignant. "If one believes that the chief function of education is to transmit the perennial truths, one cannot but strive toward a uniform curriculum and teaching. Education takes on a different shape when the major function is seen as fostering creative thinking or problem solving. As such, differences in these concepts naturally determine what are considered 'essentials' and what are the dispensable 'frills' in education" (Taba 1962, 30).

1950s   Following World War II the junior high school reaches its greatest popularity, translated into the number of schools, approximately 6,500 by 1955.

During the late 1950s and early 1960s junior high schools experience criticism from across the country. Middle schools begin to emerge in Upper St. Clair, Pennsylvania; Centerville, Ohio; Barrington, Illinois; Mt. Kisco, New York; and Saginaw, Michigan (George et al. 1992).

1957   The Russian launch of the satellite *Sputnik* throws U.S. criticism in the direction of the public school. Students are felt to be unprepared, particularly in math, foreign languages, and science, to compete in the world arena.

1960s   Just as the 1960s are a time of civil unrest, they are a time of reformation in politics, in social views, and in education. They are an era of changing perspectives and of questioning both authority and the norm. As the country becomes more urban, more pluralistic, more complex, and more open in its thinking, examination of the effectiveness of the junior high school construct becomes more honest and reveals major gaps between philosophy and practice.

During the early 1960s the work of child developmentalist Jean Piaget is translated, moving the view of the ten to fourteen year old back to the forefront of intermediate grades education.

1960   The number of junior high schools stands at more than 5,000 in 1960 (Howard and Stoumbis 1970), down somewhat from the 1950s but still high in comparison to the few hundred at the beginning of the twentieth century. The large number is in large part owing to the rise in numbers of post–World War immigrants, the postwar baby boom, and the continued influence of higher education (George et al. 1992). In this same year, 80 percent of high school graduates have experienced an elementary–junior high–high school sequence (Alexander and McEwin 1989).

The junior high schools during the 1960s maintain their replication of high school emphasis on compartmentalized subject matter knowledge, subject-by-subject student retention, and closed-door classroom teaching in which the teacher is the expositor of perennial truths that are to be memorized and repeated by students.

Students are often tracked or grouped by ability. There is little room for authentic exploration beyond specialization in preparation for high school. And teachers and administrators find themselves at the junior high level through default rather than through choice. "The junior high school, in practice, [is] shaped by the high school, by the state university, by Harvard, and by European universities established five centuries earlier" (George et al. 1992, 62). There is little curricular change appropriate for this developmental age group.

1961   A publication entitled *The Junior High School We Need* maintains that the current junior high organizational structure is inappropriate and dysfunctional. The ninth grade, which is influenced by high school graduation credits, should be moved into the secondary building, leaving a middle grades school of seventh and eighth graders and a high school, which would include grades nine to twelve.

The document calls for middle grades schools characterized by blocks of instructional time rather than by forty-
five- to fifty-five-minute periods, smaller size, flexible
scheduling, more appropriate instructional strategies, and
teachers prepared to teach this particular age group.

1965 New developmentally appropriate educational organizational structures emerge: middle school education, early
childhood education, gifted and talented education, and
special education.

Curriculum developer William Alexander, often referred to
as the father of American middle schools, along with Gordon Vars and John Lounsbury, calls for a new school organization based on clear developmentally appropriate
goals, objectives, and teaching practices. The ninth grade
belongs with the high school, leaving a sixth- through
eighth-grade middle school arrangement.

1966 Even though educators support new ways of thinking regarding student-centered schools, school planners and policymakers seek reconfiguration for different reasons. Alvin
Toffler's paper "The Schoolhouse in the City" mirrors the
sentiment in the late 1960s and 1970s that the construction
of middle schools is intended to alleviate the pressure to
contain school district racial desegregation, particularly in
large cities and in the South (George and Alexander 1993).
This perspective contradicts the philosophy of the reform
and may have stunted the early growth of the middle school
as such. Bringing together people of different racial and socioeconomic backgrounds, however, would theoretically
encourage and foster a more tolerant society. Inevitably, because schools have not proven to be effective tools for social
reform per se, their capacity to teach basic skills is impaired.
The effective marriage between social responsibility and
educational instruction is yet to happen.

LATE 1960s Overcrowded junior high schools send ninth graders to
the high school, not for curricular purposes but for purposes of accommodation.

1973   The National Middle School Association is founded and sets forth four priority belief goals that should influence individual school goals:

- Each student should be well known by an adult in the school, someone who takes responsibility for the student's guidance

- Each student should achieve mastery of basic skills and of the lifelong process of learning and should have an adult advocate to help

- All students should possess a functional body of fundamental knowledge

- All students should have opportunities to explore and develop interests in aesthetic, leisure, career, and other life activities (George and Alexander 1993, 33)

1975   The Working Group on the Middle School and the Early Adolescent Learner, established by the Association for Supervision and Curriculum Development, offers the following recommendations through its document *The Middle School We Need:* reemphasize the developmental characteristics of the young adolescent and base all instructional practices on those needs.

1980s   It is now recognized that the majority of those middle schools that evolved during the first twenty-five years after the movement's inception were middle school in name and grade only, with little curricular or programmatic response mirroring the call for developmental responsiveness in the reform model. Rather, these schools are driven by central office mandates to desegregate schools. Moving ninth graders to the high school and bringing all the district's young adolescents together would accomplish such desegregation.

Additionally, as has been true starting in the 1960s, school enrollments are decreasing on the secondary level because of the absence of the postwar baby boomers. Although there is a growth spurt in the elementary schools, high schools are facing cutbacks. Moving students out of crowded elementary schools, moving ninth graders into the less full high schools, and creating middle schools are moves to address the enrollment problems.

1983   The *A Nation at Risk* blue ribbon panel report rallies the national battle cry for more math and science for all students.

1984   Florida, through the Speaker's Task Force, implements legislation favoring middle schools with interdisciplinary teams and funds the process with grants of more than $30 million annually (George et al. 1992).

1985   The National Association of Secondary School Principals releases *An Agenda for Excellence at the Middle Level,* which supports developmentally responsive schools, advisory programs, the use of a variety of instructional strategies, school organization by teams, an adult advocate for every child, and higher education preparation specifically for middle level teachers and administrators.

1987   California State Department of Education publishes a task force report, *Caught in the Middle,* which offers support for school reorganization.

1988   The National Middle School Association adopts characteristics of effective middle level schools: the uniqueness of middle grades programs, the focus on the unique needs and characteristics of the young adolescent, the appropriateness of the interdisciplinary team for students and teachers, the significance of exploration in the curriculum, and rejection of tracking or ability grouping.

1989   The Carnegie Corporation's Council on Adolescent Development presents *Turning Points: Preparing American Youth for the 21st Century.* One of the most influential documents concerning the middle school movement because it is written by political leaders, policy specialists, and researchers, *Turning Points* contends: "Successful reform must be comprehensive and integrative, with careful attention to sequencing and establishment of some . . . building blocks on which other elements can be mounted. . . . There are clear patterns of interdependence" (1989, 547). The report urges middle schools to provide:

- small communities for learning within the larger school building
- a core academic program common for all students
- successful experiences for all learners
- empowerment for teachers and administrators in making decisions about the experiences of middle grades students
- teachers trained in teaching young adolescents
- improved academic performance fostered through health and fitness
- reconnection of schools and families in young adolescents' education
- schools connected to the community

LATE 1980s   As middle schools are increasingly better organized and operated, school personnel find this model of schooling to produce more substantive results than the former junior high model (George and Oldaker 1985a, 1985b).

1970–1990   The number of traditional junior high schools (grades seven through nine) decreases by 53 percent. The number of middle schools (grades five or six through eight) increases by over 200 percent (Alexander and McEwin 1989).

1995   The National Middle School Association writes *This We Believe: Developmentally Responsive Middle Level Schools,* which sets forth the association's major beliefs and philosophies regarding effective middle grades education.

1997   The National Board for Professional Teaching Standards (NBPTS) develops eleven categories of standards for Middle Childhood/Generalist: knowledge of students, knowledge of content and curriculum, learning environment, respect for diversity, instructional resources, meaningful applications of knowledge, multiple paths of knowledge, assessment, family involvement, reflection, and contributions to the profession.

The two-tiered system of the 1800s gave way to a three-tiered system of elementary, junior high, and high schools in the twentieth century. In the second half of the twentieth century, however, out of convenience and owing to social reasons rather than educational—facility overcrowding, racial desegregation, post-*Sputnik* criticism of the non-competitiveness and poor rigor of U.S. schools, and the jump by some to join the newest "fad"—junior high schools were replaced by middle schools designed to educate the whole child. "Public schools must accept their responsibility in this area, but they cannot do it alone. Any plan to meet the needs of all children must involve every group and agency responsible for the welfare of our children" (Rose 1999, 4).

Although public schools cannot be used as a holding tank for the troubles of our culture and then be expected to produce responsible citizens, they can be used as facilities in which thoughtful strategies for social reform may be implemented. Despite the fact that the original middle school philosophy did not include this plan of action, the struggle for social equality has become embedded in the public's viewpoint as a primary responsibility of its educational facilities. "We expect our schools to help our children become not merely good workers, but good citizens" (Riley 2000, 6). In the late 1960s through the early 1970s, amid the turmoil in the streets, America's middle schools became instruments through which a nation grappled with its own conscience.

Comparing middle schools of the 1970s to those of the 1980s shows a change in climate but not necessarily in curriculum. Many schools adhered to and benefited from the recommended middle school characteristics, yet they simply glazed over one of the most important factors of the school—curriculum. Primarily people in the movement simply added to or expanded what they already had—such as adding interdisciplinary teaming—without making curricular changes. "Overlooked is the basic understanding that for reform to be successful, it must begin with the process of how teachers teach and how students learn" (Hope 1999, 236). And "asking 'how to teach' is not the same as asking 'what to teach'" (Beane 1993, 7).

Yet, despite all the influential documents' recommendations and observations, few of the suggested actions are in fact practiced school-wide, and still fewer practiced well. Researchers contend that many schools are highly motivated to be exemplary but have not realized the full breadth of structural changes that would satisfy the needs of middle schools and their students according to the *Turning Points* document (Epstein and MacIver 1993). Reform is an evolutionary and developmental process. A minimum of five years is needed to begin to realize the full range of changes required to successfully implement the *Turning Points* recommendations (Felner et al. 1997). Just as a child's development happens in fits and starts, so too does the identity of a middle school. Progress occurs when multiple components are placed together as a functional source of improvement

Although many middle schools may have initially assembled for reasons of convenience, they have evolved into outstanding model facilities. Being placed in a new configuration forced educators to view their audience with a different perspective—one focused on the student. Offering the only child-centered, developmentally appropriate instructional and educational design in the public school system, middle schools in the 1990s through the turn of the twenty-first century began to more systematically and systemically focus on providing successful learning experiences, environments, and relationships for all students, their families, their communities, and the school personnel. In this new millennium, refinements of the middle school are still in progress. The growth of the middle school movement is directly proportional to the understanding of the young adolescent. Exploration and curiosity characterize young adolescents just as they should the environment in which they live and grow.

REFERENCES

Alexander, W., and K. McEwin. 1989. "Schools in the Middle: Programs 1968–1988: A Report on Trends and Practices." Chicago: ERIC Document Reproduction No. ED327000.

Beane, J. 1993. *A Middle School Curriculum: From Rhetoric to Reality.* 2d ed. Columbus, OH: National Middle School Association.

Carnegie Council on Adolescent Development. 1989. *Turning Points: Preparing American Youth for the 21st Century.* New York: Carnegie Corporation.

Epstein, J., and D. MacIver. 1993. "Middle Grades Research: Not Yet Mature but No Longer a Child. *Elementary School Journal* 93 (5): 529–533.

Felner, R. D., A. W. Jackson, D. Kasak, and P. Mulhall. 1997. "The Impact of School Reform for the Middle Years." *Phi Delta Kappan* 78, no. 7 (March): 528–541.

George, P., and L. Oldaker. 1985a. *Evidence for the Middle School.* Columbus, OH: National Middle School Association.

———. 1985b. "A National Survey of Middle School Effectiveness." *Educational Leadership* 43, no. 4 (December): 79–85.

George, P., C. Stevenson, J. Thomason, and J. Beane. 1992. *The Middle School— and Beyond.* Arlington, VA: Association for Supervision and Curriculum Development.

George, P. S., and W. M. Alexander. 1993. *The Exemplary Middle School.* New York: Holt, Rinehart, and Winston.

Grantes, J., F. Patterson Noyce, and J. Robertson. 1961. *The Junior High School We Need.* Washington, DC: Association for Supervision and Curriculum Development.

Gruhn, W. T. 1970. "What's Right with Junior High and Middle School Education?" *NASSP Bulletin* 54, no. 346 (May): 139–145.

Hope, W. C. 1999. "Service Learning: A Reform Initiative for Middle Level Curriculum." *The Clearing House* 72, no. 4 (March/April): 236–238.

Howard, A., and G. Stoumbis. 1970. *The Junior High and Middle School: Issues and Practices.* Toronto: Intext Educational Publishers.

National Association of Secondary School Principals. 1985. *An Agenda for Excellence at the Middle Level.* Reston, VA: Author.

National Middle School Association. 1995. *This We Believe: Developmentally Responsive Middle Level Schools.* Columbus, OH: Author.

Riley, D. 2000. "Champions of a Cause." *Teaching Pre K-8* 30, no. 5 (February): 6–7.

Rose, L. C. 1999. "The Business of Improving Public Schools." *Phi Delta Kappan* 81 (1): 4.

Taba, H. 1962. *Curriculum Development Theory into Practice.* New York: Harcourt Brace.

Toffler, A. 1968. "The Schoolhouse in the City." Chicago: Eric Clearinghouse Document Reproduction No. ED028615.

Tye, K., and B. Tye. 1984. "Teacher Isolation and School Reform." *Phi Beta Kappan* 65, no. 5 (January): 319–322.

Wiles, J., and J. Bondi. 1993. *The Essential Middle School.* New York: Macmillan Publishing.

Chapter Three

✜ Pedagogical Perspectives

Pat Williams-Boyd

It was the day to honor Dr. Martin Luther King, Jr. The entire district teaching and support staff gathered in the high school cafeteria for discussions on inclusion, diversity, and curriculum. We focused our attention on the minister from Washington, D.C. who was ready to offer his vision of Dr. King's message. With the microphone in one hand and a book of Dr. King's words in the other, he told us of his own struggles to grow into that message. "As a young man," he confessed, "I was drawn to the power of Malcolm X's philosophy, that we must take back that which was stolen by any means necessary. But as I grew older, and perhaps wiser, I began to understand the true power was not to be found in striking back. I began to understand that true strength and courage came only from love." The heads of my colleagues nodded in agreement.

At the end of his story, the minister asked for questions. My teammate spoke up from the seat right behind mine, "Just as you struggled to embrace Dr. King as a youth, our kids seem ready to fight at the drop of a hat. What can we do as their teachers?" I smiled, proud that my good friend had articulated what so many of us had been thinking. The minister's response did not disappoint. Smiling again, he removed the small reading glasses from their perch on his nose.

"It's a hard thing you do—to teach. I would pay you all $300,000 each if I could. I know how hard you work. I would ask that you do two things in Dr. King's honor. Number one, if you believe in the power of love, and I see that you do, you must model it for them. For many, you will be the only one who does. Second, believe that they hear you and see you and that the message is getting in. They

may not come around for you. They may never show you that you changed their hearts, but you do. And someday, just like it did for me, that message will transform them and then hopefully, they too will pass it on."

I'm sure that most of the people in that room were taken back to where they were when they heard Dr. King speak or perhaps what they were doing at the time of his assassination. My mind dialed up a memory of riding in the car with my mother through the rough streets of Benton Harbor. My Catholic grade school was located behind the church and along the same stretch of road that crack dealers frequently roamed out in the open. Even as a young child, I could clearly see the contrast between our nice, big house by the lake, and the run-down houses that surrounded the church. Some of the houses we passed were much grander than ours, but years of neglect had worn away all but the hints of their former selves. I once promised my mother that when I made a million dollars I would come back and fix up the broken homes, as if someone just forgot to sweep up or change the light bulbs. She smiled at me from the driver's seat, and said she hoped that I could. Some years after I had packed and left for college, the school packed up and moved to the other side of the river.

I haven't been back to that neighborhood since I was a boy, but in some ways teaching takes me there every day. I see young people in my classroom who, like those old houses, could use a little care. Just like then, I wish I could just spend a few bucks and make them all like new again, ready for the world. I know better than that; so I work hard to make my classroom a place where there is a caring adult for them. I know the minister is right when he tells me that they may hear me without listening, but sometimes that is of little comfort.

—From the journal of Richard M. Bacolor,
January 19, 2000 (Bacolor 2000, 32–33)

Middle schools are full of young adolescents and teachers with hopes and dreams—for their lives, for their careers. Some dreams are newly formed, some are being realized, and others are already deferred. Who are these young people who pose such a challenge to even the most stalwart, and what has happened to their hopes? Because if we know who they are even as they change from day to day, and if we understand how they learn, how they see themselves and their world, then designing a rigorous curriculum becomes a match game—an exercise that poses relevance and appropriateness as sentinels. Middle grades science teacher Raquel Dicks contended that "to effectively educate middle school students, it is important to recognize and respect where they are in life's journey. Like a child, they long for guidance, approval, and praise. However, they also long for responsibility and independence like an adult. Young adolescents struggle to find their identity and place in the greater culture" (Dicks 2001, 4).

Every change, addition, deletion, or activity in a middle grades school should answer the question, "How does this meet or affect the needs of young adolescents?" No other educational grouping, whether elementary or secondary, builds its policies and practices upon the developmental characteristics of its students as does the middle school. Few would argue with the contention that young adolescents pose a unique challenge. Their schooling, their learning experiences and activities must mirror this difference. Lipsitz (1984) studied four successful middle schools and concluded that "the most striking feature of the four schools is their willingness and ability to adapt all school practices to the individual differences in intellectual, biological, and social maturation of their students. The schools take seriously what is known about early adolescent development, especially its inter- and intra-individual variability. This seriousness is reflected in decisions they make about all aspects of school life" (167). There is an emerging body of research that indicates that the success young adolescents experience between the ages of ten and fourteen is a strong indicator of the success they will experience as adults.

There are adjectives commonly used to describe young adolescents, such as *awkward, clumsy, moody, distant, overly emotional, testy,* and *self-absorbed*. And there are questions that teachers commonly hear from parents, such as, "I hope I can survive this period in their lives" or "We used to be so close; what happened?" Or frequently when a teacher speaks well of a student, a parent may look askance and say, "I think you are talking about someone else's child." This was such a frequent response that I kept a school yearbook on my desk when visiting with parents so I could point out the child about whom we were speaking. Could this outgoing, thoughtful student be the same sullen, distant young offspring who spends most of her evening talking on the phone in her room? And why are there such different views of the same person?

The answer is simple enough but must be understood in context. Middle school teachers often find themselves in a familiar conversation: "What do you do?" "I'm a teacher." "Oh, how wonderful; what grade do you teach?" "Middle school." With a rolling of the eyes and a shaking of the head, the questioner responds, "Oh, my goodness; I could never work with those kids." Middle grades students are the least understood and the most conflicted group of people, owing in part to the explosion of growth taking place in so many different realms of their lives, and they are among the most rewarding with whom to work. They are neither children nor young adults, a dilemma that brings with it all kinds of obstacles, challenges, and gifts.

As a people, we unfortunately tend to distrust those who are different from us. That distrust is exacerbated when our expectations of the ways in which young people should behave, according to our own tempered recollections of our youth, go unmet. How frequently do we hear adults say, "When we were young we would never have talked back to our parents that way" or "When I was a kid I never hung out in the mall, blocked shoppers, laughed loudly, acted disrespectfully." And students say, "Please don't invite my parents to school. They will embarrass me" or "My folks just don't understand." Often from the young adolescent point of view, adults don't really like them, appreciate them, or even understand them (Mee 1997). Such a confusing stage of life, so misunderstood.

Too often adults forget that their present is what young adolescents are constructing as their past. Situations become far more complex than they often are, not only because adolescents do not have a backlog of success from which to draw but also because the young adolescent's self is at the center of a limited worldview. How then do we make sense of and then respond and teach to the unique characteristics and needs of this group of young people?

FRAMES OF UNDERSTANDING

There are four important theories of development that help shape our understanding of young adolescents in the middle grades: Piaget's cognitive developmental stages (1952), Havighurst's developmental tasks (1972), Gilligan's moral reasoning (1982; Gilligan, Lyons, and Hammer 1990; Gilligan and Brown 1992), and Maslow's hierarchy of needs (1970).

Piaget

Jean Piaget, a Swiss developmental psychologist, believed that if we could understand how young adolescents think, we could understand why they

behave and therefore learn as they do. He held that there were four separate stages of intellectual development, as illustrated in Table 3.1

Most middle grades students think at the concrete operational
stage. By the time they reach the eighth grade, many are beginning to
enter the formal operational or abstract thinking stage. Because girls are
approximately two and a half years ahead of boys in their developmental growth, girls tend to move into the abstract thinking phase before
their male counterparts. It is important to note, however, that growth
and development are not always continuous and forward moving. Because students do well on Friday's writing assignment based on abstract
thinking does not necessarily mean they will be as successful on a similar assignment on Monday. Because everyone is at different stages at
different times, middle grades teachers need to be observant and flexible in their teaching strategy.

Havighurst

Another developmental psychologist, R. J. Havighurst, contended that
there are six general stages of growth, as illustrated in Figure 3.1. As

Table 3.1
Piaget's Cognitive Developmental Stages

Stage	Description	Age	Dominant Characteristic
One	Sensorimotor	0-2	Thinking in response to the interaction with objects
Two	Preoperations	2-7	Development of language and social skills
Three	Concrete operations	7-11	Solving concrete problems that exist in the present; child becomes more social, moves from totally egocentric view, uses language more effectively, can think logically, can organize objects in a series
Four	Formal operations	11-15	Solving abstract, hypothetical problems; child expresses thoughts, ideas, and feelings and can rationalize contradictory information

Source: Adapted from J. Piaget (1977), "Problems in Equilibration." In M. Appel and L.
Goldberg, eds., *Topics in Cognitive Development,* vol. 1.

68

Figure 3.1
Havighurst's Developmental Tasks

Infancy and Early Childhood → Preparation for reading
Learning basic motor skills—walking, talking, eating, controlling body fluids
Using language to describe physical surroundings and
Social understandings

Middle Childhood ——————▶ Constructing positive self-image
Learning social skills with peers
Learning skills of reading, writing, numeracy
Learning team physical skills
Understanding social roles of male and female
Developing skills for everyday living
Developing an emerging moral self and set of values
Striving for personal independence
Developing attitudes toward institutions

Adolescence ——————▶ Developing socially acceptable and responsible behavior
Developing own set of values that form ethical behavior
Accepting one's sense of physical body
Achieving socially acceptable male and female roles
Engaging in more mature relations with peers
Achieving emotional independence from parents and adults
Preparing for economic career, marriage, and family

Early Adulthood ——————▶ Marrying, rearing children, managing home life
Establishing adult peers
Assuming place in social structure and community

Middle Age ——————▶ Reaching satisfactory position in job choice
Assisting children into adulthood
Accepting, adjusting to psychological changes of middle age
Adjusting to aging parents

Later Maturity ——————▶ Adjustment to decreasing physical strength and health, death of spouse, retirement from career

Source: Adapted from R. J. Havighurst (1972), *Developmental Tasks and Education.*

noted above, the period of adolescence presents aggressive changes. Havighurst maintained that early adolescents were confronted with:

1. Achieving new and more mature relations with age-mates of both sexes
2. Achieving a masculine or feminine social role (as much a social process as it is a biological one)
3. Accepting one's physique and using the body effectively (again as much a cultural process as it is a biological one)
4. Achieving emotional independence from parents and other adults.

As young adolescents assume the responsibility for more aspects of their lives, as they engage in the process of separation-individuation— that process of moving away from their parents and becoming their own person—there is a shift in roles for both the family and for the child. The young adolescent develops new goals, values, interests, and moral perspectives as she questions what she has been taught in the family. This is a shift that may cause stress and emotional pain for everyone involved.

Gilligan

Harvard scholar Carol Gilligan argued that there are not only different stages in moral development but also different perspectives, namely male and female. Unlike Lawrence Kohlberg, who based his moral stages of development on eleven boys and then generalized his observations to a much larger population, Gilligan noted that women and men approach situations and tend to needs according to the ways in which each group has been socialized. Women tend to rely on interpersonal relationships, whereas men approach things in a more individualistic and legalistic fashion. During the middle school years girls are encouraged to rely on fulfilling boys' needs, on developing attachments and interpersonal relationships; boys are encouraged to strike out and be more individualistic and self-sufficient. Girls are socialized to understand themselves through these relationships while boys are encouraged to define themselves in terms of occupation and accomplishment.

This apparent contradiction of roles creates discord for middle level students who are struggling to reconcile what they are taught with what they feel. The challenge for the family and for teachers is to help all students maximize their perceptions of themselves and their hopes for the future within a safe and caring environment and to mesh these two very different perspectives into a positive growth experience for everyone.

Maslow

Abraham Maslow looked at human development from the perspective of needs-fulfillment. He felt there were two general groups of needs, as illustrated in Figure 3.2.

Other Theories of Development

In contrast to the behavioral view of adolescent basic needs, a classroom teacher looked at her students and observed a different set of needs (James 1974), incorporated here into an action critique format (Table 3.2). This is a working plan that examines the student within the individual classroom and school and the response to the characteristic or need. It then asks what needs to be or could be done to improve response to all students—in other words, what action needs to be taken.

George, Lawrence, and Bushnell (1998) comparatively situated James's basic needs in the current generation of adolescents. They noted that during the country's agricultural and early industrial periods, young people were expected to share work responsibilities if the family were to survive. With the postindustrial era and with the necessary child labor–protection laws, young people no longer contributed in significant ways to or participated in the larger society. Therefore, their *need to be needed* and the attendant sense of self-integrity have been deferred. In recent years academic service learning, discussed in Chapter 6, has provided the kinds of opportunities for recognized participation in and contribution to the community that build a fundamental view of one's self-worth and self-esteem.

The *need to need* speaks to the kinds of learning activities that must value both the pride in individual work and accomplishment and the collaborative and cooperative work of peers. These kinds of activities help to develop young adolescents' burgeoning sense of independence as well as their interdependence. George, Lawrence, and Bushnell (1998) noted that young adolescents also need to master some skill or possess some body of knowledge. I would add that young people *need to be successful*; they need to know something or be able to do something that their peers and/or adults value and respect.

Figure 3.2
Maslow's Hierarchy of Needs

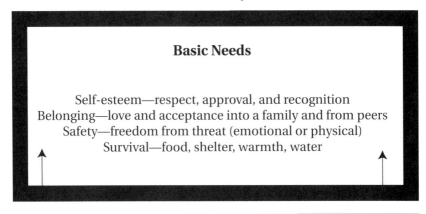

Basic Needs

Self-esteem—respect, approval, and recognition
Belonging—love and acceptance into a family and from peers
Safety—freedom from threat (emotional or physical)
Survival—food, shelter, warmth, water

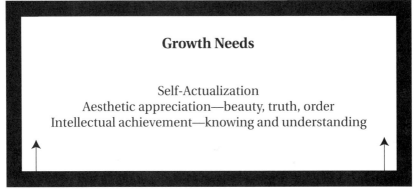

Growth Needs

Self-Actualization
Aesthetic appreciation—beauty, truth, order
Intellectual achievement—knowing and understanding

Source: Adapted from Paul Eggen and Donald Kauchak (2001), *Educational Psychology: Windows on Classrooms.*

Student choice and voice in their own learning are critical elements of effective middle grades practice. When given the opportunity to choose what they wish to study, young adolescents frequently *look inward.* They are naturally curious about themselves and about how they think, why they act the way they do, how they learn, and why they learn. And they are curious about the actions of others: Will there be a planet to inherit if there is a next generation? What is life and could there be life somewhere on the other side of the stars? Why do people love? Why do they hate? Why do they war against each other? Why do they believe as they do?

Table 3.2
Action Critique: Responding to Basic Student Needs

James's Basic Adolescent Needs	Ways My Classroom / School Responds on Behalf of All Students	Ways My Classroom/ School Can Improve Programs for All Students
Need to be needed		
Need to need		
Need to move inward		
Need to affect the outer world		
Need for intensity: need to take risks, to try, to fail, and to still be okay		
Need for routine		
*Need for imagination: creativity, myth, and legend		
Need for fact		
Need for physical activity		
Need for stillness		
Need for separateness		
Need for belonging		
*Need to succeed		
*Need to be respected		

* These items have been added to James's list.
Source: Based on C. James (1974), *Beyond Customs.*

As transescents search for answers to these questions, they begin to see the discrepancies between the reality of the world they will inherit and their own ideal views. They note that their environment has not been affected in random fashion but has been altered by the people who live in it. So they struggle to close that gap. George, Lawrence, and Bushnell (1998) thoughtfully noted of transescents that "they feel a strong need . . . to bring their efforts into the work of making the material world more nearly fit their image of what it might become. If their needs to affect the outer world are not honored by the adult community, the natural consequence is a retreat into apathy or a grasp for power in some destructive way" (20). In response the school that provides functional, hands-on activities helps students learn the consequential pattern of actions both on animate and on inanimate objects. In so doing, they enable students to experience the limits of their own power. Among the first groups to recycle newspapers, to save cans, to clean up rivers, to in essence *affect the world around them* were middle schoolers.

James (1974) described *intensity* in young adolescents as a natural "high." When youth can't find constructive ways in which they can experience a particular sense of significance, they turn to more destructive means that lead them down the path of trouble to abuse, violence, and other self-destructive acts. There is, on the other hand, little greater sense of intense accomplishment, camaraderie, and thrill than in performance.

After nearly three decades in the public school arena, I can still hear the celebratory roar of the young people's voices as the last curtain fell on that year's spring musical. With a talented and selfless colleague, Charles E. Holley, we double cast large productions that included everyone who auditioned, wrote music for a pit choir of over 150 students, wrote instrumental parts for our alumni who faithfully returned to join in the fun, and engaged the all-important parents in set design, costuming, and general production. Three weeks later we followed the musical with the Spring Fantacular, a spring concert that featured parents singing and dancing, students choreographing their own music, the select choir Excaliber, the Dance Company, the handbell choir, the guitar ensemble, all the general music classes, the faculty, and the principal. One would think that in a school of 500 with nearly 400 students performing, there would be little audience, yet extra rows had to be added to the 1,100 seats in the auditorium. People came not for the music itself, nor for the youth themselves. Those two productions became something much bigger than any of us. They were intense, with rehearsals at 6:00 A.M., after school, and through the evening, and then Saturday rehearsals for the family. They became "happenings." I recently received an e-mail from Master Sgt. Robert Buccia, standing in harm's way somewhere half a world away, that simply said, "I want you to know that when I become lonely or a tinge of fear creeps in, I always remember my days in Excaliber with you. I belonged to something special, something that made me proud of who I was. Something bigger than who I thought I could be. I felt safe. I felt valued. I felt I could take a chance and if I failed, you would be there." Bobby was in my classes nearly twenty years ago. *A need for intensity.*

Bobby's story was also a portrait of the young adolescent *need for success*. That means more than every student having her or his fifteen minutes in the spotlight. It means that effective middle schools know their students well enough to provide a variety of experiences that tap into each student's pool of talent. It also means that schools create non-traditional opportunities, that schools embrace and celebrate all students, that at the end-of-the-year awards assembly potentially every student will walk across the stage for recognition in one area or another. Every person walks with one foot on the ground and one moving forward in the air. The foot on the ground is based in success, and that compels the student to take another step, another chance, to take a risk, to try something new. The learner moves most effectively from the known to the unknown. But the learner is more willing to move to the unknown when he or she has known success, no matter how large the audience.

Although James explained intensity in terms of creativity, I would suggest young adolescents experience the *need to create*. This doesn't mean that every child is a stage musician or an artist or a performer. But it does mean that the human spirit has a sense of aesthetics, of what is beautiful in a particular way. Effective middle grades schools nurture this need through their arts education program—both aural arts (choral and instrumental music) and visual arts (for example, photography, drawing, painting, woodcrafting, weaving, string design). Every culture in recorded history has borne witness to the human need to express itself, to create—to the extent that some of the early Greek cultures and some nearly extinct cultures such as the Mayan are represented only through their art. The first record of western civilization is a Greek song or skolion found on a piece of pottery. From the Mayans we have learned about astronomical time, about astronomy, about calculations, all from their architecture. Yet, when resources become limited, arts programs that include the majority of students in every school are the first to be cut.

Similarly, James (1974) noted that as young adolescents develop their abstract thinking, they grasp the richness of many of life's deepest concepts through myths and legends. George, Lawrence, and Bushnell noted, "The myths of a culture provide its continuity" (1998, 21), when in truth, artifacts, myths, and legends tell us through music, through pottery, through the hieroglyphic legends, and through ancient papyrus, of another time. It is the *need for imagination* that both creativity and intensity shape.

Young adolescents *need routine,* but not drill and practice. The kind of environment that is consistent, reasoned, steady, and encouraging provides the fertile ground for the development of necessary skills and dispositions. In today's environment the safety, continuity, and order of the classroom are often the harbor in the midst of a societal storm.

The *need for fact* is the need for deductive and inductive logic, the ability to observe, draw a hypothesis, test that hypothesis, come to a substantiated conclusion and then to metacognitively analyze how one arrived at that conclusion, or in other words to think about one's thinking.

Anyone who infrequently comes into a middle school is quickly struck by the students' restless energy. An observer only has to spend one class period with the students in order to understand their obvious *need for physical activity.* Is it not ironic, however, that when students arrive at the middle school, recess has been eliminated?

The other half of active physical activity is just as intense but may not be as obvious. Students *need to be still* or have quiet in their own persons. They need to learn to focus, to center their energy and concentrate on a single task at hand. The ability to quiet oneself frees the mind of extraneous noise and clarifies focus to accelerate performance and to enrich the experience. Many teachers have accomplished this with their students through the use of various styles and forms of music, through self-discipline techniques, through breathing exercises, through the practice of mantras, or even through the study of nature. And in many ways this leads into James's view of the *need for separateness,* that need to intentionally and constructively remove oneself from the group, the need for privacy. When students step into a middle school, are their needs for privacy subsumed by the collective necessity for space? Some schools have rigorously analyzed their school policies as well as their use of the physical plant and again asked, "Are the needs of the students met first, or are the needs of the adult staff represented?"

And finally James concluded with the *need for belonging*—a belonging that is chosen, a belonging that fulfills the young adolescent *yearning for respect,* a belonging that teaches and affirms. These are not natural skills, and for all the power the peer group holds, middle school youth know little of the tools necessary to interpret or to understand the rules of group interaction that will augment their success within the group. Cooperative learning, discussed in Chapter 5, provides the kind of learning experiences that enable this form of skill building.

However adolescent development is framed or configured, it is clear that if a child's basic needs are not met, little if any academic learning will take place. Because the larger culture asks schools to perform more noneducational tasks, schools are enlisting the help of community organizations through the establishment of partnerships.

Society is changing at a faster pace than at any other time in recorded history. Emerging adolescents are both living in this dynamic society and experiencing more changes in their own lives than at any other time. These changes challenge adults to keep pace with adaptations appropriate to the growth of young people. Adults think they understand young people because they experienced adolescence themselves. The world as they knew it, however, is not the same as the world in which young people live today. It is in this discrepant gap that erroneous assumptions and stereotypical beliefs reside, separating young people from the adults whom they need as teachers and guides.

If we know how emerging adolescents think and grow, if we know what they believe, how they look at themselves and the world, how they reason and how they learn, we can be more effective teachers by tailoring our teaching to each student.

DEVELOPMENTAL NEEDS

There are six key developmental needs of young adolescents:

- Positive social interaction with adults and peers
- Structure and clear limits to physical activity
- Creative expression
- Competence and achievement
- Meaningful participation in families and in school
- Community support; opportunities for self-definition (Scales 1991)

To this list author and former middle grades teacher Chris Stevenson (2002) would add young adolescents' need for self-respect and the need to be liked, accepted, and successful. They want life to be fair and just. Dorman, Lipsitz, and Verner (1985) looked at adolescents as a group and concluded they need:

- Diversity (in experiencing teaching, curriculum, and scheduling)

- Self-exploration and self-definition
- Meaningful participation in school and community
- Positive social interaction with peers and adults
- Physical activity
- Competence and achievement
- Structure and clear limits

Each semester I would ask my middle level students, "If you could tell student teachers one thing they needed to know in order to be successful with you and in order for you to be successful, what would you say?" And every semester for over twenty-eight years, students would say that teachers need to set boundaries and fairly enforce them. They spoke of a just, caring, and safe environment under the guidance of an authority figure who respects them, understands them, and knows what she or he is teaching.

In constructing middle schools to meet the developmental needs of transescents, we would consider both the vast differences in and transitional nature of the student population. When asked to describe the typical middle school student, sixth-grader Jordan wrote on September 11, 2002, "The typical middle schooler is like a box of chocolates, different some loud like stomping, some soft like a melody" (Sanders 2002).

Although the students must feel safe and secure in school, they must also feel the freedom to take risks with regard to learning. Even though there is a core body of knowledge that all students need to know, as importantly the school must provide encore or elective classes that will stimulate students in the creative domain. And although the school establishes rules of conduct by which all participants are bound, students need to exercise the kind of openness that engages their opinions, respects their voices, and responds to their suggestions.

In examining effective middle schools, then, we turn to the domain characteristics of young adolescents, while acknowledging the differences students display within each domain.

INTELLECTUAL OR COGNITIVE DEVELOPMENT

Characteristics of Young Adolescents

1. Display a wide range of individual intellectual development

2. Love to learn if they see the relevance
3. Are in a transition between concrete and abstract thinking
4. Prefer active to passive learning
5. Want to work with peers or do group work
6. Consider variables but have difficulty prioritizing
7. Think a lot about what others think—they tend to think they have an audience; they are preoccupied with self
8. Have a strong need for approval and can be easily discouraged
9. Understand sophisticated humor
10. Challenge the authority of adults, always observing them
11. Develop an increasingly better understanding of themselves and their abilities
12. May demonstrate little interest in or regard for academic work, but are intensely interested in the world around them

Implications for Practice. Schools Should:

1. Differentiate instruction
2. Use real-world models; use various approaches and teaching materials
3. Frequently change groups—group and regroup
4. Provide learning opportunities that are exciting, that encourage physical movement, and that are meaningful and respectful
5. Provide learning centers, small group discussions, creative dramatics to demonstrate learning
6. Teach strategies for thinking and ordering information such as notetaking, brainstorming, and lecturing but only in eight- to ten-minute chunks
7. Link classroom studies to areas of concern in the community; role-play debates, provide learning centers, engage in community politics, provide academic service learning opportunities
8. Allow opportunities that encourage self-expression/peer group discussion of self-identity and self-understanding
9. Encourage self-expression through the study of art and drama and in role playing

10. Involve students in the planning of the curriculum based on their interest levels; engage students in their own assessments and in the preparation of a unit; have a class government and/or classroom rules generated collaboratively by the teacher and the students; provide a positive school environment of trust
11. Provide immediate and attainable goals rather than remote, delayed goals
12. Organize content around real-life concepts; develop service learning opportunities

In addition to shifting from concrete to abstract thinking, young adolescents also begin to think reflexively, that is, to think about their own thinking, a process also called metacognition. This often confuses young people as they sort out their involvement in experiences around them and in their participation in their own learning. Their newly found ability to reason on another level can be a real source of meaningful learning when used by the skillful classroom teacher. On the other hand, it can also be a source of student discouragement if the teacher is unaware. For instance, when elementary school children attempt a task that is difficult and discover they don't understand the task, they move on to an easier one. The young adolescent may begin a task that he does not understand and rather than moving to a new task, he may dwell on his inability to perform that task, especially when his peers are successful.

This new sense of reasoning not only affects the intellectual progress of students but also becomes the stage upon which other changing aspects of young adolescents' lives are played out. When their physical bodies are experiencing dramatic changes, their reasoning becomes much more comparative, sometimes to the point that they become obsessed with their appearance. Likewise, if they are not experiencing physical changes and their friends are, the obsession with themselves takes on enormous proportions to the extent that they reason that they are failing where others are succeeding, in spite of themselves. Seventh grader Tashonda said, on September 11, 2002,

> Most middle school students are crazy. They cuss, talk about people, and they get into fights more than 6th or 8th graders. Most of the stuff that's important is their appearance, like their clothes, shoes, hair, if they stink, etc. Other people worry about if they will get a E [failing mark] on the quiz or test they took the day before.

> If people wouldn't trip about the way they look, or if they are wearing the right clothes, everything would be fine. There would be no more stress. (Sanders 2002, 1)

Middle schoolers are beginning to interpret themselves and what is happening to them, to critique their surrounding world, and to form a new sense of what they believe and what they value. They are beginning to interpret events, people, and beliefs. They are beginning to interpret their place in the world. Transescents are confident in some situations and totally absent of confidence in others. They are known to frequently shift between feelings of superiority and inferiority (Wiles and Bondi 2001).

Dweck (1999) described performance-goal students. They tend to narrowly view their intelligence as fixed and concrete and are more concerned with receiving high marks and "looking good." Performance-goal classrooms emphasize evaluation and ability in contrast to classrooms that foster learning by emphasizing progress and mastery. It is in the latter classrooms that students are more likely to put forth continued effort because they enjoy learning and are encouraged to take risks and make mistakes (Wehner 2002). If students have not encountered mistakes and engaged in subsequent problem solving, they will not have the requisite experience to meet more demanding challenges that will at some point arise (Midgley, Kaplan, and Middleton 2001).

PHYSICAL DOMAIN

Characteristics of Young Adolescents

1. Grow rapidly and irregularly; often move awkwardly
2. Are restless and fatigued
3. Have bones that grow faster than their muscles
4. Experience a large flux in metabolism rate
5. Exhibit a wide range of physiological differences between students
6. Are concerned about body image
7. Need daily physical activity because of increased energy
8. Mature at different rates, girls one and a half to two years sooner than boys
9. Eat junk food rather than healthy food
10. Tire easily—are at their best between the hours of 9 and 11 A.M.

11. Have poor health habits—bulimia/anorexia, experimentation with drugs
12. Have poor physical fitness—lack endurance and strength
13. Develop sexual awareness that increases as secondary sex characteristics appear
14. Are physically vulnerable

Implications for Practice

1. Have intramural programs and physical education classes where all students can participate; limit interscholastic sports
2. Allow for exercise during school hours; provide healthy snacks; encourage parents to see that students get proper rest at home; limit late school activities; incorporate active teaching
3. Provide nutritional guidance
4. Avoid activities where physical appearance can be compared; encourage parents to assure students their body changes are natural and will eventually stabilize; provide science and health curriculum that emphasizes self-understanding about body changes; offer health and hygiene seminars; provide information about influence of drug, alcohol, and tobacco use on the body
5. Provide opportunities for daily exercise and a place where all students can be children by playing and being noisy for short periods
6. Offer different age activities: exploratories, yearbook, play, outdoor activities, music, art

To say that young adolescents are focused on their physical development and on their peers' perceptions of them would be somewhat of an understatement. Although teachers are particularly aware of the physical changes and sporadic demands of development on students, we sometimes forget the energy and space those changes consume to the extent that even the best of students sometimes tune us out. Whether it is a bad-hair day or an acne outbreak, transescents are sure the entire world knows their problems but doesn't really understand them.

Growth spurts are real and perplexing for young people. An eighth-grade boy was walking down the hallway in front of me one morning when he suddenly tripped and fell. Although I pretended I didn't see, he nonetheless turned to me and said, "My bones just grew, cause I don't see anything else I could have tripped on." In truth it was probably a normal adrenaline surge. During his eighth-grade year, Zach began to experience a great deal of pain in his joints and bones. Several physicians later, it was found he had grown so much in one year that his body had not kept pace. Finally by the beginning of his tenth-grade year the pain eased, and Zach felt comfortable inside his body.

Middle grades youngsters are developing at irregular rates. Because their hormone levels are changing, significant changes occur with metabolism, body growth, and sexual maturation (Messick and Reynolds 1992). An eighth-grade science teacher at Lincoln Middle School noted that irregular metabolism may cause individuals to experience fatigue and restlessness. Even though students at this age prefer junk food, it is important that they eat healthfully and get plenty of exercise and rest.

Girls tend to mature earlier than boys, both physically and mentally. Young adolescent girls tend to feel awkward about their bodies as they develop breasts. Likewise, boys feel uneasy about their appearance as they develop facial and body hair. Boys are also beginning to experience voice changes, which can cause them to feel self-conscious. Both genders are developing sexual awareness and are eager to learn more.

Protecting students from situations such as group showers, in which their physical development or lack of it could be compared, is the least schools can do to be more sensitive. Jay had been in my honor program for three years, and I knew him to be a gentle, thoughtful, and caring boy. Suddenly, during the last semester of his eighth-grade year, he began cutting classes. Upon more careful note, I realized that it was first the gym class he cut, then it became the alternate days in which he had physical education. Sitting out on the back step of our World War I memorial school building, Jay began to tell a story of conflict, embarrassment, confusion, and hurt. During group showers, some of the more developed basketball boys poked fun at his being overweight and underdeveloped. The harassment soon escalated into name-calling and bullying. Jay poured out his confusion over his emerging sexuality and tried to find a way to retain his dignity in the face of little self-worth. He confided that he had considered suicide but hoped I would notice his absences and in some fashion come to "rescue" him. In many ways what seventh-grade Amanda wrote on September 11, 2002, spoke about Jay: "People are becoming more followers than leaders in middle school. Like calling one person names and teasing them just because one person started doing that" (Sanders 2002, 1).

And even closer to Jay's experience, Shaquille believed, as he expressed it on September 11, 2002, that typical middle school students "act snobby and mean. They don't like nobody except the people that fears them or people they fear. What they think is important is impressing someone by picking fights with people or being bad in school" (Sanders 2002, 1).

Teacher and family understanding of the pressures young people face is critical. When young adolescents share part of their hidden fears, adults must resist saying they understand, for youngsters of this age feel no one else has experienced what they are going through and that therefore no one else really understands. What they really desire is someone to listen, and to listen with compassion. This is the antithesis to the imaginary audience, a phenomenon frequently written about in developmental literature. Young adolescents feel that everyone is always looking at them, talking about them, criticizing them—a phenomenon called egocentricism; they feel there is an imaginary audience they can't see because of the glare of the spotlights in their own eyes. In the presence of the adult confidant and in the private space of their own bedrooms are often the only places where they feel safe, free from critical observation, momentarily free from pressures.

In health education and science classes students learn about growth through self-analysis, and they discover that growth is discontinuous and sporadic. Any middle grades teacher could tell the family about the "mirror factor." Because so many students, of both genders, were constantly pulling out pocket mirrors and checking to see what had changed in the last thirty minutes or so, I always kept a mirror by the classroom door. The students could check themselves before class started and before they left my classroom. Above the mirror was a sign that said "The person in this mirror is special."

Physical development in which difference is the rule and not the exception provokes unease in transescents and understanding in teachers. Aaron was a seventh-grade boy who was six feet tall and weighed 280 pounds. His best friend Tavin was four feet five inches tall and weighed all of 110 pounds. Too often I found myself expecting more mature behavior from Aaron than from Tavin simply because of his physical presence. And although middle school students often ask themselves if they are "normal," what is normal developmentally for transescents looks quite different from what is normal at any other stage of growth and to anyone not schooled in developmental practice.

In the past two decades, television, music, films, and in particular Music Television (MTV), have portrayed a "grow-up quickly" image to emerging adolescents. With the advent of puberty, issues of sexuality become paramount in students' minds. The images portrayed in the media further confuse their individual understanding of themselves as sexual beings. It is first the responsibility and the privilege of the family to teach their children the values and beliefs they hold and then to be open to questions youth may be hesitant to ask. It is then the responsibility of the faith community to support young people as they move through this sometimes treacherous period. And it is the responsibility of the school and particularly the individual teacher to welcome students to ask questions because they know their confidence will not be betrayed. A prospective teacher in my undergraduate class said, "What if a student asks my opinion about an issue of sexuality and I hold very firm religious beliefs about that situation?" As long as a child does not share something that the teacher is legally bound to report, what is important is that the teacher listens openly, asks what the family believes, warmly validates that child and the struggle to find him or herself, and then volunteers to accompany the student if he or she feels uncomfortable and needs to talk with a parent, a guardian, a leader in the faith community, or a counselor. More times than not, students are not really asking our opinion, they are asking that we actively listen and help them work through issues. We cannot do this apart from upholding the family and the family's culture and beliefs.

Given all of these physical adjustments students are attempting to make, it is important to have them physically moving about as they learn. Young adolescents should also participate in physical education classes to develop their coordination. Students should be educated about their body changes and personal hygiene in health or science courses. It is also important that middle grades youngsters know they are not alone and that other students experience the same bodily and emotional changes and self-doubts.

SOCIAL DOMAIN

Characteristics of Young Adolescents

1. Have a strong need to belong to a group, with peer approval becoming more important as adult approval decreases in importance

2. In their search for self, model behavior after older, esteemed students or nonparent adults
3. May exhibit immature behavior because their social skills frequently lag behind their mental and physical maturity
4. Experiment with new slang and behaviors as they search for a social position within their group, often discarding these "new identities" at a later date
5. Must adjust to the social acceptance of early-maturing girls and the athletic successes of early-maturing boys, especially if they themselves are maturing at a slower rate
6. Are dependent on parental beliefs and values but seek to make their own decisions
7. Are often intimidated and frightened by their first middle level school experience because of the large numbers of students and teachers and the size of the building
8. Desire recognition for their efforts and achievements; seek constant affirmation
9. Like fads, especially those shunned by adults
10. Often overreact to ridicule, embarrassment, and rejection
11. Are socially vulnerable because, as they develop their beliefs, attitudes, and values, the influence of media and negative experiences with adults and peers may compromise their ideals and values
12. Show extreme behavior at times—daring, argumentative, overly noisy, drastic, even embracing outrageous fashions of dress
13. Remain influenced by adults other than their parents
14. Seek choice and self-responsibility within the boundaries set by nonparental adults
15. Pledge allegiance to the peer group and often tend to exhibit cruel behavior to those outside that group; strive to fit in
16. Rebel against parental values yet remain largely dependent on and reflect these same values
17. Test limits, question authority, and push boundaries
18. Step into the realm of heterosexual relationships while maintaining same-sex friendships; strive to understand the socially accepted standard for both
19. Experience traumatic breaks with important friends because of increased societal mobility

Implications for Practice

1. Establish an active student government that allows students to help establish standards for behavior and dress codes
2. Encourage students to engage in service learning and community activities
3. Use flexible teaching patterns so students can interact with a variety of adults with whom they identify
4. Schedule large-group activities rather than boy-girl events; encourage cocurricular activities
5. Assist students in establishing and reaching realistic goals
6. Promote "family" grouping of students and teachers to provide stability for new students
7. Provide an orientation program and/or "buddy system" that can reduce the trauma of transitioning into and out of middle school
8. Provide debates, plays, play days, and other activities to allow students to "show off" in productive ways
9. Work closely with the family to help adults realize peer pressure is a normal part of the maturation process
10. Encourage parents/the family to continue to provide love and comfort even though they may feel rejected
11. Encourage teachers to be counselors (advisory period)
12. Provide multiple role models through teaching teams, advisory teachers, and other adults in the school
13. Provide a diverse staff
14. Teach the importance of respecting others (Wiles and Bondi 2001)

LaShonda, a student of Rex Sanders at Willow Run Middle School, wrote on September 14, 2002: "We want to be good at something that people apreshate [*sic*]. To be noticed in positive ways. Gotta have at least one friend that you can tell what happened at school. We want to be able to talk to our teachers as if they are one of our friends. We want to be able to tell the truth about something without thinking about what someone is going to say about it to you or about you" (Sanders 2002, 1). William, another of Sanders's students, observed on September 14, 2002,

> The typical middle school students have different actions. There are the ones who are clowns, the ones that are cool, and the so-called

nerds. They start to dress differently, mature differently, and act differently. I think the most important things in a middle schooler's life is their reputation, and maybe someone to have a crush on. I have a crush on some girls, but I still stay the same as usual.

I have a reputation as the brains of the class to most people I know. I help most of them on their work. (Sanders 2002, 1)

Stress, Vulnerabililty, and the Family

If any single word could describe this period in the development of young people, it would be *vulnerable*. Self-consciousness soars during transescence. If it were not enough to feel the pressure to find oneself and to find one's peer group, while attempting to succeed academically, the outside social pressures caused by family dissolution, family trauma, and societal images create a sense of stress, which is little short of burdensome for any person, much less for one who has to date so little success navigating life's ups and downs.

What is apparent is that the upward spiral of students who emerge from this developmental period never able to fully realize their created potential is increasing. Alarmingly, in my thirty years of public school teaching, students moved from describing themselves in the 1970s as fearful of the world that they might inherit, to disengaged in the 1980s, to disconnected and apathetic in the 1990s and early 2000s. The first Carnegie *Turning Points* document observed:

> Unfortunately, by age 15, substantial numbers of American youth are at risk of reaching adulthood unable to meet adequately the requirements of the work place, the commitments of relationships in families and with friends, and the responsibilities of participation in a democratic society. These youth are among the estimated 7 million young people— one in four adolescents—who are extremely vulnerable to multiple high-risk behaviors and school failure. Another 7 million may be at moderate risk, but remain a cause for serious concern. (Carnegie Council on Adolescent Development 1989, 8)

A decade later, the second Carnegie *Turning Points* (Jackson and Davis 2000) document noted a continued rise in the number of eighth graders who experimented with tobacco, alcohol, and illicit drugs whereas the number of teenagers engaged in sexual activity reportedly decreased. What can be noted for both males and females is that the level of stress, as witnessed in various acting-out behaviors, continues to increase. Middle grades teacher and researcher Lisa Klemetson defined stress as the failure to handle real or imagined problems in a healthy, normal way (2002). It is also defined as mental or emotional tension or pressure. This inability to handle difficult situations leads to problems in any or all areas of life, health, and well-being. Navarrete noted, "According to the National Institute of Mental Health, approximately 3 to 5% of all children under the age of 18 experience serious depression. This amounts to well over 3.4 million depressed youngsters" (1999, 137).

Klemetson's critical case study of an eighth grader named Kim revealed a child without a childhood, a thirteen year old expected to care for younger siblings and take care of the house in lieu of the working mom and in the absence of a father. Klemetson noted that when the stress of home got Kim down, she stopped turning in her homework, she did not eat lunch with her friends, and she didn't like to participate in class activities. On the outside, it looked as though she were disinterested in school, but with knowledge regarding her home life, it was easier to understand from where the quiet and withdrawn behavior came.

> Studies indicate that depression can have an adverse effect on the progress of adolescent performance. Adolescents who are depressed tend to have difficulties in school, both socially and academically. They might be absent more or might even drop out. They may take part in dangerous activities such as drugs and alcohol or they may lose interest in their appearance and may have problems with relationships both within school and outside of school. (Klemetson 2002, 5)

Unfortunately, the term *dysfunctional family* has become more common. With parents abusing drugs and alcohol, neglect and abuse are facts of life for many young adolescents (Dove 2001).

> Sadly, the teaching and nurturing that many parents traditionally have been expected to provide is now deficient and lacking. It has become necessary to create a whole new vocabulary to describe youth and families of this time.
> *Latchkey kids, fatherless kids, at-risk students,* and *throwaway youth* are dangerous terms recently created to classify today's youth. Dysfunctional families, addictive families, disengaged families, detached parents, nonresidential parents and parenthood by

proxy are just a few of the phrases coined since the 1970s to illustrate society's steady displacement of the traditional meaning of the
family and parenthood. (10)

In trying to understand Kim's needs in her classroom, Klemetson
noted that studies have shown that an adolescent's low self-esteem can
be the result of a parent's being too authoritative, too demanding, or
nonsupportive. It can also be a consequence of family economic difficulties, of the parents' low self-esteem that in turn directly influences
the child's self-esteem. Other researchers argue that financial difficulties in the family can lead to depression and stress in children. There appears to be a significant correlation between parents who experience
job loss and adolescent conflict with their parents. Fathers who suddenly experience unemployment tend to hand out more penalizing
punishments, are less consistent with the firm enforcement of family
rules, and show less attention to their children (Lempers and Clark-
Lempers 1997). Families who are struggling financially have less time to
create positive family relationships. They are less likely to stay in one
place and are less likely to think of themselves as a close family unit.
Parents tend to be unaware of the cascade of problems that spills from
them to their children.

Heaney (2002) noted that children of divorce also often experience more stress owing to their family relationships and because of all
of the structural and relational changes. But because of the nature of
their families, they are also in a situation where they are provided less
support (Teybar 2001). The custodial parent may be working two jobs,
starting a new relationship, attending to the needs of the new family
members when a stepfamily is involved, or just trying to keep up with
the work of raising a family without the help of a partner. The inaccessi-
bility of the parents to the child can create many new stresses in addition to the ones the child is seeking their help in resolving.

Sidney (2002) noted that divorce had become a major factor in
Jamishia's life. This eighth-grade student had been dealing with several
levels of abandonment for years, as do most children in divorce situations. According to Carter and McGoldrick (1999), divorce is the largest
variation of the traditional family life cycle. And even though divorce is
now common, it is still an abnormality. Many families consider themselves to be "broken" or "incomplete" once divorce occurs. In turn the
child believes she or he, too, is broken in some fashion, if not responsible for what has happened to the family structure (Ahron 1999).

When young adolescents feel they are broken or don't fit in, they experience major stress. And that stress often expresses itself in erratic behavior—behavior due to sudden change, unfortunate circumstances, and in some cases growth. Sidney noted that a student like Jamishia goes through these circumstances on a daily basis. It is difficult for Jamishia and others like her to sit still or even to want to be interested in what their teacher is saying. Yet, her resilience—that ability and habit of mind that causes her to be confident, caring, and competent (Stevenson 2002) in the face of factors that could easily place her at risk—instructs wise teachers like Sidney in profound ways. Sidney noted, "Jamishia has taught me a lot about her world through body language more than through words. More importantly it is clear to see she has matured because of her life's circumstances. She plans to keep all promises she has made to herself such as being extremely responsible" (2002, 8).

Stress and Deferred Childhood

Johnson (2002) observed that societal change has brought more stress into the lives of adults, which in turn increases the stress level of young adolescents. Adults experience an increase in stress owing to fear brought on by the increase in violence. There is the fear of being alone with the higher divorce and separation rates. And there is fear of professional insecurity due to economic restructuring, rising unemployment rates, and economic inflation. When the level of stress increases, adults become self-absorbed with the demands put on them. When this happens, we unintentionally or unknowingly hurry our children to grow up sooner than is developmentally appropriate.

Johnson further noted that society adds to childhood stress by raising expectations, by exploiting children by having them dress in a more adult manner, by encouraging children to sue their parents, and by creating summer programs that offer competitive sports to perfect skills. The family often unknowingly adds stress to young adolescents, asking them to assume adult responsibilities including child-rearing chores, making their own meals, and tending to household chores such as laundry and dwelling maintenance. When the family works during the time children are home, a stressful situation may ensue. Additionally, the school adds to the stress of a child who is chronically failing. For some children, simply going to school every day is stressful enough.

Johnson's (2002) study of Arika cited a transescent who had been denied her childhood. Yet that was not the only factor that put Arika at risk. There are many factors that together cripple the chances of so many young people to maximize their immediate potential. Arika's brother was incarcerated; her mother bar hopped; and the older father for whom Arika provided care was ailing. Other transescents may change schools frequently or move from one home to another, or they may even deal with the teeter-totter of wondering which utility will be turned off that month so other bills can be paid. In the current violent and angry society, many children must deal with the death of a loved one. Any and all of these factors will cause children to grow up too quickly, to face a world for which they are not ready, a world that sees them as children and expects them to act as mature young adults. Where is the celebration of the rites of passage when the window of time between childhood and adulthood is truncated?

Stress and Depression

Because Kim's parents faced financial difficulties and were not a cohesive unit, Kim learned to deal with the pressure by escaping to her world of horses. "When she begins talking about horses and riding, it is like she is transformed into another time and place where there are no problems, just space to ride her horse and gallop into the sunset" (Klemetson 2002, 8). The results of a study of depression and teenagers found that there is a call for attentiveness to adolescent depression and the possible severe penalties depression can have. Today's educators need to be mindful of the warning signs in order to prime students for the future. Some of those signs are:

- Personality changes—a usually talkative child becomes quiet or a normally compliant child begins to break rules
- Social problems—child withdraws from friendships, does not participate in group activities
- Behavior withdrawal—child becomes withdrawn and quiet, tends to hide from certain situations
- Academic problems—child does not turn in homework; experiences low test scores when he or she is capable of much more
- Parental relationship problems—child argues with parents or is unable to resolve conflicts
- Avoidance behavior—child does not want to be noticed or chooses to be overlooked
- Disaffected engagement—child is not interested in school either socially or academically; is not interested in his or her appearance

- Low self-esteem, which causes the child to be more susceptible to drug and alcohol abuse and/or to engage in other risky behavior, makes problems seem bigger than they really are, and can lead to thoughts of suicide

Because the current generation of students will outnumber the 1940s and 1950s baby boomers, current young adolescents will have an effect on every aspect of the society. This group has a life full of challenges ahead, a world of opportunities and of pitfalls—drugs, alcohol, and violence more than their parents could have imagined (Navarrete 1999). Klemetson continued, pointing out that the situations that today's adolescent faces are much too immense for the school or one social assistance organization to address. It is the village surrounding the adolescent or school-linked services (Williams-Boyd 1996) that need to step up and become the support system for young people (Dove 2001).

Klemetson (2002) indicated that teachers could learn to avoid creating added stress in their students' lives by following some simple guidelines:

- Set definite guidelines for grading
- Share the grading system with students
- Create class routines and adhere to them
- Connect lessons to the world of the young adolescent's experience
- Avoid unnecessary interruptions that disrupt the flow of the lesson and of the day
- Help students set realistic goals
- Provide opportunities for cooperative learning activities
- Give positive feedback
- Help students find control over their situations (Lessard 1998)
- Incorporate student input into the formulation of classroom rules
- Get to know the students outside of the classroom
- Celebrate student accomplishments
- Express joy at being with the students

It is crucial that adolescents become more aware of stress in their lives and how to effectively deal with stress. In the mad political rush for states to test their students by standardized means, little attention is given to the development of social and socioemotional skills in young people. Young adolescents need to learn how to deal with verbal attacks, power struggles, and anger that might be directed toward them from parents, from peers, or from friends who are dealing with their own life's struggles (Martin and Martin 2000).

Klemetson thoughtfully observed that because Kim's only escape was her horse riding, which only happened once a week, she needed to find ways to deal with stress on a more consistent basis. Because her horseback riding could end at any time, being able to have more permanent stress management techniques was paramount to Kim's survival. As Lessard contended, "pupils are already being provided with a potentially supportive group environment that encourages open discussion concerning difficulties, doubts and worries, that can systematically encourage, identify and experiment with stress or stress management techniques, thereby strengthening their sense of control and mastery over situations. . . . Teaching coping skills to adolescents is both possible and beneficial" (1998, 16). Although Kim's current method of coping was working for the time being, it was not a method of stress relief that could take her into adulthood. Adolescents need to develop life skills that deal with day-to-day stress before the pressure becomes debilitating in their lives (Massey 1998).

The physical atmosphere of a school can greatly increase or decrease the amount of stress in an adolescent's life. For example, the lighting, the actual size of the school, the number of students, the noise level, the cleanliness of the building, and the general layout of the school are factors that can add or relieve stress in some students. Klemetson noted that during one conversation, Kim related how much calmer home was when everything was clean. If cleanliness calms one student, it is fairly safe to assume there are others who need order in their surroundings as well. Navarrete (1999) offered additional suggestions as to how to deal with adolescents who exhibit signs of depression:

- School counselors, psychologists, and other school personnel make themselves available and accessible to students in a one-on-one situation or in small groups, or during advisory period
- School personnel become aware of at-risk warning signs and then monitor students of concern. This presents some challenge because expected young adolescent behavior in any other population might well be seen as at-risk behavior. Knowing the distinction between the two during early adolescence is critical.

- Community health professionals work collaboratively with school personnel

Kim had the opportunity to work with a small group of students twice a month on developing life skills such as coping and problem solving. She has related to Klemetson her joy with the small group setting and her sense of growing knowledge about stress-relieving strategies that have already helped her deal with trying school situations.

Broader Understanding

Young adolescents are changing how they interact with their peers and adults. They are loyal to their peer groups, and many times give in to peer pressure in order to "fit in" (Messick and Reynolds 1992). They tend to rebel and argue with adults or authority figures, yet they look to them for guidance and reassurance. Unfortunately, their self-worth is often based on media images and expectations.

A student at this age likes to argue just for the sake of arguing and wants to "know the reasons for the expectations put upon him or her rather than accepting rules at face value" (Messick and Reynolds 1992, 41). These students are extremely sensitive to personal criticism and tend to have a low self-esteem at times. They tend to have intense and random mood swings. This can cause them to overreact when they feel ridiculed, embarrassed, or rejected.

In a research study conducted by O'Dea and Abraham (1999), young adolescent male and female students were given a questionnaire that helped examine the effect and interaction of gender, pubertal status, age, and body weight on self-perception. Students were asked to rank the importance of friendship, academics, appearance, romantic appeal, behavior, and physical appearance. They were also asked about their self-confidence in each area.

The results suggested that both males and females feel having close relationships, doing well at school, and being romantically appealing contribute most to how they feel about themselves. Males tended to have a greater self-esteem than females. They also had a more positive self-concept regarding academics and physical appearance compared to females. Females tended to have a better self-concept, however, when it came to forming close friendships, thus bearing out Gilligan's observations (1982). The young adolescents in the study felt body weight was an important factor in social acceptance. Overweight students felt less socially accepted.

This research affirmed the notions that young adolescents are very concerned with appearance, that their self-esteem is affected by negative messages sent by the media and society, and that peer relationships are critically important (Dicks 2001).

Gender roles are becoming more clearly defined during adolescence. Transescents seek to understand what their role is in society, and all too often adolescent girls lose sight of who they truly are and create a "false self" to fulfill society's expectations without considering their own values and feelings first

Transescents need guidance, yet they also need opportunities to be independent. They should be given chances to debate and reflect on issues that concern them, yet they should also be encouraged to examine other perspectives. Middle grades students should feel supported and encouraged by adults. Learning environments that create feelings of friendliness, concern, and cohesiveness in addition to a sense of on-task focus are most effective (Dicks 2001).

Modeling appropriate and desirable behavior for middle level students is essential. As explained by Messick and Reynolds: "Teachers do not know all, and should not pretend to. Students need reinforcement to accept the idea that it's all right not to know something and that finding out is more important than faking it or giving a flip answer. Equally important, students need examples of how to escape or handle situations in which they feel pressured to prove themselves" (1992, 4). It is important for young adolescents to feel comfortable being who they are and not compromising that to impress others. Issues of weight should be handled delicately. Students should be encouraged to exercise, yet reasonable and realistic goals should be stressed. They need to observe appropriate methods of staying healthy.

And Dicks concluded that gender roles should be discussed and evaluated. Students should discuss and understand stereotypes and how they affect people. Women role models should be included in all content areas. Inclusive language should be used so that girls do not feel excluded or inferior (Pipher 1994). For example, it is more appropriate to say "chairperson" rather than "chairman." It is important that learning environments are inviting to young girls. It is critical that they see their roles in the learning community as being of equal value to those of their male counterparts. Girls need to feel that they are capable and valued in society.

If we still hold with Oliner that "individualism is a cornerstone of American ideology" (1986, 408), then the social skills of independence, interdependence, developing relationships, adapting in shifting relationships, earning respect, knowing when one is valued as a group member, contributing to a group, participating in meaningful ways in the community, and developing one's self-identity must be explicitly taught, not assumed. Transescents need to be guided in forming a rich balance between having their own needs met and meeting the needs of a community. That balance is one with which all middle grades teachers contend, not to teach it didactically, but to help young people interpret their experiences and construct their own sense of balance. This understanding will position transescents to function even in the moment as responsible members of an interdependent community of people.

Perhaps this balance can also keep them from the precipice of drugs, alcohol, and sexual experimentation. For it is not peer pressure alone that places young people in jeopardy. Rather, there are contextual factors—developmental, social, cultural, familial, religious, and institutional processes that together affect young people. Researchers and theorists share little agreement as to any single factor, whether it be the peer group, modeling, or adaptive behavior, that will serve as a cause for stress or for risky or deviant behavior in young adolescents. What can be agreed upon is that on a daily basis schools persevere in teaching young people to respect themselves and their peers; to care for one another; to respect the traditions and values of their families; to uphold their families' religious teachings; to value curiosity, questioning, and risk taking in the service of dynamic learning; and to hold dear the promise of life that each of us has for only a moment.

EMOTIONAL/PSYCHOLOGICAL DOMAIN

Characteristics of Young Adolescents

1. Experience mood swings often with peaks of intensity and unpredictability
2. Need to release their energy, often resulting in sudden, apparently meaningless outbursts of activity
3. Seek to become increasingly independent, searching for adult identity and acceptance
4. Are increasingly concerned about peer acceptance
5. Tend to be self-conscious, lacking in self-esteem, and highly sensitive to personal criticism
6. Exhibit intense concern about physical growth and maturity as profound physical changes occur

7. Increasingly behave in ways associated with their sex as sex role identification strengthens
8. Are concerned with many major societal issues as personal value systems develop
9. Believe that personal problems, feelings, and experiences are unique to them
10. Are psychologically vulnerable, because at no other stage in development are they more likely to encounter so many differences between themselves and others
11. Lean toward the optimistic and positive view of the world
12. Have chemical imbalances due to unstable hormone levels, which frequently trigger frightening emotions that they often misunderstand; some regress to childish behavior patterns (Kellough and Kellough 2003)

Implications for Practice

1. Encourage student self-evaluation
2. Encourage students to assume leadership in group discussions
3. Design activities that help students play out their emotions—activity programs that provide opportunities to draw out shy students and calm louder students
4. Structure counseling as a part of rather than as an adjunct to the learning program
5. Help students interpret superiority and inferiority feelings
6. Design activities and opportunities in which students examine options and consequences of actions
7. Structure a general atmosphere of friendliness, concern, and group cohesiveness
8. Avoid sarcasm by adults
9. Assist students in developing problem-solving systems
10. Avoid pressuring students to explain their emotions (crying for no apparent reason). Occasional childlike behavior should not be ridiculed
11. Use literature/readings that deal with problems similar to the students' to facilitate their seeing that many problems are not unique, but shared

To say that students' self-consciousness or self-centeredness in thinking everyone and everything is about them is at its pinnacle in young adolescence could perhaps be another understatement. Yet, it is a natural part of the maturation process. Those schools that recognize this in their students tend to be more responsive, accepting, and successful than the majority of schools that, whether by choice or by design, focus only on cognitive development. Effective schools build cognitive skills upon the success students have in intentionally dealing with socioemotional stress. It is recognized that the standards movement and the race to perform on state-mandated tests pose a challenge to developmentally astute middle grades teachers and administrators. That is not to say that academic rigor and achievement are not critically important at all developmental levels. But it is to say that in order to reach the mind one has to go through the heart. In order to help students as cognitive learners, we must also see them and help them as complex psychosocial, socioemotional, and moral human beings. The large body of research on youth who have dropped out of school and on those who remain in school but who are at risk in various ways clearly indicates that these young people feel alienated, disrespected, rejected by both adults and peers, and disenfranchised by the environment of the school (Mills, Dunham, and Alpert 1988).

What are some of the reasons students may have for feeling rejected or alienated beyond the expected sense of low self-esteem natural at this developmental stage? Teacher Carol Anton (2002) spoke of a child named Dee: "Living in poverty adds layers to the difficulties a child like Dee has with her peer relations. There are many adverse effects of economic hardship on youth: socio-emotional adjustment, including impaired peer relations, low self-esteem, antisocial behavior, and internalizing problems such as anxiety and depression" (2002, 10). Anton interpreted Emon's work (2002) when she observed that poor children are more likely to be unpopular and rejected by their peers. They are also less likely to be exposed to cognitively stimulating materials and activities and are often limited in their involvement outside of school, in neighborhood and community organizations. This reduces opportunities for social interactions and for acquiring knowledge and skills other than those reflective of their social situation. Such was the case with Dee, who had shown most of these adverse effects.

But Anton took steps in her classroom to promote positive peer interactions, relations, and resilience among all students. She suggested that teachers can take a variety of actions at the classroom level as well as at the school level. A classroom fostering resilience will display many of the following traits. Anton noted the work of T. S. Bickart, who contended that children should be involved in

- Assessing their own work
- Setting goals for themselves
- Participating in developing standards for their work
- Having many opportunities to work collaboratively
- Participating in meetings to solve classroom problems
- Having opportunities to make choices
- Feeling connected in a classroom structured as a community
- Playing an active role in setting rules for classroom life (Bickart 1997)

These are considered "best practices" for all classrooms at all developmental levels but are particularly suited for the middle grades classroom.

George, Lawrence, and Bushnell (1998) suggested that in order to promote social maturity, middle grades schools should offer students the opportunity to:

- Develop leadership, expressive, sharing, and active-listening skills
- Obtain influence and recognition
- Take constructive and manageable risks in new roles
- Socialize within low-pressure, noncompetitive situations
- Clarify personal values
- Develop realistic personal goals
- Develop skills of independent self-management
- Appreciate their own strengths and accomplishments
- Develop trusting relationships
- Develop skills of giving and receiving help
- Feel accepted and valued by others
- Understand roles and responsibilities in our society and how to fit in
- Develop skills in relating to persons who are culturally different from themselves
- Develop skills for resolving conflicts nonaggressively
- Develop and apply decisionmaking and problem-solving strategies (110–111)

Transescence is the time when young people push against barriers or limits—limits set by adults in the family, school, adults in the community, and even barriers they construct around themselves. As they push, those who have set the limits for very justifiable reasons push back. How long will they talk on the phone? When will they clean their room? How late will they stay out with friends? Why must they go to the mall? The transescents sometimes stomp their feet and ask why they can't have the freedom to determine when to go to bed, what to eat, when to get up in the morning, how long to study or whether they have to study, how long they can watch television, what they can wear, what color their hair is going to be that day, how low they can wear their jeans, how short they can wear their sweaters, how many body piercings they can have, whether they can have tattoos, whom they can date, and even how loudly they can play their music. And often these moments turn into major issues, sometimes confrontational ones because they are attempting to stretch their sense of their own freedom.

The limitations placed on transescents are the regulators of responsibility and reason. When the family or caregivers hold fast to their guidelines that will ultimately teach responsibility and lead to maturity, the ensuing adolescent response is often little short of pouty, sulky, angry, pleading, and manipulative. With every familial "no" can easily come a transescent "that's not fair." Yet underneath, in moments of crisis or quiet revelation, my middle grades students confessed to me that when their folks or loved ones or teachers set limits, they knew they were cared for. Often the students would privately say, "They wouldn't do it unless they really cared about me, 'cause they know I'm gonna give them a lot of guff." And just as often they said, "I don't know why I act to them like I do, I just do."

Frequently that classroom teacher with whom the students identify will become a confidant because they know that if they share something they fear may cause adult displeasure or disappointment, the loss of a teacher's respect is far less damaging than the loss of the family's love, which is irreplaceable. This domain can be summed up in the dichotomies of dependence and independence, freedom and limitations, being a child and becoming an adult, being sophisticated and being naive, being and becoming.

MORAL DOMAIN

Characteristics of Young Adolescents

1. Are generally idealistic, desiring to make the world a better place and to become socially useful

2. Are in transition from moral reasoning that focuses on "what's in it for me" to that which considers the feelings and rights of others
3. Often show compassion for those who are suffering or disenfranchised and have special concern for animals and the environmental problems that our world faces
4. Are moving from acceptance of adult moral judgments to development of their own personal values; nevertheless, tend to embrace values consonant with those of the family
5. Rely on parents and significant adults for advice when facing major decisions
6. Increasingly assess moral matters in shades of gray as opposed to viewing them in black and white terms as is characteristic of young children
7. Owing to their lack of experience, are often impatient with the pace of change, underestimating the difficulties in making desired social changes
8. Are capable of and value direct experiences in participatory democracy
9. Greatly need and are influenced by adult role models who will listen to them and affirm their moral consciousness and actions
10. Are increasingly aware of and concerned about inconsistencies between values professed by adults and the conditions they see in society
11. At times are quick to see flaws in others but slow to acknowledge their own faults

Implications for Practice

1. Provide opportunities for students to accept responsibility in assisting setting standards for behavior
2. Help students develop values when solving their problems
3. Encourage mature value systems by providing opportunities for students to examine options of behavior and to study consequences of various actions
4. Provide opportunities for students to engage in community service and in service learning projects

5. Structure schools and classrooms to provide the environment of participatory democracy, assisting students in understanding and experiencing both responsibilities and rights

Frequently the moral domain is absent from middle grades education texts. Perhaps influenced by a small number of parents who mistakenly assume that values education means teaching secular, humanistic values, rather than building on students' families' values, teachers shy away from this critical area of young adolescent development. It is not the province of the school to teach religion. But it is the responsibility of the school to prepare young people who care about each other, who respect each other's rights, who exercise their newly developing sense of place in the democracy, who value the just community, who will not just "fit in" to the society but who will create their own place in the service of a better world.

We again use an action critique. As shown in Table 3.3, several of my graduate students who are dynamic middle grades educators (MaryLu Strimbel, Carrie Heaney, Cynthia Sidney, Holly Renko) chose one domain, in this case the moral domain, and examined their own schools on the basis of the three seminal documents spoken of earlier. Table 3.3 details the teachers' first stage—the assessment. That was followed by stage two or the plan of action.

Although Table 3.3 is by no means exhaustive, it does present a picture of the theory of adolescent development as translated into practice within the school. Action critiques provide the kind of comparative and supportive data that give rise to research-based changes necessary for schools to be effective.

Centers of Similarity

Stevenson (2002) offered another way for middle grades teachers to view their students in the service of creating active curriculum and hands-on learning. From his work as a middle grades teacher, he noted five broad conceptual domains that need to be considered in the process of change: the introspective domain houses the somatic, intellectual, communal, and familial domains. Lipsitz (1980) called these domains "centers of similarities" for middle grades students. And although they refer to particular areas of change, they are not delimited areas. Rather they are overlapping and responsively interactive.

Table 3.3
Middle Schoolers' Moral Development: An Action Critique and Assessment

Characteristics	Practices	Research	The School's Standing
Generally idealistic, want to make the world a better place	Community service opportunities; advisory	1,2,3	Fair—advisory; need more community service
Transitioning from "What's in it for me" to "How do others feel?"	Accept responsibility and set standards of behavior/set classroom rules; advisory program; help students create values when solving problems	1,3	Fair—rules up to each team; no say in school rules; advisory program in place but not practicing sound philosophy
Finding own values and yet clinging to their family's values'	Create classrooms that engage in participatory democracy; model mature value systems	1,3	Fair—up to team teachers; teachers model respect and caring
Relying on advice from adults for major decisions	Adult role models; advisory; help develop values when solving problems	1,2,3	Commendable—area of strength
Impatient with social change but not realizing the importance of the change and how they handle it	Encourage mature value system— advisory debates; role-plays; participatory democracy; service learning projects	1,2,3	Commendable—area of strength through advisory and bullying program
Quick to see others' flaws but not to see their own	Examine options of behavior vs. consequences; advisory; solve problems	1,2,3	Commendable—area of strength
Developing sense of right and wrong; larger sense of social justice	Student government	1,2,3	Poor—nothing in place

(continues)

Table 3.3 *(continued)*

Characteristics	Practices	Research	The School's Standing
Supporting outside services—exploring their ability to give beyond themselves	Academic service learning projects; clubs—environmental clubs; support charities	1,2,3	Fair—school has academic service learning projects; does not have clubs or opportunities within schools
Developing empathy	Peer mediation; advisory sessions; counseling	2,3	Commendable—area of strength
Valuing direct experience in democracy	School government; help with political elections; discussion about relationships between rights and responsibilities	1,2,3	Good—school holds class government, mock elections
Are generally idealistic, desiring to make world a better place	Provide opportunities for students to accept responsibility in setting behavior standards	1,2,3	Fair—meets expectation but only in isolated situations
Relying on adults for advice	Role models; teacher as advisor; school counselor	2,3	Poor—no school counselor; teacher as advisor is needed
Concern for social problems: animal rights, environment	Role models who champion causes they are interested in; community involvement	1,2,3	Good—school promotes values and citizenship; student nursing home partnership

Sources: #1 Document: National Association of Secondary School Principals (1985), *An Agenda for Excellence;* #2 Document: National Middle School Association (1995), *This We Believe;* #3 Document: Carnegie Council on Adolescent Development (1989), *Turning Points.*

The Introspective Domain

Stevenson contended that the introspective domain is the quintessential domain, as it includes and affects all other thinking and action and creates its individual response to change. Essentially this domain answers the hermeneutical, existential question "Who am I?"

Middle grades teacher Lynette Wehner described an eighth-grade student with whom she had worked for the preceding three years.

> Celeste thrives on attention. In 6th grade, she became known as
> "Princess" and played the part to the hilt. She would wear pink
> blouses, put pink feather barrettes in her hair, and sometimes actually
> would wear a crown to my class. When she turned in assignments, she
> would put "Princess" on her paper instead of her name. She would al-
> ways decorate any assignment with glitter or other things in order for
> her project to stand out from the others. She was in essence, attempt-
> ing to form an identity. (Wehner 2002)

Developmental psychosocial theorist Erik Erikson maintained that adolescence is a socially accepted time during which young adolescents are free to experiment with who they are, thereby putting a moratorium on their psychosocial development (Rice 1999). Erikson further stated, "The central developmental task of adolescence . . . is the formation of a coherent self-identity" (182). There are four developmental stages in the formation of identity with early adolescents at the very beginning of identity establishment:

1. Identity diffusion—A student in essence says "I don't know yet what I want to be"; confusion reigns; choices are difficult to make and are often suspended
2. Identity foreclosure—A student makes decisions based on what others (teachers, parents) expect: "I choose to be a lawyer because my father wants me to."
3. Identity moratorium—A student waits until more information is gathered to make any decisions; long-range choices such as "what do I want to do when I grow up" are temporarily suspended until late high school
4. Identity achievement—A student knows what he or she wants to be, believes, holds to be true, and is about

For the most part middle grades students are in the phase that Erikson called identity crisis or Identity versus Role Confusion because they are uncertain about who they are. The process of identity formation is a discontinuous one, sometimes progressing, sometimes regressing into periods of doubt and despair. Young adolescents, usually ages eleven and twelve, look for heroes, role models, people to emulate. When schools teach only from a European perspective, when they teach history or social studies only from the standpoint of the victors, many minority students look in vain to find themselves in roles other than subservient ones. Rather than learning about African American inventors who developed the stop light, the street sweeper, or the coupler for train cars, they see themselves mirrored only as sports stars. And teachers become frustrated in their students' singular interest in sports. African American females are never taught about the black woman who developed the first underwater cannon that became the torpedo. Native Americans are expected to celebrate Thanksgiving when a large part of their heritage was written in the death records of those who became infected from European disease or those who were shunted off to remote and desolate reservations. Cinco de Mayo passes with no notice from the classroom teacher. The point here is simply that at such an impressionable time when all students are looking for heroes, our country should not have to endure another September 11 to find the valor and courage, creativity and brilliance that resides in all of our peoples.

Female Role Models

There are many studies that support what middle grades teachers have known for a long time—that adolescence, particularly for girls, is a time of psychological risk and vulnerability (Waldecker 2002). According to Brown and Gilligan:

> Girls at this time have been observed to lose their vitality, their resilience, their immunity to depression, their sense of themselves and their character.
>
> Girls approaching adolescence are often victims of incest and other forms of sexual abuse. This crisis in women's development has been variously attributed to biology or to culture, but its psychological dimensions and its link to trauma have been only recently explored. (1992, 64)

Waldecker (2002) talked about her student, Amy, who has been fortunate enough to have a mother and grandmother who provide strong female role models. Amy's mother in particular has modeled resilience and empowerment. Her affection and control strategies have probably had an impact on Amy's development as well. Pipher (1994) noted that parents who are high in control and high in acceptance tend to produce adolescents who are independent, socially responsible, and confident. Furthermore, girls who resist the perils of adolescence tend to have close, confiding relationships with their mothers.

Waldecker further noted that Amy's positive, close relationship with her maternal grandparents appeared to be important. According to Rice, "Grandparents may be the key agents in restoring a sense of continuity in an adolescent's life, in linking the past to the present, and in transmitting knowledge of culture and family roots and thus having a positive impact on the adolescent's search for identity" (1999, 268). Additionally, if an adolescent has a good relationship with grandparents and sees them often, he or she is more likely to develop a positive attitude toward the elderly and toward aging. The sense of belonging that Amy's grandparents have provided her has helped preserve her identity (Pipher 1994).

Waldecker continued that Brown and Gilligan's quote did not describe her student Amy as it did not describe many young adolescents. Although reared by her mother and her grandparents without the support of a father, Amy is bright and positive about everything. Waldecker asked how she had been able to retain her vitality, her resilience, her immunity to depression, her sense of herself, and her character. In response to these questions, Amy indicated that she doesn't allow herself to get caught up in the "gossip and mean-spirited things her classmates say about each other. I don't do the mean things that some people do because if I do a mean thing to someone, I feel terrible" (Waldecker 2002, 4). Further, Amy said she refuses to let people have that kind of power over her and she is willing to risk unpopularity in order to do what she thinks is right. When Waldecker asked what she thought gave her the courage to say or do something like that, Amy said simply "faith in God."

Fitzell observed :

> Girls need adults in their lives who model assertiveness, strength, caring and responsiveness. They need to see the women in their lives value and foster positive relationships. Girls need to see us working to

continually improve our ability to communicate our needs, hopes, and concerns so that we nurture others but don't lose ourselves. In a world defined by clothing labels, media hype, and gender stereotypes, girls need role models who base their identity and self-worth on who they are as people, rather than how pretty or fashionable they are. (1997, 362)

Waldecker argued that there is also a connection between a young girl's courage and the opportunities she has to express her voice. In her work with adolescent girls, Rogers said, "Through the avenue of play and theatre, we call girls' voices out into the room, we listen to them and enjoy them, and we delight in their ordinary courage—played through their voices and physical poses" (1993, 116). Waldecker concluded, "Amy's singing, as well as her strong faith in God are what I think Pipher [1994] refers to as an adolescent girl's 'protected space', which are things that allow a young girl to grow emotionally healthy" (2002, 6). The protected spaces could be athletics, books, church, music, or any activity in which a child feels accomplishment and fulfillment apart from expectation. Pipher (1994) contended that possessing talent and/or being genuinely useful gives girls something to hold on to; it allows girls the continuity they need to bridge past childhood with current adolescence.

Gender and Identity Formation

It is important to note the gender differences in identity formation, because Erikson's work done in the 1960s, 1970s, and 1980s is culture-bound by earlier notions. During his writing there tended to be clear societal roles for both males and females. Males were expected to have job aspirations and to provide for the welfare of a family while being caretakers of the world, whereas females were to marry, rear children, and tend to the home. As mentioned earlier in this chapter, Gilligan (1982, 1986) argued that males and females are socialized in different ways even though they now share many of the same role responsibilities. Gilligan maintained that females form emotional bonds through interpersonal attachments whereas males establish their independence and personal achievement (Balk 1995).

Just like Celeste, most young adolescents experiment with various identity roles. "Celeste was Princess during her sixth-grade year. The role concept permeated everything she wore, what she said and how she acted in class" (Wehner 2002, 4). The establishment of identity comes through the opportunities provided for this type of experimentation. Wehner observed that the "Princess" concept no longer worked for Celeste in the eighth grade, so it was virtually nonexistent. Celeste shared the insight that "Princess was yesterday's news" (6).

Yet, although Celeste's Princess days were over, she had turned to garnering attention through striving for academic awards. "I just want to show people that I worked in middle school and did good and then in eighth-grade got an award for that" (Wehner 2002, 6). Part of a young adolescent's self-concept as represented in Celeste is the perceived position within the accepted social system, in this case, within the school. Wehner concluded that when Celeste received the desired attention, she was able to put herself on the social ladder, which in turn fed her feelings about herself. It worked for her, but only as long as things went her way. There are usually over 500 students in the average middle school, however. Can things always go the way of each child?

Stevenson noted, "Youngsters need to believe that they are becoming more skillful and competent. They prize concrete evidence of accomplishments" (2002, 81). Many middle schools are becoming more sensitive to the needs of all of their students in this regard. How often I sat in a two- to three-hour awards assembly and watched the same 25 percent of the students come up for various academic and athletic awards. Eventually the staff made a deliberate commitment to actively observe the talent in each child, acknowledge that it might assume different forms, and then reward that talent. For instance, in addition to the traditional "A" and "B" honor rolls and sports awards, we created an *Inkspots* (the name of our all-school literary anthology) Outstanding Author Award, honor choir and honor band awards, Fun Run Awards in which each student competed against his or her own best time, drama awards, yearbook and newspaper awards, photography and arts awards, citizenship awards, Acts of Kindness Awards, and a 100 percent club award for students who submitted all of their homework for the quarter. No longer did 75 percent of the student body passively sit by and watch.

Identity and Peer Pressure

Psychologist David Elkind, in his landmark work with adolescent identity formation, explained that young adolescents construct their identity in one of two ways: by substitution or by integration, which is the slower but healthier of the two. He noted that as a people we

> must encounter a great number of different experiences within which
> we can discover how feelings, thoughts and beliefs are different from
> other people. At the same time, we also need to learn how much we are
> like other people. As a result . . . of differentiating ourselves from oth-
> ers, in terms of how we are alike and yet different . . . we gradually ar-
> rive at a stable and unique perception of ourselves. (1984, 15–16)

Looking at today's young adolescents, we would not dispute the fact
that they are experiencing more pressure than did their parents a generation ago—peer pressure, adult pressure, popular culture/media
pressure, and self-pressure.

The Peer Group

As noted earlier in this chapter, Havighurst observed that the peer
group offers a sense of belonging, a community of identity that may
share mannerisms, enjoy the same music, dress alike, or achieve similar
grades in the academic work. Ryan (2001) conducted a study on the influence peer groups have on adolescent motivation and achievement.
She argued that students' grades typically decline when they enter middle school and further decline when students choose a peer group that
functions at a lower academic level. Teacher and researcher Kimberly
Toloday noted that a student named Roy maintained he was "more motivated to learn and improve his academic performance when the rest
of the group feels that way, too" (2002, 3). Roy's peer group has a good
distribution of academic achievement levels because his former lower-
achieving peer group merged with the higher achievers who serve as the
leaders of the newly formed group. "Students interact and exchange information with other students in the peer group, and such interactions
influence adolescent motivation and engagement in school" (Ryan
2001, 1138). Students tend to associate with peers of similar academic
performance. And in Roy's case, he and his peers were preparing for
high school placement exams and realized these grades had greater
consequence than the appearance on a report card.

The peer group affects not only academic performance but also
classroom behavior. The friends Roy chose in sixth and seventh grades
mirrored Roy's disruptive presence in the classroom. "Friends influence
all aspects of school adjustment, but their influence on adolescents'
disruptive behavior is strongest and most consistent. Adolescents become more disruptive at school when their friends are more disruptive,

and they have more negative interactions with friends" (Berndt and Keefe 1995, 1327).

Toloday further observed that, with his last year in middle school, Roy began to assume some leadership responsibilities within the school, a new role that motivated him and his peers to take control of their own behavior. Additionally, because the school was organized in interdisciplinary teams of teachers who offered each student more personal attention and support, Roy and his peer group demonstrated more positive classroom behavior.

Wendy Robinson's middle school has adopted William Glasser's (1999) Choice Theory as its school management philosophy. Glasser contends that students behave or misbehave in schools as they strive to have their five basic needs met, those being survival, belonging, power, freedom, and fun. Robinson's critical case study (2002) noted that her student Katie's need for belonging and power affected her need for freedom and fun.

Glasser (1999) defined belonging as the need for relationships, social connections, and networks that both give and receive affection and that offer the individual a valued place in a group. But Robinson noted that because Katie has problems with social connections, her "Quality World" is unbalanced. In Glasser's terms, Katie uses power or the process of being listened to and having a sense of self-worth in the form of her voice. This makes her appear opinionated and loud, so she can feel others are listening to her. Yet this behavior causes Katie to push away all her peers, thereby denying the fulfillment of her need for belonging. The consequences of this lack of fulfillment are severely conflicted. Katie displays dysfunctional behavior in the form of what is defined as an oppositional defiant disorder. Students with this disorder often argue with adults, swear and use obscene language, are angry and resentful toward others, actively refuse adult requests, throw temper tantrums, and have trouble accepting corrections from adults (Mason and Windle 2002).

We cannot help but question why some of our students fall prey to life's exigencies and others, like Sidney's Jamishia discussed earlier, rise above society's ills and blossom. Stevenson (2002) noted the often-cited resilience research done in 1991 by Benard, who noted that the primary growth tasks of adolescence are:

- Social Competence—flexibility, empathy, communication skills, a sense of humor in relationships and responsiveness

- Problem-Solving Skills—creativity, resourcefulness, ability to learn from reflection on experience, planning skills and divergent thinking
- Critical Consciousness—understanding one's challenges and dealing with them to the point of overcoming them
- Autonomy—personal efficacy, integrated sense of personal identity
- Sense of Purpose—optimism about one's present and one's future (88)

The Somatic Domain

The somatic domain answers the question "Who am I physically?" or rather it speaks to the question, because it could be argued that middle schoolers spend the entire transescent period attempting to answer the question. If a single word could characterize this domain it would be *puberty.* It is the marker between childhood and young adulthood, the time when girls physically become young women, able to bear children, and boys become young men, able to father children.

The view of one's body or the image of one's physical presence in the world is of augmented importance to this age group. Unfortunately, flawed self-concepts can lead to serious if not traumatic dysfunctions, such bulimia or anorexia. A form of dysfunctional somatic-domain behavior that appears particularly in females is eating disorders. The messages the popular culture persistently sends to young adolescents are ingrained in the visual images of slim, sleek, fashion-conscious (that is, according to the latest fad) young people, sure of themselves, articulate in any social situation, sexually experienced, and often angry at the imperfect world they have begun to critically observe.

Middle grades teacher Sandy Hryczyk noted that the effects of anorexia nervosa (the initial refusal to eat, which later becomes the inability to eat, which leads to emaciation and in some cases death) in adolescent girls are complex and vary with each case. In Hryczyk's study (2002), she observed that Sophia's particular struggle bore similarities to that of other young females. They include a distorted body image, an obsession with food and weight, a need to strive for perfection and to have control over some aspect of her life. And Hryczyk concluded, "If we accept the biopsychosocial model which incorporates culture as a driving force of an eating disorder such as anorexia, then the schools can become the place where we can educate young adolescents and perhaps prevent them from falling victim to the devastating consequences of anorexia nervosa" (10).

The Intellectual Domain

The intellectual domain answers the question "Who am I and what do I think?" In keeping with Piaget's work, Stevenson (2002) noted the following principles:

- Young adolescents' schemas—or networks of thinking— are different from those of adults.
- There are no concrete ages or times at which either males or females begin to shift in their thinking from formal operational to abstract. Likewise, each student moves between thinking stages in a discontinuous and somewhat staccato fashion, often influenced by adult and peer interactions beyond the school, life experiences, and maturation rates.
- Intellectual development is augmented by experiential, active, hands-on learning during which students can interact with people and with the learning they are constructing.
- Functional learning is the student's way of "making and remaking" concepts through active engagement. (100)

The Familial Domain

The familial domain answers the questions, "How do I relate to my family?" and "What is my role in the family and my family's role in my life?" The conventional picture of the relationship between the middle school child and the family is largely unsupported. Although it is true that students at this age are attempting to establish their own sense of identity apart from the family, they do not want the family to be too far removed. To return to an earlier example, when I suggested that my honor students' parents could perform in the Spring Fantacular, the common cry "They will embarrass me" echoed through the classroom. Yet when it came time for that part of the concert, the students whose families were on stage cheered the loudest and openly received the praise from their admiring peers—peers who the following year had their families in the spring concert.

This is such a critically important area of a middle schooler's life that to do service to the power the support of the family exerts on the student and on the school is best left in reference to Joyce Epstein's seminal life work in parent involvement.

The Communal Domain

The communal domain answers the questions "Where do I fit in?" and "To whom or to what group do I choose to belong?" As schools and class sizes grow larger, the fundamental need for young adolescents to socialize with an intimate group goes unmet. We need only look at the groups of youngsters in the malls, or ask a parent of a middle schooler what they have to do to get access to the phone in the evening, or watch any given class and see the number of notes students write to each other or place in each other's lockers, to bear witness to the social or communal needs of transescents. "During these years of early adolescence, youngsters shift toward other kids for acceptance and confirmation—a gradual turn from primary dependence on approval by parents and teachers to a quest for . . . belonging with age-mates and significant adults beyond parents and teachers"(Stevenson 2002, 111).

The infamous clique is part of the adolescent culture that can have devastating effects on those within and outside of it. Effective middle grades schools, however, have formed interdisciplinary teams with logos, banners, slogans, newsletters, handshakes, and songs to offer the sense of group identity and belonging so sought by transescents. They also offer academic service learning projects (as discussed in Chapter 6) to extend the students' sense of themselves beyond the clique, the team, or the school, into the community.

In contrast to Stevenson's model, which sees the young adolescent through the dominant domain of the introspective, in their classroom work teachers Wendy Robinson, Sandy Hryczyk, Holly Renko, and Mary-Lu Strimbel view the student through the emotional "goo" that permeates everything the students do (top half of Figure 3.3). And yet another group of teachers, as an in-class assignment, portrayed the students as tripartite individuals, as illustrated in the bottom half of Figure 3.3. Tom Beltman, Rex Sanders, and Lynette Wehner experience their students as a fluid interaction of the body, soul, and spirit through which the communal, intellectual, familial, and somatic domains interact. The configuration itself is less important than the realization of how a teacher sees his or her students, because through that lens student

Figure 3.3
Transescent Domain Interactions

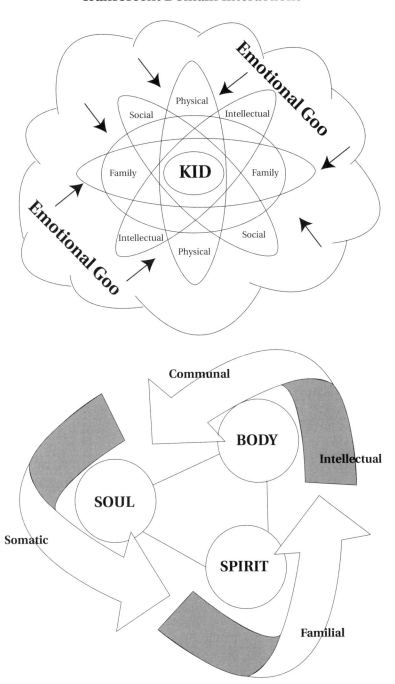

behavior will be interpreted, acted upon, and understood. How a teacher perceives her students will drive expectations, explanations for what gets done in the classroom and what doesn't, and explanations about the exigencies of life and what power the teacher has to affect students' beliefs about themselves and about their futures.

CONCLUSION: IMPLICATIONS FOR MIDDLE SCHOOLS AND THEIR STAFFS

The middle grades movement is constructed on the fundamental understandings of human growth and development, of learning domains and entry points, of young adolescent needs and characteristics. This deep understanding of emerging learners is important to the extent that it affects daily classroom teaching and learning.

Stevenson contended that when we serve our young adolescents best, "we respect their inexperience and protect their frailty from harmful societal influences as well as well-intentioned but misguided schooling practices" (2002, 114). In order to do this we must know our transescents. Teacher-researcher Carol Anton noted: "The importance of taking the time to understand what goes on in the lives of our students outside the school setting can truly give us the insight we need to attempt to reach more of the children who are not as motivated to succeed in their educational venues" (2002, 8).

Although the intellectual education of students is the prime goal of every school, because of the particular needs of young adolescents, middle grades educators strive to find a balance between academic rigor and developmental responsiveness, a balance between seeing students as learners and acknowledging them as rapidly changing young people, a balance between the intellectual and the socioemotional, a balance that shares a teacher's passion for knowledge with the intense understanding that all of the domain characteristics listed above are intermingled in the shape of an emerging young adult. In order for middle grades students to succeed academically, they must have a sense of self-identity and self-esteem that encourages them to step out and take chances in their own learning. It is the confidence students have in themselves that causes them either to believe that they can do something or, in its absence, to fear that they can't.

Dicks observed the vast number of changes that middle schoolers experience and contended that "it is important that parents and teachers guide and support them. As they look to society and try to find their place in it, they should have confidence in their abilities and values" (2000, 12).

Waldecker concluded her critical case study of a middle grades student encumbered with the vagaries of an adult world and functioning with adult tools and said, "We cannot replace our students' home environments, but we can certainly connect with and nurture our transescents, be good role models for them, and help them develop a sense of belonging and higher purpose. If that is our focus, I think we will find ourselves helping others successfully beat the odds" (2002, 8).

Effective middle schools match their teaching and learning experiences with the nature and needs of young adolescents. But, as importantly, the people who work in these schools celebrate rather than criticize these young people who are trying out new roles and personas for themselves, experimenting with new friends and new ideas, adjusting to more pressure and more responsibility, fluctuating between the desire to stand out and the desire to blend in, shifting between being a young adult and remaining a child, and developing the morals and values that will guide them in sexual and social relationships, that will shape their view of themselves in the world, and that will help them become the people they desire to be. They are not all in the storm of angst as some would believe. But they are all unique, created with talents and abilities and individual personalities unlike any other.

> Perhaps what I will take from this year's MLK celebration is the idea that we are all still a work in progress. Things are not as they should be. Our kids do not all come to us prepared to read or to write, and they most certainly do not all come to us ready to show love. Yet, there is a hope and a challenge in Dr. King's message for teachers.
>
> I truly believe that we cannot do our jobs without faith that our work with kids may someday make his dream a reality and our world a better place.
> **—From the journal of Richard M. Bacolor, January 21, 2000**
>   **(Bacolor 2000, 37)**

REFERENCES

Ahron, C. 1999. "Divorce: An Unscheduled Family Transition." In B. Carter and M. McGoldrick, eds, *The Expanded Family Life Cycle: Individual, Family, and Social Perspectives* (381–395). Needham Heights, MA: Allyn and Bacon.

Anton, C. 2002. "The Stresses of Living in Poverty: One Child's Path of Struggle and Resilience." Critical case study, Eastern Michigan University.

Bacolor, R. 2000. "Reflective Journal." Journal, Eastern Michigan University.

Balk, D. 1995. *Adolescent Development.* Pacific Grove, CA: Brooks/Cole Publishing.

Benard, B. 2002. "Fostering Resilience in Kids: Protective Factors in the Family, School and Community." In C. Stevenson, *Teaching Ten to Fourteen Year Olds.* Boston, MA: Addison-Wesley.

Berndt, T. J., and K. Keefe. 1995. "Friends' Influence on Adolescents' Adjustment to School." *Child Development* 66: 1312–1329.

Bickart, T. S. 1997. "Practicing Resilience in the Elementary Classroom." *Principal* 77 (2): 21–24.

Brown, L. M., and C. Gilligan. 1992. *Meeting at the Crossroads: Women's Psychology and Girls' Development.* Cambridge: Harvard University Press.

Carnegie Council on Adolescent Development. 1989. *Turning Points: Preparing American Youth for the 21st Century.* New York: Carnegie Corporation of New York.

Carter, B., and M. McGoldrick, eds. 1999. *The Expanded Family Life Cycle: Individual, Family, and Social Perspectives.* Needham Heights, MA: Allyn and Bacon.

Dicks, R. 2001. "W.A.C.Y. Wetlands Awareness Curriculum for Youths." Masters project, Eastern Michigan University

Dorman, G., J. Lipsitz, and P. Verner. 1985. "Improving Schools for Young Adolescents." *Educational Leadership* 42 (6): 4–49.

Dove, M. 2001. "Runaway, Throwaway, and Homeless Adolescents." *The Delta Kappa Gamma Bulletin* 68 (1): 10–15.

Dweck, C. S. 1999. *Self-Theories: Their Role in Motivation, Personality, and Development.* Philadelphia: Psychology Press.

Eggen, P., and D. Kauchak. 2001. *Educational Psychology: Windows on Classrooms.* Upper Saddle River, NJ: Merrill–Prentice Hall.

Elkind, D. 1984. *All Grown Up and No Place to Go: Teenagers in Crisis.* Reading, MA: Addison-Wesley.

Emon, M. K. 2002. "Influences and Mediators of the Effect of Poverty on Young Adolescent Depressive Symptoms." *Journal of Youth and Adolescence* 31(3): 231–244.

Fitzell, S. 1997. *Free the Children: Conflict Education for Strong Peaceful Minds.* Stony Creek, British Columbia: New Society Publishers.

George, P., G. Lawrence, and D. Bushnell. 1998. *Handbook for Middle School Teaching.* Reading, MA: Addison Wesley Longman.

Gilligan, C. 1982. *In a Different Voice: Psychological Theory and Women's Development.* Cambridge: Harvard University Press.

————. 1986. "Reply by Carol Gilligan." *Signs: Journal of Women in Culture and Society* 11: 324–333.

Gilligan, C., and L. M. Brown. 1992. *Meeting at the Crossroads: The Landmark Book about the Turning Points in Girls' and Women's Lives.* New York: Ballantine.

Gilligan, C., N. Lyons, and T. Hammer, eds. 1990. *Making Connections: The Relational Worlds of Adolescent Girls at Emma Willard School.* Cambridge: Harvard University Press.

Glasser, W. 1999. *Choice Theory.* New York: Harper Perennial.

Havighurst, R. J. 1972. *Developmental Tasks and Education.* New York: David McKay and Co.

Heaney, C. 2002. "The Effects of Divorce and Step Families on Middle School Students." Critical case study, Eastern Michigan University.

Hryczyk, S. 2002. "Starving to Be Thin: Anorexia and the Effects on a Middle School Girl." Critical case study, Eastern Michigan University.

Jackson, A. W., and G. A. Davis. 2000. *Turning Points 2000: Educating Adolescents in the 21st Century.* New York: Teachers College Press.

James, C. 1974. *Beyond Customs.* New York: Agathon Press.

Johnson, K. 2002. "Handle with Care: There's a Child Inside." Critical case study, Eastern Michigan University

Kellough, R. D., and N. G. Kellough. 2003. *Teaching Young Adolescents: A Guide to Methods and Resources.* Upper Saddle River, NJ: Merrill–Prentice Hall.

Klemetson, L. 2002. "Life Is Full of Challenges: Stresses and Successes." Critical case study, Eastern Michigan University.

Lempers, J., and D. Clark-Lempers. 1997. "Economic Hardship, Family Relationships, and Adolescent Distress: An Evaluation of a Stress-Distress Mediation Model in Mother-Daughter and Mother-Son Dyads." *Adolescence* 32: 339–356.

Lessard, J. 1998. "Adolescent Stress and Workload: From Bamboo Seed to Flying." *Guidance and Counseling* 14 (1): 15–18.

Lipsitz, J. 1980. "The Age Group." In *Toward Adolescence: The Middle School Years.* National Society for the Study of Education (NSSE) Yearbook (79: 7–31). Chicago: University of Chicago Press.

————. 1984. *Successful Schools for Young Adolescents.* New Brunswick, NJ: Transaction Books.

Martin, D., and M. Martin. 2000. "Understanding Dysfunctional and Functional Family Behaviors for the At-Risk Adolescent." *Adolescence* 35: 785–792.

Maslow, A. 1970. *Motivation and Personality.* New York: Harper and Row.

Mason, W. A., and M. Windle. 2002. "Gender, Self-Control in Adolescence." *Youth and Society* 33 (4): 479–514.

Massey, M. 1998. "Promoting Stress Management: The Role of Comprehensive School Health Programs." Chicago: ERIC Clearinghouse on Teaching and Teacher Education Document Reproduction No. ED421480.

McGoldrick, M. 1999. *The Expanded Family Life Cycle: Individual, Family, and Social Perspectives.* Needham Heights, MA: Allyn and Bacon.

Mee, C. 1997. *Two Thousand Voices: Young Adolescents' Perceptions and Curriculum Implications.* Columbus, OH: National Middle School Association.

Messick, R. G., and K. E. Reynolds. 1992. *Middle Level Curriculum in Action.* New York: Longman.

Midgley, C., A. Kaplan, and M. Middleton. 2001. "Performance-Approach Goals: Good for What, for Whom, under What Circumstances, and at What Cost?" *Journal of Educational Psychology* 93 (March): 77–86.

Mills, R. C., R. G. Dunham, and C. P. Alpert. 1988. "Working with High-Risk Youth in Prevention and Early Intervention Programs: Toward a Comprehensive Wellness Model." *Adolescence* 23: 643–660.

National Association of Secondary School Principals. 1985. *An Agenda for Excellence at the Middle Level.* Reston, VA: Author.

National Middle School Association. 1995. *This We Believe: Developmentally Responsive Middle Level Schools.* Columbus, OH: Author.

Navarrete, L. 1999. "Melancholy in the Millennium: A Study of Depression among Adolescents with and without Learning Disabilities." *The High School Journal* 82 (3):137–149.

O'Dea, J. A., and S. Abraham. 1999. "Association between Self-Concept and Body Weight, Gender, and Pubertal Development among Male and Female Adolescents." *Adolescence* 34: 69–79.

Oliner, P. M. (1986). "Legitimating and Implementing Prosocial Education." *Humboldt Journal of Social Relations* 13: 391–410.

Piaget, J. 1952. *The Origins of Intelligence in Children.* New York: International University Press.

———. 1977. "Problems in Equilibration." In M. Appel and L. Goldberg, eds., *Topics in Cognitive Development.* Vol. 1: *Equilibration: Theory, Research, and Application* (3–13). New York: Plenum Press.

Pipher, M. 1994. *Reviving Ophelia: Saving the Selves of Adolescent Girls.* New York: Ballantine Books.

Rice, P. 1999. *The Adolescent.* Boston: Allyn and Bacon.

Robinson, W. 2002. "Warning: Social Outcast Entering Middle School." Critical case study, Eastern Michigan University.

Rogers, A .G. 1993. "Voice, Play, and a Practice of Ordinary Courage in Girls' and Women's Lives." *Harvard Educational Review* 63: 265–291.

Ryan, A. M. 2001. "The Peer Group as a Context for the Development of Young Adolescent Motivation and Achievement." *Child Development* 72 (4): 1135–1150.

Sanders, R. 2002. Unpublished interviews with students at Edmonson Middle School, Willow Run, Michigan.

Scales, P. 1991. "A Portrait of Young Adolescents in the 1990s: Implications for Promoting Healthy Growth and Development." Chicago: ERIC Clearing House Document Reproduction No. ED346990.

Sidney, S. 2002. "Erratic Behavior, Divorce, and Abandonment: The Steps of an Eighth Grade Student." Critical case study, Eastern Michigan University.

Stevenson, C. 2002. *Teaching Ten to Fourteen Year Olds,* 3rd ed. Reading, MA: Allyn and Bacon.

Teybar, E. 2001. *Helping Children Cope with Divorce*. San Francisco: Jossey-Bass.

Toloday, K. 2002. "Follow the Leader." Critical case study, Eastern Michigan University.

Waldecker, S. 2002. "Against the Odds: One Middle Schooler's Success Story." Critical case study, Eastern Michigan University.

Wehner, L. 2002. "Pay Attention Please: One Girl's Struggle to be Noticed." Critical case study, Eastern Michigan University.

Wiles, J., and J. Bondi. 2001. *The New American Middle School: Educating Pre-Adolescents in an Era of Change*. Columbus, OH: Merrill–Prentice Hall.

Williams-Boyd, P. 1996. "A Case Study of a Full Service School: A Transformational Dialectic of Empowerment, Collaboration, and Communitarianism." Ph.D. diss., University of Kansas.

Chapter Four

☙ **Programs and Practices**

There are particular programs and practices that both characterize and help shape middle grades schools. Although the programs discussed in this chapter have been developed by middle grades teachers in response to young adolescent needs, many of these practices have been adopted and then adapted by both elementary and secondary schools. It is important to note that the collection of practices discussed in this chapter does not necessarily make a school a middle grades school; nor does their absence cause a school not to be deemed a middle grades school. The single defining characteristic of whether a school is a true middle school or not lies rather in the ways in which the school shapes its work around the needs of the young adolescent or in whether it ignores those needs and focuses inappropriately on programs.

Those practices that typically characterize the high-performing middle grades school are usually the advisory program, interdisciplinary teaming, block and flex scheduling, thematic instruction and curriculum integration, core explore, and the use of varied assessments. These practices are discussed in this chapter. Student-led conferences, the integration of technology, and varied instructional practices will be examined in Chapter 5.

Teaching is about relationships. And there is no more critical a relationship in middle school than that between the teacher and the student. The Carnegie Council on Adolescent Development (1989), the National Association of Secondary School Principals (1985), the National Middle School Association (1995), and Phi Delta Kappa (Wayson et al. 1982) all supported the establishment of an adviser-advisee relationship in which every middle grades child has an adult advocate.

Advisory programs have their roots in 1880s American schools where vocational and moral guidance were included in the English curriculum (Wittmer 1993). As a program devoted particularly to young adolescents, advisories can more legitimately be traced to the 1890s junior high school, which emphasized character education and preparation for citizenship (Galassi, Gulledge, and Cox 1998). Throughout the twentieth century, guidance has become the responsibility of all the school's adults.

With the middle school movement came a shift in the kind of guidance expected of teachers. Alexander et al. (1968) argued that teachers should function as advocates, mentors who help young adolescents negotiate the murky waters of personal challenges and educational dilemmas. They called for teachers to be skilled in group dynamics and in adolescent developmental tasks and charged them to be sensitive to the needs of their students. This is no simple challenge, for at a time when young adolescents need adult guidance the most, they are naturally moving away from their familial adult support systems. The charge to the advisor teacher was to at once respect this process of separation-individuation and offer adult support at a time of extreme student vulnerability. What then is this advisor-advisee relationship that is so central to the workings of the middle school?

ADVISORY PROGRAMS: THE POWER OF RELATIONSHIPS

Definitions

An advisor-advisee program assigns a teacher a small group of students to whom the teacher provides guidance based on mutual respect (George and Alexander 1993). An advisory program offers students a safe harbor with an advocate who will listen to their concerns and help them find answers. Scheduled during a specific time in the day, the advisory class provides for social interaction and offers activities that challenge students to think, stretch, and grow (Ayers 1994). The adviser acts as a connection between the students and the school (Stevenson 1998). This adult also aids in helping a student find a supportive peer group and guiding the group to academic and social success.

The advisor also becomes the bridge for communication between the school and home. "Advisory programs are designed to deal directly with the affective of transescents. In the best of these programs, transescents have an opportunity to get to know one adult really well, to find a point of security within the institution, and to learn about what it means to be a healthy human being" (Beane and Lipka 1987, 6). The Carnegie Council on Adolescent Development's *Turning Points* (1989) saw the advisory system as a deterrent to student alienation. Students need to know that the teachers who educate them are also concerned about them personally.

The transition from elementary school to middle school can be challenging. This change can be a thrilling as well as an apprehensive experience. It is an exciting time in a young adolescent's life, yet it can be full of fear. A student's status changes when he or she moves from the top grade level of the elementary school to the lowest of the next school. An advisory program helps make this transition less painful by addressing unfamiliar issues and calming the students' fears.

Advisory Functions

The main purposes of advisor-advisee programs are to provide a caring environment for social, emotional, and academic support. Additionally they:

- ensure that each student is known well at school by at least one adult who is that student's advocate
- guarantee that every student belongs to a peer group
- help every student find ways to be successful
- promote coordination between home and school
- provide every student with one adult who takes the time to talk and listen to students

Rationale

Why adult advocacy? What is it? Why is it important that adults who teach middle level students also act as their advocates? All students need someone at the school who cares. In moving from elementary to middle school students are exposed to many new experiences. Their interests and relationships change. They explore and test new boundaries; at the same time they are deluged with new daily life happenings and experiences (Burkhart 1999).

Transescents need support and affirmation, the kind that mentor teachers can provide. Students feel a sense of confidence and security from having at least one adult advocate within the school who also serves as a guide who teaches moral and civic responsibility, coping skills, conflict resolution skills, and cooperative sharing in a problem-solving atmosphere. As transescents begin to see themselves in relationship to a larger world, issues of state, national, and global concern are discussed during the advisory period, a time for honest and open discussion in an atmosphere of confidence, support, and advocacy.

Successful Programs

In order for an advisory program to work, the staff must collectively believe in their role as advocates, and they must feel comfortable with the program as a result of good preparation and latitude in selecting activities based on the interests and needs of their students (Burns 1998). Planning for a school-wide advisory program demands proper preparation and district support of the faculty.

If teachers are not trained properly, have negative attitudes toward advisory, or are given prescribed activities, an advisory program will probably fail in reaching the students. Most failures are born of mediocre planning, a lack of proper staff development and training prior to program implementation, a lack of goals, and an absence of shared vision or values. Additionally, if teachers have not been properly trained in understanding the needs of young adolescents, both the program rationale and implementation will be less likely to succeed. In such instances the advisory period often becomes a social time, a study hall, or a time to take attendance, make announcements, or hand out papers. VanHoose (1991) suggested seven reasons why advisory programs may not work:

1. Parents may not understand the concept and therefore oppose it.
2. Many administrators are not really concerned about it.
3. Most teachers have had little formal preparation for serving as an advisor.
4. Teachers do not understand program goals.
5. Advisory takes time that many teachers believe could be invested more effectively in preparing to teach their subjects.
6. Some teachers do not want to engage in a program that requires personal sharing.

On the other hand, effective advisory programs tend to have:

1. Well-defined goals
2. Well-defined curricula and learning activities
3. Ongoing administrative support

4. A balance of daily activities
5. Advisors who express a willingness to share themselves with their students (George and Alexander 1993)

Successful advisory programs tend to be guided by the same basic objectives. They:

- Promote student-teacher relationships
- Address general student self-esteem and beliefs about student confidence
- Provide a time for social exchange and peer recognition in a safe and supportive environment
- Link parents and the school
- Mediate between academic and social concerns (National Middle School Association 1995)

The curriculum for the advisory program supports both academic and social achievement by addressing a wide range of adolescents' personal and interpersonal concerns. Effective programs provide practical strategies for student success as compared to self-defeating behaviors to which young adolescents are so vulnerable.

Advisory Programs

There are various types of advisory programs. The topics covered within the program are primarily determined by the needs of the school and its students. Very few advisory programs have a district-appointed curriculum. Once the advisor has set the standards for the meeting time, students become the main focus. According to Stevenson (1998), advisors should develop a "game plan" for the advisory period, a time to explore the interests of students. In order to get student buy-in into the program, the teacher must involve every student in the goal-setting process. Frequently during advisory teachers and students decide to update daily assignment books, check daily schedules for tests and activities, review study skills, build self-esteem and confidence, and get to know each other on a personal level (Stevenson 1998).

Additionally, advisory programs:

1. Provide a culture that will foster bonding within the group so that students feel valued by the teacher and by their peers

2. Help students cope with academic demands and set goals that will help facilitate positive school experiences
3. Help students find ways to discover their own talents, uniqueness, and abilities so they might begin to appreciate the differences among people and see them as strengths to be valued
4. Help young adolescents develop positive relationships through learning experiences that challenge them to use group dynamics and group social skills
5. Promote higher-order thinking skills and critical thinking skills through discussion and problem solving so students begin to learn how to make good choices
6. Develop listening skills and a critical understanding of the power of effective communication
7. Help students build self-esteem so their confidence will allow them to assume responsibility for their actions
8. Augment student awareness of good citizenship through providing opportunities to serve the community, to make meaningful contributions to their school and to the community, and to participate in academic service learning activities
9. Provide opportunities for meaningful student involvement through shared decisionmaking
10. Improve home and school communication and relationships through active involvement and engagement. (Hoversten, Doda, and Lounsbury 1991, 6)

Advisories are student centered, for students set their own goals and are responsible for checking them as the year progresses. A community service project is a good way to start students working together. Giving students full responsibility for choosing a project, planning it, and implementing it is a great way to begin team building and leadership development (Miller 1999).

Advisory programs address specific needs and focus on particular goals and skills; for instance, an advisory program at East Middle School may have an academic focus, so that academic performance is improved through reading, writing, tutoring, and the development of study skills. South Middle School may have a community advisory program that focuses on group identity through discussion, projects, intramurals, and group management. North Middle School's skill-based advisory program may focus on developmental guidance through decisionmaking, stress management, race relations, and values clarification activities. An advocacy advisory program tends to focus on the adult-student relationship through individual student conferences and activities. The invigoration or active advisory program focuses on enthusiasm and personal qualities through student participation in intramurals, clubs, parties, and informal fun activities. The administrative advisory program attends to clerical activities such as announcements and school business. Any given advisory program may be one or a combination of these types. Morton Middle School has an emphasis on school business on Mondays, advocacy and community on Tuesday and Wednesday, academic performance on Thursday, and intramurals and clubs on Friday.

For every school and perhaps for every grade level or house, the advisory program may vary. Relationship building is always the focus of an effective program, however. What do advisory periods of relationship building look like?

Examples

In order to create a successful advisory period, students need to be involved in basic decisions. At the beginning of our year, the students and I brainstorm the jobs that will make the advisory period run smoothly and efficiently. These jobs include removing the chairs from their desktops, delivering attendance to the office, working the Ditto dispenser, functioning as counter patrol or desk patrol (cleaning the top of desks on Fridays) or board patrol (cleaning the board and its erasers on Fridays), cleaning the overhead, being the reminder for Drop Everything and Read (D.E.A.R), and being supervisor. There are usually two to three students assigned per job, so they help each other. The jobs are posted on the back wall and change every Monday by simple rotation of names.

Students exercise decisionmaking skills by deciding how each advisory during the week will be spent. Wednesdays are designated D.E.A.R., a time when all students and staff read for the first thirty minutes of the day. Fridays are job days, and at least one day of the week is teacher-led instruction. Students usually incorporate one homework day and one open topic day when they can bring up any appropriate topic for discussion. These days are important, for the topics discussed give me an opportunity to recognize, acknowledge, and validate students' opinions and thoughts.

To avoid student grade-level isolation, teachers "buddy up" with an advisory class in a different grade. For example, my seventh-grade advisory class will buddy up or partner with a sixth grade. Once a month, time is set aside for buddies to meet with each other and discuss different questions. This buddy partnership helps the younger students more easily adapt to middle school and feel more comfortable in the building because they have an "upper classman" as their buddy.

The advisory period lessons shown in Tables 4.1, 4.2, 4.3, 4.4, and 4.5 help students develop the skills they need in difficult situations.

Table 4.1

Dealing with Disrespect in a Positive Manner

Developmental Characteristics	Middle Level Curriculum Standards	Multiple Intelligences
Often overreact to ridicule, embarrassment, and rejection	Help students interpret superiority and inferiority feelings	Verbal/ Linguistic
Are psychologically vulnerable, because at no other stage in development are they more likely to encounter so many differences between themselves and others	Use flexible teaching patterns so students can interact with a variety of adults with whom they identify	Intrapersonal Interpersonal Bodily/Kinesthetic
Are socially vulnerable because as they develop their beliefs, attitudes, and values, the influence of media and negative experiences with adults and peers may compromise their ideas and values		

Objective
- Students will be able to react to a disrespectful situation in a positive manner and maintain an acceptable level of respect

Time Needed: four fifteen-minute advisory periods

Materials Needed:
- Worksheet "How Would I React?"
- Worksheet "How Did They React?"

Activities/Procedure:
1. Students need to learn how to react to disrespectful comments.
2. Ask students to remember an embarrassing moment they experienced or one that they have witnessed.

(continues)

Table 4.1 (continued)

3. Ask the following questions:
   - What was done to embarrass the person?
   - What behaviors would you interpret as being disrespectful?
   - How did the person handle the situation?
   - What are the consequences of a violent reaction?
   - How was the situation handled?
4. Discuss respect:
   - Define it
   - What does *disrespectful* mean to you?
   - What was the situation that brought you disrespect?
   - What is the best way to handle it?
   - What can you do to minimize the embarrassment?
   - How can you "save face"?
5. Choose students to role-play a personal situation. Discuss their behaviors and how they handle them.
6. Pass out worksheet "How Would I React?"

Assessment:
Informal assessment through discussion and completion of worksheet

Homework:
Worksheet "How Did They React?" due in two days for discussion

Table 4.2
How Would I React?

Directions: For each situation explain what you feel like doing and then explain what you should do.

Situation One
You are in the school hallway, minding your own business, and the school "bully" knocks your books out of your arms and does not apologize. Now you are going to be late for class and everyone around you will laugh.

1. What emotions are you feeling at this time? What do you feel like doing?
2. How should you really handle the situation?

Situation Two
A teacher calls on you to answer a question in class. You were not paying attention and do not know the answer. The teacher persists in requesting an answer from you. At this point your face is turning red, and students are beginning to laugh.

1. What emotions are you feeling at this time? What do you feel like doing?
2. How should you really handle the situation?

Table 4.3

How Did They React?

Directions: Choose three friends who are not in this class. Ask them if they have ever had an embarrassing moment at school and how they handled the situation. Then, ask them what they would do differently if they could change the way they originally reacted. (Do not use names in summaries.) Record their answers below.

Friend One:
- Situation
- Reaction
- Changed reaction

Friend Two:
- Situation
- Reaction
- Changed reaction

Friend Three:
- Situation
- Reaction
- Changed reaction

Table 4.4

Behavioral Expectations—Code of Conduct for Students during Advisory Period

Developmental Characteristics	Middle Level Curriculum Standards	Multiple Intelligences
May exhibit immature behavior because their social skills frequently lag behind their mental and physical maturity	Establish active student government that allows students to help establish standards for behavior	Verbal/Linguistic Interpersonal
Often overreact to ridicule, embarrassment, and rejection	Schedule large group activities rather than boy-girl events; encourage co-curricular activities	
Are socially vulnerable because as they develop their beliefs, attitudes, and values, the influence of media and negative experiences with adults and peers may compromise their ideas and values	Schedule debates, plays play days, and other activities to allow students to "show off" in productive ways.	

(continues)

Table 4.4 (continued)

Objective
- Students will work together to determine the behavioral expectations during advisory period including communication with peers in advisory
- Students will develop a list of expectations to be displayed in the room

Time Needed: two fifteen-minute periods

Materials Needed:
- Markers
- Volunteers to write on board
- Typist
- Poster board

Activities/Procedures:
1. Brainstorm behaviors appropriate for advisory period. Volunteers write them on the board.
   Questions to lead brainstorming:
   - What rules do you think are important when having a group discussion?
   - Do you ever feel embarrassed when someone laughs at your suggestion?
   - What can we do as a class to avoid that?
   - What rules should be followed when students are sharing ideas?
2. Discuss the importance of honesty and confidentiality regarding personal statements made during advisory period.
3. Create a list of expected behaviors. A volunteer will type up the list for each student.
4. Make a poster of the expected advisory behaviors to hang in the room.

Assessment:
Students will be informally assessed through observation during advisory period. The teacher keeps a journal, recording a few students' reactions and behavior in deciding expectations, and uses this journal to record responses throughout advisory.

Conclusion: Advisory Programs

Traditional schooling in the United States requires students to make many transitions—from home to school, grade to grade, teacher to teacher, elementary school to middle school, middle school to high school, and high school to college. Students who find transitions to be most difficult are young adolescents between the ages of ten and fourteen. These transescents are continually changing emotionally, physically, and socially. As students move from elementary to middle school, sixth graders may be influenced the most to the extent that

Table 4.5
What Others Think of Me

Developmental Characteristics	Middle Level Curriculum Standards	Multiple Intelligences
Are psychologically vulnerable, because at no other stage in development are they more likely to encounter so many differences between themselves and others	Design activities that help students play out their emotions—activity programs that provide opportunities to draw out shy students and calm louder students	Bodily/Kinesthetic
Are socially vulnerable because as they develop their beliefs, attitudes, and values, the influence of media and negative experiences with adults and peers may compromise their ideas and values	Structure a general atmosphere of friendliness, concern, and group cohesiveness	Visual/Spatial
Tend to be self-conscious, lacking in self-esteem		Verbal/Linguistic

Objective
- Students will be able to reveal positive feelings about their advisory group classmates

Time Needed: two fifteen-minute advisory periods

Materials Needed:
- Construction paper
- Pen/pencil

Activities/Procedure:
1. Split group into pairs.
2. Each student draws the outline of the partner's foot or hand.
3. Each student puts name on the paper and leaves it on the desk.
4. Students then move around the room stopping to write a positive comment on every hand or foot they come to. The comments should describe a positive feature of that person. Rotate to all the papers.
5. Break into groups of four and discuss the comments received.
6. Meet together as a whole and discuss the comments.
7. Make a collage in the room with the hands and feet.

Assessment:
- Informal assessment through discussion after activity.

this transition may have far-reaching effects in years to come. Anderman, Maehr, and Midgley (1996) stated that this is a critical time in students' lives because sixth and seventh graders run the risk of being turned off by negative academic and social experiences. They must be given attention. An advisory program could assist students with these transitions.

The middle school movement has helped ease transescents' transition from being children in elementary school and adolescents in middle school to becoming young adults in high school. The thoughtful middle school suggested by the National Middle School Association (1995) provides a superior curriculum for the students in a relaxed environment that encourages them to interact socially, learn academically, and explore their interests.

The benefits to students are a greater sense of belonging that drives a positive school environment, individual and group accomplishment, heightened peer concern, and the deliberate establishment of a culture of trust and respect. An advisory program benefits the school by establishing and cultivating positive interactions among adults, students, the home and the community; by resulting in fewer students dropping out of school; by nurturing a cooperative atmosphere of problem solving and decisionmaking in which students play an active and respectful role; by augmenting the students' abilities to discuss social issues; and by providing projects that actively place students in helping roles within the community. Whether the program is an affective or a cognitive one, when students know that they are valued, that their voice will be heard, and that they are active players in their own education, everyone benefits.

Exemplary middle schools have maximized learning opportunities through the reorganization of time. Outstanding middle schools were found to have three strikingly similar components: interdisciplinary team organization, flexible schedules, and home base or advisor-advisee programs (Alexander 1988). In the next sections, three middle grades teachers examine the use of time as a resource. Lisa Klemetson examines scheduling; Michelle Galecka examines the creative use of core explore time, and Gretchen Cline discusses the work of interdisciplinary teams.

Michelle Madden

INTERDISCIPLINARY TEAMING

Interdisciplinary teaming is the linchpin of effective middle schools because it makes possible other features, such as flexible scheduling and curriculum integration.

Life before Interdisciplinary Teaming

Prior to the middle school movement, students went from their small, neighborhood elementary school where everyone knew their name to a larger, more centrally located junior high school. Each year in elementary school they had essentially one teacher whom they came to know fairly well, with one set of rules and expectations. The junior high brought near anonymity with hundreds of students and five, six, or seven teachers each with her own set of policies, rules, and assignments. There was little time to form the quality relationships necessary for a successful academic community. This can be a daunting and unsettling change, particularly when we consider the emotional, social, and physical changes young adolescents are experiencing.

In this same junior high school the teachers were equally fragmented. Each teacher had as many as 150 students each semester, possibly in multiple grade levels. This allowed little time to focus on individual students' academic needs, let alone on their social or emotional concerns. Each hour, thirty new students marched into the room, worked according to that teacher's rules, received their homework assignment, and marched into another classroom, mostly with different classmates, and the process was repeated. Owing to the heavy student load and scheduling conflicts, there was little time for teachers to coordinate curriculum, much less to discuss an individual student's problems. The majority of each teacher's planning time was spent grading papers, doing work specific to their departments, or making parent phone calls, possibly calling the same parent another teacher was contacting. This format was used for many years, and although it is unlikely that it harmed students or teachers, we know that it did not help them to be more successful.

Historical Background

Though interdisciplinary teams have been part of the middle grades reform movement for the past thirty years, such teams have seldom been implemented in a comprehensive and integrated fashion. Coming out of the junior high school with its emphasis on the core curriculum, teaming—or the interdisciplinary team's practice—was born of junior high teachers' concern that they needed to know a few students and know them more intimately (McEwin 1997). One teacher was charged with integrating one or more disciplines for a common group of students. The same impetus drives middle grades teaming today.

What Is an Interdisciplinary Team?

An interdisciplinary team is a small group of teachers who share the same group of students. These teachers usually represent the four core areas of math, science, language arts, and social studies. Some teams include elective teachers for subjects such as art, music, theater, journalism, physical education, computer technology, or special education. The number of students on the team are correlated to the number of teachers, averaging twenty-five to thirty pupils per teacher. Oftentimes, the size and configuration of a team are based on each teacher's individual certification. For instance, a teacher who is certified in math and science may team with two other teachers, one who is certified in social studies and the other who is certified in language arts. This constitutes a three-person team. On another team, four teachers may each be certified: one in language arts, one in social studies, one in science, and one in math. This would be a four-person team. And sometimes there are two-person teams because a teacher certified in math will also frequently be certified in science and the other, certified in social studies, is often also certified in language arts. Table 4.6 illustrates the student and faculty grouping in a sixth-, seventh-, and eighth-grade middle school.

There are 183 students in the sixth grade, called a "house," and the house is divided into two interdisciplinary teams: one three-person team and one four-person team. The seventh-grade house has a total of 173 students divided into two three-person teams of 88 and 85 students respectively. And the eighth-grade house has a total of 147 students divided into 76 students on the four-person team and 71 students on the three-person team. Each house has its own guidance counselor housed within the common classroom space, and each team includes a special education teacher. During the common team planning time, the entire house of teachers plans together at least once a week and the team plans together the other four days.

Table 4.6

Central Middle School Student and Faculty Organization

6th Grade House		7th Grade House		8th Grade House	
3-Person Teaching Team	4-Person Teaching Team	3-Person Teaching Team	3-Person Teaching Team	4-Person Teaching Team	3-Person Teaching Team
90 students	93 students	88 students	85 students	76 students	71 students

Although there are no hard and fast rules about the size of a team, research indicates that smaller is better (Erb and Stevenson 1999). But it is not the size of the team that matters as much as how the teachers and students use their arrangement for the benefits of teaching and learning.

According to *Turning Points* (Carnegie Council on Adolescent Development 1989) and *This We Believe* (National Middle School Association 1995), the students on a team should be grouped heterogeneously or by mixed ability, rather than by ability levels, as has been the practice in the traditional junior high school. It is through interaction with students of varying talents and abilities that students learn most about themselves and others—skills needed for life in the real world. On some teams student groups stay together in all of their core classes; on other teams they are regrouped from class to class. Many schools allow teams to plan their own daily schedules, using a given block of time. Teaming offers teachers and students the flexibility to adjust classes and groupings based on what is needed at a given time for a particular learning activity.

As schools move to interdisciplinary teaming, they address the following formative questions:

1. How does teaming benefit the students?
2. How does teaming benefit teachers?
3. How does teaming benefit and affect the school culture?

4. What considerations need to be made in forming the teams?
5. Who should be on the team in addition to the core teachers? Elective teachers, special educators, counselors?
6. Who decides the makeup of the team? Who chooses the combination of teachers?
7. What skills and attitudes should effective team members have?
8. What does the organization of the team look like and who decides?
9. What do effective teams do?
10. How does the team evaluate its ongoing effectiveness?
11. How does the team maintain momentum?
12. If there are responsibilities/roles on the team, who decides?
13. What is the role of the administrator with regard to each team? (Bullock and Pedersen 1999)

Why Move to Teaming?

When a junior high school adopts a middle grades philosophy or when a middle school, in name only, considers more effective practice, one of the first considerations is adopting interdisciplinary teaming based on the following reasons:

1. Student achievement improves because of coordinated teaching and learning
2. Students are better known by a smaller family both within the house and within the home team
3. When students feel more connected to an adult and to each other, their sense of self-worth increases; they become more motivated to learn, and discipline problems decrease
4. There are greater flexibility in instruction and variety in instructional practice
5. There are greater curricular continuity and connections across classes

6. Teachers make better use of their own strengths and creative abilities
7. Teachers' teaching skills improve as the team develops (Forte and Schurr 1993)

The goal of a team is to create an organized learning environment. This means that rules, policies, and formats should be as similar as possible in all of the team's classrooms (Clark and Clark, 1997). Many teams meet as a house or whole group early in the school year and encourage students to brainstorm the rules for the house and for their team. This might lead to a house or a team constitution that is signed by all members. These rules would be posted in each classroom, and the consequences, again agreed upon by the team, would be the same in each classroom. Many teams go beyond agreeing on the rules to include common policies and practices. Team teachers can and should have the same policies for things such as how papers are to be turned in, what is acceptable for late or incomplete assignments, and what the grading policy will be. They coordinate homework assignments and major projects, tests, and quizzes. Outstanding teams conduct help sessions for students. They provide frequent and timely feedback on students' academic work and social progress (Forte and Schurr 1993). This continuity among classrooms saves students from having to switch gears every time they change rooms and helps to end confusion while it improves understanding of expectations.

Things Successful Teams Do

Meet Regularly

Some school districts that understand the value of teaming provide their teachers a team planning time in addition to their individual planning time, as illustrated in Table 4.7. This allows members of the team an opportunity to meet daily. Without the common planning time, teaming becomes a challenge. Interdisciplinary teams need to meet as often as possible to ensure their continued success (Erb and Doda 1989). During these meetings, teachers discuss individual students' needs, accomplishments, and talents; solve problems; meet with a student's family; and make plans for future teaching and learning. Forming

Table 4.7
Interdisciplinary Team Teacher's Schedule

Period	Responsibility
Advisory	Advisory
1	Language Arts
2	Language Arts
3	Language Arts
4	Lunch
5	Individual Planning Time
6	Team Planning Time
7	Language Arts
8	Language Arts
Core Explore	Core Explore

the team is not the end of the process, but the beginning. Failure to meet on a regular basis causes the group to stagnate and defeats the purpose of interdisciplinary teaming.

Stay Organized

An interdisciplinary team must find an organizational system that allows its members to make the most of their time and energy. Successful teams designate a specific meeting time and place free from interruptions. In supporting teams, the principal must require attendance of all team members and must emphasize the importance of interpersonal skills and group dynamics. The team itself establishes the guidelines by which it will operate and decides how decisions will be made, how it will disagree in a positive way, and what procedure for solving difficult or sticky problems will be used. Teams function more easily and respectfully after this consideration. They more readily stay on task, establish priorities, assess their own effectiveness, value confidentiality, and prize the power of humor.

It is beneficial for each team member to have a special role or task. Some schools name "team leaders," in some cases a paid position, to act as the liaison between the team and the administration (Erb and Doda 1989). They attend leadership meetings and convey information back and forth between the team and the administration. In many schools the team leader role is rotated from year to year, so that all members have the opportunity to share in the responsibility. Successful interdisciplinary teams also designate a recorder who keeps minutes of team meetings, as illustrated in Figure 4.1, and refers to them as needed. They maintain a log of communications with parents and administration.

Often on Friday the team log, which includes the minutes of the daily team meetings, is given to the principal as another form of open communication. Additionally, if the team members are mapping their curriculum (as discussed later in this chapter), they will include that information on their charts and in their log. They keep a centrally located calendar of school, team, and classroom events and inform each other of any changes made to it. They may even keep files of student work or information in a place to which they all have access. When a team is well organized, its members can spend their time dealing with student and curricular issues. Table 4.8 illustrates the way one interdisciplinary team uses its team plan time across a two-week time period. The team attempts to adhere to the schedule so it does not get bogged down in the mire of repeatedly discussing daily business or problem students. Additionally, the team holds to its goals, objectives, and mission statement as focal points in team planning time.

Integrate Curriculum

Once a team has been established, team members examine the learning in each of its classrooms, and they find ways to make connections more explicit for students. It is extremely valuable and necessary to deeper learning and understanding for middle grades students to see connections between what they are learning in their classes. Successful teams do this by integrating their curricula. This does not necessarily mean creating interdisciplinary units (or units of study with common threads or themes that run through all the classes all of the time). Those often lead to watered-down or contrived connections between classes. Rather, integrating curriculum means taking a careful look at each content area's curriculum and finding the natural conceptual overlaps. For example, the science teacher may be required to teach a unit on space, and the math teacher has to do a unit on converting fractions to decimals. In math they use their data about space to practice conversions and use the data in their presentations on the planets. Perhaps the language arts teacher teaches letter writing while the social studies teacher is doing a unit on nonrenewable resources. Students write letters to local residents and businesses, urging them to recycle and telling them about ways to conserve energy. These connections help students better understand the relevance of their learning.

Figure 4.1
Sample Team Log

TEAM LOG
EAGLE TEAM

Members Present: _____ Date: _____

Focus of the Meeting: _____

Agenda:

1. _____

2. _____

3. _____

Comments/Ideas: _____

_____

_____

Actions to Be Taken:	Actions to Be Taken:

Notes for Further Discussion: _____

_____

_____

_____

Guests Present: _____

Table 4.8
Two-Week Team Plan Schedule

Day	Team Focus
Monday	Curricular Planning
Tuesday	Student Needs
Wednesday	Family Participation
Thursday	Curricular Planning
Friday	Log, Curriculum Mapping, Curricular Connections
Day	Team Focus
Monday	Curricular Planning, Advisory Coordination
Tuesday	House Activities, Encore Teachers' Notes
Wednesday	Student Needs, Counselor's Notes
Thursday	Team Activities
Friday	Log, Curriculum Mapping, Student Needs, Student Recognition

Include the Family

Effective teams celebrate students' families as valuable resources and make sure that they are informed and involved. This might mean sending home regular team notes or newsletters to let the family know what is going on in the classroom. It means finding out what skills the family has and using them as volunteers or presenters. It means inviting all parents in for conferences and performance demonstrations. It means seeking their input early when the team recognizes that a child is in some way struggling. It means including the family's perspective in solving problems. It means inviting the family to actively participate in the daily work of the classroom.

The families of middle school students are often unsure where they fit when it comes to the education and success of their children. As the middle grades child naturally moves away from complete dependence on the family, family members are not as comfortable coming to the school as they were when the child was in elementary school. The common middle schooler's phrase, "Oh, they will just embarrass me," when a teacher encourages students to invite their families to the school, is both put in its proper developmental context and directly addressed. Effective teams provide positive experiences in which students and their families enjoy and are proud of each other. Good teams welcome the family and make sure they stay "on board."

Create an Identity

Most sports teams have a name and a mascot that set them apart from other teams and create a sense of belonging. Interdisciplinary teams also create an identity that makes students feel special. Many teams select a name, sometimes a banner or a special handshake, and even a mascot that holds some special significance (Erb and Doda 1989). Calling the students "Smith and Jones's Kids" is probably not enough. Often students brainstorm several choices and vote on their team name and on other team identifiers. This allows members of the team to feel that they really are a part of a group, something very important to the middle grades student. Once the team identity has been formed, team teachers and students find ways to market their identity and make sure that it stands for something positive. This may include team T-shirts, posters, bumper stickers, and even cheers. Students who take pride in their positive identity are more likely to maintain it and to feel that sense of family that allows them to take necessary risks in their own learning. To belong, to feel valued, to have a positive place in school spur the kind of self-efficacy that accomplishment and success command.

Build Community

When students and teachers work closely together, it is important that they understand, respect, and appreciate each other (Peterson 1992). Successful interdisciplinary teams afford their students time to bond, not just at the beginning of a school year but regularly throughout the year. They have team rituals, ceremonies, coats of arms, and banners; they have special awards such as student of the month (Figure 4.2) or a special award for a student who does something exceptional for other students or for the community; they have team meetings and games that allow students to be silly and laugh together (Peterson 1992).

Some teams allow time for class meetings, held during advisory or during core explore, often initiated by students, to openly discuss issues that occur and ensure that students' needs are being met. Group projects and particularly academic service learning projects (see Chapter 6) are a valuable and powerful way to bring students together, especially when

Figure 4.2
Student of the Month Award

Student of the Month

Awarded to
(Student's Name)

For

Teacher _____   *Date* _____

they are provided the opportunity to showcase their own unique talents. Lock-ins, field trips, and community projects also help to solidify a group.

Reflect and Revise

An interdisciplinary team is constantly evolving, amenable to change as it grows. This requires team members to constantly self-assess and to make the necessary changes. This might mean changing the schedule to accommodate a new learning activity or aspect of the curriculum not previously included. At times rules must be adjusted to deal with issues as they arise. Team members return from a conference with new ideas they want the team to try. Sometimes ideas may not be as effective as the team had hoped. They must be willing to positively learn from the event, discontinue it, and move on. Teams need an action plan, including a mission statement, goals, and objectives, in order to move forward each term, each semester, each school year (Erb and Doda 1989).

In short, following the recommendations of Stephen Covey, a nationally recognized expert on successful management, and his notions of excellence in organizations, successful interdisciplinary teams are proactive in that each team member assumes responsibility for his or her role on the team; the team members begin with the end in mind by determining what it is their students need to know, to be able to do, and to understand by the end of the school year and then plan backward; they put first things first by deciding which things they actually have control over and what their priorities will be; they think win/win, for as they develop a sense of deep trust in each other and as each person is moved by a commitment to personal integrity as well as to students, the success of the team becomes more important than the success of any one person; they seek first to understand and then to be understood, or in other words, they listen more than they talk; they synergize by viewing the differences among the team members as strengths and by engaging in perpetual reflection on their work, making adjustments to better serve their students; and they model the commitment to each other and to learning as a habit that students can emulate (Branham 1997).

How Interdisciplinary Teams Benefit Students

Academically

Research has shown that interdisciplinary teaming has a positive impact on students' academic success for several reasons (Flowers,

Mertens, and Mulhall 1999). Students on interdisciplinary teams have consistent rules, procedures, and expectations. This helps eliminate students' guesswork as to how assignments are supposed to be done. When students have difficulty understanding, they feel more comfortable asking their advisory or team teacher for help, because teaming has allowed them time to develop safe relationships. Students have many other teammates, also completing the same assignments, to whom they can turn for help. Those students may present a different way of understanding material from the teacher's. Finally, teachers make curricular connections across classes (Powell 1993). Middle grades students learn best when they see that what they are learning fits into a bigger picture and that it is connected to life in the real world (Carnegie Council on Adolescent Development 1989; National Middle School Association 1995).

Socially

At no time in a person's life is social acceptance more important to the individual's development than during the middle grades (Carnegie Council on Adolescent Development 1989; National Middle School Association 1995). Teaming allows students the opportunity to form bonds of friendship in the classroom. Instead of seeing new classmates each hour, students often stay in the same group for their four core classes. Others who don't stay together for their core classes can socialize during team activities and during the passing from class to class or block to block within the physical space of the house. They don't get lost in the school maze, because their classrooms are usually adjacent to one another or situated together in a common physical space. These students complete the same projects, often in collaborative groups, and take the same tests, which allows them to assist, support, and really get to know one another (Powell 1993). In this smaller learning community, conflicts are usually noticed earlier and can be resolved more quickly than in a traditional junior high setting.

Emotionally

Early adolescence can be a time of great emotional turmoil. Students are dealing with changes in their bodies, their minds, and their relationships with others. Being part of a team can help students deal with issues born of developmental angst. Teaming allows all students to belong to a group that is unique and special (Powell 1993). It allows students from different backgrounds to meet and see that they really are more similar than different. Students see that they are not the only person experiencing challenges and changes. The time teachers spend with students allows a trusting relationship to form more easily than in a traditional setting. Students are then more likely to seek help from their teachers. As well, this time together allows teachers to notice changes in their students and to seek assistance for them if they are troubled.

How Interdisciplinary Teams Benefit Teachers

Professionally

Teachers on teams have a lot more autonomy than their nonteamed counterparts (Erb and Doda 1989; Husband and Short 1994). They plan their own schedules, group and regroup their pupils, and make many of their own decisions based on what they think is best for their students. Their discussions help identify and solve problems for students and for other teachers. The opportunity that teams have to meet regularly gives them time to share craft knowledge and to see content or thematic connections among their curricula. Teamed teachers reinforce skills taught in each other's classrooms. And teaming helps reduce time and effort spent on issues of classroom management and behavior, creating a consistent and united culture.

Personally

Most people choose to become teachers because they have a passionate desire to help children learn and grow. Teaming enables teachers to work in a student-centered rather than a subject-centered environment, and it allows them to feel that they make more of a direct difference in the lives of their students (Erb and Doda 1989; Husband and Short 1994; Flowers, Mertens, and Mulhall 1999). Teaming provides teachers the time to express and nurture an interest in the lives of their students and to form relationships that foster student trust, learning, and growth. The opportunity to make decisions, share ideas, and solve problems together leads to greater job satisfaction, to shared or distributed leadership, and to the exercise of pedagogical and professional talent. Finally, just like their students, teachers benefit from being part of a unique group that is different from all other groups in the school.

A Look Inside One Interdisciplinary Team

The seventh-grade hallway at Pierce Middle School in Waterford, Michigan, is home to the Groovy Geese team. You can spot Groovy Goose classrooms by the giant tie-dyed flags that hang above their doors, with their motto A Gaggle of Great Kids, A Flock Full of Fun. The name of the team comes from research on the loyalty, cooperation, and trust that geese maintain as they migrate south each year. The geese are a metaphor for what the team should become.

The two-person teaching team is made up of a math/science teacher and a language arts/social studies teacher who work with approximately sixty students. Organizing the team begins each year at student registration in mid-August. The Groovy Geese teachers, wearing their team tie-dyed T-shirts, meet and greet their new students and families and distribute their team brochures. The brochures contain information about the curriculum, the teachers, upcoming events, and the supplies that students will need for the school year. Families maintain that meeting the teachers and receiving the information before school begins helps make their child and them feel welcome.

On the first day of school, Groovy Geese meet as a team, rather than going to each class, and discuss what it means to be a Groovy Goose. Teachers and students decide on class rules, and students learn the organizational procedures consistent in all core classes. Their daily schedules, proper presentation of their assignments, and submission of work on time are openly discussed. It doesn't take long for students to fully understand they really are on a team.

Later in the day, students are divided into "Flock" and "Gaggle," the two groups that will move from class to class together, and are reassured that these two groups will be rearranged and changed through the school year. The rest of the day is spent doing community-building activities and learning each other's names. Community-building activities continue throughout the year to help maintain a positive atmosphere.

Curriculum night is another important event on the Groovy Geese team. A few weeks into the school year, families are invited to the school to talk with their child's teacher about the curriculum, to meet the teachers on the team, to discuss their important role on the team, and to share with teachers their ideas about their child's education. Families are given a team handbook that includes team policies, schedules, and expectations for the school year. A volunteer sign-up sheet is distributed among the families. At the end of the evening, a raffle is held for prizes such as coffee, chocolate, and earplugs—all tools needed to jokingly "survive" their child's middle grades years. The Groovy Geese teachers try to make humor and laughter a regular part of team life.

Pierce Middle School teachers plan their own teaching schedules. They are given information on what times they will be with students, but it is up to the teams to plan what they will be teaching, to whom, and when during the blocked times. This really helps teams to tailor instruction to student needs and to easily make changes.

On the Groovy Geese team, students are first divided into two groups, named Flock and Gaggle; each group travels together to its core classes. Staying together has proven helpful in motivating students to form relationships, but when adjustments need to be made, for behavior management reasons or for learning preferences, they can easily be done.

The Groovy Geese team has many rituals and identifiers. One of the most obvious is the brightly colored team T-shirts that students wear on designated "Groovy Pride" days. Their mascot is Groovy, a plastic lawn-ornament goose, that adults outside the school may think a bit tacky but that students on the team are thrilled to take home for special events or family trips. Groovy Goose has been salmon fishing and trick-or-treating, and has even gone swimming in Florida. One of the favorite team rituals is the weekly team meeting. Each Friday, the entire house meets to discuss things happening on each team and in the school, to solve any recent problems, and to distribute "Golden Eggs." These are awards given out a few at a time to students who have done things to improve the team or themselves. This allows each child on the team to be a star at least once during the school year.

Attached to the midterm academic progress note is the "Goose Call," the team newsletter. It keeps the families informed about what their children are doing in class and about upcoming events. Families have repeatedly said how helpful these correspondences are because they keep the home and the school connected. It is just as important for families to have a way of conveying information from home to school.

Curriculum integration is an ever-evolving process on the team. Each year there are expected curricular changes as the teachers on the team attempt to add, where it best fits, at least one more aspect of integration. One example of integrated activities is the team's creation of "Cell Counties," which includes studying the parts of a cell as compared to the parts of a specific country, creating a story-telling project about a minority scientist, and using simile and metaphor in drawing creative math and science comparisons. Reading strategies are taught in all core classes. Integrated activities require knowledge of other teachers' curricula, including when particular segments of learning take place and when they are taught. This integration and coordination have proven extremely beneficial to the students.

Part of understanding and connecting with other content curriculum is understanding each other's schedules. The Groovy Geese team keeps a master calendar of all classroom events and regularly consults it when planning lessons. Projects, quizzes, tests, and assignments are all spaced out and prioritized, so that students are never faced with a night of homework from all four classes or multiple projects due on the same date. At the beginning of the school year, all of the school's students are given a planner, which the team updates daily. This helps students and teachers to prioritize their workload and encourages students to develop time management skills.

Every day the teachers on the Groovy Geese team have both an individual planning time and a team planning time, a practice the school district felt was important for effective teaming. The teaching team plans its calendars, communicates with families, meets with administration, and carries out the daily activities. Because it is a small team, it has no need for a formal team leader. Both teachers consider the team the most important factor to their students' success, so all decisions affecting the team or an individual student are made together, a process known by students, families, and administrators.

The Groovy Geese team has evolved over several years of trial and error and through continuous reflection. Each year the team has added and eliminated practices and activities, often after consulting the students about what they thought was or was not working. There are always improvements to be made, objectives to be accomplished, and goals to be reached. Being a part of a successful team has meant a lot of compromise and some conflict. At the heart of every decision, however, has been the question, "What is best for the students?"

Conclusion: Interdisciplinary Teaming

Many of the best-practice recommendations for middle grades education are met through interdisciplinary teaming. The benefits to both student and teacher are apparent. But effective teaming can only be possible when teachers, students, administrators, families, and the community are actively and positively involved. The list of descriptors for successful interdisciplinary teams is lengthy and as diverse as there are teams. Yet at the heart of every effective interdisciplinary team is the need to consistently evaluate team decisions and practices in order to

Table 4.9
Traditional Departmentalized Master Schedule

Time	Monday	Tuesday	Wednesday	Thursday	Friday
7:40–7:55	Advisory	Advisory	Advisory	Advisory	Advisory
8:00–8:55	1	1	1	1	1
9:00–9:55	2	2	2	2	2
10:00–10:55	3	3	3	3	3
11:00–11:25	4-Lunch	4-Lunch	4-Lunch	4-Lunch	4-Lunch
11:30–12:25	5	5	5	5	5
12:30–1:25	6	6	6	6	6
1:30–2:25	7	7	7	7	7
2:30–3:25	8	8	8	8	8

ensure that the academic, social, and emotional needs of all students are being met. In a world where individuals tend to be more and more isolated, the call to community—just as the call to American democracy—is answered in interdisciplinary teaming.

Gretchen Cline

BLOCK AND FLEX SCHEDULING

Although most middle level educators would agree that the developmental needs of middle level students must be addressed within their buildings, the level to which any teacher may be able to do so relies heavily on the school's master schedule. As illustrated in Table 4.9, the master schedule shows how time is divided into periods or hours for the entire school population.

The traditional discipline-based or departmentalized schedule creates the same time frame for all classes regardless of student learning needs or learning activities and regardless of whether they are core academic classes or electives. A recent survey (Valentine 1993) indicated that 94 percent of the country's middle schools use a six-, seven-, or eight-period day. This type of schedule lends itself to grouping students by ability, called tracking, a practice that categorizes students, limits teachers' expectations of student accomplishment, and tends to perpetuate stereotypic conceptions of what various groups of students can and should be able to do.

Scheduling creates the parameters within which teachers strive to use teaming to its fullest potential. A flexible block schedule gives a team one or two large blocks of time during which the four core classes (math, science, language arts, and social studies) are taught. This time may be adjusted on a daily basis to best meet the middle level student's physical, social, emotional, and academic needs; to create interdisciplinary connections; and to provide the highest level of educational experiences for the students. The most flexible team adjusts the schedule on a week-by-week, or even day-by-day, basis depending upon student needs identified during the team's common planning time in keeping with curricular goals (Kasak 1998).

Block-of-time and flex schedules are two ways to organize time during the school day. Block-of- time schedules result in longer class periods with more instructional time for one specific subject. For instance, instead of the traditional forty-five- to fifty-minute period—a practice dating back to the early 1900s—classes can be twice as long and more focused on learning. Flex scheduling means adjusting the schedule and the time of classes during the day or week to meet the needs of the students. Block scheduling and flex scheduling can be used in concert with one another, making the middle school experience more appropriate for students who need more time to make important learning connections. Block scheduling, which enjoyed nationwide attention in the 1990s, forces teachers out of a lecture mode and into more hands-on, project-based teaching and learning. This points to deeper student understanding of concepts and skills.

In today's middle schools, there are more diversity and more ethnic, racial, and socioeconomic differences than ever before (Gable and Manning 1997). As a result of the Carnegie tradition, or incremental pieces of time devoted to individual content study, on one end of the programmatic spectrum most junior and senior high schools are scheduled the same way. The class schedule is the same each day, and the amount of time in any one class is the same. On the other end of the same spectrum, middle school teachers are allowed to plan their instructional activities based on the needs of their students, not the needs of the schedule. This is where block-of-time scheduling is a useful concept (Merenbloom 1991).

A traditional schedule can be very limiting. What happens when a video lasts longer than the forty-five minutes of a class period? What happens when a group is discussing a topic and the discussion is not finished, but the forty-five-minute class period is? What happens when students begin cooperative work on a team project that will take at least ninety minutes to two hours to complete, but the bell rings after only forty-five minutes of planning? Those valuable moments are gone, and the work must be continued later, often causing discontinuous planning, implementation, and assessment. These learning activities are not then as effective as they could have been if they had been taught during an extended block of time (Beane, Toepfer, and Alessi 1986).

Change can be very exciting and energizing. Teachers can change the way they organize their lessons, their units, and their time when the traditional middle level schedule allows them the flexibility. Flexible scheduling also allows teachers the opportunity to try innovative activities that may take more time than a traditional schedule effectively allowed (DiRocco 1998–1999).

There is no single schedule that will fit every middle school, for the schedule reflects the needs, the beliefs, and the values of the staff. Hackman and Valentine (1998) suggested the following guidelines, however, when a school is considering scheduling changes. The schedule should:

1. Support interdisciplinary team organization. Because interdisciplinary teaming is a keystone to effective middle grades practice and because its value has been well documented (Dickinson and Erb 1997), the schedule should promote the implementation of an interdisciplinary curriculum.
2. Support an appropriate curriculum. The schedule should facilitate the creative work of teachers and students. Decisions about the amount of time spent on core academic subjects, on encore or elective classes, and on thematic units should be determined by the curriculum specialists in the school, the teachers. The schedule should facilitate the kinds of learning activities that help all students reach mastery.
3. Support quality instruction in all content areas. The schedule should allow all students mastery of content through varied instructional techniques such as cooperative learning, project-based instruction, integrated technology, authentic assessments, active learning, and varied group arrangements.

4. Promote student development and supportive relationships. When elementary students who were used to self-
   contained classrooms come to the middle school where
   they move from class to class, the chances of "getting
   lost" are formidable. The quality schedule offers flexibility
   and stability for students. It promotes supportive relationships developed through interdisciplinary teaming
   and nurtures young adolescents' need for self-efficacy.
5. Promote quality teacher collaboration. The effective middle school allows time for teachers to plan individually
   and to plan as an interdisciplinary team.
6. Promote teacher empowerment. When teachers are given
   the opportunity to determine the schedule, they exercise
   professional judgment and are trusted to make decisions
   on behalf of their students. The greater the teacher autonomy, the greater the innovation and creativity, varied
   instructional strategies, and techniques and ability to
   identify and address student needs (Steffes and Valentine
   1995).

Block Schedules

When a school is able to create blocks of time for instruction, there are
many opportunities for teachers to be innovative and creative in their
instructional approaches. Beane, Toepfer, and Alessi (1986) cited many
advantages of block scheduling. First, as the name implies, block schedules create longer periods of instructional time for activities and discussions. Instead of being limited to the traditional fifty-five-minute segment of time, as illustrated in Table 4.10, teachers incorporate multiple
activities during an eighty-five- to ninety-minute block of time, which
keeps students immersed in the material for longer periods of time.

This increase of time encourages students to engage in more in-
depth discussions of material while having more time to be actively engaged in their learning. Block-scheduled classes may meet for 90–100
minutes each day for a semester, or they may meet on alternating days
throughout the entire school year, with only one day as a regular six- to
seven-period day. Block scheduling allows for opportunities for more
individualized instruction because of the longer period of time. It also
provides more time to focus on lab work, project work, and on the objectives being taught (Gable and Manning 1997).

Table 4.10
Traditional 55-Minute Departmentalized Teaching Schedule

Time	Period	Course
7:40–7:55	Advisory	Advisory
8:00–8:55	1	Science
9:00–9:55	2	Science
10:00–10:55	3	Science
11:00–11:25	4	Lunch
11:30–12:25	5	Science
12:30–1:25	6	Science
1:30–2:25	7	Planning
2:30–3:25	8	Science

Types of Block Schedules

When using block-of-time scheduling or block scheduling in the middle school, educators can consider several options. A schedule may have classes divided into "A" days and "B" days, with the days on a rotating basis. The schedule might be "A" class three times the first week, "B" class two times the first week, "A" class two times the second week, and "B" class three times the second week as illustrated in Table 4.11—an alternating-day block schedule. Each block of time would last ninety–100 minutes, and the day would be arranged with three or four blocks of extended time.

Students in an alternating-day block schedule may have three or four academic classes instead of six. Classes meet every other day for ninety minutes instead of for the more traditional six forty-five-minute time slots. Students become more deeply involved in an interdisciplinary unit in English and social studies; they complete larger projects; and they engage in laboratory experiences such as literature circles, science experiments, math projects, or art and music projects. Alternating-day block schedules can be less intrusive on the general school population as well (DiRocco 1998–1999). Schools that use alternating-block schedules have reported an improvement in general school culture because students and teachers do not feel rushed to try to understand and complete assignments (Hackman 1995).

Block scheduling has the potential to create increased student academic performance because the students are engaged in learning for longer periods of time (DiRocco 1998–1999). When using block-of-time schedules, two-teacher teams might decide to work on projects in

Table 4.11

Alternating-Day Master Block Schedule—Two Weeks

Time	Monday "A" Day	Tuesday "B" Day	Wednesday "A" Day	Thursday "B" Day	Friday "A" Day
7:40–7:55	Advisory	Advisory	Advisory	Advisory	Advisory
8:00–8:45 8:50–9:35	2nd Hour	1st Hour	2	1	2
9:40–10:25 10:30–11:15	4th Hour	3rd Hour	4	3	4
11:20–11:45	Lunch	Lunch	Lunch	Lunch	Lunch
11:50–12:35 12:40–1:25	6th Hour	5th Hour	6	5	6
1:30–2:15 2:20–3:05	8th Hour	7th Hour	8	7	8
Time	Monday "B" Day	Tuesday "A" Day	Wednesday "B" Day	Thursday "A" Day	Friday "B" Day
7:40–7:55	Advisory	Advisory	Advisory	Advisory	Advisory
8:00–8:45 8:50–9:35	1	2	1	2	1
9:40–10:25 10:30–11:15	3	4	3	4	3
11:20–11:45	Lunch	Lunch	Lunch	Lunch	Lunch
11:50–12:35 12:40–1:25	5	6	5	6	5
1:30–2:15 2:20–3:05	7	8	7	8	7

one class in the morning, do lessons later in the block, and do a group review time at the end of the day (Pate, Homestead, and McGinnis 1997). When teachers have extended time to do inventive activities and lessons, they more creatively use time for varied instructional activities and strategies. When teachers decide to change the traditional schedule, they gain control over instructional time and become a part of the powerful middle grades reform.

Middle grades students have somewhat limited attention. They are all at various levels of development and have different learning needs. The more traditional schedule does not allow for the flexibility necessary to respond to these differences (Merenbloom 1991). During a block-of-time class, students learn to focus on a task by practicing the skill for an extended period of time.

Sometimes short breaks are needed during a block-scheduled class. Students at this age need to move around, walk, and stay active. Students are actively engaged in learning activities that are best suited to their age and developmental level, yet activities that challenge them to go further in what they are learning. When there are no bells to interrupt student activities, the time goes quickly (Pate, Homestead, and McGinnis 1997).

There are many advantages to block scheduling. Less time is needed for administrative issues such as attendance, because there are fewer classes during the day. Students change classrooms fewer times during the day because of the longer class periods, which can help alleviate crowded hallways and issues that arise during passing time. When there are more minutes in a class and fewer classes, teachers are able to use their time more effectively. There is also less need for the routines of beginning and ending class (Geiken et al. 1999).

Fortunately, block scheduling is not a big jump from the traditional schedule that parents and the general public are used to. This means there tend to be fewer objections from parents when schools change to a block-of-time schedule.

In addition to the traditional departmentalized schedule and the alternating-day block schedule, the third kind of schedule is the flexible interdisciplinary schedule.

Flexible Interdisciplinary Schedule

What is flexible scheduling, often called flexible block scheduling or flexible interdisciplinary scheduling? Middle grades schools that group teachers on interdisciplinary teams that share the same students often chunk time in ninety-minute to two-hour blocks, as illustrated in Table 4.12.

The use of these large chunks of time is determined by the team based on the particular learning activities in a given day or even week. For instance, on Monday an interdisciplinary team took a four-content-area block of time from 8:00 after advisory period until 11:20 (lunch) and walked their classes two blocks down the street from the school to the local river, where they began an environmental research project. Following lunch the students proceeded with their elective classes during the fifth and sixth periods and ended the day with a ninety-minute

Table 4.12

Flexible Interdisciplinary Student Block Schedule

Time/Period	Monday	Tuesday	Wednesday	Thursday	Friday
7:40–7:55	Advisory	Advisory	Advisory	Advisory	Advisory
8:00–8:45	1[a]	1	1	1	1
8:50–9:35	1	1	1	1	1
9:40–10:25	1	2	1	2	1
10:30–11:15	1	2	1	2	Math Lab
11:20–11:45	Lunch	Lunch	Lunch	Lunch	Lunch
11:50–12:35	Encore	Encore	Encore	Encore	Encore
12:40–1:25	Encore	Encore	Encore	Encore	Encore
1:30–2:15	2	3	2	3	2
2:20–3:05	2	3	2	3	2

Encore classes may include but not be limited to: choral or instrumental music, technology and robotics, physical education, foreign language, yearbook, journalism, theater and drama, art, home economics, and photography.

[a] 1 refers to Core Block 1, 2 refers to Core Block 2, 3 refers to Core Block 3.

chunk of team-determined time (seventh and eighth periods as illustrated in Table 4.12) used to begin to log their data from the morning's research project.

On Tuesday the team decided to break the morning into two chunks of time; math class during Core Block 1 was held in the computer lab, where students entered their data, and science during Core Block 2 was used to examine some of the water samples gathered on Monday. After the students had foreign language class during the 11:50–12:35 encore time and choral music during the second encore time of 12:40–1:25, they went to language arts during Core Block 3, where they listened to a local writer share his poetry on the environment. On Wednesday following advisory, the students and teaching team returned to the river to continue to gather water samples and other data during Core Block 1 from 8:00 to 11:15. After the students had participated in their Wednesday encore class of physical education followed by a second encore of dramatics, yearbook, photography, or instrumental music, they ended the day in a second core block of language arts during which they began their own poetry writing about the environment. On Thursday Core Block 1 (social studies) was spent studying the core democratic values that were tied to the students' study of the environment. Core Block 2 was spent in the computer lab with the science and math teachers, and Core Block 3 was again devoted to poetry in language arts. Friday concluded the river research study, and during an extended block from 8:00 to 10:25, students prepared their projects that displayed their data and analysis along with their poetry about the environment. The projects were then evaluated and displayed in the team's commons area (usually an open shared space) for examination by the invited city commission and the city water treatment personnel. Written comments and ribbons were awarded to every student and student-team display, and the displays were viewed by the students' families at an evening open house that concluded the week's study.

The school's master schedule is only a guide with general day-to-day instructional specifications. The teaching teams change the actual class schedule daily, weekly, or monthly. Students can be grouped or regrouped during this flexible time for specific skill lessons or topics of instruction.

Flexible scheduling can mean different things, depending on the purpose the flex time is meant to serve. For example, when educators use flex scheduling, each day does not need to be organized in the same manner. The duration of the classes flexibly depends on the subject or the lesson being taught. Flex scheduling then gives teachers an option in time use rather than having fixed time constraints of a uniform schedule (Merenbloom 1988). This type of scheduling also allows teachers to create a balance between creative and developmentally appropriate activities.

Teachers benefit from flexible scheduling because it allows them to work together toward a common objective—teaching students in a way that attends to each student's learning needs while keeping them engaged and challenged. By flexing the time spent in class and on activities, teachers gain more instances for individualizing learning. Finally, flex scheduling allows teachers to include more aspects of an effective middle school program such as advisor/advisee, special events, and presentations, as well as other accompaniments to the regular curriculum (Merenbloom 1991).

The following questions may help teachers and staff as they consider moving to flexible scheduling:

1. Are there any outside time constraints, special presentations, or activities that need to be considered?
2. Should students be regrouped? A benefit of flexible scheduling is that students are able to be regrouped to

meet their needs in special areas of concern or strength (Merenbloom 1988). These groups might be heterogeneous, homogeneous, or a combination, depending on the subject area being taught. This option depends on the flexibility of the team members and their willingness to move.

3. Teams should make choices on how the time periods for instruction will be used. Will the students have classes that meet more often or less often than the traditional five math or science classes per week or will the schedule rotate in a predetermined schedule?

4. What other staff members might be included when deciding on a flexible schedule? Consideration must be made regarding the resources that can be brought in to further individualize student instruction. The schedule creates an opportunity to focus more on individual assets and difficulties.

When choosing what type of schedule works best for an individual student-centered school, the following considerations are helpful. What is the schedule's:

1. Potential to support interdisciplinary team organization?
2. Potential to support a particular curricular model? If a school is focused on a subject area by subject area model, the traditional departmentalized schedule would be the best match. If a school engages in thematic, integrated, or interdisciplinary curriculum (as discussed in Chapter 5), the flexible interdisciplinary or flexible block schedule would be most appropriate.
3. Potential to support interdisciplinary instruction in the content areas through lengthened and flexible organization of time?
4. Support for student-centered instruction? The traditional departmentalized schedule focuses on curriculum and uses the lecture as the primary instructional practice. Flexible interdisciplinary block and alternating-day scheduling affords multiple teachers the opportunity to plan in ways that tend to individualize instruction and learning for students. Flexible scheduling offers a teach-

ing team a common planning time, which in itself creates a model of collaboration on behalf of students.

5. Support for quality teacher collaboration? There is little common planning time in the traditional schedule, whereas the flexible schedule offers a teacher both an individual planning time and a team planning time. Effective teams engage in four broad tasks during common planning time: curriculum coordination; coordination of student assignments, assessments, and feedback; parental contact and involvement; and contact with other building resource staff (Kasak 1998, 56).

6. Potential to enable teachers (Hackmann and Valentine 1998, 9–11)?

After working with a local middle school for a year, the faculty and staff of one school voted to adopt the philosophy and practices of an effective middle school. That required the addition of new faculty in order to make possible the team planning time. A thirty-one-year teacher, often thought to be rigid and somewhat resistant to change, said after the first few weeks with her interdisciplinary team, "I'm glad I taught long enough that I am no longer alone." The teacher meant that she no longer taught in the traditional schedule, which saw her close her classroom door when the bell rang. Now she teaches in collaboration with her team colleagues.

Although the flexible interdisciplinary schedule usually blocks core academic subjects together, a Midwest middle school has successfully created an exploratory block, as shown in Table 4.13, by scheduling encore classes during two consecutive periods with the same students. For instance, the same seventh-grade students who may have choir seventh period during the first nine weeks also have photography or drawing and painting eighth period. During the second half of the first semester of the arts block, the seventh-period choir students have theater and drama during the eighth period. During the first half of the second semester, the students have physical education seventh period and technology eighth period. And they finish the year with physical education seventh period and foreign language eighth period.

Much of the anecdotal information and qualitative data regarding the effectiveness of flexible block scheduling has shown a smaller student failure rate; a reduction in the number of tardies, absences, and class disruptions; an increased use and integration of technology; and

Table 4.13

Interdisciplinary Flexible Team Schedule with Encore Block

Time	Class Schedule
7:40–7:55	Advisory
8:00–11:05	Core Block (Math, Science, Social Studies, Language Arts)
11:07–11:27	Lunch
11:27–12:12	Encore (Elective Class)
12:15–1:00	Encore (Elective Class)
1:04–2:35	Core Block (Science, Math, Social Studies, Language Arts)
2:38–3:05	Core Explore

The encore or elective block of time from 11:27 to 1:00 may be used in the following manner:

First Quarter	Second Quarter	Third Quarter	Fourth Quarter
Choral Music		Physical Education	
Photography or Drawing and Painting	Theater and Drama	Technology and Robotics	Foreign Language

support from the family. On the other hand, the challenge seems to be how to include the exploratory classes so necessary to middle grades students and how to help students retain key understandings, particularly if they do not take the core classes year-round (Gallagher 1999, 13). Additionally, transferring from one school to another may be a challenge.

Conclusion: Scheduling

There will be strengths and weaknesses in any schedule, and there are as many variations of the three main models as there are middle schools (Williamson 1993). Regardless, the schedule must be based on the priorities of each school. George and Alexander (1993) suggested that the schedule reflects the priorities, values, and goals of individual schools.

Although the benefits of such a schedule seem endless, Seed (1998) contended that the two major benefits of flexible block scheduling were improved instruction and communication. In fact, "since the team has a designated section of the building and the teachers meet regularly to discuss issues and make adjustments, the students are actually held to a higher level of accountability than in more rigid school structures with fixed periods and bells"(Kasak 1998, 59).

Although flexible block scheduling can certainly enhance a middle school, there are disadvantages within this model (Williamson 1993). Administrators may find the schedule complicated by itinerant and part-time staff, pull-out programs, and lunch hours. In addition, there may be some resistance from teachers who feel the need to protect structured academic time as preparation for the high school. There will always be scheduling constraints and parameters set out by the school district, teacher contracts, and the community.

On the other hand, a flexible schedule provides opportunities for allotting different time periods to various subjects on the basis of teacher and student need while allowing options for team teachers to group and regroup children (Lappin 1997; Williamson 1993). Implementation of interdisciplinary instruction, along with large- and small-group instruction, is easily managed through flexible block scheduling.

Lisa Klemetson and Pat Williams-Boyd

CORE EXPLORE

What Is Core Explore?

There is another way of using time as a resource. Core explore is often used as a period during the day that focuses on exploration, remediation, and enrichment activities. These three types of activities are the three foci of core explore. Although they are unique entities, they are also a cohesive unit whose relationship allows for a developmentally responsive and engaging middle level experience. The core explore program provides time for students to interact with their team teachers and for teachers to address the numerous and varied needs of middle level learners.

- Enrichment is an opportunity to enhance and deepen the current curriculum, to provide interdisciplinary connections, to make available hands-on or real-world experiences that might not otherwise be shared, and to foster growth above and beyond the content areas.

- Exploration is an opportunity to investigate student interests; to share real-world experiences; to learn new skills, crafts, or trades; to realize personal talents; to gain new understandings; and to encounter a sense of endless opportunities.
- Remediation is an opportunity to work with smaller groups of students in order to differentiate and individualize instruction, to encourage individual growth in areas of weakness, to reteach skills not mastered, and to provide a forum in which success is fostered.

Enrichment Opportunities

Enrichment of the core curriculum (math, science, social studies, and language arts) provides for a deepening of knowledge and encourages a broadening perspective while making connections between content areas and real-world applications. Interdisciplinary teams naturally integrate curriculum in middle level education. The National Middle School Association (1995) defined curriculum as integrative "when it helps students make sense out of their life experiences. This requires curriculum that is itself coherent, that helps students connect school experiences to their daily lives outside the school, and that encourages them to reflect on the totality of their experiences" (30).

Although a common team planning time provides the opportunity for teachers to integrate the curriculum, they often struggle with making the connections that would extend and enrich learning for their students. The most effective curriculum is collaboratively planned by teachers and students. "The themes are derived from student curiosity about their interests and needs as they relate to their world" (Beane 1990, 27). Integrated teaching allows the team to focus on learning processes such as problem solving, rather than on what might well be "accidental connections" coming out of state-mandated curriculum (Kain 1996). Then the content objectives are connected to the overall theme. Within interdisciplinary teaching, teachers may "share class time with their team members, adjust the order and substance of units or activities to accommodate other subject areas, and combine classes for specific activities related to the content they [are] teaching" (176). Flexible block scheduling facilitates the frameworks necessary for implementing an integrated thematic unit.

A middle level educator striving to meet the needs of individual students through enrichment in core explore should ask the following questions:

1. Would the core content areas (math, science, social studies, language arts) lend themselves to enrichment activities during this time frame?
2. How could the encore classes be involved in core explore?
3. Are there activities that would enhance the current curriculum that could be managed better in smaller groups?
4. Could portions of an interdisciplinary unit be enhanced and enriched during core explore?
5. Would students facilitate an enrichment experience?
6. What is the difference between extending the current curriculum and deepening this curriculum?
7. Are there students who would benefit from a challenge within certain content areas?
8. Could core explore be an avenue to manage some differentiated learning activities (as discussed in Chapter 5)?

Exploration Opportunities

An interdisciplinary team who uses a flexible block schedule has the opportunity to provide students with exploration activities. Guerrero (1995) found that most teachers underestimated their students' readiness for more sophisticated instructional experiences and learning activities. Joe Renzulli, a nationally recognized expert in teaching gifted children, maintained that authentic learning has a definite place in the middle level classroom, in what he terms "enrichment clusters" (1998, 2). He further defined authentic learning as the application of relevant knowledge, thinking skills, and interpersonal skills to the solution of experienced problems. Authentic learning requires a real-life problem with "a personal frame of reference for the individual or group pursuing the problem. [It does] not have existing or unique solutions for persons addressing the problem . . . [yet those pursuing a solution] want to create new products or information that will change actions, attitudes, or beliefs on the part of a targeted audience . . . a real audience" (2).

Renzulli went on to suggest that students use authentic learning in enrichment clusters, which are nongraded groups of students who come together for perhaps half a day per week because of the common interest they share and because of their willingness to work together within a somewhat unstructured learning environment (1998). The teacher is a facilitator with no set curriculum to follow. The students devise their own course of action and learning and in the end create a product or a provide a service. These enrichment clusters encourage active learning, which helps students analyze, criticize, and select solutions to problems. They also present situations in which students— whose own systems of beliefs, values, and attitudes are just emerging—experience the value of working cooperatively together in creative and constructive ways.

A second method of providing exploration opportunities is through minicourses or a series of one- or two-week courses from which students may choose based on their interest. Minicourses promote skills development, interpersonal skills, and a sense of self-worth and accomplishment. They also provide outlets for individual creative expression while motivating the students to work together (Dunham 1995). These minicourses also provide a more teacher-directed curriculum than the enrichment clusters. They also offer students exploration and enrichment in topics that extend the core curriculum but in ways that are of particular interest to the students.

Because the use of core explore reflects an individual team's values and perspectives, much of the following discussion regarding exploration is framed in questions the team needs to consider:

1. Middle level students enjoy an opportunity to explore a variety of topics, interests, and activities. Do the teachers on the team have certain interests, hobbies, or pastimes that they would like to share with the students?
2. How could students share their interests with their peers?
3. Minicourses are an opportunity for students to experience different activities that may be of interest to them. Would each member of the team be interested in preparing a one- or two-week minicourse on a topic of his or her choice? (As an example, this could include arts and crafts, chess tournaments, creative writing, orienteering.)
4. How can the encore teachers be involved in exploration during core explore?
5. Would self-exploration, including one's goals, one's talents, and one's beliefs, become a part of core explore?
6. Are there hands-on activities that are more conducive to a smaller group that could be held during core explore?

7. How could core explore provide an opportunity for career exploration and real world experiences?

Remediation Opportunities

Middle level learners need time for remediation. As with all age levels, middle school students progress at different rates, and although some students are ready for enrichment and extension, others need remediation before moving ahead. MacIver and Epstein (1991) argued for providing an extra class period during the school day for students who would benefit from remediation opportunities: "Remediation activities that occur outside the regular school day . . . are often not well attended by the students who need the most extra help to master basic skills and pass courses. . . . Remedial programs using the extra-subject-period approach may be preferable to pull-out programs because students do not miss part of their other academic instruction" (606).

Remediation should not be limited to those students requiring special services because they have special needs. Because most middle grades students are in a transitional thinking stage, vacillating between concrete and abstract, they need more manipulative, more demonstrative, and more active learning activities to help them grasp abstract concepts. Therefore, on any given day there will be students who do not master the concepts. A time period called core explore, as illustrated in Table 4.14, would be most beneficial to the middle level learner who needs reteaching, a different presentation of material, or further time to process information or develop skills.

In order to create a time frame for core explore, the passing time or time designated for students to move from one class to another is abbreviated within the block. This works easily because of the large chunks of time, in the morning from 8:00 to 11:05 and in the afternoon from 1:04 to 2:35, and because middle grades schools tend to have a team's classrooms in close proximity. The time for the encore classes is preserved, and in this case, the team ends the day with core explore.

The following questions may help teams as they examine core explore and remediation:

1. How do teachers diagnose individual student's needs?
2. What are the procedures used to determine whether a student needs assistance?
3. Does the same population of students need remediation all of the time?

Table 4.14

Interdisciplinary Flexible Team Schedule with Core Explore

Time	Class Schedule
7:40–7:55	Advisory
8:00–11:05	Core Block (Math, Science, Social Studies, Language Arts)
11:07–11:27	Lunch
11:27–12:12	Encore (Elective Class)
12:15–1:00	Encore (Elective Class)
1:04–2:35	Core Block (Science, Math, Social Studies, Language Arts)
2:38–3:05	Core Explore

4. How is remediation individualized, and should instruction look different from the daily classroom?
5. Would there be opportunities for students to request help from various teachers within and outside of the team?
6. Would the students be a part of a peer-tutoring program?
7. Could the students make up work and/or tests from when they were absent?
8. Is it possible for parents and other community members to be involved during this time for remediation purposes?
9. Would students be allowed to make choices about whether or not they would like help with a particular content area, or would teachers group students for assistance?
10. How is remediation different from a "study hall"?

In planning core explore and the kinds of service and activities involved, interdisciplinary teams may well ask:

1. Will the team plan all activities for core explore together at a team meeting, or will individuals be responsible for certain activities?
2. Will students always remain with their assigned core explore teacher, or will they rotate through the other teachers?

3. What will the role of the teacher be during enrichment (that is, facilitator, leader, coordinator)?
4. How will teachers determine students' needs and the methods by which they will address these needs?
5. Will there be a set weekly schedule for core explore (for example, Mondays and Tuesdays are set aside for certain types of experiences), or will teams plan according to need?
6. How often will advisory activities take place?
7. What will be the balance of enrichment, exploration, and remediation?
8. How will teachers assure that all children have a balance of enrichment, exploration, and remediation?
9. Will students have a choice as to activities in which they will be participating?

Core Explore in Action

In order to facilitate many of the components necessary for a developmentally responsive middle school, Novi Middle School in Michigan created an enrichment/physical education program that offers students a core explore experience and an advisory program in addition to a year-long physical education program, as illustrated in Figure 4.3.

Novi's Enrichment Model serves the needs of middle grades students and staff members by:

1. Encouraging and supporting academic success
2. Giving all students the benefit of having physical education for the entire school year—something not achievable in the past
3. Promoting physical fitness and well-being
4. Providing small class sizes for core explore and advisory activities within enrichment
5. Offering a forum to achieve the goals of an advisory program, thereby addressing the social and emotional needs of middle grades students
6. Providing an adult advocate for every student
7. Solving scheduling issues through the use of a flexible block schedule

Figure 4.3
Novi's Enrichment Program

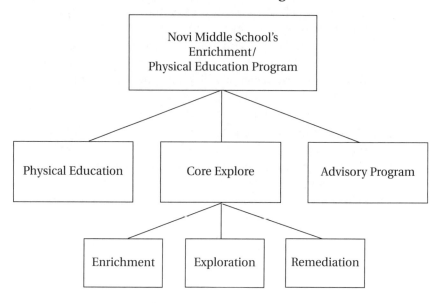

Keeping in mind that all activities would be based on students' developmental needs, when Novi's teaching teams were ready to implement core explore, they had attended to the following questions:

1. Would there be a structured seating arrangement?
2. Would students feel more willing to share or participate sitting in a circle or on the floor?
3. Would there be one activity going on in the classroom, or would students be varyingly engaged at multiple stations?
4. Would more than one group of students be combined for core explore?
5. Would the movable classroom walls be opened to join two or more classrooms?
6. Would all the activities need to be inside the classroom, or could some be outdoors or in other areas of the building?
7. Would the students be able to go out into the community during core explore, or could community members come into the school?
8. Would music be appropriate during core explore activities?
9. How do students' needs help determine these choices?

Just as importantly, Novi's teams were concerned with how students would be grouped. Again, because every school will respond differently based on its beliefs and assumptions about students, issues of how students will be grouped are shaped in the following questions:

1. Will the students remain with their assigned core explore teacher for every class period?
2. How will students be involved in decisionmaking about student grouping?
3. If stations are set up, could students group with peers of their choice to accomplish the tasks for the day?
4. When each teacher would like all of the students to benefit from a particular experience in a small group, will the team set up a rotation so that each core explore group of students would rotate through the four-teacher team over a period of four core explore class times?
5. Would certain activities work with all of the core explore students grouped together and managed by all four teachers?
6. Will there be multiple opportunities for small-group and larger-group experiences?
7. Could two core explore groups work together?
8. Could more than one team of students come together to share a core explore experience?
9. Would students benefit from the expertise of teachers on another team?

Because the advisory period was such an integral part of the Novi enrichment program, the teams asked themselves the following questions to help determine how they would best shape the advisor-advisee relationship:

1. How will the team facilitate each student's having an adult advocate?
2. How will advocates for individual students be determined?
3. How do advocates create a safe, caring community that will support the needs of its members?
4. How often will student needs, behaviors, and situations determine advisory activities?

5. How can teachers be aware that students' voices are valued and affirmed?
6. Do current events, whether global, local, or individual, influence the advisory program?
7. Will the advisory be included once a week, in week-long blocks throughout the year, or in a different shape?
8. How will teachers interact with students to identify advisory issues?
9. Would core explore provide time for community service or academic service learning opportunities?

As core explore evolves, demands will be placed on this program. Middle level educators are encouraged to inventory these demands and to determine whether the suggested activities belong in core explore and whether the daily schedule will need to be reassessed to accommodate these needs. For example, issues of school business always arise. Novi's teaching team dealt with these matters by asking:

1. Are there student council activities that could be managed through core explore?
2. Could this be a time period in which various school clubs could meet?
3. Would there be opportunities for surveying and data collection within core explore?
4. Would this be a time for students to work together to brainstorm suggestions for making their school a better place?

Because Novi Middle School had determined reading to be one of its schoolwide goals, the team also had to ask itself:

1. Would the team like to allow time for silent reading for pleasure within core explore?
2. Would there be a team program with guidelines for reading material selection; for example, should a certain genre of text be chosen, books of a certain length or reading level; should reading be informational or narrative?
3. Could students simply select books and/or magazines of their choice?

Timberlane Middle School in Pennington, New Jersey, uses core explore as core enrichment in which each individual teaching team develops a series of courses directly tied to the content of one particular teacher's curriculum. Their frame of reference in developing these courses is their attempt to offer students concrete applications of learning and to include technology in content areas. Timberlake offers the following three frameworks, based on student and teacher interest and need, during each of the four grading periods:

1. *Framework One:*

   - The students take an eight-week teacher-developed course and participate in a one-week team activity focused on research or study skills
   - All students take all four courses (each course developed by one of four team teachers), one per grading period

2. *Framework Two:*

   - The students take a seven-week teacher-created course
   - All students participate in a two-week interdisciplinary unit developed by all the team's teachers
   - All students take all four courses and choose an interest area for interdisciplinary unity

3. *Framework Three:*

   - The students take a three-week course developed by each teacher on the team
   - All students participate in two three-week interdisciplinary thematic units, with student choice
   - Each student takes four courses and chooses an interest area for eight thematic interdisciplinary units.

Timberlane has capitalized on teacher and student creativity with such exploration topics as "Speak Up," which focuses on speaking before groups, with activities in pantomime, critical analysis of famous speeches, and presentation of persuasive speeches; "Life By the Numbers," a guided exploration of math applications in the twenty-first century that offers activities in virtual reality, topology, perspective drawing, hypercubes, knot theory, and mapping; and "Crime Scene Investigations: Real-Life Science," in which students conduct lab tests and think critically to solve various crimes and function as forensic scientists.

Conclusion: Core Explore

In order for core explore to be a dynamic middle grades experience, it must be based on the developmental needs of all learners. Therefore, educators must answer the following questions:

1. Does this activity promote opportunities for interaction with peers and adults?
2. Are we utilizing task-focused strategies to divert attention from social and ability comparisons and moving toward achievement?
3. Are we fostering feelings of belonging?
4. Is competence achieved through authentic assessment based on personal goals, progress, and improvement?
5. Are we recognizing the desire for autonomy and identity by providing learning strategies that involve choice, a curriculum based on social and individual interests, and opportunities for exploration within a safe environment?
6. Do we use a flexible classroom structure with hands-on activities that incorporate the need for physical activity?
7. Are we including service projects and project-based learning strategies that capitalize on students' creative expression and the need for meaningful participation and experimentation with identity within community, including the need for cultural expressions of identity?
8. Do content area standards guide classroom experiences, combining students' needs and societal expectations?

Given the diversity of middle grades learners and the characteristics of effective middle schools, we can begin to see that the issues of flexible block scheduling; student grouping; advisory programs; and enrichment, extension, and remediation opportunities are intimately connected and interdependent. These components that reflect the middle school concept are fundamental when considering developmentally appropriate practices. Although researchers do not comment directly on an enrichment/physical education block of time as conceived by the Novi Middle School, research provides many implications for the implementation of advisory programming along with enrichment, extension, and remediation opportunities for middle grades learners.

To this point, we have examined the defining characteristics of middle grades theory, its organizational structure, its commitment to the needs of young adolescents. This discussion is, however, only the scaffolding that allows middle grades curriculum to be responsive to the needs of a very diverse population. Interdisciplinary teaming sets the stage for integrated curriculum, for thematic instruction, and for active teaching and learning.

Michelle Galecka

THEMATIC INSTRUCTION, CURRICULUM INTEGRATION, AND CURRICULUM MAPPING

Curriculum integration is a tool used to teach the life skills necessary for participation in a democracy. Integrating the curriculum makes sense of content knowledge through intentional applications made to the young adolescent's perception of the real world. This is an ongoing, flexible process as the world changes and as social issues shift in importance.

In developing and using integrated curriculum, the notion of "core understandings" or "common learnings" plays a prominent role. What are these life or generic skills that all middle grades students should have? There are three groups of theorists who reflect different positions:

1. *Schoolwide goals for student learning.* The National Study of School Evaluation (NSSE) and the Alliance for Curriculum Reform (ACR) divided the schoolwide goals for all students into six groups: learning-to-learn skills, expanding and integrating knowledge, communication skills, thinking and reasoning skills, interpersonal skills, and personal and social responsibility (Fitzpatrick 1997, xi).
2. *Life skills.* The Mid-Continent Research for Education and Learning (MCREL) Laboratory examined national standards and content-area documents and divided "essential knowledge" into thinking and reasoning, working with others, self-regulation, and life work.

3. *Core standards.* The Texas-based Center for Occupational Research and Development (CORD) examined academic organizational standards and compared them to the call from the workforce. The center created fifty-three integrated standards that include a spectrum of skills from computer literacy and statistical analysis to ethics and self-concept. (National Middle School Association 2002)

The way a school community chooses to shape its shared understanding of common skills often dictates the ways in which the curriculum itself is implemented and manipulated. Based on this conceptual foundation, middle grades theorists are often at odds regarding three critical views of middle school curriculum:

1. Middle schools should teach a general education curriculum that focuses on young adolescents' concerns with a larger view of the world around them rather than concentrating particular attention on specific content areas
2. Middle school curriculum ought to serve the needs of early adolescents in each particular school
3. Middle schools are little more than holding areas for the young caught in the quagmire of hormonal development, whose angst needs to be mediated by a variety of catchy extrinsic motivators (Beane 1991)

Middle level practitioners tend to find a balance among the three approaches—although the third approach is demeaning to middle grades students and sets a stage for low expectations—by integrating curriculum that parallels the questions young adolescents have about themselves and their world and through attention to standards-based content. What emerges are rich themes found at the intersection between the world's concerns and the concerns students have (Beane 1993). They are themes that challenge creative thinking, critical thinking, problem solving, and social advocacy. They are themes that recognize and are responsive to students' ideas and questions. They are themes that are born and developed in a constructivist philosophy that will be addressed in the next chapter. And they are themes that spur both the cognitive and the affective development of middle schoolers.

First, let's examine integrating curriculum in general, thematic instruction in particular, and how thematic instruction can naturally emerge from curriculum mapping.

Integrated Instruction

When teachers choose to integrate their curricula, they are choosing a method of instruction that will energize and excite their students. Learning is constructed in an innovative and purposeful way that shows relationships between what happens within and outside of school. "Curriculum is organized around real-life problems and issues significant to both young people and adults" (Vars and Beane 2000). Some themes are transitions, change, relationships, responsibility, justice, advocacy, community, dependence, and democracy in action.

There are four levels of curriculum integration (Erb and Doda 1989) that differ in the amount of group planning time required to integrate the different subject areas into a thematic way of teaching:

1. *Pre-integration.* This level requires the least planning, for there is no real integration of subject content. By including flexible scheduling, teachers have more freedom to incorporate field trips and assemblies and to try instructional strategies previously impossible in the traditional forty-five- to fifty-five-minute class schedule.

2. *Coordinated or overlap teaching.* This level requires more of a group effort than level one, but it is still relatively uncomplicated. It requires that an instructor be familiar with the topics being taught by other members of the team or group. On this level of integration, teachers teach similar, individual, and themed units or lessons at the same time as other members of the team. There is some actual integration of material, but there is more parallel teaching than integrated teaching.

3. *Cooperative teaching.* This level of integration requires more planning and flexibility, for teachers make alterations in their teaching to focus specifically on a team-chosen topic. This is not simply a skill of the week, where there might be a certain skill taught in one subject area that is reinforced in other subject areas throughout the week. Rather it requires changing when

certain concepts and skills might be taught in order to better align with the same theme being taught in other subject areas.

4. *Interdisciplinary thematic unit.* The final level in the integration paradigm is fully incorporated thematic instruction. This level involves more than one teacher in the planning of the instructional unit, a unit that focuses around a common theme and includes various subjects in the curriculum. Dramatic results can occur when teachers collaborate with other teachers and when they orchestrate activities that reinforce more than one objective or skill. (99)

The process itself of creating an integrated curriculum can be described in six easy-to-follow steps.

1. Select a theme. Just as Pate, Homestead, and McGinnis in their own curriculum integration process asked their students to assist them in developing ideas, students must be actively involved from the beginning.
2. Create spotlight questions. Students are asked what questions they might want answered about the unit's main theme.
3. Ask students what skills might need to be developed in the content they are going to explore. Align these skills with the curriculum.
4. Provide students the opportunity to choose how they will be evaluated and how they will demonstrate their learning.
5. Identify resources needed for the unit.
6. Locate and access these resources. (Pate, Homestead, and McGinnis 1997)

Although this process involves the students in the decisionmaking process, the same steps may be followed while integrating curriculum without the students' perspective. Either way, successful integration occurs when teachers create a curriculum that makes sense and demonstrates how various subjects are connected and related.

The effective creation and successful implementation of an integrated curriculum involves all teachers. There are six suggested keys found to be helpful in this process:

1. Patience and perseverance are important when planning an integrated curriculum. Change takes time, often longer than anticipated.
2. Teachers are the change agents for their own curriculum integration.
3. Teachers engaged in the change process need support, release time to plan, and training for professional development in new pedagogical skills.
4. Pressure sometimes facilitates change. Teachers and administrators offer each other the incentive to become involved through their support, encouragement, and modeled example.
5. This is a collaborative process. No one can do the task alone.
6. Team brainstorming sessions, learning from other teams also in the process of curriculum integration, analyzing existing quality thematic units, and reviewing and reflecting on the work of the team are beneficial. (Sprague, Pennell, and Sulzberger 1998)

A sample team examined the results of their own content integration and found the following:

1. Students were more responsible and self-directed
2. The integrated curriculum held deeper meaning and richer opportunities for learning owing to connections deliberately created between the world beyond the classroom and the students' learning.
3. Through curriculum integration the students were able to recognize these connections in a process of discovery.
4. The teachers functioned as facilitators or guides for student learning rather than as lecturers about discrete pieces of information.
5. Students willingly worked cooperatively with other students.
6. Students were accountable for their own learning.
7. Students were confident in making choices as effective explorers in their own learning. (Pate, Homestead, and McGinnis 1997)

Curriculum integration enjoys its most profound effectiveness in middle grades because of its student centeredness and because of its crafted connections to "real life," so important to young adolescents. The emphasis in student learning is on cooperative work, on higher-order thinking skills, and on conceptual human values with which young adolescents are only just beginning to grapple.

Because students are the focus of integrated curriculum and because they are engaged in the development of the curriculum and in its constructed meaning, the shift in relationship between the student and the teacher is of great consequence. Teachers who integrate curriculum:

- Share curriculum and other decisions with their students
- Focus more on the reality of their students' perceptions or on their concerns than on content guides
- Present themselves as colearners with their students
- Place great value on meanings constructed by the students
- Advocate for their students' rights to study in this fashion (Beane 1997)

Curriculum theorists maintain that there are three pillars on which effective middle grades programs are built: the philosophical, which addresses purposes and values; the psychological, which addresses both the learner and learning; and the sociological, which addresses social and educational constructs. In integrative curricular terms the psychological sees students more motivated and actively engaged with issues that reflect young adolescents' perspectives. The sociological prepares students for lifelong learning because it addresses social problems. And philosophically integrative curriculum examines common concerns, values, and active democracy and, therefore, more prudently prepares students for citizenship (Vars 2001).

Thematic Instruction

Rich learning seldom happens within the traditional classroom where students sit passively and the teacher stoically stands at the front of the classroom and lectures to students, who take notes and then repeat them on a paper and pencil test. This fragmented approach to learning, or mere transfer of information, is most understood by teachers rather than by students. That is not to say that what we know about ourselves and the context of our own reality is not examined. It is to say that the traditional compartmentalization of knowledge does not offer students the constructed opportunity to examine and grapple with ideas in a larger, more interrelated fashion. Too often those voices that have been marginalized by the majority culture go unheard. History is taught from the victor's position; science becomes the discrete acquisition of facts rather than the study of life itself; math is taught as the memorization of formulas and the development of particular skills rather than examined as a rich study of pattern; and language arts is all too often taught as the use of proper grammar, correct spelling lists, and the study of male European authors rather than as the strivings of generations of peoples to communicate with each other, to move each other through shared passion, joy, and despair conveyed in the written word.

Effective middle grades teaching and learning are connected to the adolescents' lived experience. Learning that includes movement, creative presentations, and activities spurs on disconnected students (Moss and Fuller 2000). Interdisciplinary thematic units of study provide teachers an opportunity to create a wide variety of learning experiences while addressing different student readiness levels, interest areas, and learning profiles. At the same time such units provide meaningful learning experiences that give new life to often-used concepts and less-than-exciting objectives (Erb and Doda 1989).

A thematic unit can be thought of as an umbrella under which curriculum is organized. The big idea or focus questions are the umbrella's framework and represent what is taught in the classroom. This is where connections can be seen and ideas come together, where concepts and skills are organized and materials and activities are designed (Mitchell and Young 1997).

The first steps in creating a thematic unit are to identify major content strategies and main concepts. Looking at a map of the curriculum, the team can identify common themes as they naturally emerge from within the content areas (Sprague, Pennell, and Sulzberger 1998). This is the starting point for a thematic unit. Teachers refer to district curriculum guides and state standards and benchmarks to identify required concepts. They then share their own interests with each other and with students and build a thematic unit on these combined interests and strengths.

The introduction of a thematic unit depends on its purpose and intent. Some thematic units are meant to be taught at the beginning of the year, because their goal is to acquaint students with certain units of study. Other units are intended to be presented more in the middle or end of the school year when students have had more experience with the skills and concepts included in the thematic unit. Some units focus on a holiday, a special event, or a certain time of the year (Erb and Doda

1989). The intent of the thematic unit dictates the appropriate time to incorporate it into the school year.

Before beginning a thematic unit, there are some formative questions that need to be addressed:

1. What is the unit's topic, main question, or idea?
2. Why is this unit worthy of study? If the teacher creating the unit is unable to see the connections, then the students cannot be expected to.
3. Brainstorm all ideas related to the thematic unit being created. Is there enough information to create a unit? What will be the main focus of the unit? How will the students be motivated and ready to learn?
4. What are the potential student activities? What different kinds of activities could the students work on during the unit?
5. What kinds of materials might be needed for the thematic unit? In what ways and with what materials might learning be enriched?
6. What skills will be included in the unit? Which subject area skills need to be taught, emphasized, or reviewed for the unit?
7. What instruction skill work needs to be developed in the unit?
8. How does the class need to be organized? How does the classroom environment need to be arranged?
9. What would the introductory activities and culminating projects look like?
10. How will students be graded and assessed during the thematic unit? (Mitchell and Young 1997)

Students are successful when the theme of the unit creates opportunities for authentic and motivating engagement, problem solving, and decisionmaking that are connected to their perceptions of reality.

What constitutes a successful interdisciplinary unit (ITU)?

- The unit is based on content standards, benchmarks, or district curriculum objectives:
    1. The unit encompasses concepts, skills, and information as well as important life skills

2. The unit includes skills in personal development and problem solving, in developing peer relationships and self-worth

3. The ITU includes a variety of objectives that will push each student out of her comfort zone (Erb and Doda 1989)

- The ITU has distinctive parts:

  1. The ITU grabs the attention of the students. An engaged student will want to learn more about what is being presented.

  2. The student is responsible for learning. The student needs to be held accountable for his or her own learning.

  3. Students should be able to apply what they have learned to real-life situations.

  4. Teachers need to anticipate each of these pieces by planning backward—starting with the end or knowing where the students' learning will be at the unit's completion—and working back through the unit to the beginning.

  5. The ITU should have a sense of balance in the activities being chosen. There should be both long- and short-term goals with a balance of teacher-directed and student-directed activities.

  6. A successful ITU offers a great assortment of student activities that assist learning. There are limitless possibilities in the kinds of activities in an ITU, and this sparks interest in students who may be disinterested in more traditional types of learning environments.

Thematic activities help students to create more enduring understanding when they:

- Are linguistically, cognitively, socioculturally, and developmentally authentic
- Provide students opportunities to use various communication systems such as visual and aural art, dance, language, and mathematics—to learn both the concepts and the generalized understandings within the theme

- Provide students opportunities to use thinking processes to form conceptual understandings in various disciplines
- Provide opportunities to use communication systems for a variety of functions and purposes
- Integrate the language and culture of the home with the language and culture of the school
- Represent a range of literacy, thinking, and creating abilities
- Engage students in independent as well as collaborative and cooperative activities
- Provide students opportunities—with "safety nets"—to take risks and to problem solve and engage in divergent thinking
- Challenge and encourage students to assume multiple perspectives
- Engage students in creating their own meaning
- Encourage students to integrate and synthesize new meaning with prior understandings (Kucer, Silva, and Delgado-Larocco 1995, 56–57)

Because students are able to see connections between and among various content subjects in thematic units, they internalize what they are learning, making that learning more meaningful (Moss and Fuller 2000). Themes may naturally emerge from what teachers are already teaching and for which they are held accountable. All too often, a well-meaning middle school may stop teaching its curriculum and artificially engage in all the work required for a fun-filled unit on the rain forest, after which everyone returns to their required curriculum. This is not the intent of integrated thinking, teaching, and learning. Curriculum mapping may help this process become more natural.

Curriculum Mapping

The amount of time spent teaching a specific concept has a direct correlation to the depth of student learning. By using a curriculum map, teachers can visually examine the length of time they spend on a specific course of study, unit by unit, and week by week. Some teachers map their curriculum by keeping a diary. Day by day, they record what they did in their classroom, how much time the activity took, what reactions were noted, and what adjustments might need to be made next time the lesson is taught. This type of curriculum map assists teachers in identifying excessive instructional time for a specific skill and instances where not enough time is being used for another skill (Clough, James, and Witcher 1996). Other types of curriculum maps can be made on large sheets of paper, divided by months, and filled with Post-it Notes or pieces of paper that explain what was taught each month.

Some schools that map their curriculum include for each month the processes, objectives, and essential skills taught in addition to the length of time spent on an idea, skill, or behavior. Additionally, they include the concepts, the goals of the unit, and the types of assessments used. Because there are so many ways of doing curriculum mapping, the type of map and the detail of the information should match the reason the curriculum is being charted. Information in a map may be focused on one grade level throughout a school, or it can show the curriculum students experience as they move from one grade to the other (Jacobs 1997).

A rather painless way of mapping the curriculum, when the intent is to find common themes and to note what content standards and benchmarks are being taught, is demonstrated in Table 4.15. At the end of each week, each content-area teacher (represented by a different colored Post-it), simply writes the number of the week in the top left-hand corner, the concept taught, and the standard and benchmark in the bottom right-hand corner. As the grading period progresses, themes begin to emerge, and teachers who may have been otherwise unaware of what their colleagues were teaching, particularly if they are not in interdisciplinary teams, can see what content areas have been examined. In Table 4.15 the team begins to see the potential for a unit on genres or forms of expression as noted in the language arts area in weeks three and seven, in the music classes in week three, in foreign language in week three, and in forms of government in social studies in week seven. Post-its from those particular weeks are then copied and moved together to potentially form an integrated unit for next year. A potential unit on patterns emerges from music in week one, math in week seven, and language arts in week three. And similarly, a unit on rights and responsibilities emerges from social studies in week three, music in week seven, foreign language in week three, and science in weeks three and seven. Of the three potential units, rights and responsibilities and interdependence would be particularly poignant for middle grades students who are beginning to question their place in the social context.

Table 4.15
Curriculum Map for Selected Weeks of One Grading Period

Week	*1*	*2*	*3*	*4*	*5*	*6*	*7*	*8*	*9*
Language Arts	1 communication 3.2		3 genres—poetry 4.2				7 genres—short story 1.2		
Math	1 triangles 4.1		3 angles 3.1				7 symmetry 2.1		
Science	1 conservation 3.3		3 conservation & energy 4.3				7 conservation & wetlands 2.4		
Social Studies	1 core democratic values 1.1		3 rights & responsibilities 5.2				7 forms of government 4.6		
Foreign Language	1 communication —greetings 3.1		3 culture & appropriate forms of conversation 2.1				7 culture & communication for travel 4.3		
Music	1 rhythmic patterns 4.2		3 forms or genres—ensemble of musical expression 5.1				7 performance & responsibility to other performers 1.3		

A Thematic Unit

The following excerpts from a thematic unit entitled "Another World" were created by middle grades teachers John Steinhebel, Tim Podlewski, and Beth Harris. In constructing the unit, they brainstormed first with their students and then together and shaped the unit around two broad goals:

1. Students will interact with elders in their community and with people from other regions of the world in order to examine the similarities and differences in their cultures
2. Students will examine the ways in which geographic location, age, natural resources, and economy affect culture (Steinhebel, Podlewski, and Harris 2000)

Their unit rationale stated:

> Early adolescents have many concerns and interests as they move from childhood to adulthood. They have concerns about their bodies, their image, their choices, their society, and their world. This unit attempts to address many of the concerns of young adolescents by looking at various aspects of culture.
>
> The unit will address psychological, intellectual, cultural, and physical questions and concerns. Students will examine themselves as individuals and as members of a particular culture. They will be asked to look at the cultural, regional and generational similarities and differences among others and themselves. Based on several state standards and benchmarks, the unit will teach students to be respectful of others and of themselves, to take responsibility for those who are in need and to "see" the world from a variety of perspectives. (Steinhebel, Podlewski, and Harris 2000, 3)

Figure 4.4 visually presents the unit in concept-map format, and Table 4.16 acknowledges the students' prior knowledge on which the unit is based. Table 4.17 notes the skills all students will develop through the course of the unit, and Table 4.18 states the unit's cognitive and affective outcomes. Table 4.19 presents the two-week unit in daily format for language arts, science, math, and social studies.

Table 4.20 is a sample lesson that offers the flavor of the kinds of lessons the unit includes. It is presented as part of the text to demonstrate the types of decisions made regarding lesson construction. Con-

Figure 4.4
Integrated Thematic Unit: Another World Concept

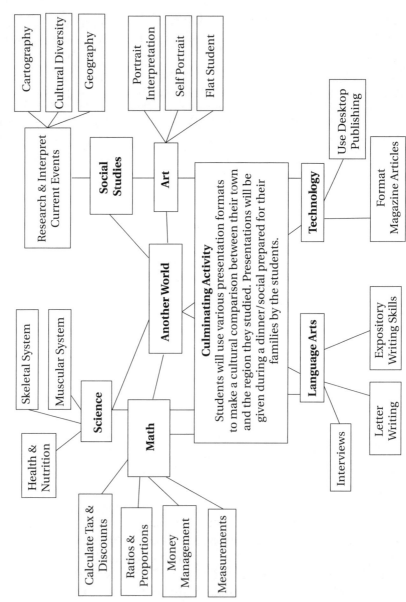

Table 4.16
Integrated Thematic Unit: Another World, Prior Knowledge
Assumptions

Language Arts	Science	Social Studies
1. Writing process	1. The four basic food groups	1. Basic map reading skills
2. Paragraph construction	2. General knowledge of the human body	2. Preconceived ideas about African culture
3. Basic grammar rules	3. Basic math computational skills	3. A basic understanding of cultural diversity
4. Basic word processing skills	4. Use of the scientific method	4. An understanding of current events
5. Interpersonal skills	5. Basic lab safety procedures	5. Knowledge of how to use and interpret periodicals
6. Proofreading marks	6. Rubric scoring	6. An understanding of how to search the Internet for information
7. Basic reading skills		7. Rubric scoring
8. Familiarity with different poetic styles		8. A basic understanding of geographic locations
9. Oral presentation skills		
10. Rubric scoring		

tent standards and benchmarks, young adolescent developmental
characteristics, learning differences as portrayed in multiple intelligences, and content topics are some of the initial considerations.

The culminating activity for the unit is presented to the students
in the following way:

- The purpose: To demonstrate your understanding of the
  similarities and differences among cultures in the city of
  Ann Arbor and in your chosen region of Africa.
- Your task: Compare and contrast your culture and its history with the culture and history of a region in Africa. You

Table 4.17

Integrated Thematic Unit: Another World, Skills Incorporated in the Unit

Study Skills	Higher Level Thinking Skills
1. Taking notes	1. Analyzing data
2. Organization of current work and Research	2. Making predictions
3. Recording auditory information	3. Looking for patterns
4. Synthesizing notes	4. Applying knowledge to real-world contexts
5. Paraphrasing	5. Drawing conclusions
6. Studying for quizzes	6. Reflecting on conclusions
7. Reciting interview questions as practice	7. Synthesizing information
8. Completing homework assignments	8. Comparing and contrasting past and present
9. Brainstorming	9. Translating thoughts into writing
10. Practicing oral presentations	10. Evaluating outcomes
11. Using library and reference materials wisely	11. Justifing a position
12. Using the Internet and other computer programs as resource tools	12. Varying writing techniques
13. Setting goals	13. Constructing interview questions
14. Organizing tasks	14. Critiquing self and others
15. Budgeting time	15. Creating a writing piece based upon research
16. Editing notes	16. Reorganizing data
17. Being physically nourished	17. Organizing and integrating research into a particular writing style
18. Getting help from teachers or family members	
19. Using research to form questions	
20. Using charts to organize data	

Table 4.18
Integrated Thematic Unit: Culture

Content-Specific Knowledge	Skills and Attitudes
1. Natural resources and economical land use based on geographic location	1. Develop sensitivity to diverse backgrounds
2. The effects of geographic locations on culture	2. Develop an appreciation for historical events and places in their hometown
3. Cultural effects on diet and nutrition	3. Understanding the effects of nutrition and exercise on the human body
4. The effects of natural resources and economics have on culture	4. View technology as a tool for research
5. Use of multimedia as a form of communication	5. Demonstrate interview skills
6. World geography	6. Engage in social interactions with peers and adults
	7. Develop an appreciation of cultural diversity
	8. Develop an appreciation of the value of communication with senior citizens
	9. Understand the relationship between culture and the events that affect that culture

will focus on things such as food/diet, physical activities, geographic location, climate, natural resources, fashion, beliefs, attitudes toward the elderly, attitudes toward the young, religion, hobbies, and other areas of interest.

- Your resources: You will use information gained from your senior friend, your pen pal, your parents/family, social studies and science classes, your research on the Internet and in books, magazines, newspaper articles, and pamphlets.
- Your choices: Please choose one of the following ways to demonstrate your new knowledge or suggest one of your own:

Table 4.19

Another World Thematic Unit: Culture

Unit Calendar	
Week 1—Monday	*Week 2—Monday*

Language Arts/Social Studies
- Use information from current event articles to write letters to pen pals
- Parts of a friendly letter activity

Social Studies
- Ongoing current events activity focusing on one region in Africa
- Take an interest inventory as a preassessment tool

Science
- Introduction of the food pyramid
- Work on journal checklist assignment

Art
- Introduction to self-portraits

Computer Technology
- Introduction to PowerPoint

Language Arts
- In the media center, research the history of students' town
- Use information to formulate questions for interview

Social Studies/Math
- Use grids to expand map drawings
- Use class time to complete maps; any remaining work will be completed at home

Science
- Demonstration: Knot a Bone
- Name that Bone game

(continues)

1. Magazine—at least eight articles of varying content, pictures, and advertisements related to the topic
2. Scrapbook—include pictures with journaling, mementos from your senior friend and pen pal, newspaper articles, maps, and so on
3. Dramatic Performance—dramatize a typical day in the life of someone in Ann Arbor and someone in your chosen region in Africa
4. Video Presentation—You may do a newscast, talk show, or other television format. Be sure to get permission from everyone you tape.

- Your Audience: Your presentation will be enjoyed by your family, friends, school and administrative staff, senior friends, and other community members.

Table 4.19 (continued)

Week 1—Tuesday	Week 2—Tuesday
Language Arts • View a television interview and write a critique • Discussion of good interviewing techniques **Social Studies (#3)** • Introduction to Africa map projects • Sort teams for the culminating activity • Form culminating activity teams • Decide on type of map to design **Science** • Discovery of the skeletal and muscular system • Share conclusions **Art** • Continue self-portrait lesson throughout week 1 **Computer Technology** • Continue PowerPoint and reinforce research techniques throughout the remainder of the unit	**Language Arts** • Continue from Monday **Social Studies** • Prepare 3" x 5" cards for map presentations • Review the components of a good speech • Begin map project presentations • Video tape presentations **Science** • How Muscles Move Bones activity • Review for skeletal and muscular systems oral quiz on Wednesday

Week 1—Wednesday	Week 2—Wednesday
Language Arts • Continue from Tuesday **Social Studies** • Go to the media center to gather research for map projects **Science** • Introduction to skeletal system • Review of skeletal and muscular system diagram • Put together the skeleton assignment	**Language Arts** • Role-play the setting up of interviews • Confirm time, date, location of the senior friend interview **Social Studies** • Continue Africa map project presentations • Begin watching taped presentations during Core Explore for reflection purposes **Science** • Skeletal and muscular system oral quiz

(continues)

Table 4.19 (continued)

Week 1—Thursday	Week 2—Thursday
Language Arts • Continue from Wednesday **Social Studies** • Complete research in the media center • Share African current events • Play current events bingo **Science (#3)** • Focus on muscular system • Flexercise • Microscope investigation	**Language Arts** • Team field trip to Bortz Health Center to conduct senior friend interview **Social Studies** • Complete Africa map project presentations • Share current events • Play current events bingo • Map project video reflections will continue during Core Explore until completion; Core Explore will focus on reinforcing proper speech techniques

Week 1—Friday	Week 2—Friday
Language Arts • Whole day field trip (walking tour of Ann Arbor) • Respond to tour through drawing and writing	**Language Arts** • Senior friend interview learning contract **Social Studies** • Introduction to African region articles • Using Africa article assignment sheet, decide upon responsibilities • Review and discuss Africa article scoring sheet **Science** • Begin muscle fatigue lab

Week 3—Monday	Week 4—Monday
Language Arts • Continue working on learning contracts **Social Studies** • To media center to begin research for African region articles **Science** • Complete muscle fatigue lab	**Language Arts** • Continuation from Friday **Social Studies** • Continue presentations

(continues)

Table 4.19 (continued)

Week 3—Tuesday	Week 4—Tuesday
Language Arts • Continue working on learning contracts **Social Studies** • Continue from Monday **Science** • Begin skeletal and muscular relationships system lab	Culminating activity to present prepared meal and cultural comparison project to senior citizen pals, families, friends.

Week 3—Wednesday	Week 4—Wednesday
Language Arts • Complete learning contracts **Social Studies** • Final day of research in the media center **Science** • Continue lesson from Tuesday	Continuation of culminating activity

Week 3—Thursday	Week 4—Thursday
Language Arts • Introduction of the culminating activity **Social Studies** • Work on the layout of their magazines • Prepare presentations for classmates • Share current events and play current events bingo **Science** • Work on the culminating activity or move on to a new unit	**Social Studies** • Final sharing of African culture current events • Play current events bingo

(continues)

Table 4.19 (continued)

Week 3—Friday	Week 4—Friday
Language Arts • Work on culminating activity • Time can also be used for science and social studies lessons if necessary **Social Studies** • Begin African culture article presentations	Final sharing from Thursday

• Assessment: Your final product will be based on the attached rubric (Table 4.21), which will be discussed in class.

The culminating activity becomes a celebration of learning in which all stakeholders participate in the work of the school.

Assessment

The rubric shown in Table 4.21 is an example of the kind of authentic assessment that becomes a tool to further inform teaching and an instrument through which students have greater ownership in their own learning. The term *authentic assessment* is frequently used interchangeably with *alternative assessment* or *performance assessment.* Whichever term is used, the assessment looks different from a traditional assessment and serves a different purpose. A traditional assessment becomes its own objective in that it passively documents learning; it tends to be individual and is concerned with information. An alternative assessment is an active process intended to facilitate learning through some sort of inquiry process, often in a collaborative fashion. The traditional assessment is administered in a hierarchical model, the teacher holding power and testing the student, whereas the alternative format is a cooperative venture in which learning is shared by the teacher and the student.

An authentic assessment offers students an opportunity to demonstrate their learning in a variety of ways that tend to be more critical and meaningful and more culturally relevant. It requires students to think on higher levels, to problem solve, and to integrate knowledge across content areas. Just as in the material in Tables 4.20 and 4.21, the

Table 4.20

Lesson #2 Language Arts: Another World

Introduction to Interviews	
Topics	*Content Standards/Benchmarks*
• Learn the characteristics of interviews and interview questions • Learn how to give and receive constructive criticism	**Content Standards 3: Benchmark 3** • Read and write fluently, speak confidently, listen and interact appropriately, view critically, and represent creatively. Examples include reporting formally to an audience, debating issues, and interviewing members of the public **Content Standard 7: Benchmark 2** • Monitor their progress while using a variety of strategies to overcome difficulties when constructing and conveying meaning, and develop stgrategies to deal with new communication needs **Content Standard 4: Benchmark 1** • Compare and contrast spoken, written and visual language patterns used in their communication contexts, such as community activities, discussions, mathematics and science classes, and the workplace **Content Standard 3: Benchmark 5** • Select appropriate strategies to construct meaning while reading, listening to, viewing, or creating texts. Examples include generating relevant questions, studying vocabulary, analyzing mood and tone, recognizing how authors and speakers use information, and matching form to content
Developmental Characteristics	*Multiple Intelligences*
1. Tend to be self-conscious, lacking in self-esteem, and highly sensitive to personal criticism 2. Prefer interaction with peers during learning activities 3. Are capable of and value direct experience in participatory democracy	1. Verbal/Linguistic 2. Interpersonal 3. Intrapersonal

(continues)

Table 4.20 (continued)

Introduction to Interviews
Lesson #2

Objectives:
The Student Will Be Able to (TSWBAT):
• Determine characteristics of interviews and interview questions
• Respond verbally and in written form to an interview shown in class
• Work in small groups to prepare well-written interview questions
• Work with a partner to prepare a practice interview to be critiqued by class-mates
• Critique and offer constructive criticism to others about their interviews
• Accept and use constructive criticism based on a practice interview

Time Needed: 3–4 50-minute class periods or one blocked chunk

Materials Needed:
Videotape of sports interview; questions to help students respond; examples of "good" interview questions taken from the sports interview; camcorder with blank tapes; "3 x 5" cards; critique sheets; interview checklist; learning contracts

Vocabulary:
• open-ended question
• "yes-no" question
• constructive criticism

Activities/Procedures:
1. Students will watch an interview between a famous sports personality and a sports broadcaster
2. Students will use the questions given them to respond to the television interview; done in small groups
3. The class will discuss the differences between open-ended and "yes-no" questions and their responses to the interview
4. Students will be asked to use a learning contract to respond to the interview seen in class
5. The teacher will offer students choices for collecting interview information (3" x 5" cards, notebook paper, tape recorder, camcorder)
6. Students will work with a partner to choose a topic (teacher will give choices) and write five well-written interview questions
7. Students will practice interviewing each other using the questions they have written together
8. Interviews will be videotaped in class and everyone will be asked to offer constructive criticism, using the critique sheet, to the interviewer/interviewee
9. Students will be given the opportunity to view their own videotapes in order to improve their interviewing techniques and will be asked to critique themselves in writing

Assessment:
Students assessed on the basis of their learning contract work, self-critiques, critiques of others, and participation.

Table 4.21

Cultural Comparisons Project—Scoring Rubric

Scoring Criteria	Poor (1)	Fair (2)	Good (3)	Excellent (4)	Points
Compare • Describe similarities between Ann Arbor and your region in Africa • Information is accurate	Comparisons were not clearly explained; some info inaccurate				____x5 (20)
Contrast • Describe differences between Ann Arbor and your region in Africa • Information is accurate			Evidence of thoughtful research and writing; could be more developed		____x5 (20)
Personal Experiences • Experiences from your senior friend's life are included • Information gained from your pen pal is included	Experiences were minimal and not explained clearly			Experiences were richly developed; the reader could see the senior friend in the writing	____x5 (20)

(continues)

Table 4.21 (continued)

Scoring					
Criteria	Poor (1)	Fair (2)	Good (3)	Excellent (4)	Points
Creativity					
• Demonstrates time and thought		Some good ideas were begun; somewhat disorganized			_____x5
• Eye catching					
• Organized					(20)
• Unique					
Visual Aides					
• Map of African region					
• Map of Ann Arbor					_____x5
• Colorful					
• Neat					(20)
• Accurate					
					Total _____

purpose of the assessment is to challenge students to take risks, to use various modes of demonstrating learning.

Authentic assessment allows students to work on their strengths as well as their weaknesses, for it takes into account a variety of learning profiles, readiness levels, and areas of interest. Therefore it nurtures self-worth and self-efficacy while it honors all efforts. And most important, alternative assessment, because it is based in shared choice, focuses on an alternative to failure. There are basically three types of authentic assessment—performance, product, and portfolio—and often teachers use a combination. When an assessor views an actual performance of a predetermined task using agreed-upon measures, the assessment is said to be a performance assessment. A portfolio is a collection of student work that may demonstrate outstanding pieces of a variety of kinds of assignments, or it may chronicle the progress of a student across time. A product assessment is one that judges a set project or an observable piece such as a videotape, a diorama, an exhibit, a journal, or an experiment. In the "Another World" unit, the team of teachers offered the students an opportunity to choose the way in which they felt they could best present their learning. One student may choose the PowerPoint presentation and as such have a product assessment. Another may choose the drama and be evaluated through a performance assessment.

In developing the culminating experience and its rubric for the "Another World" unit, Steinhebel, Podlewski, and Harris deliberated and included the following:

- A clear definition of what the students were to learn
- A rubric and accompanying explanation with directions that were clear and understandable to all students
- Choices that would motivate, challenge, and respect all learners
- Reasonable time lines for the completion of each part of the task so students could better manage the task's full completion
- Resources and materials that were easily accessed and available for all students so those who did not have materials or support at home could also complete the tasks.
- Learning contracts that allowed both learners and teachers to easily follow student progress
- Presentation of the project that involved the community and the family

These teachers shared some common assumptions about their students, which are reflected in their unit and in the assessment. They believed that all of their students could learn and master the unit's major concepts if they were given an appropriate and respectful way in which to learn and in which to demonstrate that learning. The pre-assessments gave the teachers valuable information regarding what the students already knew, how each student learned best, and how they felt they could most successfully share their learning. The teachers also believed the family and the community to be valuable resources in their students' learning. And they felt the students' cultural beliefs and values were an important and viable part of all learning. Teachers who use alternative assessments share these same assumptions about students, about their learning, and about their families.

Conclusion: Integrated Learning

Can integrated curriculum and thematic instruction survive in a standards-based environment? The simple answer is yes. Often when a team backmaps its curriculum or on Friday of each week notes the concepts taught, the content standards addressed, and the assessments used during that particular week, it is easily seen what, if any, concepts are being excluded from instruction or if perhaps too much time is spent on a given area.

Frequently, when students are invited to participate in understanding content standards and in charting their examination within the classroom, students experience one more level of problem solving from which they had been previously excluded. Teachers who engage in curriculum integration hold certain beliefs about middle grades students. They believe that young adolescents should have the opportunity to do authentic work, to think creatively and critically, to shape their own sense of values and judgments, and to be challenged to think beyond the moment or beyond that particular class hour. They believe students should be given a guided chance to see the world in all of its connections, to be able to examine it, and to be able to contribute to its becoming a better place in which to live.

Lisa Klemetson and Pat Williams-Boyd

REFERENCES

Alexander, W., E. Williams, M. Compton, V. Hines, and D. Prescott. 1968. *The Emergent Middle School*. New York: Holt, Rinehart, and Winston.

Alexander, W. M. 1988. "Schools in the Middle: Rhetoric and Reality." *Social Education* 52 (2): 107–109.

Anderman, E., M. Maehr, and C. Midgley. 1996. "School Reform and the Transition to Middle School." Paper presented at the annual meeting of the American Educational Research Association, New York. ED 396 440.

Ayers, L. R. 1994. "Middle School Advisory Programs: Findings from the Field." *Middle School Journal* 25 (3): 8–14.

Beane, J. A. 1990. *A Middle School Curriculum: From Rhetoric to Reality*. Columbus, OH: National Middle School Association.

———. 1991. "Integrated Curriculum in Middle Schools." *Educational Leadership* 49, no. 2 (October): 9–13.

———. 1993. *A Middle School Curriculum: From Rhetoric to Reality*. 2d ed. Columbus, OH: National Middle School Association.

———. 1997. *Curriculum Integration: Designing the Core of Democratic Education*. New York: Teachers College Press.

Beane, J. A., and R. P. Lipka. 1987. *When the Kids Come First: Enhancing Self-Esteem*. Columbus, OH: National Middle School Association.

Beane, J. A., C. Toepfer, and S. Alessi. 1986. *Curriculum Planning and Development*. Newton, MA: Allyn and Bacon.

Branham, L. 1997. "Stephen Covey Comes to Middle School: The Seven Habits of Highly Effective Teams." *Middle School Journal* 28, no. 5 (May): 14–20.

Bullock, A., and J. Pedersen. 1999. "Looking in the Mirror to Create an Interdisciplinary Team in Middle Level Teacher Education." *Middle School Journal* 30 (3): 21–27.

Burkhardt, R. M. 1999. "Advisory: Advocacy for Every Student." *Middle School Journal* 30 (3): 51–54.

Burns, J. 1998. *National Middle School Association 25th Anniversary Interview*. Las Cruces, NM: Author.

Carnegie Council on Adolescent Development. 1989. *Turning Points: Preparing American Youth for the 21st Century*. New York: Carnegie Corporation.

Clark, S., and D. Clark. 1997. "Exploring the Possibility of Interdisciplinary Teaming." *Childhood Education* 73 (5): 267–271.

Clough, D., T. James, and A. Witcher. 1996. "Curriculum Mapping and Instructional Supervision." *NASSP Bulletin* 80 (September): 79–82.

Dickinson, T. S., and T. O. Erb, eds. 1997. *Teaming in Middle School: We Gain More than We Give*. Columbus, OH: National Middle School Association.

DiRocco, M. D. 1998–1999. "How an Alternating-Day Schedule Empowers Teachers." *Educational Leadership* 56 (December/January): 82–84.

Dunham, D. 1995. "Mini-Courses: Promoting Interdisciplinary Relationships, Creative Expressions, and Social Skill Development." *Schools in the Middle* 4 (4): 20–22.

Erb, T., and N. Doda. 1989. *Team Organization: Promise, Practices, and Possibilities.* Washington, DC: National Education Association.

Erb, T., and C. Stevenson. 1999. "What Difference Does Teaming Make?" *Middle School Journal* (January): 47–50.

Fitzpatrick, K. 1997. *Indicators of Schools of Quality.* Vol. 1: *Schoolwide Indicators of Quality.* Schaumburg, IL: National Study of School Evaluation.

Flowers, N., S. B. Mertens, and P. Mulhall. 1999. "The Impact of Teaming: Five Research-Based Outcomes." *Middle School Journal* (November): 57–60.

Forte, I., and S. Schurr. 1993. *The Definitive Middle School Guide: A Handbook for Success.* Nashville, TN: Incentive Publishers.

Gable, R., and L. Manning. 1997. "In the Midst of Reform: The Changing Structure and Practice of Middle School Education." *The Clearing House* 71 (September/October): 58–62.

Galassi, J., S. Gulledge, and N. Cox. 1998. *Advisory: Definitions, Descriptions, Decisions, Directions.* Columbus, OH: National Middle School Association.

Gallagher, J. 1999. "Teaching in the Block." *Middle Ground* 2, no. 3 (February): 10–15.

Geiken, N., J. Larson, D. Van Deusen, and J. Donham. 1999. "Block Scheduling: Opportunities for Challenges and Collaboration." *Teacher Librarian* 27 (October): 26–31.

George, P., and W. Alexander. 1993. *The Exemplary Middle School.* New York: Holt, Rinehart, and Winston.

Guerrero, J. 1995. *Serving the Advanced Middle School Learner in the Heterogeneous Classroom.* Chicago: ERIC Document Reproduction Service No. ED 385 361.

Hackman, D. 1995. "Improving the Middle School Climate: Alternating-Day Block Schedule." *Schools in the Middle* 5 (1): 28–34.

Hackmann, D. G., and J. W. Valentine. 1998. "Designing an Effective Middle Level Schedule." *Middle School Journal* 29 (5): 3–13.

Hoversten, C., N. Doda, and J. Lounsbury. 1999. *Treasure Chest: A Teacher Advisory Source Book.* Columbus, OH: National Middle School Association.

Husband, R. E., and P. Short. 1994. "Interdisciplinary Teams Lead to Greater Teacher Empowerment." *Middle School Journal* (November): 58–60.

Jacobs, H. 1997. *Mapping the Big Picture: Integrating Curriculum and Assessment K–12.* Alexandria, VA: Association for Supervision and Curriculum Development.

Kain, D. 1996. "Recipes or Dialogue? A Middle School Team Conceptualizes Curricular Integration." *Journal of Curriculum and Supervision* 11 (2): 163–187.

Kasak, D. 1998. "Flexible Organizational Structures." *Middle School Journal* 29 (5): 56–59.

Kucer, S., C. Silva, and E. Delgado-Larocco. 1995. *Curricular Conversations: Themes in Multilingual and Monolingual Classrooms.* York, ME: Stenhouse Publishers.

Lappin, S. 1997. "Flexible Master Scheduling." *Michigan Middle School Journal* 21 (2): 34–36.

MacIver, D., and J. Epstein. 1991. "Responsive Practices in the Middle Grades: Teacher Teams, Advisory Groups, Remedial Instruction, and School Transition Programs." *American Journal of Education* 99 (4): 587–622.

McEwin, C. K. 1997. "Trends in Establishing Interdisciplinary Team Organization in Middle Schools." In T. Dickinson and T. Erb, eds., *Teaming in Middle Schools: We Gain More than We Give* (313–324). Columbus, OH: National Middle School Association.

Merenbloom, E. Y. 1988. *Developing Effective Middle Schools.* Columbus, OH: National Middle School Association.

———. 1991. *The Team Process: A Handbook for Teachers.* Columbus, OH: National Middle School Association.

Miller, H. M. 1999. *Making the Most of Advisory Programs.* Reston, VA: National Association of Elementary School Principals.

Mitchell, D., and L. P. Young. 1997. "Teaching Ideas: Creating Thematic Units." *English Journal* 86 (September): 80–85.

Moss, S., and M. Fuller. 2000. "Implementing Effective Practices: Teachers' Perspective." *Phi Delta Kappan* 82 (December): 273–276.

National Association of Secondary School Principals. 1985. *An Agenda for Excellence at the Middle Level.* Reston, VA: Author.

National Middle School Association. 1995. *This We Believe: Developmentally Responsive Middle Level Schools.* Columbus, OH: Author.

———. 2002. *Meeting the Standards.* Westerville, OH: Author.

Pate, P. E., E. Homestead, and K. McGinnis. 1997. *Making Integrated Curriculum Work.* New York: Teachers College Press.

Peterson, R. 1992. *Life in a Crowded Place: Making a Learning Community.* Portsmouth, NH: Heinemann Educational Books.

Powell, R. R. 1993. "Seventh Graders' Perspectives of Their Interdisciplinary Team." *Middle School Journal* (January): 49–57.

Renzulli, J. 1998. *How to Develop an Authentic Enrichment Cluster.* Available at <http://www.gifted.uconn.edu/semart01.html>.

Schurr, S. L., J. Thomason, and M. Thompson. 1996. *Teaching at the Middle Level: A Professional's Handbook.* Edited by John J. Lounsbury. Lexington, MA: D. C. Heath and Company.

Seed, A. 1998. "Free at Last: Making the Most of the Flexible Block Schedule." *Middle School Journal* 29 (5): 20–21.

Smith, D., N. Pitkin, and M. Rettig. 1998. "Flexing the Middle School Block Schedule by Adding Non-Traditional Core Subjects and Teachers to the Interdisciplinary Team." *Middle School Journal* 29 (5): 22–27.

Sprague, M., D. Pennell, and L. Sulzberger. 1998. "Engaging All Middle-Level Learners in Multi-Disciplinary Curricula." *NASSP Bulletin* 82 (December): 60–66.

Steffes, R., and J. Valentine. 1995. "Organizational Characteristics and Expected Outcomes of Interdisciplinary Teaming." Paper presented at the Annual Convention of the National Association of Secondary School Principals, San Antonio, TX.

Steinhebel, J., T. Podlewski, and B. Harris. 2000. "Another World." Interdisciplinary unit, Eastern Michigan University.

Stevenson, C. 1998. *Teaching Ten to Fourteen Year Olds,* 2d ed. New York: Addison Wesley Longman.

Valentine, J. 1993. *Leadership in Middle Level Education.* Vol. 1: *A National Survey of Middle Level Leaders and Schools.* Reston, VA: National Association of Secondary School Principals.

VanHoose, J. 1991. "The Ultimate Goal: A/a across the Day." *Midpoints* 2 (1): 1–7.

Vars, G. 2001. "Can Curriculum Integration Survive in an Era of High-Stakes Testing?" *Middle School Journal* 33, no. 2 (November): 7–17.

Vars, G., and J. Beane. 2000. *Integrative Curriculum in a Standards-Based World.* ED 441618. Chicago: ERIC Clearinghouse Document Reproduction.

Wayson, W. W., G. G. De Voss, S. C. Kaeser, T. Y. Lasley, S. S. Pinnell, and the Phi Delta Kappa Commission on Discipline. 1982. *Handbook for Developing Schools with Good Discipline.* Bloomington, IN: Phi Delta Kappa.

Williamson, R. 1993. *Scheduling the Middle Level School to Meet Early Adolescent Needs.* Reston, VA: National Association of Secondary School Principals.

Wittmer, J. 1993. "Developmental School Guidance and Counseling: Its History and Reconceptualization." In J. Wittmer, ed., *Managing Your School Counseling Program: K-12 Developmental Strategies* (2–11). Minneapolis, MN: Educational Media Corporation.

Chapter Five

❧ Diversity among Middle Level Students

Before middle grades teachers can begin to use a variety of instructional strategies appropriate for the diverse needs of young adolescents, they must first motivate their students to want to learn and then sustain that interest. Various research studies have chronicled the fact that too many middle schoolers are bored with work that does not relate to their experience or that they find disrespectful, too challenging, or lacking in stimulation (Eccles and Midgley 1990; Larson and Richards 1991).

Rather than looking at a home environment that may or may not be conducive to learning, we look at the classroom, for that is the only arena in which faculty and staff can affect student learning. This chapter will examine varied instructional practices and varied perspectives healthy for the growth of young adolescents.

MOTIVATION

What are some successful motivational strategies teachers can use with middle schoolers?

1. Adult modeling. Teacher beliefs and expectations that students observe and experience have a profound effect on academic performance. Teachers who share and model the value of learning provoke intrinsic motivation to learn in their students, the kind of motivation that is long lasting.
2. Schoolwide practices. Schools that stress learning mastery and effort, rather than test performance, encourage students to take risks in their own learning.

3. Classroom environment and school practices and policies. Whether a student feels safe, considered a valuable part of a class, celebrated, or even noticed affects student learning, attitudes, and beliefs.
4. Achievable tasks. Tasks should be challenging but achievable, and they should be contextualized or explained in ways that tie their importance to the students' world of relevance and experience.
5. Defined tasks. Tasks that are clearly defined and broken into small, achievable steps and expectations, as well as reasons for engaging in a particular activity that are understood by everyone, tend to stimulate the student.
6. Frequent and formative feedback. Teachers who help guide students through tasks provide ongoing support.
7. Authentic assessment. When students are given choices in how they will demonstrate their learning and when these choices tend to be more authentic than a paper and pencil test, students are more engaged.
8. Personal connections. Teachers who know their students and use their names in daily lessons make learning more personal and engaging; for example, "Wai-wen, do you agree with Thunderhawk's statement?" or "LaMurvin, I'll ask you question two in a few moments. Be ready with your response."
9. Teacher enthusiasm. A teacher's enthusiasm about the content of the class, the learning activities, the students in the class, and life itself is infectious.
10. Total success. A classroom in which all students can succeed is one of the greatest motivators.
11. Student investment. When middle schoolers play a thoughtful role in the development of class rules and in their own learning, they tend to be more invested.
12. Varied instructional strategies. Changing the teaching-learning format sustains a sense of vitality in the classroom (for example, Socratic seminars, games and simulations, differentiated learning, inductive and inquiry-based learning, court briefs, student-created court briefs, commercials, travel brochures, letters to the editor, presentations to the city commission, cooperative learning, the use of task cards, learning con-

tracts, learning centers, and students as active researchers).

13. Lesson vitality. When lessons are humorous, exciting, and
    vivid, students are more curious and motivated to learn,
    in part because they realize the teacher has made an ex-
    tra effort to stimulate them (for example, students and
    teacher dressing in costume for the reenactment of a Civil
    War battle; the teacher pointing with a plunger to infor-
    mation listed on the board; the teacher dressing in a
    tribal mask when teaching about symmetrical geometry).

14. Student interest. Teacher flexibility encourages students
    to actively examine their own interests in relationship to
    particular learning.

15. Problem solving and questioning. When learning is cen-
    tered around key concepts and questions, students be-
    come active problem solvers in a world full of challenging
    situations.

16. Matching content. When teachers know their students'
    interests, learning profiles, and readiness levels, they can
    match the content to the students' entry points or they
    begin learning where they are and then nudge them
    slightly out of their comfort zones (Hootstein 1994).

Fortunately, there are no prescriptions for "the" motivational
strategy that will work for all students. What is successful with one student or one group may well be unsuccessful with another. The teacher
as a craftsperson of the profession exercises her best judgment, matching learning tasks to student interests, learning levels, personal experiences, and perceived relevance.

What can be done to help those students in every classroom who
tend to be unmotivated?

1. Self-worth. Even when students engage in self-defeating
   acts such as cheating, procrastination, or simply turning
   in no work, recognize that they are attempting to protect
   their sense of self-dignity (Raffini 1993).

2. Attribution retraining. Help students concentrate on the
   tasks rather than on the failure. Respond to frustration by
   discovering alternative solutions. Attribute failure to lack
   of information, dependence on ineffective problem solv-

ing, or insufficient effort rather than on lack of ability (Brophy 1986).

3. Student focus. Help students see their work as investment rather than risk, skill growth as incremental and domain specific, and mastery of content as the goal (Lumsden 1994).

4. Choice. Through student choice, motivation becomes a natural response to the student's curiosity. When students experience shared ownership in their learning, they are more willing to take risks.

When schools are safe, orderly, vibrant places in which adults are trained to motivate and teach young adolescents, we can turn our discussion to effective instructional practices.

DIFFERENTIATING INSTRUCTION

Developing curriculum for middle school students can be somewhat of a challenge, given the wide variance of adolescent learning needs. Therefore, middle grades educators pay special attention to the prior experiences, cultural backgrounds, learning styles, interests, and readiness levels of all students. If we teach all students in the same manner, using the same approach, and providing the same learning activities, we inherently "lose" two-thirds of our students. The students who are functioning above grade level are bored because they already know the content, and the students who are functioning below grade level are lost and confused. Perhaps only the students who are functioning at grade level are being challenged enough to gain any measure of success in their education. For these reasons, and to maximize the exuberant energy and the joyful curiosity and to accommodate the widest variance in cognitive and social skills that middle schoolers may bring with them, the curriculum in the classroom needs to be differentiated in order to effectively challenge all students.

Although teachers have for many years offered students learning choices and placed them in various learning groups and may have offered enrichment activities to stimulate the "higher-ability" students and have required fewer problems of the students who struggled, differentiated instruction is an intentional process of thoughtful choices, activities, products, and assessments the teacher matches to the learners' needs and talents.

Definitions

Differentiated instruction involves actively and respectfully engaging all students in the mixed-ability classroom. A common middle school phrase is "That's not fair," which students freely apply to any number of situations. When a teacher begins to intentionally differentiate instruction, that phrase takes on new meaning, and it represents a shift in how the business of school is conducted. *Fair* no longer means "everyone gets the same"; *fair* means "what everyone needs." This necessitates a process of relearning: for the student, the teacher, the staff, and the family. It creates a new beginning point, a different process, and a more equitable perspective.

1. The beginning point is the student: What does the pre-assessment for the unit reveal about the student's interests, understanding of the content, and learning profile? This information is used by the student and the teacher to match instruction; it naturally changes from unit to unit.
2. The teacher notes exactly what concept, skill, or understanding is key to the student's learning for the daily lesson as well as for the unit.
3. Together, the student and the teacher create and modify learning activities that push the student just outside of his or her comfort zone of understanding.
4. The teacher as a facilitator and a craftsperson carefully scaffolds success for the student by offering choices, guiding and facilitating student progress, and noting daily work and interaction with other students.
5. The teacher then modifies the content of the lesson/unit, the learning activities, and the products that demonstrate student learning.
6. A guiding principle for the student is self-efficacy: helping the student become an independent learner who experiences success and who is then willing to take new risks in his or her own learning.

The curriculum is concept based (discussed below); the methods used to teach the concepts vary according to the interests, readiness levels, and learning profiles of the students. Students are continually assessed and grouped and regrouped in order to exercise their strengths and buttress their weaknesses in different areas. For example, in a language arts classroom, a student may be a very strong reader who is able to comprehend complex concepts and ideas and yet struggles to create an organized, logical essay. During a unit of instruction in which students must read and respond to a piece of writing, this student may be placed in a group with others who are functioning above grade level. If the teacher decides to have students write an essay about a novel they have recently completed, however, that same student may be placed in a group with others who are at grade level.

Before we begin looking at various methods and strategies for differentiating instruction, it is important to understand what differentiation is not. Many critics of this type of instruction believe that differentiation requires the teacher to create a different lesson plan for every student in the classroom, somewhat reflective of the IEP (Individual Educational Plan) movement of the 1970s. Although lessons are planned to accommodate different students, these students are placed in groups whose work is all very similar but whose impediments to learning are removed or motivators to learning are included.

Differentiation is also not something added to the curriculum. Often teachers say "You don't understand. We have so much we have to cover already. We don't have time to add something else." When asked how their students are performing on state tests or on other measures, they respond that "'they are not doing well at all." Perhaps that is an indication that teachers may have "covered" the curriculum, but the students have not "uncovered" or created any understanding of the content. Differentiation is a way of looking at how teachers teach differently the same content for which they are currently responsible and how students can grow in their current learning, and how this can be done collaboratively.

Likewise, differentiated instruction does not mean that students at higher readiness levels do more work or that students working below grade level complete less work. No doubt we all remember when group one in math had to do fifteen problems, group two had to do ten, and group three only had to do five. The number of problems assigned somehow left the latent message that to be "smart" meant you had to do more work. Today's students figure that out rather quickly and become suddenly cognitively challenged as they ask to be put in group three. The key to effectively differentiating instruction is to make all of the work for all of the students challenging, meaningful, and accomplishable, which therefore has little to do with varied amounts of work. Busy work or work that is "dumbed down" (for example, worksheets) will only lead to bored students who also quickly understand what the teacher's expectations of them are. Bored middle school students tend to become disruptive middle school students.

How to Establish a Differentiated Classroom

On the basis of the seminal work of Carol Ann Tomlinson (1995), who made systematic what thousands of teachers were doing piecemeal and intuitively, differentiated instruction is noted as often successful when guided by the following ideas:

1. Talk with your students about differentiation. Have them begin their own learning portfolios, complete with learning profiles and examples of their progress. Explain that together you are changing the usual business of school and of what *fair* means.
2. Keep parents informed. Because this is not the way they have experienced their own schooling or their child's, parents can become strong allies when invited to be part of the new classroom from the beginning.
3. Start slowly. Such things as offering students choices in assignments, in book selection, in their groupings (pairs, teams, cooperative groups, alone), in seating arrangements, in kinds and levels of questions, and in setting goals are good ways to experience success as a teacher creating a differentiated classroom.

Initiation into Differentiation

At the beginning of the school year, each student is given a piece of graph paper on which to draw the *x* and *y* axis. Students may draw a line or a bar graph. This works well for seventh graders, who are usually reviewing charts and graphs in science and math. The class brainstorms a list of adjectives they use when someone is very good at something. All the words are placed on the board and then ranked according to the meaning of each word. For example, if they choose *excellent, good, very good, outstanding, awesome,* or *outa-sight,* then they decide *excellent* might be highest, followed by *outstanding,* then *very good,* and so on. This is then repeated with adjectives when someone is not very good at something.

Students then create a continuum that starts at the bottom of the *y* axis with words such as *horrible, awful, very bad* on up to *sweet, awe-*

some, fantastic, and *way cool.* Students are given a list of activities such as good at math, good at cleaning my room, good at doing homework, and good at singing or playing a musical instrument. Students then add three things of their own to the list or totally create their own on their x axis. For homework they are to think about the activities on the x axis and rank themselves.

Students bring their graphs the next day, and they are put in the hallway or the classroom. By small group, students look at the graphs and make general notes and then discuss their observations. Students are amazingly insightful. They are then asked, "Why did we do this activity?" Typical responses are that some people are good at things that others aren't; people added things to the x axis that they are good at and nobody is good at everything; sometimes a person is good in one subject, but not in another; and students in school are not always good at the same things.

This is a fertile time to explain differentiation to students: During the school year there will be times when everyone will be working on the same concept or unit, but not everyone will be doing the same kind of activity. This becomes a point of reference for later in the year when students observe they are not all doing the same thing.

It is important to keep parents up-to-date about the classroom, especially when it comes to units that are differentiated. Characteristically parents appreciate teachers who take the time to notice that their child has strengths and weaknesses and who design activities to suit those needs. Every parent wants his or her child to succeed, and when a teacher takes an active role in helping the child accomplish his or her goals, it helps the parents become copartners in their child's education. Never leave parents in the dark. Their support is essential to the success of the classroom and to the success of the child.

Getting Started

Start Small

Before moving to what Tomlinson (1995) called high-preparation differentiation, begin to talk with students about how they learn best, about the ways that stimulate their thinking creatively, and about choices. Making the teaching-learning process both an interactive dialogue and an intentional one for both teacher and student is an effective way to begin. Talking about differences in learning, about things that students excel at or are challenged by, and about strengths and weaknesses overall and then in particular content areas sets the stage for more complex differentiation.

Support Success

Using a variety of instructional tools (as examined in this chapter), including graphic organizers, study guides, guide sheets for projects, manipulatives, and particularly modeling, is a way to buttress success as the teacher begins to nudge students out of their comfort zone of knowledge.

Scaffold Your Own Success

As the teacher begins to experience her own levels of success in differentiation and moves to more complex preparation, she chooses a unit that is already in the curriculum so that new materials do not have to be created. It takes a lot of work to prepare a differentiated unit/activity that is more complex, so taking small steps is the best way to begin.

The Successful Environment

It is important to understand student dispositions and skills necessary for work in this new environment. Anchor activities help to keep the entire class focused while the teacher moves from group to group giving instructions, answering questions, and getting the different groups started. With multiple groups, the teacher never gives instructions for each group to the entire class. One could easily see the line of students at the teacher's desk. "I don't understand what we are supposed to do." Explain anchor activities and behaviors to the class and practice performing these activities before ever beginning a differentiated unit.

In this case, anchor activities are meaningful things students can do on their own with little or no instruction. They may include, but are not limited to, vocabulary activities, crossword puzzles, sustained silent reading, or choices of books. Anchor activities should never be busy work. In other units, the anchor activity could be a long-term project based on unit content that the student has individually contracted with the teacher to complete. Sometimes these are preparing large exhibits or dioramas, assembling a poetry book, conducting ongoing science experiments that are recorded in lab books, creating a broadside or newspaper that is connected to a unit on the American Revolution, or working on an architectural drawing of a new sports venue for a math unit on angles. All students have anchor activities in this type of unit. And for students who may never complete their work early in class and therefore are never able to work on their projects, special days during the week are designated as anchor activity days, for it is these students in particular who need to be engaged in the more hands-on exciting projects fashion.

The teacher then decides how to differentiate the unit and how to group students. Students may be grouped according to readiness level (a more flexible term than ability level), interest, or learning profile. The lesson may be differentiated according to the process by which the students will complete the activity, the content of the lesson, or the product they will produce in order to demonstrate their understanding.

Basics of Differentiation

A teacher who differentiates teaching and learning first thinks about what all students need to know, to be able to do, or to understand in a given unit of study. In the current environment in which no child shall go untested, the compassionate teacher is more concerned that every child is seen as unique and special. When the teacher matches the beginning point of study with the knowledge of the student as a learner, and with the content standards and benchmarks, no child is left behind.

1. Identification of content, skill, or basic understanding. The teacher notes the basic concept or skill that all students need to know or be able to do.
2. Preassessment. As illustrated in Tables 5.1 and 5.2, preassessing student knowledge of a given topic provides an entry point to match learning with students' knowledge, interests, or learning profile.
3. Creation of different ways to differentiate content. The teacher determines what the students will learn; the process or the opportunities through which students will construct understanding; and the products or the ways students will demonstrate what they have learned.
4. Differentiation. The teacher does this according to readiness, interest, or learning profile.

Table 5.1
Pre-Assessment

The American Revolution
Karry Carter

These are some of the topics we will be studying in our next unit on the American Revolution. What are you most interested in? Number the items below from 1 to 10 with 1 being the most interesting and 10 being the least interesting.

——Clothing/Uniforms	____Food & Recipes
____Religious/Political Beliefs	____Architecture
____Important Battles	____Causes of the War
____Roles of Women & Children	____Music and Art
____Role of Non-Whites (Native Americans, Blacks)	____Other (What interests you that is not on the list?

What do you already know about the American Revolution?
Write whatever you know in response to the questions below.

1. What was everyday life like in the American colonies before the Revolution?

2. Why did the colonists rebel against Britain?

3. What famous people can you list from the Revolutionary War era? What are they famous for?

4. If you lived in the Revolutionary War era, what would your life be like?

5. If you could go back to the Revolutionary War era for one day, what would you be most interested in seeing or doing?

Table 5.2
Pre-Assessment: Learning Inventory

How Do You Learn Best? **Place a mark in the *Yes, No,* or *Sometimes* column** **for each of the following questions.** **Karry Carter**			
	Yes	*No*	*Sometimes*
1. I study best when it is quiet.			
2. I am able to ignore the noise of other people while I'm working.			
3. I like to work at a table or desk.			
4. I like to work on the floor.			
5. I work hard for myself.			
6. I work hard for my teacher or parent.			
7. I will work on my assignments until I complete them no matter what.			
8. Sometimes I get frustrated with my work and do not finish it.			
9. When my teacher gives assignments I like to have exact instructions on how to finish them.			
10. When my teacher gives assignments I like to know what is expected and then make my own steps to get there.			
11. I like to work by myself.			
12. I like to work in pairs or in groups.			
13. I work best when I have an unlimited amount of time to work on an assignment.			
14. I work best when I have a specified amount of time to work on an assignment.			
15. I learn best by moving and doing.			
16. I learn best while sitting at my desk.			
17. I learn best when I research the material myself.			
18. I learn best when I have lots of material available for me to read/examine.			

Content

Differentiated content focuses on key concepts, principles, dispositions, and skills associated with the concepts. It also includes the resources that students will use during the learning process. Content that is developed around key concepts tends to be more flexible in meeting individual learner needs and provides natural avenues for interdisciplinary connections.

Some sample concepts that have interdisciplinary ties to science, social studies, language arts, math, life skills, and the arts are perspective, choice, revolution, interdependence, power, survival, energy, force, discovery, and exploration.

Varied resources might include a selection of texts or materials written at varying reading levels, books on tape, videos, computer software, Internet web sites, interviews, and court briefs.

Strategies for differentiating content include:

1. *Compacting.* Compacting essentially means not teaching students what they already know. For students who perform well on a preassessment, sitting through material they already know is not a motivating use of time. Moving them directly to a learning contract or to a large-project activity tied conceptually to the unit, provides them with richer exploration.
2. *Individualized learning contracts. Contracts* offer students choices and position students and teachers as collaborators who agree on what specific tasks each student will complete as well as the specific criteria for those tasks (see Figure 5.1).
3. *Independent Study.* Students pursue topics of interest to them, identify questions they have regarding the topic, conduct research, and report their findings to a specific audience.

Process

Process is the means by which students will construct knowledge and personal meaning of the content. Usually this is done through various activities that are structured to remove barriers that inhibit struggling learners and make more complex the problems for higher-readiness students, but provide challenge that is motivating and respectful for learners of all levels. Using tiered activities for students of varying readiness levels can be very helpful. Also, including a variety of activities and ensuring that students are active participants in their learning are key to motivating transescents. Activities could include graphic organizers, simulations, small-group discussion, writing assignments, lab activities, and learning centers or stations.

A more complex grouping tool called a tiered activity is illustrated in Table 5.3. The teachers identify the concept that all students

Figure 5.1
Learning Contract
Heroes, Villains, Conflict, and Compassion
Lisa Klemetson

Culture	*Heroes & Villains*	*Relationships*
☐ Make A collage of pictures and objects from the Hispanic culture you've read about in the book	☐ Compose A letter written by Pearl Buyers explaining responses and refusal to treat the baby's bite	☐ Write A letter of advice to Kino and Juana
☐ Draw A book cover or movie poster for *The Pearl* that represents the true feeling of the book	☐ Make a list Of all the villains in the story and explain their villainous traits	☐ Write A newspaper article that reports the finding of the Pearl of the World; include a headline with your article
☐ Draw A map of the Baja Peninsula where the story takes place	☐ Explain How the story might be different if the doctor had helped the baby the first time	☐ Prepare A persuasive speech to give to Kino and Juana about why they should help the Pearl
☐ Create A map of the village where the story takes place	☐ Write An argument in support of Kino's argument throughout the story	☐ Compose A journal entry from Juana's point of view about her relationship with Kino
Student Choice #1 _____ _____	Student Choice #1 _____ _____	Student Choice #1 _____ _____

are to know and understand; in this case, it is the relationship between muscles and bones. Because they have decided to differentiate this activity according to readiness, they begin by designing the activity for the at-grade-level students. As the teachers move to below grade level, they ask, "What would get in the students' way of learning the major concept?" If dissection were the focus skill, all students would be required to dissect the frog; because the major concept is a relational one, however, the teachers decide the tediousness of identifying each bone and muscle and labeling them with push pins would become an impediment to learning. So they remove it by offering the students a computer program in which they can click and drag. As well, because writing in this case may not be the focus skill, the students are asked to write a more engaging physician's report on their patient—motivating and yet accomplishable. For the "above grade level" students, the teachers ask themselves, "How can we make this more challenging?" They begin the directions with the students creating a whole new "being."

Table 5.3 uses task cards as the explanatory tool to help students become independent learners. Clear directions written in verb format on 3" x 5" index cards explain exactly what the students are required to do. Everyone is working on the same concept but at varying levels of intricacy and complexity. Everyone is engaged in motivating and respectful work.

Product

Product is how students demonstrate their grasp of the key concept, principles, and facts through the use of varying types of assessment. Various product choices could include creating a game to be explained, demonstrated, and played with the class; writing and performing a short skit reenacting a significant historical event; creating and presenting a PowerPoint show; writing court briefs, letters to the editor, petitions to politicians, journal entries; creating cartoons, commercials, radio broadcasts, coffee house poetry reads, art exhibits, and project fairs.

Flexible Grouping by Readiness

A significant underpinning of differentiation is flexible grouping. Were students to remain in readiness groups throughout the semester, we would be tracking them. When they know that the groups in which they are placed will be changed in either the next lesson or the next unit, they are much more willing to participate. Teachers always ask about

Table 5.3

Tiered Activity Based on Readiness

Skeletal and Muscular Systems—Relationships
Beth Harris, John Steinhebel, Tim Podlewski

At Grade Level:
- Dissect a frog
- Identify and label the muscles in the leg
- Pull back the muscles of the leg to expose the bone
- Identify the bones in the leg using the textbook
- Use color-coded push pins to label each bone in the leg
- Write a paragraph that explains how bones and muscles appear to work together

Below Grade Level:
- Using a computer program and your frog, dissect the frog
- Click and drag to identify the major muscles of the leg
- Compare them to the dissected frog
- Click and drag to identify the major bones of the leg
- Write a brief physician's summary about the relationship you found between bones and muscles

Above Grade Level:
- Create a new "being"
- Focus on designing the skeletal and muscular systems
- Label the major muscular systems in the leg of your being
- Compare the new being's muscles to your own muscles
- Label and state the function of the bones in the leg
- Write a paragraph comparing the relationship of the skeletal system to the muscular system; compare the relationship in your new being to the systems in your own body

---

the stigma of placing individuals in particular groups, as if students were not already aware of the variability among their peers. We do not hand out task cards and announce that the below-grade-level group meets in a particular part of the classroom and the above-grade-level students meet somewhere else. Rather, we return to our definition of what is fair.

Sometimes when grouped by readiness, students ask to move up a group. The wise teacher will always negotiate with the student and say, "If we move you to that group, will you do me a favor and quietly let me know if it becomes too difficult?" All too often, until students understand that the above-grade-level group does not do more work than the other groups, they want to be in the lower groups. Again negotiate with students. When they know that in a few days they are going to be regrouped by interest, they quickly understand that that will mix up readiness levels.

Flexible grouping also provides variety in whole-group instruction, individual assignments, small-group work, pairs, and independent work. Flexibility is the key.

Flexible Grouping by Interest

Grouping by interest is a way of tapping into the creative individuality of students, a motivator for learning at all ages. The Middle Ages, Industrial Revolution, Renaissance, or Roman Empire, for example, all are significant in European history, but with the topic's broad scope and time constraints, it is often impossible to teach them all with much depth. If a unit is differentiated by interest, students learn the conceptual basics of all eras, then choose the era they are most interested in. They research that era and give presentations that benefit all the students.

Flexible Grouping by Learning Profile

Each learner has a collection of information about how he or she learns best; students have particular ways each makes sense of the world. A variety of tools and theories can help teachers think about their students' learning styles: True Colors; the Myers-Briggs categories; Dunn and Dunn's learning inventories; Robert Sternberg's learning styles (abstract, sequential, concrete and so on), and Howard Gardner's multiple intelligences (intrapersonal, interpersonal, logical/mathematical, musical/rhythmic, visual/spatial, verbal/linguistic, naturalistic). How the student most comfortably works—either in pairs or on a team, in a cooperative group or independently—is also noted, as well as whether the student is a part-to-whole (just show me small pieces of the project at a time) learner or a whole-to-part (show me the entire project so I know where I'm going) learner.

As with the implementation of any new theory, it is important to start small and gradually add new things. Providing choices in a homework assignment or in the levels of books based on the same concept may eventually lead to developing learning centers or lessons differentiated by interest. What's important is not how much a teacher does in the beginning, but that the teacher begins.

Example: Seventh-Grade Language Arts/Social Studies Unit— World War II and the Holocaust

Differentiation according to Interest and Product

Students in the seventh-grade language arts classes are studying the events that took place in the world between 1939 and 1945 and the effect they had on Anne Frank and her family. In their social studies they are learning about World War II and the Holocaust. In both classes students are examining several different topics as they relate to this period of history. We want to give them an opportunity to look more deeply at a topic of interest and then create a project that demonstrates their research. The students and teacher brainstorm the following list of suggested topics: the atom bomb, concentration camps, Pearl Harbor, Anne Frank's *The Secret Annex,* artillery used in the war, progression of the war, Adolf Hitler, the SS *St. Louis,* music of the Holocaust, Navajo code language used in the war, Japanese internment camps in the United States, the Dutch Resistance, uniforms worn by various participants in the war, and war propaganda.

Students had one week to research in the media center and one week to create their projects, which included display boards, timelines, models, mobiles, performances, radio broadcasts, advertisements/posters, written biographies, brochures, and persuasive essays. The results were tremendous. Students were working who had not done anything else all year. They were engaged and interested in their work, and consequently behavior problems were virtually nonexistent—the reason this text does not include a discussion of discipline.

Constructivism

These students had constructed their own understanding when they interacted with objects, ideas, information, skills, and concepts in ways that engaged them as active participants with choice. The foundation for the learning that transpired or the mind map of learning is a schema or representation of the connections the mind makes between the known and the unknown. Vygotsky contended that social interactions between peers ensure quality learning because students use higher-level thinking skills with each other to make sense of information (Weld 1997).

Learning by doing, as Dewey would contend, assists students as they move back and forth between concrete and abstract thinking. As a theory, constructivism focuses on the learning process and on the learners as they challenge their own preconceived ideas and as they move through the various phases of interaction, analysis, and reorganization. In so doing it places greater significance on what is not known rather than what is (Association for Supervision and Curriculum Development 1997). This challenges the general flavor of contemporary teaching, which places emphasis on the acquisition and replication of discrete bits of information. Constructivism then is a theory of learning rather than of teaching, although teaching can be considered constructivist in perspective and design.

Bethany Harris, Laurie Wahlstrom, and Pat Williams-Boyd

CONCEPT-BASED INSTRUCTION

Curriculum and Concepts

Much of the focus of middle school reform has been on schools' becoming more developmentally responsive to young adolescents. The constructivist classroom, differentiated instruction, integrated instruction, inquiry-based instruction, advisory, teaming, and block scheduling are just a few key middle grades practices that have their foundation in concept-based instruction. Middle grades reform expert James Beane contended that any discussion of reform must include what students are expected to learn (1993).

If we know students need to construct their own knowledge, what should the curriculum be based on? What is the best way to state objectives, if we know students can learn the same objective in a variety of ways? How do we ensure that thematic instruction and content integration also result in deep, enduring understanding? Does being child centered preclude academic rigor? The answers to these questions may require a dramatic shift in thinking about the basis of curriculum.

The junior high school model is still mired in teaching that emphasizes discrete pieces of information, or fact-based teaching, whereas the middle grades curriculum is concept based, a process founded on the natural constructs that run seamlessly through all areas of academic content.

Although the national and state content standards have been important tools in defining what students should know and be able to do, they were never intended to become the curriculum itself. Nevertheless, the importance of scoring well on tests has led many talented teachers on wild goose chases through the state or local documents trying to "cover" as much information as possible. This leads to several problems. First, at best, the focus on coverage rather than on depth of meaning results in the students' getting mostly factual, or low-level, knowledge. Unfortunately, breadth-over-depth type of learning is frequently forgotten within twelve hours after a test, and even our most capable students merely achieve superficial knowledge acquisition.

A second problem with a fact-based design is that it reduces assessment to very limited types of performances, the most common being the ubiquitous multiple-choice exam followed by outcome-based instruction. Perhaps the most used tool in writing these outcomes is Bloom's Taxonomy of Knowledge, a hierarchical categorization of intellectual verbs and tasks. Student performance of tasks at various cognitive levels is equated with learning. Examples of topic-based statements are given in the left column of Table 5.4.

The focus in the left column is on facts, whereas the focus of concept-based teaching is on why things are important. Both lists in Table 5.4 require various levels of thinking, yet only concepts keep students truly engaged with important ideas. For example, from the left-hand column information, a student might create a wonderfully accurate model of an ocean ecosystem, but the act of making it does not necessarily require an understanding of the ecosystems.

A third problem with reductionist curriculum design is that it leads students on a dead-end search for relevance. Students are easily motivated when the learning experience is personally relevant. When curriculum is organized around facts, relevance often becomes a hit-or-miss proposition. Students who have already experienced success in a traditional setting or who have the right support structures may do just fine in a setting without much personal relevance, but students who suffer from issues of self-efficacy are often the first to turn off academic learning and turn on to other things.

How Concepts Make Meaning Last

How do we create curriculum that meets content standards while focusing on deep meaning and personal relevance? And how can we help students develop a healthy worldview as they face the rapid changes of life in the Information Age?

The brain's process of making meaning involves at least two distinct memory systems: one for rote memorization and the other for the

Table 5.4

Topic and Concept-Based Comparison

Topic-Based Understanding Statements	*Concept-Based Understanding Statements*
Students will be able to: • Name the oceans of the world (knowledge) • Explain the formation of the oceans (comprehension) • Show the oceans on a map (application) • Compare the oceans on the basis of size (analysis) • Create a model of the oceans (synthesis) • Explain the importance of the oceans (evaluation)	Theme: Oceans (concepts noted in italics) • *Topographical features* create natural *boundaries* (social studies) • *Organisms* in an *ecosystem* are *dependent* on each other for survival (science) • *Predictions* can be based on known *cycles* and frequencies (math, science) • *Natural forces* affect both living and nonliving things (science/language arts) • The *motion of currents* can be used to *transport* other objects (science, social studies)

assimilation of experiences. Research on cognitive functioning (Caine and Caine 1991) indicated that the focus of learning needs should shift toward the experiential, concept-based side, where students can take advantage of the brain's innate ability to integrate experiences into natural knowledge. In this framework, concepts are natural categories or the organizers of our perceptions.

Structuring the curriculum around big ideas and broad concepts provides multiple entry points for students: some become engaged through practical responses to problems, some analyze tasks on the basis of models and principles, and others interpret ideas through analogies from their own perspectives (Brooks and Brooks 1993).

Once students are engaged by the idea, deep learning can take place because teachers can provide situations where tension exists between the student's naive conceptions and his or her new experiences. Learning based on topics and facts rarely creates such tension because it requires the learner to accumulate information rather than assimilate it.

Popular illusionist David Blaine's street magic provides an example of how this process works. During one of his television specials, he can be seen performing illusions for people in such diverse settings as New York City, Cuba, and Africa. Though he cannot even speak their languages, his illusions still inspire wonder and amazement. His magic, like a well-written concept, is timeless and universal, requiring an examination of what one knows and accepts to be true. Fortunately, good teaching doesn't require magic or illusions, but it does begin by going beyond the level of factual knowledge and into the realm of helping students read their world by questioning and expanding the things they know to be true. Next, let us consider how concepts become curriculum.

Step One: Finding Appropriate Concepts

A concept is what ties together all of the facts in a universal way; it is the basic idea we strive to deepen and enhance through instruction. Some sample concepts arc presented in Table 5.5.

It is also important for students and teacher to be able to generate concepts from the state standards documents. For instance, a Michigan 2000 science benchmark is to "describe the arrangement and motion of molecules in solids, liquids, and gases." As it is written, the benchmark calls for a behavior ("describe") and recall of the facts ("arrangement and motion of molecules") associated with solids, liquids, and gases. Take the benchmark and begin to question why this is important information in the field of science. General concepts then start to emerge: change, energy, matter, order. They are appropriate because knowing the facts of the benchmark deepens and expands one's understanding of each concept.

Step Two: The Big Ideas, Generalizations, and Enduring Understandings

The second step of concept-based design is to identify the big ideas that students should be developing as a result of instruction. Concepts, written as one- or two-word ideas, provide the lens for learning the content and process, but they must be combined in order to be useful in any meaningful way. Change, matter, energy, and order are excellent examples of concepts, but in isolation they act more like themes.

If one links the ideas together into generalized statements of understanding, however, we then have something rich in meaning and value on which instructional units can be founded. Such a statement could be that physical properties change as the result of the loss or gain of energy and that the amount of energy in matter is inversely related to

Table 5.5

Content Area Concepts

Content Area	Sample Concepts
Science	Cycles, energy, equilibrium, forces, matter, organisms
Math	Relationships, symmetry, proportion, probability, quantity
Social Studies	Culture, relationships, society, governments, power, rights, responsibilities
Language Arts	Communication, purpose, reality, fantasy, curiosity, independence
Integrated Concepts	Beliefs, change, conflict, interactions, groups, populations, patterns, dependence, independence, interdependence, order, systems, struggle, survival, power and authority, responsibility

the order of its molecules. These are the "big ideas" we want students to include in their education and might be viewed as a form of intellectual currency. They are the lasting and transferable changes in thinking and behavior that reside at the true heart of education.

Step Three: From Concepts to Instructional Units

Practicing teachers were not only trained to use fact-based models but were students of the model as well. So they will at first find concept thinking a bit challenging. Once the concepts and generalizations are established, however, the process of designing instruction moves toward the more familiar territory of choosing assessments and creating lessons. Teachers must remain mindful that the essential content and skills are included to reinforce or exemplify the big idea, but in and of themselves are not the goals of instruction. Again, teachers are not covering material; rather, they are helping students "uncover" the truth contained within the concept (Wiggins and McTighe 1998).

Designing a unit begins at the end and moves backward, meaning the teacher begins with the big ideas and associated essential questions, then chooses how true understanding of the big ideas might be assessed. This often occurs through an authentic performance in a culminating experience. The final step of curriculum design includes making a determination of what the students need to know and to be able to do and choosing activities that would allow the desired understanding to develop naturally. Table 5.6 is a guide to organizing units with a conceptual focus.

Conclusion: Concept-Based Instruction

Several signs point to concept-based learning as the next logical step for curriculum design. First, the type of thinking required of people in the Information Age goes beyond rote memorization of facts or the development of discrete skills. Many of the jobs our students will be doing beyond high school may not currently exist. Second, the ability to create and share information is expanding at a rate far greater than any one person's ability to retain it all. Finally, the lessons of brain-based research tell us that the current system of education simply does not effectively use all that the brain is capable of doing. Therefore, curriculum must move up the ladder of knowledge. Educators must look beyond current content and skills and help students delve into the deeper meanings and abilities held within.

Moving to concept-based design may present several roadblocks. First, there is the tendency to rely on fact-based teaching because it is relatively easy to present and to assess. The widespread use of multiple-choice questions on standardized tests and of outcome-based objectives are two examples. Second, concept-based teaching requires a leap of faith by both the learner and the teacher. For the learner, it means that she must trust the ideas that form in her own mind. She must be willing to self-correct and let go of ideas that no longer function in light of the present experience or situation. The teacher must provide the opportunity for the learner to naturally make this leap. Teachers used to being judged on how well their students perform on state tests or standardized tests will not find this an easy task.

Despite these obstacles, practitioners of concept-based curriculum will find considerable support among the proponents of brain-based schooling (Caine and Caine 1991), differentiated instruction (Tomlinson 1999), constructivism (Brooks and Brooks 1993), and developmentally responsive middle schools (Beane 1993). Armed with these methodologies, middle grades teachers stand ready to put adolescent theory into practice for the benefit of all students.

Just as constructivist teachers organize information around enduring concepts, they also tend to shape conceptual clusters of problems and inquiries (Sprague and Dede 1999). They provoke and support student inquiry through the use of thoughtful, open-ended questions.

Richard Bacolor

Table 5.6
Concept-Based Unit Planning Guide

Theme:

Organizing Concept:

Enduring Understandings/Generalizations:

Essential Questions:

Key Content and Skills:

Assessments:

Culminating Experience:

Activities:

Resources:

INQUIRY-BASED INSTRUCTION

Inquiry-based instruction is founded in constructivist learning theory. Individuals use prior knowledge and experiences to make sense of new information. Until learners understand that their preconceived ideas may be wrong or not entirely correct, however, new concepts or ideas will have little significance (Colburn 1998). Once they realize they have a limited or inaccurate understanding, they are able to open their minds and view things differently. Through active and meaningful encounters with their surroundings, students are able to construct new knowledge (Fosnot 1996).

As a result of Jean Piaget's and Lev Vygotsky's studies, the constructivist learning theory, more specifically inquiry, has become a popular method of instruction. It challenges students to rethink their preconceived ideas. Since students are naturally curious about the world around them, they are motivated to ask new questions. This is what essentially drives the curriculum (Weld 1997). They work cooperatively with their peers as they investigate real-life problems and propose solutions. They are encouraged to ask more open-ended questions that promote inquiry (Collins 1994).

Teacher's Role and Responsibility in an
Inquiry-Based Classroom

The teacher's role in an inquiry-based classroom is that of a facilitator. Teachers who have a mastery of the content and of questioning techniques stimulate student involvement. Questions are used to retrieve information or knowledge the students currently hold, to encourage them to recognize misconceptions, and to guide them in discovering new concepts. Questions that stimulate students' open-ended thinking and reveal why they are thinking what they are, and what predictions they have about future investigations prove to be the most thought provoking and encourage students to share in an environment free of right or wrong answers.

As teachers plan for an inquiry-based classroom, they work collaboratively with students to select problems that represent real-world situations relevant to students' lives. Outcomes that are undetermined cause students to truly search for answers, rather than model an outcome that has already been established. When students are investigating questions, analyzing data, and critiquing outcomes, they use a variety of resources (Ramos 1999). To encourage them to research and find answers that satisfy them, they should have an unrestricted amount of

Table 5.7
Comparative Teacher-Student Roles

The Teacher	The Student
• Creates a student-centered classroom • Facilitates the lesson • Implements appropriate questioning techniques • Acknowledges that learning best occurs when posed as real-to-life examples • Realizes the importance of being flexible with outcomes	• Actively acquires new knowledge • Functions as a problem solver • Utilizes critical thinking skills • Realizes his or her involvement in the world, which increases motivation • Spearheads the outcomes of the lesson

time (Klein and Merritt 1994). Although this might not always be possible, students who are not rushed to find answers, but are instead encouraged, produce quality work because they are active participants in their own learning. Table 5.7 illustrates the interplay between teacher and student in the inquiry-based classroom.

Student's Role

As active participants, students are responsible for thinking, problem solving, and discovery as modeled by their teachers, rather than for the accumulation of discrete pieces of information (Ramos 1999). Students use such active-learning tools as collaborative learning, cooperative learning, investigational work, problem solving, small-group work, and experiential learning (Jacobsen, Eggen, and Kauchak 2002).

At the beginning of a unit, what the students know about the topic shapes the unit. When students generate a list of what they would like to know, they are essentially creating their list of questions to investigate. This curiosity evokes an ownership that motivates students, for they experience the worth of their ideas. They proceed by designing investigations, analyzing data, and reviewing outcomes to see if there are further questions that need to be answered. Placing the focus on the student rather than on the teacher shifts emphasis from the textbook to the students' curiosity.

An observer in a constructivist-based classroom would see actively engaged students making observations, asking and answering questions, recording responses in a journal, and discussing what they have discovered with their peers or with their teacher (Colburn 1998). For students who may need extra assistance, the teacher can:

- Generate a list of what they want to know
- Create investigations based on questions
- Engage them in discrepant events
- Present them with a problem to investigate

Learning occurs when students actively construct knowledge rather than when they passively record information from a lecture. For this kind of critical inquiry to be successful in developing a more complex understanding, students must engage in continuous discussion (Fecho 2000). Table 5.8 presents an example of an inquiry lesson.

Implementation of Inquiry-Based Instruction: The 5E Model

Table 5.8 uses the 5E inquiry-based model of instruction developed by the Biological Science Curriculum Study of 1993. The five phases of the model are:

1. Engage—motivate the students through the activation of prior knowledge.
2. Explore—encourage students to work with peers to observe, predict, make inferences about the concept, share their ideas, and listen to the interpretation of others.
3. Explain—students reflect on their experiments (or experiences) and integrate new vocabulary and terms. The teacher introduces the students to new ideas.
4. Expand—apply new understandings in new situations.
5. Evaluate—students reflect on the total experience and identify questions they still need answered. Teachers assess the amount and sophistication of student learning (Colburn 1998, 27–28).

Table 5.9 offers an inductive thinking example of the 5E model that poses students as active researchers.

Authentic Assessment

In a constructivist learning environment, authentic assessment partners the teacher and the student as they examine new knowledge and

Table 5.8

Lesson: What Type Are You?

ENGAGE

In an open forum, the teacher poses the following questions :
1. What are the functions of blood?
2. What does it carry?
3. What is the composition of blood?

EXPLORE

1. The students find out their blood type.
2. Use colored Post-it notes representing different types.
3. Collect the Post-it notes.
4. Organize the Post-it notes on the board by blood type as a bar graph. (Frequency of blood type in the United States is: A—40%, B—10%, AB—4%, and O—46%)
5. Calculate how many potential donors are present for each blood group.

EXPLAIN

1. What is the general distribution of blood type in our region?
2. Which group has the most potential donors?
3. Which blood type is most limited when it comes to donors?
4. Given the national percentage of blood types, does our class match?
5. What factors might influence the local patterns of blood types?
6. What is the component of blood that determines the type?

EXPAND

1. What are some of the blood disorders?
2. What component of blood do they affect? (sickle cell, shape of RBC)

EVALUATE

1. The students will use the microscope to observe blood samples with prepared slides and identify red and white blood cells.
2. They will sketch what they observe. (Can they identify the blood type? Can they obtain anti-A and anti-B serum and can they demonstrate clumping of RBC's with blood from beef?)

habits of mind (Klein and Merritt 1994). Informally, teachers monitor student progress through notes kept on student comments, questions, and observed behaviors. Formally, teachers assess journals, portfolios, daily notebooks, projects, reports, and presentations. And self-evaluation communicates what students have learned and where improvement has been and can be made. The emphasis here is on the learner and the value of prior knowledge and past experiences. In the traditional reductionist approach, assessment is deficit driven and reflects the emphasis on incremental or fractional learning.

Table 5.9

Lesson: Drivers versus Environmentalists

Activity/Procedures:

1. (ENGAGE) Distribute the "Drivers versus Environmentalists" scenario and read it to the class as they follow along. Ask students how they would react if this were to happen in their community.

"Drivers versus Environmentalists" Scenario

Several community members are furious! An active environmental group convinced the township council to ban the use of salt to de-ice roads. Citizens are concerned about road safety during the winter months. How will drivers get from one place to another safely? What about children being transported by buses to and from school? Their lives will be in serious danger!

2. (EXPLORE) The students' task is to determine what the environmentalist group said to the township to convince them to discontinue the use of salt. What caused the committee members to ban salt usage?

3. To the students: "How will you begin to find the answer?" (Research.) "Remember you want to know what the environmentalists said to cause such a drastic reaction." (The effects salt has on the environment.) "What else should you find out?" (Possible alternatives and effectiveness.) "You will design an investigative plan to demonstrate the effect salt has on the environment." Students may struggle. As a last resort, offer some materials to use or give several options so their investigation is original.

4. Distribute and discuss the requirements for the project. Group 2–3 students heterogeneously by readiness. Students will assign tasks or jobs: an Internet researcher and someone to look up information on Encarta.

5. Students complete research and begin to design their investigation, getting teacher approval concerning procedures. (Check only for safety—do not correct or troubleshoot for them. They need to learn from their errors and correct themselves.) Encourage students to go back to the drawing board if their investigation doesn't show what they want it to. They need to practice their investigative presentation before presenting it to the class. Everyone on the team must participate. Students sign up for the day they want to present—this way they can be prepared with materials. If there aren't any volunteers to go first, draw numbers.

6. Groups are given ten minutes at the beginning of the hour to collect materials prior to their presentations.

7. (EXPLAIN) Students finish presentations and share their critiques of their own and of other projects (strengths/weaknesses—whether the group demonstrated what they learned).

8. (EXPAND) Students share what they discovered about the alternatives to salt. Why don't more communities use them?

Assessment: (EVALUATE)

Students are informally assessed through teacher observation and formally assessed on research, argument summary, investigation, presentation, evaluations of other groups, and journal entries.

(continues)

Table 5.9 (continued)

Student Task: Determine what the environmental group said to the township council to convince them to ban the use of salt. What scared the township so much that they refused to allow salt on the roads?

Requirements:

1. Research—learn all you can about salt and the effects it has on the environment	20 pts_____
2. One page summary of what the environmentalists could have said to the township council to cause them to ban salt on the roads (Regulations?)	10 pts_____
3. Investigation that demonstrates or proves what your group believes changed the minds of the council	20 pts_____
4. Presentation	10 pts_____
5. Your evaluations of peers	10 pts_____
6. Self-evaluation	10 pts_____
7. Peer evaluation (group members)	20 pts_____

Learning Cycle

The learning cycle is a constructivist inquiry model that divides learning into three to five phases—exploration, concept introduction, and concept application (Barnum 1996) (as illustrated in Table 5.10). Ideally, each phase leads to the next one through assessment and discussion.

> *Exploration*—Students examine, observe, and describe the phenomena. Through discussion and sharing they develop hypotheses, and they identify, collect, and analyze data. Students' prior knowledge determines their responses.
>
> *Concept Introduction*—Students develop terminology and concepts related to the phenomena. They actively compare data, construct models, and communicate ideas. Through debate and discussion, they evaluate their choices and integrate new ideas with prior knowledge. Once they have explored the concept, they need to be able to explain it.

Table 5.10
Lesson: On My Last Nerve!

EXPLORATION

The teacher suddenly makes a loud noise. How did the students react? Teacher poses the question: "What inside your body caused these involuntary reactions called reflexes?"

Tape dominos about an inch apart to a meter stick. The tape needs to be made into a hinge connecting the back of the domino to the ruler. Use extra tape to reinforce the hinges.

Place the meter stick with the taped dominos on a desk. Flick the first domino with your finger to make it fall. What happens?

CONCEPT INTRODUCTION

In an open forum, discuss the follow question:
1. What are the two divisions of the human nervous system?
2. What components make up each division?
3. What are the four main parts of the human brain?
4. Describe the major function of each part.
5. What is the function of sensory neurons? What is the major function of the motor neurons? Why are reflexes so quick?

CONCEPT APPLICATION

1. How fast are you?
2. Lab partners work together to test how fast the students' reactions are.
3. One students holds a ruler in the air then drops it; another student attempts to catch the ruler as fast as possible.
4. Record the centimeters at which the students were able to catch the ruler.
5. Give the students a table to convert distance on the ruler to reaction time. This activity is designed to measure student response time. Why is the activity not just testing a simple reflex?
6. To extend the activity, students compare their auditory and touch cues while attempting to catch the ruler with previous visual cues.

Concept Application—Students are required to apply their new knowledge to both new and familiar situations, and they ask questions. This is the phase during which students will take action. New information becomes internalized and used in daily life situations. Once the students have the opportunity to explain the concept learned, they apply it.

In inquiry-based classrooms, teachers are able to help students accomplish four fundamental elements of active research common to all disciplines:

1. Pose questions after examining compelling data
2. Learn how to access a variety of resources and data points
3. Construct their own understanding of the information
4. Present their new understandings by using a variety of tools (Zorfass 1998, viii)

Conclusion: Inquiry-Based Instruction

Inquiry-based instruction improves students' ability to problem solve and think critically about the world around them. They generate their own questions to ponder and exercise the skills necessary to reach logical conclusions. They are actively engaged in the process of learning rather than mimicking already-existing ideas and answers. In this kind of successful learning environment, teachers place students at the center of learning.

Audrey Bolden and Raquel Dicks

PROBLEM-BASED LEARNING

It is more important for students to construct deep conceptual knowledge through experience with problems and how to solve them and through understanding the importance of questioning than it is for them to memorize discrete facts. One way that teachers can better help prepare students to meet the ongoing challenges of demanding state and national benchmarks and the nature of making these deep knowledge connections in the content-area subjects is through problem-based learning and teaching.

Problem-based learning, much like inquiry teaching, focuses on the process rather than on content and is a practice in which the learning is centered on a central problem around which the entire lesson is built. A loosely "structured" or open-ended problem relevant to the students' experiences is posed. Students are encouraged and required to develop their understanding of the problem through asking/answering their own questions, through minds-on and hands-on experiences, and through conducting active research much in the vein of a scientist who uses the inductive process to form and test a hypothesis and come to a conclusion (Goodman and Bernston 2000).

Each lesson is structured in a problem-based learning format and becomes a project as well as an adventure in which students are active participants who are responsible for developing their own understanding. Furthermore, students become active researchers, mathematicians, authors, and even social agents who are continually self-monitoring and checking for their development of the central problem.

Teacher's Role

Just as in the inquiry-based classroom, the teacher is a facilitator of in-depth discussion, investigative research, and group work. Students generate and pose new questions in response to teachers' probes. Teachers monitor students in their interactions to see where help is needed. Discovery is the process most compatible with deep conceptual knowledge, for the learners become the active participants in shaping necessary information, concepts, and application (Palinscar, Magnusson, and Collins 2001).

Problem-Based Learning and Expectations

"What are my expectations of my students?" is a pivotal question a teacher asks when considering whether or not to use problem-based learning. The school setting (urban or rural, private or public) is of little consequence when a teacher sets expectations and standards for his students and for himself. Lessons that truly get at the nature of instructional and learning standards are much more involved than fact-based models would hold and usually require more work of the teacher and of the student.

An understanding of the nature of middle school students helps us understand why expectations are set high. How many times do we hear middle schoolers say how bored they are? Problem-based learning increases student interest because students are actively applying their skills in classes that previously had them sitting and taking notes. Added interest leads to better attendance to the content and in school in general (Leonard, Speziale, and Penick 2001).

Through student responsibility and accountability, problem-based learning gives students ownership, freedom, and independence in their learning, which is developmentally what young adolescents seek. As student interest increases, so too does achievement. Students' abilities to question, write thought-provoking responses, research, and conduct formal investigations and presentations lead to a general increase in achievement on state and national standardized tests and to a particular increase on the constructed response pieces that are traditionally the most difficult questions for middle schoolers to answer (Leonard, Speziale, and Penick 2001).

Problem-based learning teaches students how to think about the problems they are presented, how to develop a plan, and how to carry it out. Low student performance on state and national standardized tests in many cases is not attributable to the students' lack of content knowledge but rather to their deficiencies in being able to patiently reason and work through problems in a logical and efficient manner. Problem-based learning helps to combat this problem.

Problem-based learning programs also positively affect students across race and gender lines, groups, and special education boundaries (Palinscar, Magnusson, and Collins 2001). This form of learning allows teachers to monitor student progress more effectively, to provide some individual attention to students who are struggling, and to offer opportunities to differentiate instruction as described below. Even the lowest-functioning students have questions and ideas. Most students prefer to use activity-based, hands-on experiences to help them make sense of difficult and abstract concepts. Problem-based learning is designed to reach all students' interests and developmental levels while allowing the teacher to work more closely with groups and students who need extra attention.

A Problem-Based Design Format

In order to integrate problem-based learning in the classroom, we must first look at the organizational structure that facilitates this type of learning.

1. Teacher's understanding. The development of a problem-based unit begins with the teacher's depth of content and pedagogical understanding. This frees the teacher to think creatively, to focus on student mastery, and to promote inquiry.
2. Scope and sequence. The scope and sequence reflect the key overarching questions that help shape the unit. This

part of the design gives the unit a sense of direction and sequences the learning in a logical manner most beneficial for middle level students. This step also provides the focus for each individual lesson and gives students a sense of where they are going in their thinking process.

3. Pre-assessment. The preassessment examines where the students currently are in their understanding. This is an important step in the process because middle level students often come from vastly different cultural and educational backgrounds. The spectrum of learning needs presents some challenges that dictate how lessons should be differentiated. This step helps to "personalize" the instruction and create a more successful learning environment.

4. Lesson development. After analyzing the preassessment—identifying the major skills, concepts, or understandings built on content standards—the teacher develops the lesson.

5. Assessment. The assessment and lesson design are intertwined because the teacher is constantly negotiating lesson design or reshaping the lesson on the basis of the ongoing assessment of student learning and understanding.

A Unit Using the Problem-Based Design

Now that we have a format or design for creating a problem-based classroom, let's examine each step in depth by developing a sample problem-based middle grades science unit on ecology and its relationship to pollution. The unit focuses on students as active researchers and social agents within their own community.

Teacher's Understanding

The teacher first clarifies his own understanding of the concepts and their relationships. A concept map, as illustrated in Figure 5.2, visually presents the unit's major concepts and their relationships, in this case, ecology and pollution. The use of concept mapping is a suggested tool because it can later be used as a strategy to help middle schoolers develop, connect, and refine their understanding of the concepts. It is also an easy-to-use visual tool for teachers and parents to help in clarifying their own understanding.

Figure 5.2
Ecology Unit Concept Map

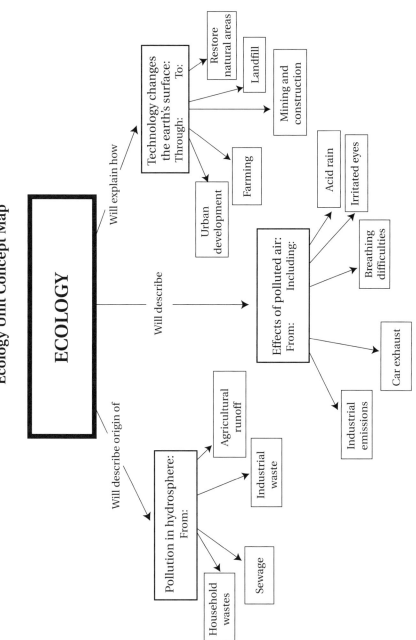

Scope and Sequence

Using the concept map (Figure 5.2), a series of questions is developed around which the unit and lessons are shaped. We will examine one of the major concepts: "Technology Changes the Earth's Surface." We would first create the key overarching question that reflects what the students need to know. Table 5.11 (Scope and Sequence) shows how that arm of the concept map is reworked by posing the question "How does technology alter the surface of the Earth?" Although this may not seem profoundly different from the statement as it appears on the concept map, it now begins to move the lesson to an inquiry focus.

From this overarching question, the teacher creates individual lesson questions that reflect key concepts from the map and that in turn get at the central roots of the larger question. Table 5.11 shows four lessons with accompanying assessments. Each lesson reflects a key concept from the Figure 5.2 map. For example, to address mining, construction, and urban development concepts of pollution, lesson one poses the following questions: How do urban development, mining, and construction change the surface of the Earth? What are the long-term effects? These lesson questions now guide student inquiry.

Pre-Assessment

The pre-assessment phase is important because it allows the teacher to thoughtfully craft lessons for a particular student group. Depending on the complexity of differentiation within the lesson, the pre-assessment will vary from time to time. For example, if we were to create a pre-assessment for the first key overarching question in Table 5.11 and we wanted to differentiate by readiness, the pre-assessment might look like Table 5.12.

Notice that all questions deal with the students' understanding at this entry point. As a result of the pre-assessment, the teacher:

1. Groups students
2. Creates and modifies learning experiences
3. Compacts students out to work on enrichment or anchor activities

If we were differentiating by interest or learning profiles, the pre-assessment questions might be:

Table 5.11
Unit 5, Scope and Sequence, Ecology

Key Overarching Questions	Lessons				
	Lesson 1	*Lesson 2*	*Lesson 3*	*Lesson 4*	*Lesson 5*
How does technology alter the surface of the Earth?	How do urban development, mining, and construction change the surface of the Earth? What are the long-term effects?	How does farming change the surface of the Earth, and what practices are used to help cause soil conservation?	What are landfills and how are they changing the surface of the Earth? How have they changed from early landfills?	How do we restore natural areas, and what processes are involved?	*Assessment: Land Restoration Plan*
How does surface water in Michigan reach the oceans and lakes and return again?	What is the water cycle and how does it work?	How do run-off, rivers, creeks, and streams contribute to the water cycle?	How are wetlands and the Great Lakes responsible for part of the water cycle?	What is the relationship between snow melt, rainfall, gravity, and the water cycle?	*Assessment: How can we create a working water cycle through terrariums?*
How does water exist below the ground?	What is groundwater and how does it get there?	What are filtration and saturation, and how are they related to the function of the water table?	What is the water table and how can it be altered?		*Assessment: Digging the well: where is the best spot?*
What are the origins of pollution in the Hydrosphere and how do we control it?	What are industrial wastes and how do they contribute to pollution?	What is agricultural run-off and how does it play a role in pollution?	What is sewage and how does it play a role in pollution?	What are the long-term effects of pollution and what are some possible solutions for change?	*Assessment: Pollution debate: Who is right? Who is wrong?*

Table 5.12
Pre-Assessment, Ecology

Key Overarching Question 1:

Directions: Answer the following questions in any manner (picture, model, examples, sentences, etc.) you wish to show your current understanding of the questions at this point in our class.

1. How do urban development, mining, and construction change the surface of the Earth? What are the long-term effects?

2. How does farming change the surface of the Earth, and what practices are used to help cause soil conservation?

3. What are landfills and how are they changing the surface of the Earth? How have they changed from early landfills?

4. How do we restore natural areas, and what processes are involved?

- Where do you see pollution in your neighborhood?
- What pollution issues do you consider to be a problem in your world today?
- Have you ever seen mining or construction either on television or in action?
- What did you notice?
- Have you ever done anything to reduce the pollution when new city development has happened near your home?
- If so, what have you done? If not, why?
- What kinds of technology do you have around your house that cause pollution?

Further, the pre-assessment responses will help in developing the direction and critical design of lessons.

Problem-Based Lessons

We have used questions to guide us through the scope and sequence and the pre-assessments. Now we use them for lesson design.

For continuity, lesson two (Table 5.13) from the Ecology unit reiterates the scope and sequence's formative question. The lesson begins under day one with a question intended to draw out student understanding to focus thinking. Students are asked to share their questions and ideas in the development of key conceptual understandings, using textbooks only for ancillary information. In step two (Table 5.13), students are presented with the problem: How can you develop more ecologically sound farming practices. Students first record their own opinions; they share them with a partner and then with a group or team (a cooperative learning technique called Think-Pair-Share that actively invests everyone). The group has to devise a method for securing background information on the topic and then has to pose questions, the answers to which will help them develop their plan for land conservation. They will use these to access various sources and to interview guest experts. The students are now active researchers.

During day two (Table 5.13) student groups interview experts by using the inquiry process and the team's prepared questions. To conclude the lesson (day two, step two), students are asked to take their research and interview knowledge one step further. Having created their

Table 5.13
Lesson Two

How Does Farming Change the Surface of the Earth, and What Practices Are Used to Help Cause Soil Conservation?

Objectives: The student will be able to:
1. Describe and explain how farming can change the surface of the earth
2. Work with and interview agriculturists to discover innovative agricultural practices that help in conservation of the soil
3. Discover what strategies agriculturists use in soil conservation and implement those strategies through development and observation of an investigation
4. Develop concern for current farming practices and appreciate the value of organic procedures

Time Needed: One block of 120 minutes or two 30–60 minute periods

Materials: performance notebooks; farmers or agriculturists; aluminum trays with soil and seeds preplanted and now sprouting; organic items for fertilizers; video: *Smart Farming for America's Future,* Southern States Cooperative, Inc., 1994.

Procedure:
Day 1:
1. Pose the lesson's question. Allow time for students to respond in their notebooks and then time to share with a partner. Report back to the class and elicit ideas through questioning that may lead to: precious natural resources are being endangered as a result of our current agricultural practices. Plants are a renewable resource, that is dependent upon the soil. Soil is a limited resource that is of major importance in the production of food and fiber. Land for crop production is becoming more and more scarce as we see an increase in housing and industrial development. As we become more conscious of the world around us and our impact on that world, we need to consider ways in which we can become better stewards of the land. As agriculturists, we need to continue to practice new technologies and find more ways to be environmentally friendly. Also discuss ideas of erosion, contamination from fertilizers and pesticides, and tractor scares.
2. Pose the question: How could we find ways that will increase farm production and at the same time conserve the quality of the soil? Allow time for response in their notebooks, and time for sharing with partners and the class (Think-Pair-Share). Allow students to form teams. Elicit the idea that we could bring in some speakers and have experts demonstrate ways to conserve the soil. Ask students to write three to five questions they will ask the speakers.

Day 2:
1. Have speakers available from an agricultural school and have students use their questions discussed in their notebooks and in the class to interview the

(continues)

Table 5.13 (continued)

guests. The goal is to develop alternative strategies to conserve soil and its quality (organic farming, integrated pest management, use of nonmechanical plows). Some speakers may bring in activities to demonstrate their practices. Require all students to ask at least one written question.

2. To conclude the lesson and establish ongoing investigations, students in groups of three or four set up trays (plots of land) with seeds (crops), on which they can implement some of the ideas. They can simulate farming situations (erosion, use of organic farming versus chemical farming and pesticides) to get a sense of what can happen with land conservation. Students should create a table that they can check every three to five days to make observations and note when they add chemicals. A follow-up conclusion is included after 15–20 days. This portion of the lesson can be optional because it is ongoing even as you continue through other lessons.

Evaluation comes in notebooks, in interview questions and responses to guest speakers, and in the farming trays. Lesson 5 serves as an evaluation tool for all lessons under key question 1. A sample rubric follows in Table 5.14.

own investigation, they now apply the knowledge and skills gained through research, interview, and revision of their hypotheses. These are the synthesis and deep knowledge stages of learning that are so rarely reached in junior high schools.

Constantly in this lesson students are researching, writing, investigating, and revising their ideas and observations as recorded in their notebooks. Throughout, the teacher monitors, facilitates, and poses and elicits questions. The lesson then belongs to the students.

How will we know what the students have learned? In problem-based learning, objective assessment during each lesson can be somewhat difficult. Rubrics aid both in the process and in the evaluation of learning, however. Table 5.14 is a sample rubric for the previous lesson that pays particular attention to whether or not the student has met the academic objectives.

The category "Understanding of the Key Question" allows the teacher to objectively assess whether the student has mastered the concept or needs further work. Unfortunately, teachers feel they need to move on without really looking at whether students are ready. Many times students may grasp some but not all of the conceptual ideas. By adding this area of critique, we create a balanced form of assessment, one that supports self- and teacher-monitoring of learning.

Table 5.14
Sample Rubric

| | Ecology—Key Question 1, Lesson 2 | | | |
	6 pts.	3 pts.	1 pts.	0 pts.
Performance Notebook	Notebook contains complete opening questions' responses and student observation grid is complete, as well as a final conclusion from experimentation.	One of the following is missing or incomplete: opening questions' responses, student observation grid, or a final conclusion from experimentation. All are completed, but could be more thorough.	Two of the following are missing or incomplete: opening questions' responses, student observation grid, or a final conclusion from experimentation. All are completed, but could be much more thorough.	No responses given and no grid completed and no response or conclusion. Work is severely incomplete.
Interview Questions	Student completes three to five interview questions and asks at least one significant question to a guest speaker.	Student completes 2 interview questions and asks at least one somewhat significant question to a guest speaker.	Student completes only 1 interview question and/or asks a question already stated to the speaker.	Student does not participate in the questioning of the guest speaker and/or does not prepare any interview questions prior to the interview.

Farm Investigation	Experiment and hypothesis are designed, tested, and completed, and all observations are made at the appropriate intervals. Conclusions are made.	Experiment and hypothesis are designed, tested, and completed, and some observations are made at the appropriate intervals. Conclusion is somewhat made.	One of the following incomplete: Experiment, hypothesis, observations made at the appropriate intervals, or conclusion.	Experiment not completed, or severely incomplete work.
Understanding of Key Question	Student met all three objectives as demonstrated by the notebook, interview questions, and follow-up investigation.	Student met two objectives as demonstrated by the notebook, interview questions, and follow-up investigation.	Student met one objective as demonstrated by the notebook, interview questions, and follow-up investigation.	Student met no objectives as demonstrated by the notebook, interview questions, and follow-up investigation.

The Assessment

Traditional textbook assessments, particularly in science, are not developmentally appropriate for middle schoolers. Table 5.15 is a sample assessment for key overarching question number one. The assessment comprises only two questions, but they will require research, thought, and the ability to apply newly acquired content knowledge to a new situation in the role of an environmentalist. Even in the assessment, students are active researchers and problem solvers and now also advocates for their own neighborhoods.

In question one of Table 5.15, students are asked to:

1. Become environmentalists
2. Examine two cases of land destruction and alteration
3. Determine short- and long-term effects of farming/mining on the land
4. Develop a land restoration plan that would begin to restore the land

This is a more viable and thought-provoking task than asking a student to name three long-term effects that mining can cause on the earth's surface. The decisions students are asked to make in question two of Table 5.15 reflect a sound understanding of the inquiry method and how to approach a new situation with new concepts. The assessment, just as other parts of the lesson, is problem based, authentic, and performance based.

Conclusion: Problem-Based Learning

Now that you have created a problem-based, inquiry-focused classroom, what should you expect to see? Students' interest, not only in science but in other subjects, will take on new enthusiasm. Students who once fell to the bottom of the class or who did not participate start to make new strides and gains. Students have been given back the opportunity to think, to ask questions, to conduct research, and to reason through problems regardless of the format (classroom assessments, standardized tests). This is the goal of a problem-based classroom.

One of the problems middle grades teachers face is how to help students create deep conceptual knowledge when so many concepts and ideas in various content areas are so abstract. Further, how do you

Table 5.15
Assessment

How Can We Restore the Land?
Creating a Land Restoration Plan

For the final assessment, students will examine photographs of different situations (agricultural site, construction site, mining site, landfill site, or urban development site). Their task is to identify within the image what the attributes are and how the earth's surface has been altered. They also should identify the possible short- and long-term effects. Lastly, they develop a plan and explain the rationale for their strategies as to how they could/would restore the land as close to its original condition as possible. Students will draw from all their research and experiences in class to defend their plan. They may work in groups, in pairs, or alone using their notebooks.

Affective Objective: Students will become concerned activists about their environment and promote ways in which we can preserve our land.

1. On your desk are several pictures of various sites around your neighborhood where land has been altered in some fashion. You are an environmentalist working for the Environmental Protection Agency, and your job is to choose two of the situations and identify how the land has been altered (as many things as you see), the possible short-term effects and long-term effects, and how you would restore the land to its original condition.

   Within your answer you should include:
   a. What techniques would you use?
   b. Why these?
   c. What are the long-/short-term effects?
   d. How would you test to see if the restoration is working?
   e. What would a rough estimate of the cost be?
   f. How would the wildlife, etc., be protected?

2. This question is an extension activity.

   You and your family have 60 hectares of land, which you depend on for your livelihood. Ten hectares are cleared and grow enough food for your family. Fifty hectares are forested. You rely on the trees from your forested lands for fuel, since your house has no electricity. Your family has adequate food, clothing, and shelter, but everyone must work hard and there are no luxuries, such as running water, in your home.

   If you clear more land to grow soybeans for export, your family will have more money available for the "extras" in life. However, you also are aware that forested lands are rapidly disappearing in your area. You've heard that this can even cause changes in climate or in the productivity of your land. You must decide whether the long-term effects are worth the short-term gains. What will you do?

(continues)

Table 5.15 *(continued)*

Decision to be made: Will you clear forests to grow soybeans as a cash crop?
a. What are the short-term advantages of clearing the land?
b. What are the long-term advantages of clearing the land?
c. What are the short-term disadvantages of clearing the land?
d. What are the long-term disadvantages of clearing the land?
e. What is your decision and why?

help students relate those concepts to their own world so that it all makes sense? The answer lies in problem-based, inquiry-focused curricula. Overall the teacher is faced with the challenge of helping students develop a sound conceptual understanding of the content and helping them manipulate and apply that knowledge to their world both now and in the future.

Middle grades students engaged in hands-on, minds-on strategies in the problem-based classroom that uses inquiry-based techniques will demonstrate higher achievement on standardized tests and classroom assessments and will demonstrate more interest in their other classes.

Richard Schaffner

PROBLEM SOLVING

Since the 1970s students in the United States have achieved at lower levels in problem solving than students in other industrialized nations (Sorenson et al. 1996). As a result, professional organizations in social studies, language arts, and science have also stressed the importance of incorporating problem solving into the curriculum.

Problem solving involves working to obtain the solution(s) to a problem and engaging in a task in which the method for obtaining the solution is not readily available or known in advance (National Council of Teachers of Mathematics 2000). Problem solving may require students to use a variety of strategies and require several minutes, hours, or even days to arrive at a solution. Problem solving requires rigor and the use of higher-level thinking appropriate for middle grades students. There are three different methods of teaching problem solving:

1. Teaching for problem solving

2. Teaching about problem solving
3. Teaching through problem solving.

Teaching for Problem Solving

Some teachers and researchers argue that the best way to help students become better problem solvers is by teaching for problem solving, because the emphasis is placed on the student's acquisition of necessary skills, knowledge, and understanding (Southwell 1998). This involves teaching students basic skills and facts. No problem solving is explicitly taught. For example, math students may learn that they need to find a common denominator to add and subtract fractions without learning why or when. Language arts students may learn vocabulary words but fail to use the words correctly in a sentence. Social studies students may learn the core democratic values without learning why these values are important. And science students may learn that objects weigh less in space without understanding why.

Teachers who teach for problem solving often focus on memorization of facts rather than on a deep understanding of the content. They claim that students cannot become good problem solvers without knowing the basic skills. Therefore, they spend all of their time teaching students basic skills rather than challenging them to apply these skills to real-world situations.

Teaching about Problem Solving

Among those who argue against teaching for problem solving are teachers who teach about problem solving. This approach ensures that the student can use strategies or heuristics necessary for problem solving (Southwell 1998, 54). In order to become better problem solvers, students must understand the strategies and have the resources necessary for effective problem solving. The eleven most commonly used strategies for problem solving include:

- Guessing and checking
- Estimating
- Working backward
- Finding a pattern
- Making a map
- Making a chart or table

- Making a model
- Using lateral thinking
- Drawing a picture
- Using cooperative learning
- Solving a simpler version of the problem

Necessary resources may include manipulatives, graphs, charts, a risk-free environment, and the opportunity to work in cooperative groups.

Teaching about problem solving involves teaching students how to use each problem-solving strategy and resource, when to use the strategies and resources, and the most efficient and effective strategy or strategies to use when solving specific problems. Teaching about problem solving provides students with the tools necessary for becoming better problem solvers. It involves teaching problem solving as a separate entity, however, for it involves teaching lessons on problem-solving strategies and other lessons on basic skills. Students are taught each strategy, memorize and practice the strategy, and are then tested on the strategy. Therefore, no connection is drawn to how the strategy is connected to the rest of the curriculum.

Teaching through Problem Solving

Teaching through problem solving is the most widely used method across content areas because, unlike the other two approaches, it incorporates problem solving into every lesson. It is the mode through which all of the curriculum can be taught. Students learn the basic skills and facts through the use of problem solving itself.

There are several strategies for teaching successful problem solving:

1. *Use of manipulatives.* Manipulatives are objects that give students a physical representation of an idea and often enable students to make sense out of abstract ideas. For example, in studying areas of shapes, students can better understand relationships when they can physically manipulate plastic circles, wooden triangles, or paper parallelograms.
2. *Student discovery.* Students construct their own knowledge by performing experiments, by looking at how things work, or by relating something to personal experi-

ence, beliefs, or values in the constructivist sense. Chemistry students perform an experiment and discover how chemicals react. Students read a piece of literature and may come up with totally different conclusions based on differences in personal experience.

3. *Asking of open-ended questions.* Unlike closed questions, where responses are either right or wrong, open-ended questions require an explanation based on higher-order thinking. They often have more than one correct solution, thereby promoting student risk taking. These questions provide a means by which students can make sense of and explain their discoveries, for they require students to have a deep understanding of what they have learned. Students develop their ability to reason and think logically, rather than merely striving for errorless learning.

4. *Problem posing.* This is a strategy used to develop students' higher-order thinking skills, for it involves students' formulating their own problems and enables them to understand the significance of what they are learning. When students pose their own problems, teachers do not hear the dreaded question, "When am I ever going to have to use this?" Rather, the students pose questions that have applications to everyday life (Verzoni 1997). Problem posing is most effective at the end of a problem-solving activity because it demonstrates students' understanding of necessary strategies and of the relationship between the completed activity and the problem they posed. It helps students become more aware of the ingredients of well-formulated and poorly formulated problems, improves their problem-solving abilities, enriches their understanding of basic concepts, causes them to think in more diverse ways, and improves their attitudes toward the concepts being taught (English, Cudmore, and Tilley 1998).

5. *Cooperative learning.* Cooperative learning, which is examined following this discussion, is a strategy that encourages students to share ideas and frequently communicate.

Teaching through problem solving is the most effective means by which teachers can help students become accomplished problem solvers. It also meets the developmental needs of middle grades students because it embraces problem posing, student reflection, cooperative learning, alternative assessments, real-life applications, and various problem-solving strategies. Problem posing provides students the opportunity to make sense of concepts in their own way.

Often students of low socioeconomic status (SES) have difficulty understanding concepts because they are unfamiliar with the context in which the concepts are taught (Lubienski 2000). When they are involved in problem posing, students create the context for their problems and thereby feel a particular sense of autonomy.

Incorporating Problem Solving in the Classroom

In an English unit on persuasive essays, the teacher explains the parts of an essay. Students read several examples of essays, discuss how persuasive essays differ from other essays, and then read *Twelve Angry Men*. The students pay particular attention to the evidence given in the case. They are then divided into groups, each of which takes a side regarding who the criminal was. As a team, they present supporting evidence for and justify their conclusion. The debate is followed by a field trip to a courthouse. The students then choose how they want to be assessed: write a persuasive essay on a topic they feel strongly about or in a group of three or four create a script regarding a criminal case. The script must explain the case, evidence found, witness accounts, and arguments presented by both sides. The case is then presented to the class.

In a social studies unit on the Civil War, students begin by brainstorming sources of information. The students may write a newspaper or create a newscast regarding the events of the conflict. Topics that need to be addressed are the precipitating events, subjugation and slavery, religion, particular conflicts, economic power, war strategies, equipment, and life during the war for all groups of people. The class is divided according to its interests, and students are placed in groups of six, each with a particular role. The newspaper includes a front page, local news, cartoons, illustrations, and advertisements. Each group presents its final product to the class and then discusses how the group members solved their initial charge: "How does the Civil War affect us today?"

In teaching through problem solving in an art class, the teacher challenges the students to draw objects from different viewpoints (top, side, front, inside out, three-dimensional). The teacher begins the unit by taking students outside the school building and asking them to draw the building as they see it, moving from front, to side, to back. The students explain how and why the drawings are different. Students are then asked to predict what they think the top of the building would look like and draw it.

A science teacher teaches the scientific method through problem solving. He explains the six parts of the process and with the class creates an experiment. The students state the problem and then share their answers with the class, whose members critique the responses and choose the best statement of the problem. The students complete the experiment, share the results, and brainstorm possible individual experiments. Upon completion, each student presents his or her experiment in a science fair judged by professionals.

A math class is engaged in a unit entitled "Ratios, Proportions, and Percents." I use Matchbox cars to begin to explain ratios, as illustrated in Table 5.16. The cars contain a number on the bottom that shows the ratio of the Matchbox car to the dimensions of the actual car. In cooperative groups the students measure the Matchbox car and then calculate the length, width, and height of the actual car. This way students discover real-world applications of ratios. They then justify their calculations. In their cooperative groups they discuss how best to explain the methods they used. They share their findings with the rest of the class and learn from each other.

The final assessment of the unit is differentiated according to readiness. All students write a word problem that requires writing a proportion to solve. The lower-readiness students may write a word problem, however, in which the solution is any value. The at-grade-level group must write a word problem in which the solution is a decimal or fraction; finally, the higher-readiness group writes a word problem in which the solution is a specific answer that I give to them. All students demonstrate their understanding of proportions by posing problems that require setting up proportions to solve. Additionally, they connect proportions to their culture or personal experiences by posing a problem that involves something with which they are familiar.

To conclude the unit, we discuss percent of change. Students discover how they can use their knowledge of percents to solve problems involving discounts and price increases. The class is divided into groups of two based on readiness. Each group is given a list of items containing the original price of the item and the discount percentage. Students in the lower-readiness groups must formulate a shopping list of things they will buy. The items after the discount must total between $157 and

Table 5.16
Ratios, Proportions, and Percents

Unit Six, Lesson Two: Ratios and Proportions

Topic Question: How Are Ratios and Proportions Used in Everyday Life?

Content Standards Met:
- Select and use appropriate tools; measure objects using standard units in both the metric and common systems, and measure angles in degrees
- Use proportional reasoning and indirect measurements to draw inferences
- Apply measurement to describe the real world and to solve problems
- Express a numerical comparison as ratios and rates

Key Concepts: Ratios, proportions, models
Lesson Objectives: The student will be able to:
- Recognize how ratios and proportions are related
- Discover how ratios and proportions apply to real-life situations
- Use proportions to discover actual lengths of objects
- Work with other students productively
- Understand how models are used
- Measure lengths of models
- Justify their reasoning

Group Roles: (1) measure the model; (2) record the measurements
Materials Needed: Matchbox cars (must contain ratios written on the bottom), Measuring Models worksheets, centimeter rulers, camera, Solving for Unknown Heights worksheets, picture, map

Introduction: Show the students a picture, a map, and a Matchbox car. Ask the students if the measurements of these models are the actual measurements of the real objects. Ask them if the parts of these models have the same locations as the real objects.

Guided Practice:
1. Explain how the models from the introduction are drawn in proportion to the actual objects
2. Explain that proportions are two or more ratios that are equal
3. Go over the Measuring Models activity

Individual Practice:
1. Divide the class into groups of two; give each group a centimeter ruler, a Matchbox car, and the Measuring Models worksheets
2. Have students complete their measurements for their Matchbox car and then switch Matchbox cars with other groups until each group has completed their measurements for each Matchbox car
3. Have students complete the Measuring Models worksheets

Assessment: Students need to do the Solving for Unknown Heights activity.

$160. Students in the at-grade-level group create their shopping list in which items after discount and after adding 6 percent sales tax total between $157 and $160. Students in the above-grade-level group create their list in which items after discount have a total price of exactly $160. They calculate the total price of the items after adding 6 percent sales tax. All students then create an advertisement. To enhance their interest and to further their sense of autonomy, they choose what they want to advertise and can present it in a poster, brochure, video, newspaper ad, magazine ad, or tape recording. They all write the original price and the percent of discount and explain how they calculated the sale price before and after adding sales tax.

Conclusion: Problem Solving

Teaching through problem solving applies to all subject areas and grade levels. For successful experiences using problem solving, teachers should keep in mind:

- Engaging students actively on a daily basis
- Involving students in a variety of activities
- Using hands-on activities, student discovery, cooperative learning, and problem posing
- Helping students recognize the significance of the concepts by relating them to real-world problems
- Giving students autonomy
- Showing the interrelationship of concepts
- Differentiating learning tasks to ensure that all students are challenged but experience success

Problem-solving skills are extremely important in fostering critical thinking strategies. Students need to learn how to solve the problem, not just discrete facts. Harden and Davis (1998) identified three important steps that place emphasis on the process of solving a problem and that activate prior knowledge:

1. Introduce relevant vocabulary before students examine the problem
2. Present the problem and have students identify and study related learning issues
3. Apply the concepts they have mastered to answer the problem

To arouse curiosity or reveal misconceptions, teachers often give students a discrepancy investigation. This is an activity used to create conflict in students' thinking—what they believe will occur and what really happens (Appleton 1997). This technique not only dispels misconceptions but also is a tool that encourages students to ask questions about what they observed. Then the students design experiments to answer their questions. By analyzing and researching data, by engaging in problem solving itself—including defining the problem; gathering facts; generating possible solutions; refining solutions; designing, building, and constructing solutions; and evaluating solutions—they begin to construct new schemata or knowledge. Discrepant events arouse students' curiosity and encourage them to apply problem-solving skills while they explore possible outcomes.

In inquiry-based, problem-based, and problem-solving classrooms, cooperative learning is an important instructional strategy. The National Council of Teachers of Mathematics (2000) called for students to be able to learn from each other and to communicate effectively. Students of low SES and low achievers generally learn best in cooperative learning environments (Banks 1988; Irvine and York 1995). All students learn valuable socialization skills from schools and in particular through cooperative learning.

Matt Admiraal

COOPERATIVE LEARNING

Cooperative learning is a name applied to a group of instructional techniques that thoughtfully place a small number of students together to accomplish a group task. Rather than simply a grouping mechanism, cooperative learning has four specific elements, each of which must be present for the strategy to be considered cooperative:

1. Social interaction that is face to face
2. Positive interaction among all members of the team
3. Interdependence that prevents the team from completing the task unless each member fulfills the designated role
4. Individual accountability that charges each member to contribute to the task

Not only does the team (usually grouped by mixed ability) accomplish the designated learning task, the members also benefit from the affective interaction of successfully working together, often with students with whom they may not have otherwise worked. Given the social and intellectual characteristics of young adolescents, cooperative learning is one of the best suited instructional practices. Developed by Johnson and Johnson (2000), cooperative learning has proven to increase academic performance, improve student self-worth at a time of particular vulnerability, contribute to a burgeoning sense of individual accountability and responsibility, challenge students to problem solve and therefore engage in higher-level thinking, and hone group skills necessary for democratic participation.

Of the 120 forms of cooperative learning, some of the more frequently used groupings are:

1. Role Playing—After groups have been selected, students are assigned a "role." For example, students are asked to build a tower that would hold the weight of a given textbook. They are assigned the "roles" of recorder (write down the thought processes of the group), reporter (share the processes and results with whole group), budget analyzer (determine the construction cost and materials used), and construction engineer (supervise the building project). The roles increase both individual and group accountability, provide an avenue for communication within the group, and foster self-esteem by providing students with a valuable part in the completion of the task. Groups are mixed socially, racially, ethnically, and by readiness levels. When students are placed in heterogeneous groups, they are more likely to hear views that differ from their own, learn to appreciate differences, and be more accepting of other opinions (Leonard and McElroy 2000).

2. Checkmates—Groups compare homework answers or class assignments. Answers that differ should be circled and discussed. Groups teach each other various methods for answering a problem, and a consensus is drawn as to the correct answer. Once an agreement is made, students may not change their answers. In assessing accountability, teachers may randomly choose students to answer problems for the whole class. Students must be able to communicate and explain the team's thought processes in determining the answer. If unable to do so, the group is redirected for further discussion and teaching among the group.

3. Roundtable—One group member has pencil and paper (guidesheet). He or she reads the question aloud. Group members consult and refer to text /notes /reference materials in order to agree on an answer. The group member with the pencil and paper writes the answer. The answer sheet is then passed to the next group member and the process is repeated. A variation on this technique is to answer questions in rounds, setting a time limit on answering questions. Students answer as many questions as possible in a given amount of time. Answers are then shared, discussed, and verified by the whole group. Students also discuss strategies that help them accomplish the task as a team. Students return to another round of questions.

4. Team Consulting—All group members have a worksheet. All pencils remain in the middle of the table as students discuss a question. When the group has reached a consensus, all students write the answer. The teacher randomly collects one sheet from the group.

5. Group Consulting—This technique may be used alone or in conjunction with the above method. Students work in groups to complete a given assignment. Papers are then traded with another group to be analyzed and discussed. Students write comments or answers with which they disagree. Positive comments are added to answers they feel are especially well written. Once groups trade back papers, students revisit questions with comments and reevaluate answers, changing answers if necessary.

6. Group Investigations—Groups of students work to complete a given project. Although projects are varied, all place an emphasis on higher-level thinking skills. Example projects include creating a cartoon, song, or poem; illustrating a concept related to a unit of study; forming a debate team in which members of the team form subgroups to defend the viewpoint of a given societal issue; or creating a mnemonic device to help remember key terms in a unit of study. In each example, students have a hand in determining which project they will complete and how the final outcome will be achieved. This will increase student ownership and accountability from the project.

7. Jigsaw—This method is especially useful with text information. Students are placed in groups to learn part of a

specific topic. They are responsible for becoming "experts" on the given topic. "Experts" from each group then meet with "experts" from others groups and teach each other the information they have learned. Finally, "experts" join their original groups to discuss information learned. If any questions arise, members may return to the "experts" for clarification.

Other often-used forms of cooperative learning include Student Teams Achievement Division (STAD), Teams Games Tournaments (TGT), and Think-Pair-Share.

Conclusion: Cooperative Learning

In mainstreamed schools in the United States, where special education students are active members in "regular" classrooms, cooperative learning has proven to be effective both in socialization and in academic achievement for all students. Given the competitive spirit of a capitalist society, educating young people to work together is not only productive but also morally sound.

Kim Phelps

VARIED PERSPECTIVES

It is worthwhile to frequently pause and ask "To whom do schools belong?" The answer to that question resonates in the kinds of programs and practices in which the school engages and provides for its students. Schools are for students and their families. It is the responsibility of all who are in decisionmaking positions to maximize both the potential for growth and the civic principles of community that our schools represent. Traditional school practices may not seem intimidating from the teacher's vantage point; but when examined from the student's or the family's point of view, we may draw other conclusions.

STUDENT-LED CONFERENCES

Parental involvement plays a pivotal role in student achievement. Student-led conferences can be used as an effective tool to engage middle level students, parents, and teachers in an authentic partnership. Students are enabled to reflect upon their own educational progress in a format that allows them to present their own work and their critical thinking about it to their families. Frequently when family members sees their child's work in this setting, they more often support homework.

During the middle grades years, the need for effective family-teacher communication increases as students move from the security of the self-contained elementary classroom to the potentially less personalized environment of middle school. With a developing need to increase independence, students tend to be reluctant to share school information with their family.

As students progress through middle school, they are expected to assume responsibility for their academic progress. They are usually excluded from traditional parent-teacher conferences (Hackman 1996). Students tend to view these conferences then with distrust, seeing teachers and their family "talking behind their backs." Instead of encouraging open communication among parents, students, and teachers, traditional conferences exclude the student.

Students possess the most intimate knowledge about their academic progress; therefore, they should have the opportunity to participate in their conferences to the extent of taking responsibility for the conference's content, implementation, and assessment. During the student-led conference, family and students are given the opportunity to focus on the student's academic progress in a one-on-one guided setting with the teacher present. Students provide the rationale for their academic progress, based on prepared portfolios, as opposed to a teacher using a grade book and speculating about the positive and negative reasons for that child's academic performance.

The primary purpose of a student-led conference is to encourage students to accept personal responsibility for their academic progress and for reporting it to their family (Guyton and Fielstein 1989). When students take ownership of their academic progress, they are more likely to achieve success. This also recognizes young adolescents' steady progress toward adolescence and their need to assume greater control over their personal growth.

Portfolios

A portfolio is a collection of the student's work and reflections, teacher's observations, and information gathered as a result of learning inventories and assessments. Portfolios can help teachers:

- Make instructional decisions and recommendations about learning activities
- Monitor educational outcomes
- Identify and share information about the student's strengths and needs (Salend 1998)

Organization

The type of portfolio used should effectively meet the goals of both teacher and student. Items to be placed in the portfolio are usually kept in individual working folders, accordion file folders, three-ring binders, or boxes located in an accessible location. The contents of the portfolio vary, but usually include student's goals and objectives and examples of major projects for all core and encore classes. Often portfolios are organized by student interests, thematic units, or in chronological order. Students frequently personalize their portfolios by covering them with photographs, pictures, or logos.

Teachers and students are beginning to use technology and multimedia applications to store and organize portfolio materials (Edyburn 1994; Stiggins 1997). These include videocassettes, work scanned onto a computer diskette or laser disk, compact disk (CD) writers, and photo CD technology to record pictures and add sound and text.

Item Selection

Teachers may select assignments or projects that represent major conceptual understanding. Projects, tests, and papers can be included and are often identified by the students during a special selection day. When students share their portfolios with each other, their sense of self-assessment is given an authentic context. Effective portfolio development finds educators initially guiding the item selection process; as students become more experienced with portfolio selection, however, they assume a greater role in the selection.

Reflection

Many educators feel portfolios are particularly valuable because they provide students opportunities for self-assessment and self-reflection. In many school settings, students are not involved in self-assessment and generally have restricted views of their strengths and limitations, goals and achievements. Through portfolio development, students are directly involved in self-assessment as they organize, select entries, share their work with others, and evaluate their own work for their portfolios.

An important part of the evaluation process is the student's identification of his or her own strengths and weaknesses. Additionally, students are given the opportunity to elaborate about the changes they would make if given the opportunity to redo the assignment. The focus of self-reflection is never negative but encourages honest recognition of strengths, areas to work on, and subsequent goal setting.

Conference Preparation

Students begin their portfolios by setting goals for their school year (Table 5.17). Emphasis is placed on showing academic improvement throughout the year. Students take the goals home to be evaluated and signed by themselves and their family. These goals then become the first section in their portfolios. During the fall conferences, students and families examine the goals and talk about strategies that will help students reach their goals.

Emphasis throughout the year is placed on students' reflecting on their work, as illustrated in Table 5.18. They are told that certain assignments specifically chosen by each content-area teacher will be included in the portfolios. Students who have not completed required work samples are asked to fill out a "My Excuse" form. On this form the student identifies the project and explains in his or her own words the reason for not completing any assignment not included in the portfolio.

Students have the option to include in their portfolios any assignments of which they are particularly proud. They also have "Student Choice" assignments followed by a reflective piece that asks them to analyze why the work was successful. Encouragement to keep an organized portfolio leads to a more effective presentation.

Three weeks before the scheduled conference date, letters are sent home that:

1. Explain the student-led conference process (Table 5.19)
2. Invite the family to attend the portfolio presentation (Table 5.20)
3. Ask the family to choose convenient times to attend their child's conference (Table 5.21)

Table 5.17
Goals for Success

West Middle School Goals for Success

Name _____ Date _____ Grade _____

My strengths are:
   A.
   B.
   C.

I need to work on:
   A.
   B.
   C.

My First Goal…

_____

_____

To achieve this goal, I will
   A.
   B.

My Second Goal…

_____

_____

To achieve this goal, I will
   A.
   B.

My Third Goal…

_____

_____

To achieve this goal, I will
   A.
   B.
People who can help me attain these goals are:

Distractions that get in the way of accomplishing these goals are:

_____   _____
Student Signature   Parent Signature

272

Table 5.18
Assignment Reflection

Portfolio Assignment Reflection

Name _____ Date _____

Assignment Name _____ Class _____

What did you like about this assignment?

_____

_____

What do you feel was your greatest strength in completing this assignment?

_____

_____

What do you feel was your greatest weakness in completing this assignment?

_____

_____

What can you do to improve this weakness?

_____

_____

What did you learn through the completion of this assignment?

_____

_____

If you could start this assignment all over again, what changes would you make?

_____

_____

If you were to rate the amount of effort you put into this assignment on a scale of 1–10 (1 being the least amount of effort and 10 being the best you can possibly do) how would you rate yourself? Why?

_____

_____

_____

_____

Table 5.19
First Family Letter

February 19, 2002

Dear Team 7B Parents,

Spring conferences are around the corner, and I wanted to inform you of a change this semester regarding conferences. Instead of the traditional conference setting, we are going to a student-led conference format. A student-led conference allows students to share with you their academic progress, show you what they have learned, and discuss their future plans. You could learn more about your student's progress by talking with them, rather than with the teachers alone. By following the student-led conference format, the student will be involved and not excluded as in the traditional conference. I believe this style of conferencing will help students achieve several goals:

- Accept more responsibility for their work
- Learn to organize, present, and communicate
- Learn to self-evaluate
- Become more accountable

The student-led conference format will promote student goal setting, reflection, and responsibility for meeting their goals. Of course you can also speak to any teacher privately by setting up another conference time. I hope this will be a positive experience for everyone involved. I am so convinced that student-led conferences can be a beneficial component at West Middle School, I am evaluating the process as a main component of my Master's degree thesis. I will welcome parent, student, and teacher feedback. Your evaluations will be used in the further development of the student-led conference format.

*If you have any questions or concerns please feel free to contact me. I look forward to seeing you at conferences.

Sincerely,
Mr. Podlewski

The letters indicate that scheduling requests will be honored in the order in which they are returned. There are usually three conferences going on simultaneously in a classroom. Usually conferences run from fifteen to twenty minutes each, and the teacher participates for five minutes before moving to the next family.

One week prior to the conferences, students revisit their goals for success (Table 5.22). Students assess themselves in each subject area con-

Table 5.20
Second Family Letter

Team 7B 2001–2002
Spring Student-Led Conferences
Mrs. Bryant and Mr. Podlewski

Dear Parents of _____,

Thursday, March 7, and Friday, March 8, have been selected as conference days for student-led conferences (portfolio presentations).

Your child will be taking some time to prepare for a one-on-one conference with you to discuss current progress report grades and his or her self-evaluation of the efforts to achieve those grades. We are hoping this will be a positive and meaningful experience that will open up added communication and evaluation at home.

Listed on the following page is a time schedule. You will be scheduling a conference with your child's first hour teacher _____. Please select a time during one of the scheduling opportunities listed on the next page. Number the choices 1-2-3 so that we can best accommodate you with a time that is suitable for your busy schedule. We will do our very best to schedule your first choice. Please keep in mind that this scheduled 20–25 minute conference is an opportunity for your child to present the portfolio and reflect upon academic progress. You may continue the conference at home, or schedule an additional (traditional) conference with your child's teachers on another day.

Our students have been working very hard to prepare their academic portfolios. In addition, they will be spending time over the next few weeks preparing for their presentations. The main goal of these conferences is to provide students with the opportunity to take ownership of their academic progress. Please make every effort to attend the scheduled conference time.

*If you have any questions, please feel free to call Mr. Podlewski.

---

tained within the portfolio (Table 5.23). Teachers then use the same subject area assessment (Table 5.23) and rate the students' work. This form also allows teachers to make personalized comments for each student.

The next stage of preparation is the organization process. The teaching team generates a table of contents used as an organizational tool to gauge whether major assignments have been completed. The students then write brief letters to their families, introducing their portfolios. They also state some of the strengths and weaknesses of the portfolios (Table 5.24).

Table 5.21
Third Family Letter

Dear Parents/Guardians,

This year's student-led conference days are scheduled for Thursday, March 7, and Friday, March 8. Conferences will be held with your child's first hour teacher. Afternoon and evening time slots are available. Please indicate you first, second, and third choices for the times listed below. We will do our best to accommodate your first preference. Up to three conferences may be held concurrently in each classroom.

*Mr. Podlewski is the wrestling coach at West Middle School. Unfortunately, the team has a meet scheduled for Thursday March 7, in the late afternoon/evening. As a result, afternoon conferences on March 7 will be scheduled in Mrs. Bryant's room only. Evening conferences scheduled on Friday, March 8, will be held in Mr. Podlewski's room.

List in order your 1st, 2nd, and 3rd choices.

Thursday, March 7	Friday, March 8 (Mr. Podlewski's room only)
_____ 12:30–1:00	_____ 3:00–3:30
_____ 1:00–1:30	_____ 3:30–4:00
_____ 1:30–2:00	_____ 4:00–4:30
_____ 2:00–2:30	_____ 4:30–5:00
_____ 2:30–3:00	_____ 5:00–5:30
(Mrs. Bryant's room only)	_____ 5:30–6:00
_____ 5:00–5:30	_____ 6:00–6:30
_____ 5:30–6:00	_____ 6:30–7:00
_____ 6:00–6:30	
_____ 6:30–7:00	
_____ 7:00–7:30	
_____ 7:30–8:00	

_____   _____
Student Signature   Parent Signature

Honoring of scheduling requests will be based on the order in which the letters are returned, and on availability.

Sincerely,
Mrs. Bryant and Mr. Podlewski

Table 5.22
Goals for Success

West Middle School Goals for Success—Revisited

Name _____   Date _____   Grade _____

My First Goal was:

_____

_____

List two things you have done (or are doing) to meet this goal.

1. _____

_____

2. _____

_____

What are two things you can do (or continue to do) to make sure you are successful in meeting this goal?

1. _____

_____

2. _____

_____

Circle the word that describes your effort to date in meeting goal #1:

None   Little   Some   Good   Excellent

My Second Goal was:

_____

_____

List two things you have done (or are doing) to meet this goal.

1. _____

_____

2. _____

_____

What are two things you can do (or continue to do) to make sure you are successful in meeting this goal?

1. _____

_____

2. _____

_____

Circle the word that describes your effort to date in meeting goal #2:

None   Little   Some   Good   Excellent

(continues)

Table 5.22 (continues)
_____

My Third Goal was:
_____
_____

List two things you have done (or are doing) to meet this goal.

1. _____
   _____

2. _____
   _____

What are two things you can do (or continue to do) to make sure you are successful in meeting this goal?

1. _____
   _____

2. _____
   _____

Circle the word that describes your effort to date in meeting goal #3:

None   Little   Some   Good   Excellent
_____

The final part of the portfolio preparation is the inclusion of a Family Homework letter (Table 5.25). Through this process, the family writes a letter to the student that is a positive personal note about the conference. The students then spend a few days prior to the conference practicing the presentation. The gains in ownership of one's work, in responsibility, and in academic achievement far outweigh the time some may see as questionably spent.

Conference Implementation

The students practice their portfolio presentations using a script (Table 5.26). Students are encouraged to write any notes on their script to help them during the conference. They engage in "mock" presentations with a peer who then offers supportive suggestions and the roles are reversed. In this way students experience what their family is going to be examining. Table 5.27 offers an example of the assessment students use to practice in preparation for the family presentation.

After setting up tables in each of the three classroom areas and a main table where the family signs in and greets the teacher, postconfer-

Table 5.23
Self-Assessment

Math

Name _____
Teacher _____   Class Period _____

Class Expectations	Ratings:	Student	Teacher
1. Works well independently		_____	_____
2. Works well with others		_____	_____
3. Completes assignments on time		_____	_____
4. Uses time wisely in class		_____	_____
5. Has a positive attitude		_____	_____
6. Treats people with respect		_____	_____
7. Participates in class		_____	_____

Missing Assignments: (See Progress Report)

Key to Ratings:
+ Exceeds Expectations   ✔ Meets Expectations   –Needs Improvement

Comments:

_____
_____
_____
_____

_____

ence questionnaires are made available for the student (Table 5.28) and for the family (Table 5.29).

After securing materials from the main table, students guide their families to the designated area of the classroom. The students then present their portfolios and use their script. Teachers move from group to group and answer questions. Usually the conferences are focused on academic achievement. Any conduct or affective concerns on the part of the family are directed to another time, either scheduled during team time or after school. What consistently happens, however, is that as students and their families move through conference presentations, students' behavior in class no longer merits any particular attention apart from its role in supporting further academic growth.

Table 5.24

Family Introduction to My Portfolio: "Dear Parent" Examples

Dear Mom,   2-20-02

Welcome to my mind-blowing portfolio. You will be seeing my magnificent work from various classes. These classes are Language Arts, Math, Science and Social Studies. I'm really excited that you will get to see my divine piece of writing that I did in Language Arts.

My greatest strength is that I work independently. My greatest weakness is I don't always get my work in on time.

Thank you for coming. I hope you learn from all this that I work really hard.

Love,
Sara

Dear Mom and Dad,   2-20-02

In this portfolio are some samples of my work from school.

Even though I haven't been here long, I have done lots of work. Some are good examples and some I still need to work on.

A subject I like a lot is science with Mr. Podlewski (He is the best science teacher ever). Another subject I like is Math with Mrs. Bryant. I know I have a few missing assignments, but I plan to work very hard to do better.

Love,
Your Son,
William

Conference Evaluation

The first assessment of student-led conferences focuses on family attendance. A local Title I school consistently saw only 9–10 percent of its families come to traditional parent-teacher conferences. When the staff moved to student-led conferences—following staff development and planning over the summer—the next conferences saw 92 percent of the entire school's families.

Table 5.25
Family Homework

Family Homework

Dear Parent/Guardian,

THANK YOU for participating in your child's conference. Now you have some homework.

Please write your child a positive personal note about the conference. Below are some areas you might think about including as you write:

- What I noticed about your work was . . .
- I was proud of you for . . .
- Keep up the good work on . . .
- I know you have difficulty sometimes, but . . .
- I'm glad you are making an extra effort in . . .
- How can I help you?

We hope this experience was as rewarding to you and your child as the process was to us. Thanks again for taking the extra effort!

Sincerely,

The Seventh Grade Team B Teachers

The evaluation process involves analyzing the questionnaires and making necessary modifications. Student-led conferences can be developed not only to enhance academic development but also to set in motion the notion that the voices of the student and of the family are fundamental to a school culture of openness and ownership.

Timothy S. Podlewski

TRANSITIONS: LIFE PRESERVERS

Just as middle grades students are experiencing physical, emotional, psychological, and social transitions, the school that is mindful of the educational transitions students experience are often able to make a smoother segue for them among institutions (elementary, middle grades, high school). There has been a great deal of research conducted on the transition from elementary to middle school (George and Alexander 1993;

Table 5.26
Conference Script

Student Procedure for Conferencing

1. Introduce your parents or guardian to the attending teacher.

2. Explain that you will be presenting your academic portfolio during the conference.

3. Briefly review the Table of Contents to give an overview of what is in your portfolio.

4. Read your "Dear Parent" letter.

5. Present your work.
   For each class:
   a. Share the information on the cover sheet.
   b. For each assignment share:
      • What the assignment was
      • What knowledge or skills you learned by doing the assignment
      • What process you went through to complete the assignment
      • What grade you earned on the assignment
      • Main ideas from your Assignment Reflection piece by reading them aloud

6. Share your third marking period progress reports (compare to first marking period progress reports).

7. Share West Middle School Goals for Success.

8. Share and discuss Goals for Success—Revisited.

9. Give your parents their "Assignment Sheet" and ask them if they would be willing to write you a note as explained on the sheet. What they write can be kept at home or returned to school to put in your portfolio.

10. Thank your parents for attending your conference.

Forte and Schurr 1993; George et al. 1992). There has been little focus on the transition from middle school to high school, however.

The goal of most ninth-grade programs (given that middle schools continue through eighth grade) is to assist students in finding a path to calm the white-water years of adolescence. Umphrey (1998) identified the following areas of concern for upcoming ninth-grade students:

Table 5.27
Observation Format

Student-Led Conference Observation

The job of the observer is to watch the speaker (student) and make a check that represents how well the speaker (student) did in each category, from A being the best to E being the worst.

A B C D E

☐☐☐☐☐   Student is making good eye contact.

☐☐☐☐☐   Student is organized in following his/her outline.

☐☐☐☐☐   Student is speaking with good English and with a normal tone of voice.

☐☐☐☐☐   Student is talking at a normal rate of speed.

☐☐☐☐☐   Student is being positive about himself/herself and about the conference.

☐☐☐☐☐   Student is not fidgeting in his/her seat while presenting.

☐☐☐☐☐   Student is being sincere (honest) while presenting.

☐☐☐☐☐   Student is explaining why he/she got his/her grades

☐☐☐☐☐   Student is showing responsibility for his/her work. (I got this grade because . . .)

☐☐☐☐☐   Student is showing responsibility for his/her behavior.

Additional comments:

_____

_____

*Please review assessment and comments with the presenter.

---

1. Large amounts of homework
2. Larger number of students and more crowded hallways
3. More complex schedules
4. Being unable to find classrooms
5. Limited amount of study time during the school day
6. Less guidance
7. Long writing assignments for which they feel ill prepared
8. Balancing the demands of increased homework and social activities
9. Receiving less attention than they enjoyed in middle school

Similar studies (Rossi and Stokes 1991) showed that students soon to be high schoolers express the same fears they felt coming into

Table 5.28
Post-Conference Student Questionnaire

Post-Conference Student Questionnaire

Dear Student,

Thank you for participating in Student-Led Conferences this year. We hope you found this experience to be rewarding. Your feedback is very important in helping to plan for future conferences. Please feel free to make additional comments on the back.

7th Grade Team B Teachers

Student Name _____

1. I like the Student-Led Conference format.

Strongly Agree	Agree	Not Sure	Disagree	Strongly Disagree
1	2	3	4	5

2. Children should be accountable for their own academic progress and should make plans for improvement.

Strongly Agree	Agree	Not Sure	Disagree	Strongly Disagree
1	2	3	4	5

3. I took responsibility for my learning.

Strongly Agree	Agree	Not Sure	Disagree	Strongly Disagree
1	2	3	4	5

4. I learned more about myself through this Student-Led Conference than from the traditional Parent-Teacher Conference.

Strongly Agree	Agree	Not Sure	Disagree	Strongly Disagree
1	2	3	4	5

5. I will need the skills practiced in Student-Led Conferences in the future.

Strongly Agree	Agree	Not Sure	Disagree	Strongly Disagree
1	2	3	4	5

6. I found keeping and maintaining an academic portfolio was beneficial this year.

Strongly Agree	Agree	Not Sure	Disagree	Strongly Disagree
1	2	3	4	5

Table 5.29
Post-Conference Family Questionnaire

Post-Conference Parent Questionnaire

Dear Parent/Guardian,

Thank you for coming. We hope you enjoyed your visit. Please take a moment to answer the following questions before you leave. Your feedback is very important in helping to plan for future conferences. Please feel free to make additional comments on the back.

7th Grade Team B

Parent Name _____   Student Name _____

1. I like the Student-Led Conference format.

Strongly Agree	Agree	Not Sure	Disagree	Strongly Disagree
1	2	3	4	5

2. Children should be accountable for their own work, communicate about their learning, set goals, and make plans for improvement.

Strongly Agree	Agree	Not Sure	Disagree	Strongly Disagree
1	2	3	4	5

3. My child took ownership of his/her learning.

Strongly Agree	Agree	Not Sure	Disagree	Strongly Disagree
1	2	3	4	5

4. I learned more about my child through this Student-Led Conference than from the traditional Parent-Teacher Conference.

Strongly Agree	Agree	Not Sure	Disagree	Strongly Disagree
1	2	3	4	5

5. My child will need the skills practiced in Student-Led Conferences in the future.

Strongly Agree	Agree	Not Sure	Disagree	Strongly Disagree
1	2	3	4	5

6. All of my questions/concerns were addressed by my child or the teacher (if needed).

Strongly Agree	Agree	Not Sure	Disagree	Strongly Disagree
1	2	3	4	5

middle school and undoubtedly will feel when they enter higher education: fear, anxiety, self-doubt, excitement, anticipation, confusion, and wonder.

There are some critical transition points that appear to be troublesome for outgoing middle schoolers:

1. Changing from self-contained classrooms to departmentalized classes
2. Changing school buildings
3. Moving to a school level where the philosophical approach and instructional process are different, although high schools are beginning to adopt many middle grades programs and practices (George 1995)

When students are really experiencing transition problems they display poor attendance, inappropriate behaviors, and failing grades. Often high schools tend to be more informal, larger, and more impersonal. With a larger number of curriculum choices and extracurricular activities comes a measure of self-doubt and a more negative view of oneself that—without the critical support of friends—could place the student in jeopardy. This becomes a charge for ninth-grade programs that could determine a student's future success.

The middle school has overcome many obstacles to redefine its organizational structure and to keep students in school when they were dropping out. The high school can replicate many of these very ideas to develop its own student-responsive programs.

High School

The high school is a bureaucratic organization that processes students through to graduation. It is very fragmented and highly departmentalized. It is an organization that does something to the students, not with them. As an organization it is isolated and compartmentalized. The bureaucratic standardization of American education has created one best system for teaching all students, even though students are individuals with different needs. High schools need to restructure their teaching of children. "We deal with adolescents' hearts as well as brains, with human idiosyncrasies as well as their calculable commonalities" (Darling-Hammond, Griffin, and Wise 1992, 8). Students are not products; they are humans with individual needs, curiosities, and desires.

High schools are run in a mechanistic way, with a formulaic routine to teaching a class. They speak of "delivering a service" to students by means of "instructional strategies." These terms are products of a factory model and include the preconceived notion that education is something that someone does to somebody. They thereby underrate the mystery, challenge, and complexity of learning and, as a result, operate at an extraordinarily wasteful level. One school's model that takes exception to the one-size-fits-all high school is the student-centered approach that is the basis for Project START (Student Transition and Readiness Team).

Transition from Middle to High School

Project START's main goal was to personalize the high school by providing support and encouraging involvement of the ninth graders. Project START's team (ninth-grade teachers, counselors, student assistance person, police liaison officer, school social worker, school psychologist, special education consultants, and administrative staff) provided communication, services, programs, and resources that promoted student growth, development, and academic achievement. Ninth graders were assessed through individual student meetings, parent contacts, classroom performance, traditional parent-teacher conferences, attendance records, and evaluations.

Athletic coaches and sponsors of academic and extracurricular clubs visited the middle school to advertise their programs. One week prior to the opening of school, ninth graders participated in an orientation tour of the school, their schedule, and a school handbook.

The ninth grade director (a special administrative position) established an after-school study program, and counselors were ready with peer tutors. Students were placed on weekly progress reports to assess their academic growth. Communication with the home was frequent because people were assigned only to the ninth grade. Additionally the team:

1. Sent monthly newsletters home
2. Ran small-group counseling sessions for study skills
3. Planned with a social worker, psychologist, student assistance person, and the family for students who were failing academically
4. Invited the family to meet with them
5. Coordinated support staff

6. Communicated and coordinated issues between staff, students, and the family
7. Provided personal counseling
8. Assisted with ninth-grade special programs
9. Met weekly to assess students of concern

Ideal Ninth-Grade Transition Program

Project START is only one example of many effective transition programs. After examining various programs, the following would be the type of program that would meet both the academic and the socioemotional needs of all students:

Team Members

Ninth-grade director, ninth-grade core academic team, ninth-grade counselors, department chairperson of special education, student assistance person, police liaison office, school social worker, and school psychologist.

Responsibilities:

Ninth-grade director: coordinates support staff; oversees students' attendance and behavior issues; communicates and coordinates issues among staff, students, and the family; oversees ninth-grade programs

Ninth-grade core: provides support system for academic team ninth-grade participants (120 in the Project START school); creates an integrated curriculum

Ninth-grade counselors: provide academic counseling for students; schedule ninth-grade students; provide personal counseling; lead academic and social support groups; and assist with ninth-grade programs

Special education chair: manages ninth-grade special consultants; manages education case load and the high at-risk student caseload; teaches study skills; assists with ninth-grade programs

Student assistance person: provides support and assistance for students experiencing severe emotional turmoil

School social worker: provides additional support for students experiencing severe emotional turmoil

School psychologist: assesses at-risk behavior and provides
support
School liaison officer: supports school on legal matters

Programs

Programs include such things as a ninth-grade academic school-within-a-school program, orientation, incoming ninth-grade parent night at the end of eighth grade, ninth-grade parent night at the beginning of ninth grade, welcome barbecue, Big Siblings Program, first day of school program, peer tutoring, study hall program, Jump START Camp, study skills program, academic and social support groups, and business partnerships.

Conclusion: Transitions

To meet the changing needs of society, schools must meet the needs of their students. Ninth-grade students are at a complex developmental phase in life. High schools are only beginning to realize the need to personalize the school for students. Instruction needs to be individualized and so do the programs offered to students. Yet, the high school must establish a way to provide students what they need with the resources available.

The school is no longer a place where students go just to receive an academic education. Schools are responsible for providing academic, social, and emotional support to all students. The insecurities of adolescent students can directly impact their success during this time of transition. The call for responsive programs is a call for a commitment to the next generation.

Jill Adamczyk

CHAPTER SUMMARY

The cultural diversity that paints the canvas of contemporary American society is an image of the nation's middle schools where all young adolescents learn how to work together, respect each other, celebrate their differences, struggle to find themselves, think critically and creatively, respect the culture and values of their own peoples, and learn what it means to become an educated person, a contributing member of the democracy.

Middle schools in the United States have not shied away from this great challenge. They have embraced their communities, their families, their students, their profession, and their nation's demands. They examine themselves, how they respond, and how they prepare young people for a world about which we have little conception. The teachers and administrators who have shared their successes in this text are champions of all that is right and good in our country. Daily they stand before and beside American youth, and their joy in their work is unparalleled. If freedom, as Camus believed, is nothing else than the chance to be better, then America's middle schools are places where people are free indeed.

REFERENCES

Appleton, Ken. 1997. "Analysis and Description of Students' Learning during Science Classes Using a Constructivist-Based Model." *Journal of Research in Science Teaching* 34 (March): 303–318.

Association for Supervision and Curriculum Development. 1997. *Constructivism.* Inquiry Kit. Alexandria, VA: Author.

Banks, J. A. 1988. "Ethnicity, Class, Cognitive, and Motivational Styles: Research and Teaching Implications" *Journal of Negro Education* 57: 452–466.

Barnum, C. 1996. "Bridging the Gap between the Old and the New: Helping Teachers Move toward a New Vision of Science Education." *Issues in Science.* Arlington, VA: National Science Teacher Association and National Science Education Leaders Association.

Beane, J. 1993. *A Middle School Curriculum: From Rhetoric to Reality,* 2d ed. Columbus, OH: National Middle School Association.

Brooks, J. G., and M. G. Brooks. 1993. *The Case for Constructivist Classrooms.* Alexandria, VA: Association for Supervision and Curriculum Development.

Brophy, J. 1986. *On Motivating Students.* Occasional Paper No. 101. East Lansing, MI: Institute for Research on Teaching. ED 276 724.

Caine, R. N., and G. Caine. 1991. *Making Connections: Teaching and the Human Brain.* Alexandria, VA: Association for Supervision and Curriculum Development.

Colburn, A. 1998. *Constructivism and Science Teaching.* Bloomington, IN: Phi Delta Kappa International. ERIC ED 426860.

Collins, R. P. 1994. "Middle School Science: A Problem-Solving Orientation." *Clearing House* 68 (1): 5–6.

Darling-Hammond, L., G. A. Griffin, and A. E. Wise. 1992. *Excellence in Teacher Education: Helping Teachers Develop Learner-Centered Schools.* Washington, DC: National Education Association.

Eccles, J., and C. Midgley. 1990. "Changes in Academic Motivation and Self-Perception during Early Adolescence." In G. R. Montgemayor, and T. Gullotta, eds. *From Childhood to Adolescence* (134–155). Newbury Park, CA: Sage.

Edyburn, D. 1994. "An Equation to Consider: The Portfolio Assessment Knowledge Base + Technology + the Grady Profile." *LD Forum* 19 (4): 35–37.

English, L. D., D. Cudmore, and D. Tilley. 1998. "Problem Posing and Critiquing: How It Can Happen in Your Classroom." *Mathematics Teaching in the Middle School* 4: 124–129.

Erickson, H. L. 1998. *Concept-Based Curriculum and Instruction: Teaching beyond the Facts.* Thousand Oaks, CA: Corwin Press.

———. 2001. *Stirring the Head, Heart, and Soul: Redefining Curriculum and Instruction.* 2d ed. Thousand Oaks, CA: Corwin Press.

Fecho, Bob. 2000. "Developing Critical Mass: Teacher Education and Critical Inquiry Pedagogy." *Journal of Teacher Education* 51, no. 3 (May/June): 194–199.

Forte, I., and Schurr, S. 1993. *The Definitive Middle School Guide.* Nashville, TN: Incentive Publications.

Fosnot, C. 1996. *Constructivism: Theory, Perspective, and Practice.* New York: Teachers College Press.

George, P. 1995. "Strengthening Transitions." *The High School Magazine:* 4–7.

George, P., and W. Alexander. 1993. *The Exemplary Middle School.* New York: Holt, Rinehart, and Winston.

George, P. S., C. Stevenson, J. Thomason, and J. Beane. 1992. *The Middle School and Beyond.* Alexandria, VA: Association for Supervision and Curriculum Development.

Goodman, L., and G. Bernston. 2000. "The Art of Asking Questions: Using Directed Inquiry in the Classroom." *American Biology Teacher,* no. 7 (September): 473–476.

Guyton, J., and L. Fielstein. 1989. "Student-Led Parent Conferences: A Model for Teaching Responsibility." *Elementary School Guidance and Counseling* 24, no. 2 (December): 169–172.

Hackman, D. 1996. "Student-Led Conferences at the Middle Level: Promoting Student Responsibility." *National Association of Secondary School Principals* 80, no. 578 (March): 31–36.

Harden, R. M., and M. Davis. 1998. "The Continuum of Problem Solving." *Medical Teacher* 20 (4): 317–322.

Hootstein, E. 1994. "Motivating Middle School Students to Learn." *Middle School Journal* 25, no. 5 (May): 31–34.

Irvine, J. J., and D. York. 1995. "Learning Styles and Culturally Diverse Students: A Literature Review." In J. A. Banks, ed., *Handbook of Research on Multicultural Education* (484–497). New York: Macmillan Publishing.

Jacobsen, E., P. Eggen, and D. Kauchak. 2002. *Methods for Teaching: Promoting Student Learning.* Upper Saddle River, NJ: Merrill–Prentice Hall.

Johnson, R. T., and D. W. Johnson. 2000. "How Can We Put Cooperative Learning into Practice?" *Science Teacher* 67, no. 1 (January): 39.

Klein, E. S., and E. Merritt. 1994. "Environmental Education as a Model for Constructivist Teaching." *Journal of Environmental Education* 25 (1):14–21.

Larson, R., and M. Richards. 1991. "Boredom in the Middle School Years: Blaming Schools versus Blaming Students." *American Journal of Education* 99: 418–443.

Leonard, J., and K. McElroy. 2000. "What One Middle School Teacher Learned about Cooperative Learning." *Journal of Research in Childhood Education* 14, no. 2 (Spring–Summer): 239–245.

Leonard, W. H., B. Speziale, and J. Penick. 2001. "Performance Assessment of a Standards-Based High School Biology Curriculum." *American Biology Teacher* 63, no. 5 (May): 310–316.

Lubienski, S. T. 2000. "Problem Solving as a Means toward Mathematics for All: An Exploratory Look through a Class Lens." *Journal for Research in Mathematics Education* 31: 454–482.

Lumsden, L. 1994. "Student Motivation to Learn." Eugene, OR: ERIC Clearinghouse on Educational Management. ED 370200.

National Council of Teachers of Mathematics. 2000. *Principles and Standards for School Mathematics.* Reston, VA: Author.

Palinscar, A. S., S. Magnusson, and K. C. Collins. 2001. "Making Science Accessible to All: Results of a Design Experiment in Inclusive Classrooms." *Learning Disability Quarterly* 24, no. 1 (Winter): 15–32.

Raffini, J. 1993. *Winners without Losers: Structures and Strategies for Increasing Student Motivation to Learn.* Boston: Allyn and Bacon.

Ramos, E. 1999. *Teaching Science Constructively: Examining Teacher's Issues When Teaching Science.* New York: ERIC Document Reproduction No. ED 436391.

Rossi, K. D., and D. Stokes. 1991. *Middle Level Education: Policies, Programs, and Practices.* Alexandria, VA: National Association of Secondary School Principals.

Salend, S. 1998. "Using Portfolios to Assess Student Performance." *Teaching Exceptional Children* 31, no. 2 (November/December): 36–46.

Sorenson, J. S., L. R. Buckmaster, M. K. Francis, and K. M. Knauf. 1996. *The Power of Problem Solving.* Needham Heights, MA: Allyn and Bacon.

Southwell, B. 1998. "Problem Solving through Problem Posing: The Experience of Two Teacher Education Students." In C. Kanes, M. Goos, and E. Warren, eds., *Teaching Mathematics in New Times* (2: 524–531). Gold Coast, Australia: Mathematics Education Research Group of Australia. ERIC Document Reproduction Service No. ED 429813.

Sprague, D., and C. Dede. 1999. "If I Teach This Way, Am I Doing My Job? Constructivism in the Classroom." *Learning and Leading with Technology* 27, no. 1 (September): 6–9.

Stiggins, R. 1997. *Student-Centered Classroom Assessment.* New Jersey: Prentice Hall.

Tomlinson, C. 1995. *How to Differentiate Instruction in Mixed-Ability Classrooms.* Alexandria, VA: Association for Supervision and Curriculum Development.

———. 1999. *The Differentiated Classroom: Responding to the Needs of All Learners.* Alexandria, VA: Association for Supervision and Curriculum Development.

Umphrey, J. 1998. "Mission Impossible? Creating Positive Transition for Students." *Leadership* 26 (9): 20–25.

Verzoni, K. 1997. "Turning Students into Problem Solvers." *Mathematics Teaching in the Middle School* 3: 102–107.

Weld, J. 1997. "Teaching and Learning Science." *Educational Horizons* 76, no. 1 (Fall): 14–16.

Wiggins, G., and J. McTighe. 1998. *Understanding by Design.* Alexandria, VA: Association for Supervision and Curriculum Development.

Zorfass, J. 1998. *Teaching Middle School Students to Be Active Researchers.* Alexandria, VA: Association for Supervision and Curriculum Development.

Chapter Six

⚫⚬ **Democracy Education**

Middle schools are charged with perpetuating the values and enduring concepts upon which our society is built. Among these formative ideas are democracy, human dignity, and cultural diversity (Beane 1993). If the process and practices of democracy are fundamental to the vitality and vigor of a society, they must be critically examined, exercised, and experienced by young adolescents as they begin to construct their sense of themselves in the world.

In this chapter, two award-winning middle grades teachers pragmatically grapple with the concept of democracy and transescents. Andrew Lindsay examines "Teen Regime," a democratic community that he and his students have created in their classroom based on Lindsay's critique of three basic questions:

1. How do classroom teachers understand what is meant by democratic teaching?
2. Why is teaching in a democratic fashion both important and developmentally appropriate for middle grades students?
3. How can a model of democratic teaching be constructed so that it is aligned with national and state standards to enhance student learning?

Lindsay contends that the importance of the role of education in developing and maintaining a democratic society is unquestioned. He believes that in order to appropriately prepare people to be active participants in a democratic society, an educational system must promote the values of community, liberty, and diversity. Perhaps one of the aims of education is to reconcile differences among the citizens in the community, differences regarding questions of who has authority and within what moral boundaries (Gutmann 1999). In developing theories about the social compact, Jean-Jacques Rousseau examined the role community plays in the formation of a democratic society; Thomas Jefferson wrote extensively on the preservation of basic liberties and inalienable rights; and Horace Mann recognized the need to educate all people, not just the wealthy elite. Democratic education requires students to bring the ideas of Rousseau, Jefferson, and Mann into a cohesive understanding of the democratic process.

According to John Dewey, the awareness of what a democracy is and what it means must be taught in a manner consistent with the ideals that a democracy represents. Further, education is a social process that must promote, the values of the society to the youth, but not impose them. "Such a society must have a type of education which gives individuals a personal interest in social relationships and control, and the habits of mind which secure social changes without introducing disorder" (1944, 23).

In other words, students are provided both a safe environment and a meaningful opportunity to engage in learning, to become empowered to make decisions, and to learn from the success or failure of those choices. Lindsay constructs his classroom on the following beliefs:

1. *Personal growth.* When educators approach education with the purpose of facilitating growth toward achieving personal potential for public good, the democratic nature of education is preserved as well as that of the community.
2. *Critical thinking.* An important part of developing individual potential for public good involves cultivating the mind to be capable of critical deliberation.
3. *Equitable access.* Democratic education must provide for equitable access to valued knowledge and full public demonstration of its result (full disclosure of successes and failures).

In "Academic Service Learning," Matthew Harbron looks at the young adolescent and democracy in the community through the lens of academic service learning. Both teachers translate the moral imperative of democracy and dignity into action in the growing lives of young adolescents.

TEEN REGIME: FROM CLASSROOM TO COMMUNITY

Democracy is the worst form of Government except for all those
other forms that have been tried.
                              —Winston Churchill

Although Winston Churchill was not speaking about middle schools, his statement about democracy holds true for the middle level environment just as much as it does for the political world. Middle level educators are beginning to realize that the healthiest, most developmentally appropriate classroom environment follows a democratic model that provides for meaningful student input in decisionmaking. To support their beliefs, theorists such as James Beane, Alfie Kohn, William Glasser, and others advocate involving students in the educational process with regard to curriculum, classroom management, and assessment of learning. According to *Turning Points 2000,* teachers should know how to create safe and supportive interpersonal school environments that promote proper, equitable outcomes for all students (Jackson and Davis 2000).

The purposes of democratic education are to provide an environment for students to experiment with critical problem solving and to offer rich experiences that engage students in the democratic process, so that in the end, students will become active participants in the democratic community. Teachers in the traditional teacher-centered classroom argue that allowing students to influence the curriculum and management of the classroom creates a muddled, undisciplined class without direction or focus. In today's standards-based environment of high-stakes testing, teachers argue that a tight schoolhouse leash is necessary in order to use every instructional minute to its fullest. As a result, students are becoming less and less responsive to teaching methods that they perceive as more oppressive.

In my classroom, I struggle with the constant battle of teaching important standards-based content while not losing my students to exasperating boredom. As students become more and more frustrated in a classroom that does not meet their developmental needs, they act out, seeking fulfillment of their needs to get up and stretch or to find out what their neighbor is doing. These actions, obviously, contradict what I am trying to accomplish in the lesson, and as a result, I take time from teaching to refocus and redirect my students to what I believe to be appropriate student behavior. The students are again frustrated, and I have lost precious moments of the instructional day. Furthermore, the more I push the lesson, the more students resist in the form of misbehavior or noncompliance. Schoolwide, students often ignore homework and come to class unprepared. The angst between teachers and students increases even more. Teachers begin to complain about students, and the students complain about the teachers. A hostile, adversarial environment has developed. A wall has been built.

The program called Teen Regime begins chipping down this wall of hostility without sacrificing any attention to required content standards. Class time is devoted to students' voicing their concerns about classroom issues, ranging from instructional methods to field trips, to issues as trivial as the number of blue colored pencils they have at their disposal. My students want to be seen and respected as equal partners in the classroom. In *This We Believe . . . and Now We Must Act,* the statement is made that middle school students should be provided an environment where they are able to "make their own decisions and increasingly take control of their own learning . . . [where] students 'own' the program" (Erb 2001, 37). Significant opportunities should be offered for students to take responsibility for the curriculum and school life. To provide opportunities for students to become more empowered in their education, we have developed a classroom government model that provides students an opportunity to give direction to classroom operation while also learning experientially about our nation's government, after which the model is fashioned. I want my students to be excited about school and about what they are capable of achieving through a democratic classroom government.

The curriculum of a democracy should allow student choice and self-direction with teacher facilitation in a collaborative, nonconfrontational manner. Adolescents need to experiment with dilemmas, problems, and roles that may or may not become part of their eventual identity as an adult. Furthermore, adolescents should all have a safe and secure place where these experimentations might occur. Middle schools provide the greatest opportunity for adolescents to find new friends, seek out new beliefs, and develop new ideas about themselves and the world around them

What Is Democratic Curriculum/Education?

The phrase *democratic education* eludes a singular, consistent definition acceptable to educational scholars and theorists. There is disagreement over its meaning, its development, its components, and its practices. For some scholars, democratic education is developed by the structure of the educational system in our nation and in our schools (Barber 1993; Bellah 1999; Meier 1995a; Sizer 1985 and 1992). For others, democratic education is developed within the curriculum and among relationships with students and teachers (Beane 1993 and 1998; Noddings 1999). And yet for others, democratic education is developed with certain theoretical aspects that must be present within the structure, curriculum, and relationships within the educational community (Gutmann 1999; Glickman 1990, 1991, and 1998). Democratic education may not be easy to define, but the diversity of opinions about its meaning is testimony to the importance of the concept.

Within education are issues of social relationships and control, cultivating certain habits of mind, as well as the perpetual concern of helping society progress without crumbling into chaos. For a democratic society, these concerns are paramount. In a democratic society, authority over control and social relationships does not reside in the authority of the state but rather with the people. Therefore, people must choose to use their personal talents and resources in a manner consistent with maintaining the state. Since education is imperative in a democratic society, what curricular implications does democracy provoke in helping people exercise their roles as citizens?

Democratic curriculum is developed in five basic ways. It:

1. reflects student diversity
2. meaningfully reflects and responds to student interests
3. connects the students with important, diverse, and current knowledge
4. inspires students to find joy in new discoveries
5. challenges students to imagine a greater world than the one in which they live (Barber 1993; Beane 1998; Glickman 1990, 1991, and 1998; Noddings 1999).

A democratic curriculum must provide all students the opportunity to learn a common body of knowledge in a meaningful and accessible way. Students should explore themes that emerge from their personal or social concern. After selecting a theme for examination, the students and teachers collaboratively determine what to explore in terms of concepts, problem solving, or issues without considering subject matter specificity (Knowles and Brown 2000).

The teacher develops curriculum based on observed capacities and needs of the individual students within the class. The curriculum developed by the teacher must adapt content to create experiences that respectfully challenge the needs of all students. In so doing, the teacher must walk the tightrope between creating learning opportunities that are flexible enough to, as Dewey stated, permit free play for individuality of experience and yet firm enough to give direction toward continuous development (1938). The curriculum the teacher creates should be premised on the belief that education is basically a social process. Within the development of these learning experiences, a teacher has a unique responsibility to foster appropriate interactions among the students. The quality of the social interactions helps define whether or not the learning experience has been beneficial. Again Dewey would agree that "when education is based on experience and educative experience is seen to be a social process . . . the teacher loses the position of external boss or dictator but takes on that of leader of group activities" (67).

Students should be empowered by their education to examine real issues and situations, to construct knowledge that enables them to critically analyze issues, and to develop ideas on how to take action. Young adolescents in particular are just becoming aware of the greater need for social order and their place in constructing beliefs and systems of accountability on issues of moral principle (Kohlberg 1970). Students should be treated with a commensurate respect that offers them a curriculum that challenges their views on meaningful issues and allows them to experiment with consequential decisionmaking in a safe, secure environment (Beane 1998). Real issues should help students make well-informed decisions.

In a democratic society in which citizens choose any means to satisfy their desires, the importance of knowing how to make sound decisions assumes an even more essential role. To make wise choices requires the ability to critically analyze information. The role of the teacher in guiding the students in developing good decisionmaking skills becomes keenly important (Noddings 1999). Students should be given the opportunity to question the validity of what they read or see. They should be taught to challenge what they perceive as truth and to critically extend their knowledge.

Part of inspiring students to experience the joy of learning is to foster in each child a vision of a better future. Democratic education challenges students to imagine a better world and to experiment with ways of making the world a better place. Students are given the opportunity to expand their knowledge beyond the capricious standards and benchmarks set by politicians and former educators who are divorced from the classroom. The students are challenged to see the democracy of the nation in its purest form and not through the vision of corporate leaders who kneel at the altars of greed, profit, and avarice. To be democratic a nation must be inclusive, not divisive; it must be progressive, not exclusive; and finally it must be cooperative, not insensitive.

Teachers' Roles in the Democratic Classroom

Teacher as Mentor

A teacher who believes in and practices democracy in the classroom must always be aware of the dual role of teacher and democratic participant. The ultimate responsibility for what happens in the classroom belongs to the teacher, so the teacher must always retain some form of authority. Authority that is gained by coercion or force alienates students, however, and erodes the democratic spirit. A teacher who wishes to engender democratic dispositions in the students must walk the tightrope between maintaining a classroom environment that reflects professional responsibilities while presenting opportunities for students to offer both voice and direction in the establishment and maintenance of the classroom environment.

In a democratic classroom, the teacher trusts the students. Periodically, a teacher takes a step of faith in creating opportunities for the students to guide the flow of the class. It is a faith guided by a trust that the students can and will make sound classroom decisions. Of all the characteristics of a democratic classroom, teacher trust of and for the students is the most foundational. The trust cannot be superficial either. Teachers cannot determine arbitrarily which issues to allow student input on and which to reserve exclusively for themselves. Students sense the hypocrisy as well as the evident lack of trust, and the opportunity to truly learn in a democratic setting fails to occur. By allowing meaningful student input into important classroom decisions, however, teachers allow students to learn how to make decisions, work together, and manage consequences in a supportive environment. The consequences for poor decisionmaking out on the street are quick and severe. There may not be an opportunity for an adolescent who makes a poor decision to rectify the situation without facing stringent consequences. In the classroom, however, students may make mistakes and learn from

them and be better prepared to make appropriate decisions independently later in life or even later in the same day.

Unfortunately, teachers often assume that students will always
seek to make decisions that are not in the best interests of curriculum or
classroom management. This assumption presupposes that students
purposely seek to do anything possible to thwart the efforts of the
teacher. In reality, students are decent, honest people who not only realize that they are in school to learn, but who want to learn if they are
taught in engaging, age-appropriate ways. The basic belief in the integrity of the students goes hand-in-hand with the assumption that
teachers must trust their students.

When disrespected, however, students, like their adult counterparts, will not (and should not be expected to) conform willingly to the
dictates of adults who are perceived as uncaring and unworthy of respect. Adolescents see adult role models all around them. They yearn
for respect from their parents, their teachers, and other adult authority
figures in their lives. Adolescents aspire to assume an appropriate place
among adults as a mark of passage from childhood to adulthood. When
treated with respect, young adolescents learn to treat others similarly.
When treated with disrespect, adolescents learn inappropriate coping
and communicating skills.

When a teacher assumes that students are decent and honest,
she will provide a classroom environment that accentuates the mutual
respect among all the participants in the classroom, including the relationship between the teacher and the student. In this classroom environment, students are willing to accommodate the needs of the teacher,
even if the efforts required by the student are not particularly desirable.
In return, the teacher accommodates the needs of the students at times
when it may not be the most convenient thing to do.

It is important to note, however, that in accommodating the
needs of the students, the teacher maintains final accountability for the
activities and actions that occur within the classroom. In a developmentally appropriate democratic fashion, the teacher always maintains
the role of the professional educator who is in charge of and responsible
for the classroom. The students respect the job that the teacher has to
do, because the teacher shows respect for the students in the lessons
that are planned as well as in the manner in which the classroom is
managed. The students learn appropriate behavior by following the
model presented to them by a teacher who serves as a mentor and who
addresses their unique adolescent cognitive, social, physical, emotional, and moral needs.

Teacher as Advocate

In constructing a classroom that acknowledges and accounts for the unique developmental needs of adolescents, a middle school teacher assumes an advocacy role for her students. As such, the teacher places herself in a position of concern for many different aspects of her students' learning and developmental growth. The role of an advocate in the middle school has many dimensions. From making sure that each student feels a sense of belonging at school to helping students find success within the academic and social environments, to fostering stronger communication between the home and school, the teacher, as advocate, embodies the commitment to the best interests of students.

Within the democratic classroom, a middle school teacher's role is to develop within each student a greater sense of citizenship and community. A healthy democracy depends on active, knowledgeable citizens capable of making meaningful and important decisions that impact the entire community. By presenting a classroom that provides for student voice and community, teachers forge a constructivist environment that focuses on students' becoming aware that there are greater responsibilities that must be accounted for prior to the apt exercise of authority. Students must assume a greater maturity for the tasks that must be accomplished in order to be seen as capable of credible, competent decisionmaking in the classroom. In other words, the students' approach to the use of shared authority in the classroom is mitigated by how they live according to democratic dispositions. Credible student decisionmakers must present themselves as democratic citizens in order to be effective leaders in a classroom democracy.

Democracy is much more than a means to govern. Democracy is also a way of life. The observed student responses to the following questions serve as a guide to the exercise of democratic attitudes:

- How well are all students accepted in a group?
- Are students invited to join each other's groups regardless of social standings, race, academic readiness, or other segregating factors?
- Are students comfortable about expressing their opinions openly without fear of rebuke?
- Are all students involved in some capacity?
- Are student leaders continuously aware of the needs of their peers?

Table 6.1
Lesson Calendar

Activity	Length of Time	Description
Lesson 1	1 period	Building a sense of belonging
Lesson 2	1 period	Explaining democracy
Lesson 3	1 period	Understanding rights and responsibilities
Lesson 4	1 period	Setting classroom and personal goals
Lesson 5	1 period	Creating classroom rules
Class Meetings	1 period, scheduled throughout the school year	Taking time to discuss issues of concern to the teacher and the students as well as plan for activities
Government Activities	1 period or less, varies throughout the school year	Using time to legislate additional rules, clarify existing rules, or plan activities
Service Learning Activities	1 period or more, depending on the activity	Engaging in activities to benefit others in the school and community to help connect with the idea that democracy is a way of life as well as a form of government

To begin to present practically the concepts of this form of democracy in the classroom, Table 6.1 offers an overview of sample lessons, class meetings, and activities that successfully challenge and celebrate students.

Lessons that Help Facilitate a Democratic Classroom

The lessons presented here are adaptable to the individual needs of different classrooms. There are several enduring understandings that the students will be able to learn and utilize as citizens in a democracy.
    The students will understand that:

- The diverse skills, talents, and experiences of a group are needed in order to create a stronger community
- Everyone can contribute to a group

- Together everyone achieves more
- A healthy democracy relies on the involvement of every-one
- Democracy is more than a form of government; it is a way of life
- Self-discipline, responsibility, and accountability are nec-essary in a strong, connected democratic community

Essential Questions

In addition to the enduring understandings that students will develop, there are questions to help guide teachers as they engage in instructional practices throughout the lessons. As all teachers know, lessons rarely fit exactly from one classroom to the next. These essential questions are a guide for teachers, however, as they adapt each day to meet the unique needs of their classrooms and their students. These questions keep the lesson focused and provide direction when "teachable moments" occur.

- How is the concept of community an essential part of a healthy democracy?
- How does diversity promote community strength?
- In what ways can freedom be protected by a system of rules and laws?
- How does an established system of rules and laws protect individual rights?
- How is authority distributed in a democracy?

To present specifically the ways in which students are observed in the practice of democratic disposition, particularly in response to the above questions, the lesson in Table 6.2 poses the critical question, "Do I belong?" The entire lesson plan is presented here in order to demonstrate how the unit may begin and how to initiate the discussion of a democratic classroom. The lesson in Table 6.3 and the diagram in Figure 6.1 continue to challenge students to compare and contrast forms of authority and ways in which their classroom may represent these forms.

In acting as an advocate, a middle school teacher must be wary of appearing to be a buddy or a best friend to the students. Students' friends are their peers. Students expect teachers to be responsible professionals who retain ultimate responsibility for classroom activities.

Table 6.2
Lesson 1

Do I Belong?

Objectives:
- The students will be able to discuss the feelings of being part of the group or not being allowed to be a part of the group.
- The students will be able to identify important reasons why it is important to be honest and trustworthy in group situations.
- The students will be able to express their ideas on several topics.

Concepts and Topics	*Content Standards*
Creating Community	Social Studies Benchmark: Strand VII, Citizen Involvement, Content Standard 1, Middle School 1 *Use laws and other ethical rules to evaluate their own conduct and the conduct of others.*

Developmental Characteristics	*Middle Level Curriculum Characteristics*	*Multiple Intelligences*
Have a strong need to belong to a group, with peer approval becoming more important as adult approval decreases in importance	Promote "family" grouping of students and teachers to provide stability for new students	Interpersonal Verbal-Linguistic Bodily-Kinesthetic
Prefer active over passive learning experiences	Encourage students to engage in service learning and community activities	
May exhibit immature behavior because their social skills frequently lag behind their mental and physical maturity	Design activities that help students play out their emotions—activity programs that provide opportunities to draw out shy students and calm loud students	
Often overreact to ridicule, embarrassment, and rejection	Help students interpret superiority and inferiority feelings	
Are increasingly concerned about peer acceptance	Structure a general atmosphere of friendliness, concern, and group cohesiveness	

(continues)

Table 6.2 (continued)

Time Needed: one class period

Materials Needed:
- Large sheets of butcher-style paper
- Felt markers
- Index cards

Vocabulary: No specialized terms

Activities/Procedures:
1. An Internet bulletin board is a nonthreatening way that many people post their ideas on a variety of topics. The Ideas Kiosk is a similar way for students to express their ideas in a safe, nonthreatening way.
   a. Post several sheets of butcher-style paper around the class on bulletin boards and chalkboards.
   b. Write a sentence starter on each Ideas Kiosk that is posted.
      - School is …
      - Students are …
      - Teachers are …
      - I would like for our class to have …
      - It's tough being an 8th grader because …
   c. Tell students that they may add ideas to the appropriate Ideas Kiosk at appropriate times during the school day.
   d. Provide as few ground rules as possible. Some ideas would possibly include: (1) no names, (2) everyone participate, (3) no poking fun at other students, (4) no bad language—which includes language that may not be swearing but is bad nonetheless, and so on.
   e. Teachers may wish to allow students to post ideas then and there or leave the Ideas Kiosks up for a few days or even leave an Ideas Kiosk up permanently. It is important, however, that the ideas that are posted are discussed.
2. The teacher will give a brief explanation telling the class that they will be beginning a contest. There are two ways to win the contest.
   a. Each person in the class will be given an index card that may or may not have a small dot on it. (For every five blank cards, one should be made with a small dot.) The students will draw index cards at random. Once each student has a card, the game begins at the teacher's direction.
   b. Students will attempt to form into groups who have cards WITHOUT a dot. The students who have an index card with a dot will attempt to infiltrate one of the groups of students without a dot.
   c. The largest group of students without any dots wins. The single student who has a dot that spoils it for the group of students without dots is also a winner.
   d. The teacher should lead a debriefing-style discussion linking the activity to what are important behaviors to remember when working in a group.

(continues)

Table 6.2 (continued)

Assessment:
• The students will be assessed by teacher observation and their ability to discuss what happened in the activity as it relates to group dynamics.

Homework:
• There is no homework as reinforcement for this activity.

As an advocate as well as a role model in the classroom, a middle grades teacher needs to place himself or herself in a position of leadership, but not of dominance. Much of the sense of community is generated by the students themselves. A good analogy would be that of a clock. To keep accurate track of time, the clock must be periodically set to account for imperfections in the clock's mechanisms or for standard time changes. For the most part, however, the clock keeps time without constant tinkering. In much the same way, the teacher who seeks to create community within the classroom gives students the opportunity and the freedom to make choices and to develop without constant tinkering. Students will make mistakes. Not giving students the opportunity to learn from their mistakes is to truncate their learning experience. Middle school students need the opportunity to handle the consequences of their decisions as they develop. As an advocate, the middle grades teacher has the arena in which to debrief students and facilitate appropriate socialization and critical thinking activities. Table 6.3, the next lesson in the unit, and Figure 6.1, which accompanies the lesson, do just that. They shape the opportunity for the students to construct their understanding of rights and responsibilities, to distinguish the differences between democracy and a dictatorship.

The goal of a teacher in a democratic classroom is to facilitate democratic dispositions within the students. Part of that process is sharing authority, advocating for student interests, and establishing an engaging, interactive learning environment.

Full authority in the classroom is not given to students. Within the democratic classroom, clear roles are established for both the teacher and the students. The teacher and the students work together to establish the parameters and the roles for both, but a clear separation exists between teacher and students. As the teacher shares power, the students accept that the teacher retains responsibility for the class. The teacher retains a separate identity from that of the students within the democratic dynamic that is created.

Teacher as Facilitator

The students' ability to participate in classroom governance creates open acknowledgment of certain student rights. Students should be

Table 6.3

Lesson 2

Why Are We Here?

Objectives:
- The students will be able to distinguish between a democracy and a dictatorship.
- The students will be able to describe some of the rights and responsibilities incumbent upon citizens in a democracy.

Concepts and Topics	*Content Standards*
Creating Community Government Structures	Social Studies Benchmark: Strand VII, Citizen Involvement, Content Standard 1, Middle School 1 *Use laws and other ethical rules to evaluate their own conduct and the conduct of others.* Social Studies Benchmark: Strand III, Civics, Content Standard 1, Middle School 2 *Distinguish between representative democracy in the United States and other forms of government.*

Developmental Characteristics	*Middle Level Curriculum Characteristics*	*Multiple Intelligences*
Have a strong need to belong to a group, with peer approval becoming more important as adult approval decreases in importance	Promote "family" grouping of students and teachers to provide stability for new students	Interpersonal Verbal-Linguistic Visual-Spatial Logical-Mathematical
Prefer active over passive learning experiences	Provide opportunities for students to accept responsibility in setting standards for behavior	
Are dependent upon parental beliefs and values but seek to make their own decisions	Design activities that help students play out their emotions—activity programs that provide opportunities to draw out shy students and calm loud students	
Are generally idealistic, desiring to make the world a better place and to become socially useful	Help students to develop values when solving their problems	

(continues)

Table 6.3 (continued)

Developmental Characteristics	Middle Level Curriculum Characteristics	Multiple Intelligences
Greatly need and are influenced by adult role models who will listen to them and affirm their moral consciousness and actions by being trustworthy role models	Structure a general atmosphere of friendliness, concern, and group cohesiveness	
Increasingly assess moral matters in shades of gray as opposed to viewing them in black and white terms characteristic of young children	Individualize instruction; group and regroup	

Time Needed: one class period

Materials Needed:
- Paper
- Pencils

Vocabulary:
- Dictatorship
- Rights
- Democracy
- Power
- Citizen
- Authority

Activities/Procedures:
1. The teacher will divide the students into groups of two or three. The groups should be different from previous activities.
2. The teacher will ask the student groups to list as many characteristics, names, terms, words, and ideas related to the concept "dictatorship" as possible.
3. After the students have finished, the teacher will ask the students to do the same for the concept "democracy."
4. The students will report their lists to the class, initiating a discussion of what a dictatorship is. Toward the end of the discussion, if it has not already been described, the teacher needs to direct the discussion to the role of a citizen in a dictatorship.
5. After the discussion of a dictatorship, the class will use their lists to discuss what a democracy is. As with the discussion of a dictatorship, it is necessary to discuss the role of a citizen in a democracy.

(continues)

Table 6.3 (continued)

6. As the class discussion progresses, the teacher should record student comments on a visual medium observable by the entire class. The teacher should make a three column chart without titles and as students give out new ideas and concepts, the teacher should record them in one of the following categories: (1) fair competition among individuals and groups for positions of power, (2) involvement in selecting the leaders and laws of the society, and (3) existence of civil and political liberties.
7. After enough characteristics have been listed, the teacher will initiate a discussion of the three essential conditions of a democratic system of government. In discussion it is crucial that these three conditions are explained in a manner that all students will understand. Comparisons in the discussion can (and should) be made to school, family, and the community to foster a greater understanding of the role of the three essential conditions of a democratic system of government.

Assessment:
• The students will be assessed through teacher observation and class discussion
• The students will be required to complete a Venn Diagram comparing a dictatorship with a democracy

Homework:
Dictatorship and Democracy Venn Diagram

able to speak among themselves about issues of concern as long as the discussion is maintained in an appropriate manner, even if the issues are not comfortable for the teacher to hear. Discussing classroom issues such as seating charts is good practice for perhaps discussing zoning laws that they may encounter later in life.

Table 6.4 presents a learning activity that challenges young adolescents to construct their own understandings of the causal relationship between rights and responsibilities. Along with the newly shaped student rights and responsibilities comes the examination of the ways in which students may exercise both. Through the analysis of and classroom comparison to the preamble to the Constitution, Tables 6.5 and 6.7 show how to ask students to set their own goals for the classroom.

In addition to being able to speak freely, students should be able to question authority. To do so effectively, however, requires the use of appropriate tone and proper language. The electorate of any democratic community would not sit idle while its leaders trampled public concerns. A free democracy responds to an active electorate that openly

Figure 6.1
Venn Diagram

Directions:

A Venn Diagram is used to compare two different topics, concepts, or ideas. In the diagram below, place similarities in the area common to both boxes. Place differences in the areas that are not shared by both boxes.

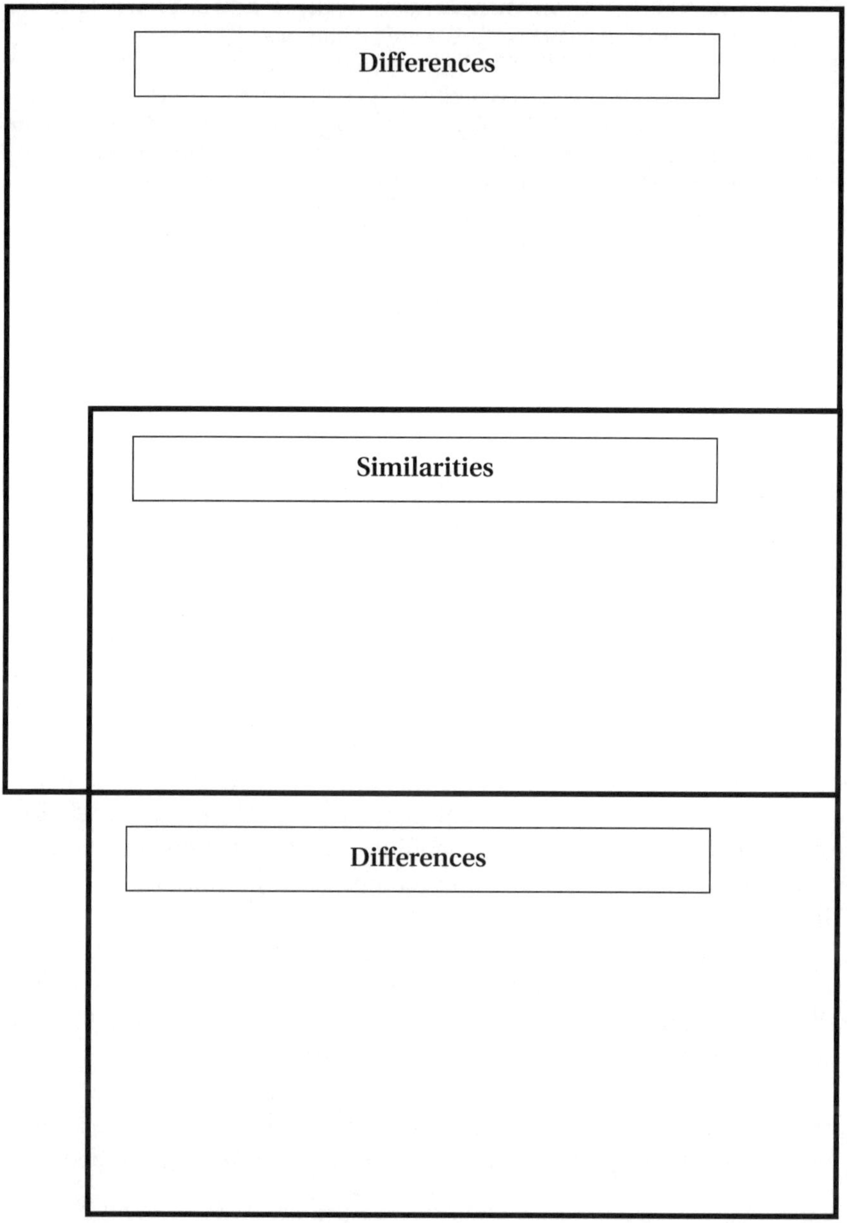

Differences

Similarities

Differences

Table 6.4
Lesson 3

"What Can We Do?"

Objective:
• The students will be able to describe some of the rights and responsibilities incumbent upon citizens in a democracy.

Concepts and Topics	Content Standards
Creating Community Government Structures	Social Studies Benchmark: Strand VII, Citizen Involvement, Content Standard 1, Middle School 1 *Use laws and other ethical rules to evaluate their own conduct and the conduct of others.* Social Studies Benchmark: Strand III, Civics, Content Standard 1, Middle School 2 *Distinguish between representative democracy in the United States and other forms of government.* Social Studies Benchmark: Strand III, Civics, Content Standard 1, Middle School 3 *Explain how rule of law protects individual rights and serves the common good.*

Developmental Characteristics	Middle Level Curriculum Characteristics	Multiple Intelligences
Have a strong need to belong to a group, with peer approval becoming more important as adult approval decreases in importance	Promote "family" grouping of students and teachers to provide stability for new students	Interpersonal Verbal-Linguistic Visual-Spatial
Prefer active over passive learning experiences	Provide opportunities for students to accept responsibility in setting standards for behavior	
Are dependent upon parental beliefs and values but seek to make their own decisions	Design activities that help students play out their emotions—activity programs that provide opportunities to draw out shy students and calm loud students	

(continues)

Table 6.4 (continued)

Developmental Characteristics	Middle Level Curriculum Characteristics	Multiple Intelligences
Are generally idealistic, desiring to make the world a better place and to become socially useful	Help students to develop values when solving their problems	Logical-Mathematical Intrapersonal
Greatly need and are influenced by adult role models who will listen to them and affirm their moral consciousness and actions by being trustworthy role models	Structure a general atmosphere of friendliness, concern, and group cohesiveness	
Increasingly assess moral matters in shades of gray as opposed to viewing them in black and white terms characteristic of young children	Individualize instruction; group and regroup	

Time Needed: one class period

Materials Needed:
- Paper
- Pencils

Vocabulary:
- Citizen
- Rights
- Authority
- Power

Activities/Procedures:
1. The teacher will divide the students into groups of two or three. The groups should be different from previous activities.
2. The students should work together to create a T-chart. The two sides of the T-chart should be labeled "Rights Students Have" and "Rights Students Should Have." The title of the T-chart should be "Student Rights."
3. When the students have finished, a class discussion should held considering the nature of these rights, both given and desired.
   a. During the discussion, the Core Democratic Values should be examined by the students in light of student rights.

(continues)

Table 6.4 *(continued)*

___

b. It is important for the students to consistently consider why they either have certain rights or why they feel they deserve certain other rights. Are the rights grounded in democratic ideals?

4. For each of the rights of the students, the teacher asks the students what responsibilities come with those rights. For example, does the right to free speech extend to saying hateful things or endangering the public? Does the right to free speech require citizens to be responsible enough not to do terrible things with their freedom?

5. These rights and responsibilities should be recorded.

Assessment:
- The students are assessed through teacher observation and class discussion.
- The teacher may wish to use discussion tools such as the "Stop and Go" index card device. (The students each have an index card folded in half at their seats, and if they have already added to the discussion, the "Stop" side of the card faces the teacher. If they have not contributed to the discussion, the "Go" side faces the teacher. It is helpful to color code these cards by using red for stop and green for go.)
- The students are assessed on the homework assignment.

Homework:
- Students write five rights adults have as citizens and the responsibilities that go with those rights.

___

questions authority in a responsible way. Part of adolescent development is questioning the adult authority.

Middle grades students are setting their values, testing new moral boundaries, and trying to establish the standards by which they will live. It is incumbent upon teachers to demonstrate both the sanctity of critical questioning and the appropriate ways to be respectfully successful. The lesson in Table 6.7 helps students form the laws and rules by which their self-established democracy will function.

Recently, stories of adolescent rampages have been an unfortunate regular part of evening newscasts. They show how some middle school students use violence and gunfire to get revenge, to assert their power, or to voice a concern. Establishing authority by coercion begs upheaval by similar means. Allowing students to openly question authority in responsible ways can be a learning experience for both the students and the teacher. The students learn appropriate democratic behaviors while the teacher can, if he is a reflective practitioner, realize that his teaching practices might need to be altered to be more developmentally appropriate and in tune with the students' needs.

Table 6.5

Lesson 4

"How Can We Do It?"

Objectives:
- The students will be able to describe some of the rights and responsibilities incumbent upon citizens in a democracy.
- The students will be able to develop a series of goals for the classroom that justify the purpose of the class.

Concepts and Topics	*Content Standards*
Creating Community Government Structures	Social Studies Benchmark: Strand VII, Citizen Involvement, Content Standard 1, Middle School 1 *Use laws and other ethical rules to evaluate their own conduct and the conduct of others.* Social Studies Benchmark: Strand III, Civics, Content Standard 1, Middle School 1 *Describe how the federal government in the United States serves the purposes set forth in the Preamble of the Constitution.* Social Studies Benchmark: Strand III, Civics, Content Standard 1, Middle School 3 *Explain how rule of law protects individual rights and serves the common good*

Developmental Characteristics	*Middle Level Curriculum Characteristics*	*Multiple Intelligences*
Have a strong need to belong to a group, with peer approval becoming more important as adult approval decreases in importance	Promote "family" grouping of students and teachers to provide stability for new students	Interpersonal Verbal-Linguistic Visual-Spatial
Prefer active over passive learning experiences	Provide opportunities for students to accept responsibility in setting standards for behavior	
Are dependent upon parental beliefs and values but seek to make their own decisions	Design activities that help students play out their emotions—activity programs that provide opportunities to draw out shy students and calm loud students	

(continues)

Table 6.5 (continued)

Developmental Characteristics	Middle Level Curriculum Characteristics	Multiple Intelligences
Are generally idealistic, desiring to make the world a better place and to become socially useful	Help students to develop values when solving their problems	
Greatly need and are influenced by adult role models who will listen to them and affirm their moral consciousness and actions by being trustworthy role models	Structure a general atmosphere of friendliness, concern, and group cohesiveness	
Increasingly assess moral matters in shades of gray as opposed to viewing them in black and white terms characteristic of young children	Individualize instruction; group and regroup	

Time Needed: one class period

Materials Needed:
- Paper
- Pencils
- Copies of the United States Constitution
- "Unlocking the Meaning of the Preamble" handout

Vocabulary:
- Welfare
- Union
- Tranquility
- Domestic
- Common
- Secure

Activities/Procedures:
- The students should list on a piece of paper five goals to achieve for the school year. These goals should be written in complete sentences.
- The teacher will divide the students into groups of two or three. The groups should be different from previous activities.
- The student groups will each be given the "Unlocking the Meaning of the Preamble" handout.

(continues)

Table 6.5 (continued)

- The teacher will assign each group one of the six goals of the Constitution as found in the Preamble.
- The students will work together in their groups to unlock the meaning of one of the phrases in the Preamble.
- After the students have finished their handouts, they will present what they have learned to the rest of the class. Once the group is finished, the class will discuss what that particular goal of the Constitution means to a classroom of students. The teacher will facilitate and redirect the discussion as necessary.
- In the discussion, the teacher should focus the class to develop class goals similar to those in the Constitution for the classroom constitution.
- IMPORTANT: The teacher should take these goals and write them in a paragraph to serve as the Preamble to the classroom constitution.

Assessment:
- The students will be assessed through teacher observation and class discussion.
- The teacher may wish to use discussion tools such as the "Stop and Go" index card device. (The students each have an index card folded in half at their seats and if they have already added to the discussion, the "Stop" side of the card faces the teacher. If they have not contributed to the discussion, the "Go" side faces the teacher. It is helpful to color code these cards by using red for stop and green for go.)

Homework:
There is no homework assignment for the evening.

In understanding adolescent needs, teachers in the democratic classroom must not assume the same maturity as can be expected among adults in a democracy. The students should be free to experiment in democratic decisionmaking. At times, because of their age and developmental level and because they have freedom to choose, students will not make the best choices. In a democratic classroom, students will make mistakes. The teacher should not intervene. Unless it jeopardizes student safety or compromises agreed-upon classroom or school rules, the consequences of the choices that are made provide a much better lesson than any lecture could. The lesson's impact is greater since the success or failure of the students' endeavor is a product of their own decisions and planning.

Ultimately, the role being defined for the teacher in the democratic classroom is that of a facilitator. The teacher does not necessarily construct lessons that address the unique learning opportunities that arise from the democratic process. The teacher helps guide students

Table 6.6
Preamble Analysis

**Unlocking the Meaning
of the Preamble to the United States Constitution**

Directions:
With a partner using the phrase assigned to you by the teacher, respond to the
following questions and prompts completely.

1. Write the phrase of the Preamble to the Constitution that has been assigned
   to you completely—word for word.

2. What words in this phrase are used in a way that you are not familiar with?
   Look them up and provide the definition that makes sense as the word is
   used in this phrase.

3. What does this phrase mean? (The person who wrote the phrase wanted the
   United States to become better in a certain way. In what way does the
   phrase assigned to you make the United States a better place?)

4. Rewrite the phrase in words that you understand more clearly so that it
   means the same thing, but in different words.

Table 6.7

Lesson 5

What Are Our Rules?

Objectives:
- The students will be able to create a number of rules and laws for the class to follow based on the characteristics agreed upon as those of quality students as well as the goals of the class.
- The students will be able to explain why rules and laws are necessary.
- The students will be able to describe the value of popular sovereignty.

Concepts and Topics	*Content Standards*
Creating Community Government Structures	Social Studies Benchmark: Strand VII, Citizen Involvement, Content Standard 1, Middle School 1 *Use laws and other ethical rules to evaluate their own conduct and the conduct of others.* Social Studies Benchmark: Strand III, Civics, Content Standard 1, Middle School 3 *Explain how rule of law protects individual rights and serves the common good.* Social Studies Benchmark: Strand III, Civics, Content Standard 1, Middle School 4 *Explain the importance of limited government to protect political and economic freedom.* Social Studies Benchmark: Strand III, Civics, Content Standard 2, Middle School 3 *Explain the means for limiting the power of the government established by the U.S. Constitution.*

Developmental Characteristics	*Middle Level Curriculum Characteristics*	*Multiple Intelligences*
Have a strong need to belong to a group, with peer approval becoming more important as adult approval decreases in importance	Promote "family" grouping of students and teachers to provide stability for new students	Interpersonal Verbal-Linguistic
Prefer active over passive learning experiences	Provide opportunities for students to accept responsibility in setting standards for behavior	

(continues)

Table 6.7 (continued)

Developmental Characteristics	Middle Level Curriculum Characteristics	Multiple Intelligences
Are dependent upon parental beliefs and values but seek to make their own decisions	Design activities that help students play out their emotions—activity programs that provide opportunities to draw out shy students and calm loud students	Visual-Spatial Logical-Mathematical
Are generally idealistic, desiring to make the world a better place and to become socially useful	Help students to develop values when solving their problems	
Greatly need and are influenced by adult role models who will listen to them and affirm their moral consciousness and actions by being trustworthy role models	Structure a general atmosphere of friendliness, concern, and group cohesiveness	
Increasingly assess moral matters in shades of gray as opposed to viewing them in black and white terms characteristic of young children	Individualize instruction; group and regroup	

Time Needed: one class period

Materials Needed:
- Paper
- Pencils
- Copies of the classroom preamble
- 10–12 Post-it Notes per student pair

Vocabulary:
- Popular sovereignty
- Laws

Activities/Procedures:
1. Prior to the start of class, on the chalkboard, the teacher should write the goals for the class as agreed upon in the previous lesson's activities. The goals should be written individually, spaced across the chalkboard so that Post-its can be attached below each goal.

(continues)

Table 6.7 (continued)

---

2. The teacher begins a brief discussion of why it would be important to have students help make class and school rules. The teacher facilitates the discussion and helps students flesh out the meaning of "popular sovereignty." This discussion should take no longer than five to seven minutes.

3. The teacher should then hand out copies of the classroom preamble that was established from the previous lesson's activities. The teacher should illustrate how the classroom preamble is the classroom goals in paragraph form.

4. After discussing the classroom preamble, the teacher should explain to the class that rules must be made that will enable the class to achieve its goals.

5. For each of the goals in the classroom preamble, at least one rule should be written by the students so that the goal can be attained.

6. The students will divide into student pairs. (Students should not partner with those they have been partnering with in previous activities.)

7. Each student pair will be given ten to twelve Post-it Notes. On each Post-it, the students should write one law.

8. After finishing their Post-its, the students should place them on the chalkboard under the goal that the rule relates to most closely.

9. After all the sticky notes have been placed, a classroom discussion should be held to answer the following questions.

    What laws mean basically the same thing?
    What laws are not in the right category?
    What laws can be combined with others that are in the same category to make one law?
    What laws do not really achieve the goal of a quality classroom?

10. A list of laws should be created from those that remain.

11. For the remainder of the class time, the students should write a journal entry. The topic for this journal should be: "After today's activity, do you see rules as things that prohibit students from doing things or as things designed to achieve goals? Is it important for those following the rules to be part of creating them?"

Assessment:
- The students will be assessed through teacher observation and class discussion.
- The teacher may wish to use discussion tools such as the "Stop and Go" index card device. (The students each have an index card folded in half at their seats and if they have already added to the discussion, the "Stop" side of the card faces the teacher. If they have not contributed to the discussion, the "Go" side faces the teacher. It is helpful to color code these cards by using red for stop and green for go.)
- Journal entries will also serve as an assessment device.

Homework:
- Finish journal entries if they were not finished in class.

---

through the democratic process by providing a choice of various avenues to follow. In a democratic classroom, the teacher works with students to develop their plan of action. Since the teacher's understanding of the school environment or even the political structure of the surrounding community exceeds that of the students, she becomes a consultant of sorts for the students as they think about a classroom or community issue, plan a strategy for resolving the issue, and then act on their plan. The teacher helps the students achieve their plan rather than uses the students to achieve the teacher's plan. The teacher promotes democratic dispositions in the classroom by facilitating democratic processes among students in the classroom.

Class Meetings

Class meetings are the regular opportunities for the students and teacher to take time to discuss issues of concern, plan activities, and follow up on actions taken in the past. Each day in every school across the nation and undoubtedly around the globe, there is a student who feels that a teacher did something unfair. In these same buildings, there are always teachers who believe that a student or group of students is not living up to potential or is acting disobediently. The key to understanding each other as teachers and students is communicating with one another. This is the purpose of class meetings.

Purposes of Class Meetings

1. Expressing Concerns: Class meetings give students an opportunity to express their concerns over increased homework and give a teacher the chance to explain why there may be increased homework. Many times educators do not take into consideration what the students may be feeling, and at the same time, students do not realize that there are factors that compel a teacher to assign more homework.

2. Time to Communicate: A class meeting provides time to communicate in a manner that is nonthreatening, collegial, and positive. Students may wish to discuss homework loads, consequences for misbehavior, field trips, pizza parties, or even classroom policies about sharpening a pencil. Teachers may wish to discuss student behavior, homework completion, field trips, service learning opportunities, or even classroom policies on placing student names on assignments. The point is that students and teachers have concerns that should be shared with the entire class in a mature, responsible fashion. A student wishing

to discuss a consequence for misbehavior is most likely not seeking to subvert the teacher's authority; rather the student may well be seeking an explanation or clarification because of a misunderstanding. Many middle school students are developing their own belief systems and will test the values and rules of adults in authority. At the same time that they are testing these rule structures, adolescents are seeking to validate the importance of them. Communicating in an open, nonhostile manner about the importance of a particular rule or procedure allows a middle school student to consider what is being said without being threatened by the message.

3. Sharing Information: There are two important reasons why taking time to share is important and developmentally appropriate. Adolescents experiment with many hobbies and activities. By sharing, middle school students have the opportunity to learn about different pastimes and diverse interests. Also, adolescents crave recognition of their achievements. By using class meeting time to share, adolescents have a supportive audience who knows what is going on in their lives. Sharing information can also be a powerful tool for a teacher to humanize herself. By sharing a little bit about herself, a teacher opens some of her private life with the students and becomes seen as a person as well as a teacher. By letting the students know about a sick dog, a daughter's first steps, or a family game of baseball, a teacher is seen as a whole person with feelings, interests, and passions just as the students have. The students can connect with the teacher's experiences and share common joys and sorrows.

4. Decisionmaking: Class meetings are a place for decisionmaking. Most decisions made in a classroom are traditionally made by the teacher. Class meetings give students an opportunity to voice opinions and concerns about classroom decisions that affect everyone. Students will be more likely to invest themselves in a classroom or lesson if they played a role in its development. Teachers do not have to accommodate students' every whim. Class meetings give teachers an equal chance to explain why rules, lessons, and procedures are structured in certain ways. Middle school students may not agree with the teacher, but their voice has been given credibility and respect by those in authority. If the teacher discovers an alternative solution through collaboration with the students, however, the lesson in democratic partnership will have lasting effects. The students will see the efficacy of handling issues of concerns properly and will have a significantly greater respect for their teacher who has proven that student voice and concerns matter.

5. Planning: Class meetings can be used for planning. Teaching includes field trip preparations, fund raising, web site construction, finding guest speakers, at the very least. The "extra" duties of a teacher are time consuming and exhausting. Class meetings can actually take some of the burden off of the teacher for many of these extra duties. For instance, students can help plan field trips, organize fund raisers, build web sites, write letters to prospective guest speakers. In assuming more responsibility for the activities of the class, middle grades students have increased latitude over the planning of activities, which gives them an opportunity to engage in meaningful decisionmaking in a protected environment that allows for some mistakes while enhancing the development of democratic dispositions.

6. Reflection: One of the most powerful uses of class meetings is in the reflection. Involving the students in reflective practices can prove to be a powerful tool in promoting a positive classroom environment, a stronger academic curriculum, and an engaged, active class of students. Class meetings are the perfect opportunity to reflect on what is going on in the classroom. Expectations can be reinforced in a nonthreatening manner so that future difficulties can be avoided. On the other hand, if the teacher takes time to reflect on a positive activity in the classroom, the students understand the importance of their success and find meaning in what they do in the classroom. Reflection is not a time for the teacher to lecture about the dos and don'ts of a particularly grating student problem. Reflection is a meaningful discussion in which both the teacher and the students present a view of what the classroom should be like.

7. Preparing for the Future: Using class meetings for sharing, deciding, planning, and reflecting is not only developmentally appropriate and democratically sound but is also a practice in preparing students for later success. When asked what traits were most valuable in new employees, personnel directors from several large companies suggested the following:

- Basic competence in whatever subjects or majors they had studied
- Good interpersonal skills
- Good communication skills, both verbal and written
- Resourcefulness and initiative
- Knowing where and how to find information
- Literacy in technology, particularly in computer usage
- Familiarity with foreign languages (Glickman 1998)

Class meetings promote most of these skills, in particular those that emphasize working cooperatively. Class meetings, though not directly connected to curriculum, are a sound use of academic time. Class meetings offer opportunities for middle school students to engage in active learning experiences that directly promote democratic dispositions while simultaneously developing the very characteristics that corporate employers find most valuable in their employees.

How Is a Class Meeting Constructed?

For class meetings to be a healthy, positive use of class time, several guidelines should be followed (Nelsen, Lott, and Glenn 2000).

- Student Ownership: Students decide most of the topics, instead of discussing teacher-generated topics. In order for students to decide the topics to be discussed during a class meeting, the teacher needs to post a list to permit the students to add issues of concern. The agenda for the class meeting is developed from this list and also from items of business and concern from previous meetings.
- Access to the Agenda: Both the students and the teacher can add to the agenda using this list. The agenda is posted in a regular location for easy student and teacher access. An important thing to remember is that although class meetings help stimulate democratic dispositions and build community within a classroom, at no time should a class meeting or any other feature of a democratically disposed class go against or serve in place of school rules and procedures unless approved and supported by the school's administration.
- Involving Everyone: The entire class is involved, instead of a select few who are chosen to learn certain skills, such as conflict management. Every person's views are treated equally. The teacher's involvement in a class meeting discussion, therefore, must be treated carefully. Students naturally defer to a teacher's authority, so a teacher's participation must be used at appropriate times. When a class discussion goes off task or hurtful comments are being made, a teacher should intervene. All student opinions are welcome given the purpose and the goals of class meetings.

- Specific Format: There is a specified format that creates the kind of order that allows more freedom for everyone involved. Public meetings throughout the United States use Robert's Rules of Order to provide structure and procedures to their proceedings. Students are not too young to follow a condensed version of Robert's Rules (see Appendix A). Students are able to follow an agenda, make a motion, understand the difference between old business and new business, vote, and carry on the business of a meeting.

The meeting format that is used in a class meeting is typically a little different than that of a public meeting. Teachers can adapt this format to fit their individual class needs, but a typical model of a class meeting agenda is as follows:

I. Call to Order: The Call to Order is the symbolic statement that the meeting is to begin.
II. Circle of Encouragement: The Circle of Encouragement is the time during the meeting to share with the rest of the class positive things about interests, news, and hobbies.
III. Teacher's Report: The Teacher's Report is a discussion of the state of the class. At this time the teacher explains concerns about behavior or grades or praises the class for proper attitude or a field trip that was well planned and executed.
IV. Old Business: Old Business is the time to follow up on items from previous class meetings or discuss them further.
V. New Business: New Business is the part of the meeting in which any new issues of concern are brought up and addressed. Items from the agenda list most often are brought up during New Business.
VI. Reflection: Reflection is time for the teacher and the students to discuss their progress in terms of the goals and purposes that have been set for the class.
VII. Announcements: Announcements is a time to remind students of important dates in the school calendar or for a student to remind her classmates of a party that she is having.

VIII.   Adjournment: Adjournment is the symbolic conclusion of the meeting, usually brought to a close by the chair or president of the class.

A healthy democracy involves citizens of all backgrounds, talents, interests, and strengths. A classroom democracy should not be dominated by a select few. Class meetings are an opportunity to voice concerns, address issues of conflict, plan activities, and reflect on the purpose for being in a democratic classroom. In short, a class meeting is the tool of communication necessary to make a classroom democracy truly the voice of the students.

Class Government

The classroom government model brings to life the federal government's three branches of power. Each class elects a president, a congress, and a court. The duties of the three branches mirror those of the federal government. The president carries out and enforces the mandates of the congress, which makes the laws. The court assumes the judicial role of determining the fairness and constitutionality of the laws that are created. Because of the unique needs of different classrooms, the powers given to a particular branch of government are not set in stone. Some teachers may feel uncomfortable with a classroom congress sharing a voice in how classroom rules are made. Other teachers may feel that for students to experience democracy fully, more authority should be given to the classroom government's court to decide the fate of those who have disrupted class. As the students and teacher write the constitution for the class, issues of authority and power are addressed and decided in a manner unique to the particular situation.

In a classroom government based on the federal model, students assume roles similar in nature and authority to those of the president, the Congress, and the Supreme Court. For instance, the president has many executive roles. During class meetings, she serves as the chair, she may appoint an attendance courier to distribute papers, she reviews laws and vetoes them as necessary, and she travels as a representative to other governing bodies such as student council.

The student congress makes laws (see Table 6.8). Throughout the school year new situations arise that require both teachers and students to examine existing rules and adapt them to a new situation. One of the responsibilities of the student congress is to write legisla-

Table 6.8
Congressional Bill

Title of the Bill: _____

Proposed Law:

_____
_____
_____
_____
_____

Why is this bill needed?

_____
_____
_____

How is this bill going to be carried out?

_____
_____
_____

Congressional Votes: (PLEASE SIGN IF YOU WOULD LIKE TO SEE THIS BILL PASSED INTO LAW.)

_____   President's Signature:

_____   _____

_____   (PRESIDENT SHOULD WRITE "VETO" IN THE

_____   SIGNATURE LINE IF THE LAW IS TO BE VETOED.)

_____

_____

tion that clarifies these situations. The classroom congress has more duties than just passing laws. The classroom congress may vote to impeach the president or a judge. The classroom congress has the authority to override vetoes. The legislative body of the classroom will hopefully represent the diverse nature of the student population in the class.

The class court is the judicial arm of the class government. It mediates disputes and determines the constitutionality of class laws. For instance, a student may wish to resolve a conflict with a peer concerning the location of their seats in class and use the petition shown in Table 6.9. Or the teacher may wish to clarify whether existing constitutional language such as "the students will attempt to do their best" means that students not turning in their homework are in violation of the constitution.

The foundational premise for classroom government is not only that adolescents are capable of participatory democratic government but also that a classroom government helps students understand more fully what rights and responsibilities really mean. A democratic classroom government, by giving students the opportunity to experience democratic decisionmaking, develops a greater understanding and appreciation for the American democratic system and prepares the students to be capable of active participation later as adults in our own government.

Teachers as Active Communicators

Teachers in all disciplines have the ability and opportunity to teach in a democratic fashion. From teaching style to classroom management, there are many different forms and practices of democratic education. For teachers seeking to alter their teaching style to become more democratic, a good place to start is to look at their instructional methods. A healthy democracy relies heavily on students who have experienced critical thought processes, rather than on those whose minds have not been challenged, as is the case with students who have used only the typical drill and practice worksheets.

Another critical element of democratic teaching across content areas is the two-part communication process between teacher and students. First one speaks, and then one listens. Teachers, as extremely busy individuals, are very good at the former with their students but not very well practiced at the latter. For adolescents, an explanation of why

Table 6.9
Petition for a Court Hearing

Name of Petitioner: _____

Why I am petitioning the Court:

_____
_____
_____
_____
_____
_____
_____
_____
_____
_____

How does this situation violate our classroom constitution?

_____
_____
_____
_____

Which Core Democratic Value supports your petition of the Court?

_____
_____
_____
_____

DEMOCRACY IS NOT JUST A SOCIAL STUDIES WORD

something is being done, whether it is a behavioral consequence or a class activity, suffices to justify its purpose. Teachers must try to understand the students' point of view. This does not necessarily mean that the teacher agrees with what the student is saying but that the teacher has made a concerted effort to listen to and understand students. The teacher models appropriate communication skills, conflict-resolution strategies, and respect for others. There is a powerful democratic lesson in what is typically not considered an academic school activity.

Conclusion: Teen Regime

In helping students understand what democracy as a way of life means, some teachers provide opportunities for students to assume authority in the classroom. Whether students are involved in making rules or determining whether someone has broken a rule, there are many different levels of democratic integration in classroom authority. A teacher does not necessarily have to have a formal classroom president, congress, or court to include students in important classroom management decisions. An informal kangaroo-style court can be instituted for situations in which a student feels that her classroom rights have been taken away from her. The teacher and students may work together to write a contract for classroom expectations that is signed and posted on the wall to hold the students and the teacher accountable to the agreement. The students may create an appeals process for complaints in the classroom so that a grievance that is made can be heard and appealed if it was not treated properly. All of these examples can occur in any classroom, not just a social studies class. The key to all of them is meaningful student involvement in making decisions that impact everyone, including the teacher, in the classroom.

As institutions funded by tax dollars, public schools have a responsibility to prepare students to become capable, active participants in the democratic system in the United States. In an era of high-stakes standardized testing and tightly micromanaged national and state benchmarks, it is intimidating to suggest to teachers that they reduce the emphasis on rote recall of facts, events, formulas, and themes. By implementing democratic processes in the classroom, however, teachers will find that their efforts to achieve the highest academic standards are more attainable. The students will become partners in the learning process rather than adversaries, and they will be better prepared for life outside of the classroom.

Everything boils down to a simple statement that has been a part of many societies for thousands of years. In ancient China, the saying is credited to Confucius. In the Christian world, the phrase is credited to Jesus Christ. For Buddhists, the Buddha preached these words. "Do unto others as you would have them do unto you." When you treat others, especially your students, the way that you would like to be treated, you will find greater satisfaction in the achievement of students, the behavior of adolescents, and your relationships with these very special human beings.

Andrew Lindsay

ACADEMIC SERVICE LEARNING

As societies become more and more complex, the amount of subject matter that needs to be integrated into the student's experiences also increases. Many educators see subject matter as being a vital part of a student's experience, yet independent of any direct associations the student may or may not have with the subject matter (Dewey 1944). In other words, students do not automatically relate to the subject matter being taught (Lindsay 2002). They may not assimilate the experiences of others into their own experience, and then their learning is not as complete. Academic service learning is one effective way of constructing a vital connection between the worlds of school and community. In 2002 former North Carolina governor James Hunt encouraged educators to embrace service learning as a natural way for students to learn civic responsibility and to experience how their commitment to their community can change lives.

Service Learning

Academic service learning promotes the middle school philosophy and taps both the developmental and democratic interests of middle school students. Service learning includes interdisciplinary strategies, team-building activities, and a concern for the developing middle schooler. Where young adolescents have been disengaged in school, service learning provides the important link between the classroom and the real world. Where young adolescents from poorer neighborhoods have been the recipients of well-intended acts and gifts, through service learning they become the givers. As young adolescents begin to see a bigger world, a place of social and moral dilemmas, service learning provides the opportunity for them to become an exciting part of possible solutions.

Academic learning, personal development, and group citizenship—three goals of effective middle schools—are accounted for in a service learning program. Just as *Turning Points* recommended, "Recognizing that students learn by doing, service learning provides a vehicle to effect change, to increase social awareness, and to enhance overall student learning" (McAleavey 1996). Students actively become involved in the process of education instead of merely being a passive product of it. Even though service learning meshes with the philosophy of middle school, educators must understand the dynamics of service learning in order to properly implement it.

Definition of Service Learning

Service learning connects a community service activity with curricular objectives in order to achieve academic goals. It promotes the cognitive, affective, and psychomotor development of growing transescents by engaging them in real-life experiences in real-world settings as they service the community. The service learning experience is thoughtfully organized by teachers who value academic success as well as meeting the needs of their students. The main focus is the authentic creation of knowledge that fosters depth of understanding and the development of self while also acquiring an awareness of civic responsibility. Service learning:

- extends beyond the classroom
- involves real learning, integrated into the curriculum
- requires real service to meet real needs in the community
- provides time for reflection
- promotes personal growth and community responsibility
- celebrates accomplishment

In general the goals of academic service learning are to:

- enhance student learning by joining theory with experience and thought with action
- fill unmet needs in the community through direct service that is meaningful and necessary
- enable students to help others, give of themselves, and enter into caring relationships with others
- assist students to see the relevance of the academic subject to the real world
- enhance the self-esteem and self-confidence of students
- develop an environment of collegial participation among students, faculty, and the community
- give students the opportunity to engage in important and necessary work
- increase the civic and citizenship skills of students
- assist agencies in better serving their clients through the infusion of enthusiastic volunteers
- expose students to societal inadequacies and injustices and enable students to problem solve and engage in solutions
- develop a richer context for student learning

- provide cross-cultural experiences for students
- prepare students for their careers/continuing education
- foster a reaffirmation of students' career choices
- keep students in class and serve as a tool for retention
- give students greater responsibility for their learning
- impact local issues and local needs
- illustrate commitment to program participation by and with diverse populations

Academic service learning is developmentally appropriate for middle grades because it addresses the following transescent needs:

- Positive Social Interactions: to know a variety of adults from different backgrounds and occupations, have freedom to take part in the world of adults, and receive support and guidance from adults who appreciate their promise as well as their problems
- Structure and Clear Limits of Physical Activity: to test value systems in authentic and safe settings and have opportunities to make real decisions within appropriate limits
- Creative Expression: to speak and be heard and feel as if they can make a difference
- Competence and Achievement: to practice abilities and discover new skills and be recognized for accomplishments
- Meaningful Participation in Families, School, and Communities: to participate in projects that have visible outcomes
- Opportunities for Self-Definition: to discover a place for themselves and create a vision of a personal future

When a school or district implements service learning, the facilitators identify the needs and craft the program accordingly. Service learning is an interdisciplinary instructional strategy that encourages students to recognize civic and social responsibility in addition to fostering the growth of knowledge and skill advancement (Burns 1998). Shelton (1999) agreed when she stated that "the term 'service learning' can be loosely defined as an educational activity, program, or curriculum that seeks to promote student learning through experiences associated with volunteerism or community service" (52).

An important factor to remember when devising a service learning program is that the service activity must link "with what students are actually learning in their classes. This is the essence of service learning" (Barlow 1999, 38). Students must somehow connect the relevancy of their academic learning to the importance of life in their community. Realizing that link strengthens the community and school team effort and emphasizes the importance of the student's role in his or her neighborhood. If the service projects are not related to the core curriculum, they at least need to be connected to the student's future plans—possibly accomplished in an exploratory class. "The proponents of service education insist on real service, real learning and opportunity for reflection" (Bennett 1999, 58). As illustrated in Table 6.10, the teacher connects the service activity to meet the objectives of the classroom curriculum. In a four-step process, the teacher begins with the curriculum, encourages participation from the students as to a possible service learning activity, makes explicit the connection, and structures an authentic form of assessment and reflection.

Service Learning versus Community Service

Many teachers believe that service learning consists of a public service performed by individuals or a group for the benefit of a community. This is partly true. And certainly "one purpose of our schools is to produce a well-educated workforce" (Riley 2000, 6). But the individuals participating must also be engaged in a structured learning process. Service learning allows "structured time for a student to think, talk, or write about what that student did and saw during the service activity and provides chances to use newly acquired skills and knowledge in real-life situations in their own communities" (Burns 1998, 38).

Tice (1999) suggested that service learning is a process that incorporates reflection, as suggested in Table 6.11, and enables transescents to use their current abilities to expand. Service learning includes cognitive, psychomotor, and affective objectives, whereas community service generally focuses only on psychomotor and affective objectives.

Because of the judicial system's use of the term *community service*, it can falsely be perceived as a punishment if an academic connection does not exist. The implementation and facilitation of an effective program integrates the idea of social responsibility as well as attends to curricular objectives. The legal system intends community service as a punishment, whereas the educational system promotes pride and self-worth as a result.

Table 6.10
Connecting Objectives and Activities

Teacher's Planning Page
Connecting Curriculum Objectives and Service Activities

A	Which part of the core curriculum (content or objectives) would flourish with a service learning experience? What could be enhance or further explored? *Example: core democratic values in social studies or themes of heroes in language arts.* 1. 2. 3.
B	What are some possible service learning activites? *Example: work with local mental health facility to promote awareness* 1. 2. 3.
C	How can A and B be connected? *Example: have a walkathon to raise money for the birthday fund of facility residents while helping others to embrace differences of fellow citizens* 1. 2. 3.
D	What types of structured reflections could be used to assess students? *Example: journals, drawings, videos, presentations, writings, original music* 1. 2. 3.

Table 6.11
Journal Suggestions

Teacher's Planning Page
Journal Suggestions

Of course, you will want to make the journal as meaningful as possible for transescents. Here are some sample questions you give students who are "stuck" for a topic. It is important to note that a journal must be kept on a steady basis and the topic must be relevant to the issue at hand on that day. Allow students to write their own questions as well as giving them focused suggestions.

1. What is a healthy society?

2. Why do we have social problems?

3. Who is affected by social problems?

4. How do you define yourself?

5. What are your values?

6. Today I felt . . .

7. When . . . happened, I . . .

8. How do people solve social problems?

9. What is the role of a citizen?

10. What evokes change?

11. What is the purpose of a team?

12. How do you fit into a team?

13. What is important to you?

14. How does the character in your book relate to you?

15. What does this activity make you feel like?

16. I like myself when . . .

17. I feel good about myself when . . .

18. How has involvement with the community organization affected your life?

19. What do you see yourself doing in 10 years?

20. How does a person become successful?

21. My cooperative learning experience was good/bad because . . .

22. Why was the guest speaker important to the service learning activity?

23. If I could change something else, it would be . . .

24. I want people to remember me by . . .

25. What does work ethic mean to you?

If an exorbitant emphasis is placed on the curricular content rather than balancing it with the active part of service, students may view the activity as simply extra work or as being less important. The expectations of a service learning project must be defined and clearly and understandably presented; otherwise, the project is perceived by young adolescents—who tend to be very astute in quickly grasping the intent of an activity—as a punishment, additional work. The focus and intent of the learning activity will have been defeated. Successful service learning experiences share common specific characteristics. As well, they identify curriculum goals and objectives; teachers can ask themselves such questions as what they want their students to know, what they want their students to be able to do, and what qualities they want their students to strengthen.

Characteristics of Service Learning

Successful service learning programs are characterized by the following. They:

1. include objectives that are outlined in the curriculum
2. relate curriculum content and apply service learning to real-life situations
3. provide collaboration between students and community organizations (Burns 1998)

Just as it is important for middle grades students to have a meaningful voice and active choice in their learning, success in service learning results from students' taking responsibility for choosing the topics, for developing plans, for engaging in meaningful community action, and for assessing their own growth through the experience (Bennett 1999). More particularly, effective service learning projects:

1. engage people in responsible and challenging actions for the common good
2. provide structured opportunities for people to critically reflect on their service experience
3. articulate clear service and learning goals for everyone involved
4. clarify the responsibilities of each person and the organization involved

5. include training, supervision, monitoring, support, recognition, and evaluation to meet service and learning goals
6. illustrate commitment to program participation by and with diverse populations (Shelton 1999, 53)

Several prestigious organizations—The Student Service Alliance established by the Maryland Department of Education, the Kentucky Learn and Serve Project, and the National Association of Secondary School Principals—advocate for four steps in a service learning project:

1. preparation
2. action
3. reflection
4. demonstration and celebration

Preparation

As in any initiative, the most critical stage of a service learning project is the preparation. Table 6.12 provides a format for thoughtful planning. Preparation involves assessing the needs of the community, identifying the core content, identifying and inviting interested community leaders and organizations to become involved, and collaboratively planning the instructional unit or project. The roles and responsibilities of the school, community leaders, and organizations are identified and clarified. The students are prepared to assume their roles, and it is through this implementation and demonstration of mature social behaviors that deeper understanding of the learning outcomes occurs. Appendix B includes excerpts from an academic service learning curriculum entitled "Making a Difference" (Harbron 2000).

Action

There are several steps in the process between the identification of the problem and the assessment of the posed solution. Action involves facilitating students' work on and development of the knowledge and skills needed to be successful in the project. During this phase the teacher facilitates student planning, research, and problem solving and poses choices for authentic evaluation of the proposed project prior to implementing the activity/strategy. Tables 6.13 and 6.14 provide examples of lesson plans and process planning sheets that help students problem solve in a step-by-step fashion.

Table 6.12
Planning the Activity

Teacher's Planning Page
Planning the Service
Learning Activity

Community

Partnership:

Contact People:

Determined Need:

Service Learning Activity:

Academic Input

Curriculum Objectives:

Reflection Experiences:

Logistics

Time Span:

Meeting between Students and
Organization:

Funding:

Celebration:

Assessments

Experiences:

Strengths:

Challenges:

Table 6.13
Lesson Plan: Overview

Addressing the Concern

Topics

Brainstorming a local concern
Setting a goal for a solution
Planning the culminating activity

Content Standards & Benchmarks

Social Studies: Public Discourse and Decisionmaking
CS 2: Engage their peers in constructive conversation about matters of public concern by clarifying issues, considering opposing views, applying democratic values, anticipating consequences, and working toward making decisions.
B 1: Engage each other in conversations which attempt to clarify and resolve national and international policy issues

Social Studies: Citizen Involvement
CS 1: Consider the effects of an individual's actions on other people, how one acts in accordance with the rule of law, and how one acts in a virtuous and ethically responsible way as a member of society
B 2: Engage in activities intended to contribute to solving a national or international problem they have studied

Multiple Intelligences

Visual/Spatial
Verbal/Linguistic
Bodily/Kinesthetic
Interpersonal/Social

Developmental Characteristics

Are in a transition period from concrete thinking to abstract thinking

Prefer interaction with peers during learning activities

Have a strong need to belong to a group, with peer approval becoming more important as adult approval decreases in importance

Are increasingly concerned about peer acceptance

Often show compassion for those who are downtrodden or suffering and have special concern for animals and the environmental problems that our world faces

Middle Level Curriculum Characteristics

Work in small groups and advisory programs promote opportunities for interaction with peers and adults

Service projects and project-based learning strategies capitalize on students' creative expression and need for meaningful participation and experimentation with identity within community, including need for ethnic expressions of identity

Table 6.14
Lesson Plan

Addressing the Concern

Days 3, 4, and 6

Objectives

Students will brainstorm a relevant concern of the group
Students will work cooperatively in a team environment
Students will use speaking and listening skills
Students will analyze a realistic problem and solution situation

Time Needed
Three 50-minute class periods

Materials Needed

Arrangement of groups and space, six handouts, writing utensils, open minds

Vocabulary

Cooperative learning, concern, conceivable, responsibility

Activities/Procedures

1. Divide students into cooperative learning groups of 4 people. Since one objective is to create a team environment, randomly place students in groups. Consequently, they will be with both people they are familiar with and people they are unfamiliar with.

2. Allow group members to appoint classmates to cooperative learning roles.

3. Give students time to converse about and complete the *Brainstorming Concerns* handout. Once everyone is finished, the class needs to have a conversation about the groups' responses and decide on a concern—even if it is tentative—that they will address during the class.

4. The cooperative groups can continue discussing and working on the *Concern* handouts and present information when all are completed.

5. The teacher needs to keep notes on the board or overhead projector as the students present their information.

6. When the process is finished, the class will decide on the most effective solution, local organization to be contacted, and culminating experience.

(continues)

Table 6.14 (continued)

Assessment
Completion of the seven *Concern* handouts and oral presentations by the speaker, of the cooperative groups

---

Homework
Journal entry

Teacher Notes

Reflection

Students are asked to reflect on the project/activity and on their relative place within it. There are ongoing opportunities to review and think about their actions through writing and through speaking activities. Table 6.15 is a lesson plan that introduces journaling as an important aspect of growth in the service learning paradigm. Reflection is important during the planning and implementing stages. Teachers facilitate continuous student investigation and research, they engage students in assessment and evaluation of the project, and they connect activities and the classroom so students have the opportunity to understand the meaning and impact of their efforts.

Demonstration—Celebration

Students demonstrate their knowledge and understanding of service learning and of the goals and objectives of the project by reporting to peers, to faculty and/or community members, and to their families. They write publications both within the school and in the community at large. Table 6.16 presents information to help a teacher plan for the celebration part of the completed project. And during this public phase, students, teachers, and community members are recognized for their

Table 6.15
Journaling: Overview and Lesson

Journaling

Topics

Learning the purpose of a journal

Content Standards & Benchmarks

Language Arts
CS 12: Develop and apply personal, shared, and academic criteria for the enjoyment, appreciation, and evaluation of their own and others' oral, written, and visual texts.
B 4: Create a collection of personal work based on individual, shared, and academic standards, reflecting on the merit of each selection

Developmental Characteristics

Are preoccupied with self

Are dependent on parental beliefs and values but seek to make their own decisions

Seek to become increasingly independent, searching for adult identity and acceptance

Are in transition from moral reasoning which focuses on "what's in it for me" to that which considers the feelings and rights of others

Middle Level Curriculum Characteristics

Increase in desire for autonomy and indentity addressed through learning strategies involving choice, curriculum based on social and individual interests, opportunities for exploration of topics in exploratory programs and prevalence of safe environment for experimentation

Multiple Intelligences
Verbal/Linguistic
Intrapersonal/Introspective

(continues)

344

Table 6.15 (continued)

Objectives

Students will document personal growth
Students will construct meaning in a thoughtful manner
Students will be open to others' opinions

Time Needed
One 50-minute class period

Materials Needed

Paper, folders, writing utensils, art supplies, *The Diary of Anne Frank*
(The teacher may want to view the suggested questions in the *Teacher Planning Section.*)

Vocabulary

Journal, commitment

Activities/Procedures

1. Engage students in a conversation about a journal, establishing what the purpose is: recording personal growth, feelings, thoughts, inspirations, downfalls, successes. Make sure students realize that journaling is not listing tasks they did that day but rather documenting their search for "self."

2. Read a section of *The Diary of Anne Frank* as an example of quality journaling and pass the book around the class so every student has an opportunity to hear and see it.

3. Have students write their first journal entry: *What is the purpose of my journal?* (Discuss length, proper paragraph structure, and *daily commitment.*)

4. Allow volunteers to share their entries with the class.

5. Have students decorate their journal folders in a way that is demonstrative of their personalities and appropriate for school.

Assessment
Completion of the journal, group discussions, and private teacher/student interaction

(continues)

Table 6.15 *(continued)*

Homework
Journal entry 2—a topic of their choice as long as it reflects the purpose of the journal

Teacher Notes

learning/achievement and for accepting social responsibility (Burns 1998).

Reasons for Service Learning

Service learning is based and exercised in America's own neighborhoods. Successful programs require knowledge of the environment and a sense of commitment to the area and to the people who live there. Service learning establishes a stronger sense of self within the community. "Concern for the development of young people socially, psychologically, and intellectually and interest in the transformation of schools and learning" certainly add validity to the practice of service learning (Hope 1999, 237). Varlotta (1997) emphasized the "common good"—a core democratic value students study in required social studies curricula.

Middle schools embrace life skills as well as academia in order to fully equip young adolescents to be responsible citizens in the democracy. "The awareness of a sense for civic care and responsibility is alarmingly low" (Tice 1999, 38). The concept of helping our fellow human being has perhaps been lost somewhere along the way. To encourage that philosophy, teachers and parents must instill a sense of community pride in students by extending opportunities for them to become a worthy part of that community. Once actively involved in the culture of the local community, students quickly detect the need for others to participate, and they identify their own contributions as valuable.

By incorporating service learning into our current curricula, "we are communicating that civic involvement should be an integral aspect of everyone's life" (Wysocki 1999, 350). The communities we live and grow in reflect who we are and what we will leave behind. People learn

Table 6.16
Planning the Celebration Activity

Teacher's Planning Page
Planning the Celebration

At the end of every service learning experience, the
participants should celebrate their accomplishments, new
friends, and learning. At this celebration, recognition is
given to students, teachers, local organizations, members
of the community, administrators, parents, and anyone
else involved with the project. It is here that the
persuasive speech has the most impact. Students may also
display their portfolios. The class—not the teacher—should plan and make
arrangements for the celebration. Here are some guidelines to follow.

Who	*When*
Who will be invited and how?	What will the date and time be?

What	*Where*
What activities will happen?	Where will it be?
What supplies/refreshments will be needed?	

from and through experience. In order for students to embrace and benefit from the tenets of service learning, they need to witness, to encounter, to experience themselves as caregivers and reflect upon the ways they may incorporate aspects of service learning into their everyday lives.

Interdisciplinary teaching—a hallmark of middle schools and a recommendation of *Turning Points*—is a perfectly formatted structure for service learning. All subject areas are well suited for service activities. For instance, language arts classes discuss themes in literature that focus on commitment to the community or to our fellow human being. Social studies acknowledges the integrity and character of those involved in the civil rights movement. Following suit, students study architectural barriers that would prevent nonambulatory students or families from full access to the school facility or to stores, restaurants, and other buildings in the community. They then present their findings to the city commission, and in company with the local health organization, the community, and the school, they rectify the obstacles. Dedication to the environment is studied in science. Students take water samples across a number of months, chart their findings, and then propose a water cleanup project to the city building and grounds committee. The school's choir raises funds each year to purchase uniforms; because they have extra funding, they adopt senior citizens, visit them, and buy them gifts, since they are studying music with lyrics that speak of commitment to our brothers and sisters. The art classes are studying beautification projects, and the students gain permission to paint a mural on the side of an abandoned building that is an eyesore to the community. They study other mural painters in other urban areas, present their ideas for their own mural, paint it, and celebrate the culture of their own neighborhood. The math classes are studying right triangles. The students are placed in teams and are paired with elementary students. Together each team will create its own to-scale drawing of a new playground, full of right triangles. The winning team has help from peers, parents, and the local lumber yard, and a new playground emerges on the elementary school's playground. The opportunities for service learning projects abound in every school's curriculum.

In 1993, Wake County Public Schools in North Carolina instituted a comprehensive character education program with service learning. Since then, their schools have become a more supportive and positive learning environment. "That has translated into more students who complete high school and better student behavior in all grades" (Riley

2000, 7). The effects are long lasting. According to former secretary of education Richard Riley, students who successfully pursue the goals of a strong service learning program form an enduring understanding that transfers to future situations.

Because project participants establish roots in a variety of ways (emotionally, loyally, financially), service learning provides an opportunity to bond together. "It is a dynamic process that is fundamentally about investigating the connections among culture, power, knowledge, authority and meaning" (Hytten 1997, 50). Students who participate in service learning projects experience a fundamental responsibility toward the community and an intrinsic sense of belonging. Not only do they recognize and reflect upon the nature of their own status as citizens, but they are able to value others' positions in society as well.

The kinds of service learning projects are as diverse as are schools. Those that promote advocacy and student leadership are particularly poignant for middle grades students. As illustrated in Table 6.17, tutoring younger children or working with culturally diverse people, assisting a community in recovering from a natural disaster, restoring historical sites of hometowns, or relating environmental issues to specific communities are exciting examples of linking learning between school and the community. Some schools have organized clean-up committees after particularly devastating storms or have raised funds for families whose homes have been destroyed; still others have created health brochures. Any activity that draws the school's curriculum into a worthwhile experience for the student involving the community will reap the benefits of service learning.

These activities foster self-worth and exploration—important aspects of healthy transescent development. Middle grades teachers realize that the curriculum needs to be relevant to students' lives in order for students to be motivated to learn and in order for that learning to be deeply understood. Yet "it is the rare student who, on his own, makes connections between what transpires in the classroom and the 'outside world'" (Hope 1999, 236). Constructing learning opportunities in which students experience the "outside world" at the same time they are learning curriculum content bridges the gap between school and community. "If we adhere to the premise that schools exist to help students learn the skills, knowledge and attitudes they need to live productive lives and participate as responsible citizens in their communities, then service learning has a place in our middle schools" (237).

Kahne and Westheimer (1996) contended that service learning teaches civic responsibility, self-development, and academic achieve-

Table 6.17
Planning for the Culminating Activity

Teacher's Planning Page Culminating Activity Suggestions

Examples of Service Learning Experiences

Forming a partnershp with a senior citizen facility to bridge a generational gap

Raising money for playground construction

Establishing peer tutoring programs

Building a skate part for middle school kids

Instituting a recycling program

Enhancing local areas with beautification tasks

Providing homeless people with warm clothing

Starting a literacy program

Cleaning up local rivers

Holding a clothing drive for homeless people

Helping others understand learning disabilities

ment. It involves students in activities that respond to the needs of the community while advancing academic goals.

Through service learning, students acquire essential skills in real-life contexts. They contribute to the welfare of the community and actively experience their importance as community members. There are opportunities to respond to the needs of others, opportunities that are potential chances for learning more about being a compassionate person. Reflection opportunities strengthen students' skills in becoming lifelong learners (Swick 1999).

Whatever the service learning activity may be, it is important to also consider assessment of the experience before developing, planning, and implementing the activity.

Assessing Service Learning

To date one of the more challenging and relatively undeveloped areas of service learning lies in the assessment of student progress. "Identifying the specific curricular learnings from a project and assigning a formal grade are challenges for teachers" (Cairn and Cairn 1999, 66). Teachers tend to be less familiar with and less sophisticated in using performance-based assessment. In addition, because service learning is so directed toward affective objectives, evaluating a student's value progression is difficult, primarily because teachers have not been schooled in affective objectives or in authentic assessment; neither have they experienced them as students. "To fail to give adequate attention to these affective needs within the school setting can be detrimental to the success of the school in motivating students," however (Barkley 1989, 43). Obviously in a performance-based class, students must display enthusiasm and interest. Therefore, careful examination of alternative authentic assessment will reveal appropriateness of the assessment according to the age of the transescent, to skill level, to the task being performed, and to the student's ability to reflect.

When developing assessment measures, teachers inform students as to how they will be evaluated. Since service learning can, on the surface, be construed as very open-ended and lacking in structure, many students interpret the grading criteria to be relaxed. "The fact is that there is more to observe and consider in making evaluative judgments about students" (Wysocki 1999, 348). Common forms of assessment for service learning projects have typically been journals and drawings. As indicated in Tables 6.18 and 6.19, however, there are a wide range of assessment possibilities and a variety of constituents from and for whom evaluations would be useful.

Dialoguing personal experiences has proven to be a worthwhile method. Skills strengthened during this activity include predicting, inferring, summarizing, and paraphrasing. The most important aspect in constructing service learning assessments is the inclusion of opportunities for students to reflect upon their own values, beliefs, accomplishments, disappointments, and visions as a result of the project.

Having students create a portfolio is one very effective form of self-assessment. Table 6.20 offers students a thoughtful plan for the construction of their growth portfolios. Students categorize their finest pieces in order to demonstrate what they believe best illustrates what they have learned. A variety of kinds of work is required to comprise a quality portfolio. Students "know that the more active they are, the more involved they are, the better they're going to perform" (Cairn and Cairn 1999, 67).

Cairn and Cairn (1999) also maintained that agency site supervisors could assess student performance by using a checklist provided by

Table 6.18
Assessment Options

Assessment: Options for Reflection	

One day a week is designated "Reflection Day." Please consider the following assessments as options. Do not limit teaching or learning to only these reflections. It is vital to meet the needs of students. If other assessment/reflection activities will better promote student identities and the recognition of self, please substitute. Some reflections can be repeated; however, the collection of reflections should include a variety of assessments. Also give students the opportunity to create their own reflections that best demonstrate their identity.

Journals

Journals must reflect what is inside the student—values, beliefs, thoughts. They should convey feelings, concerns, insights, doubts, fears, and positive experiences, not simply be a list of tasks and dates. They should also include critical questions about the issue and people involved. Most important is the discovery of *self*. Students should be able to express where they stand on particular issues and recognize a development or evolvement in their journals. Honesty in writing encourages self-discovery and growth.

Photo Scrapbooks

Photos can allow others to view what is most important to students. Scrapbooks should be a collection of the most inspiring, disappointing, motivating, successful, and "ah-ha"moments throughout the service learning activity. They should include images that explain the meaning of the service and the contribution made by the student. The photos chosen should represent the growth and learning of the student through this experience.

Videotapes

A creative expression that extends the opportunities for students to be stars is videotaping. The filming can be handled in a variety of methods: mini-movie, documentary, or play. It can incorporate site visits or homemade sets, real characters or actors and props. The tape must include a representation of how the experience evoked growth and show a direct correlation between the community service and academic learning.

Group Discussions

Giving opportunities for students to converse with peers about the same experience allows them to express the growth that they have made and witness others' growth. Sharing perspectives is a part of development and adds to the reflection process. Group discussions should incorporate the ideas of everyone in the group. The atmosphere needs to be inviting, welcoming, and comfortable. Disagreements must be allowed as long as a mature conversation style ensues.

(continues)

Table 6.18 (continued)

Artwork

Artwork can be in the form of drawings, sculptures, collages, cartoons, or any other creative expression the students think of. Artwork must be authentic to the student and illustrate meaning from the experience. Comparison/constrast or before-and-after situations may further demonstrate the students' message.

Role Playing

Role playing allows students to gain insight of other participants in the service learning activity and strengthens problem-solving skills. Role playing scenarios should include representatives of all groups involved (students, school personnel, parents, community members, members of the organization, etc.). It shoudl include a knowledge of speaking and listening skills and demonstrate a problem and solution with input from every role player.

Writing Pieces

Writing pieces can use various genres—poems, short stories, letters, essays. The writing must deliberately convey the meaning the student gained from the service learning experience. It should include proper writing format and express feeling. The writing must express reflection.

Original Music/Song

Making music is a sincere form of expression. It gives students a chance to display emotion in a manner that isn't embarrassing. Students are most willing to share original music with others, and others are most apt to remember and gain meaning from it. Original music should include an emotion or meaning the student gained from the experience. It should be story-like and personal to the individual creating it.

---

instructors. Supervisors rank items that may include "Student established good rapport with clients and staff" and "Student's service has allowed the staff to do things they would not have been able to do otherwise" (68).

Barbara Wysocki teaches a one-year class called "Social Advocacy: History, Theory, and Practice." The problems she encountered in her class specifically centered around assessment. Her methods of assessment "were not measuring the key elements of service learning—critical and reflective thinking, personal growth and understandings, and the degree to which the students were assuming adult responsibilities" (Wysocki 1999, 346). So along with a colleague, Wysocki devised four assessment strategies they believed would encompass the meaning of the program and promote service learning outcomes for students.

Table 6.19
Student Reflection

Reflecting and Assessing:
Remembering Your Experience

*This form is for the **STUDENT** to complete. Name* _____

You have now finished a service learning experience! You have worked rigorously and productively during the past weeks. Take some time to reflect on what you wanted to do, what you actually did, and how you feel after accomplishing such a meaningful task.

Was the concern you focused on addressed effectively? Explain.

Were all of your expectations during the service learning process fulfilled?

What would you have done differently?

How do you feel now that the experience is over?

Do you feel better about yourself? Explain.

What effect did the journal and other assessments have on you?

Do you have a better idea of "who you are"? Explain.

Table 6.20
Portfolio Planning Guide

Portfolio:
Acknowledging Our Accomplishment
and Growth

A portfolio gives you the opportunity to showcase you. It is the collection of work that you take pride in and display for others to better understand who you are. Part of the identity of the portfolio includes the selection of pieces that are thoughtfully chosen by you. Read the following information before you begin constructing your portfolio.

PURPOSE	We construct portfolios as a means of collecting work that is representative of our personal growth and to share with others the meaningful journey we experienced.

SELECTIONS	You should choose the pieces that will best represent who you are as a person. Which pieces did you really put your heart into? What identity do you want people to recognize you as?

ORGANIZATION	You want to organize your reflection pieces in a meaningful way. For some, that might be chronological (moving in order from the first reflection to the last); for others, it might be by categories (all writings together, all artwork together, etc.); and for some, it might be by personal growth (some reflections were more meaningful than others).

REQUIREMENTS

1. *Creative Cover* that reflects the personality of the student
2. *Table of Contents* that includes titles of reflections and page numbers
3. *Seven Reflections* organized in order of the table of contents
4. *Written Comment* about each reflection piece describing the meaning to the student and why it was chosen
5. *Self-Assessment* of the portfolio by the student
6. *Future Goals* based on the student's needs, interests, and self-assessment of the portfolio
7. *Parent Portfolio Assessment Feedback Form* including comments, feedback, and encouragement

1. Her students were first evaluated on class participation. Active engagement including discussing insights and sharing past experiences, and asking questions was expected.

2. Students had to write in a journal in order to document their personal experiences of serving and learning and to reflect on how the "self" was being shaped. Teachers read the journals and responded with questions, affirmations, and statements of focus.

3. Next, Wysocki and her co-teacher assessed the students' volunteer experience. Visitations to off-campus sites allowed the teachers to make determinations not only on the students' progress but on the placements as well. By attending a session of the service learning activity, the teacher could also see if the students were actively participating with members of the community or simply filing papers in a back office.

4. And finally, students were required to write. Several options were available to accommodate student interest and the nature of the activity. Students could select a literary work, whether it was fiction or nonfiction, contemporary or historical, for analysis. They could write a "day in the life of" short story. Students could write a sociological portrait that would cause them to reflect on how their actions and surroundings might have reflected a particular social group. It would also give students experience with conducting a sociological or qualitative ethnographic study. The last writing assignment, called "Living Poor in America," enabled students to measure primary and secondary needs of poverty-stricken people.

Wysocki created assessment tasks that cover an array of skills and performances and that alleviate pressures of conformity. Although her students are required to complete four assessments, they are given a choice. By allowing students to choose the journal questions, service activity, literature, and writing assignments, she ultimately makes students responsible for their own learning, causing student ownership.

Summary: Academic Service Learning

Academic service learning responds in meaningful ways to the mandates of middle grades education—the dual concern that young adolescents learn critical social skills and academic content. Service learning challenges the often ego-centered young adolescent to look beyond his or her limited world of experience and step into someone else's world. When the student does so, the complex attitudes of empathy and compassion and the skills of group work and cooperation assume new places in the student's learning career.

Service learning meets students where they are by acknowledging their abilities rather than their deficits and by offering students experiences in which they can perceive themselves as capable, thoughtful, and respected. As well, service learning challenges the teacher to flexibly look beyond the classroom and see the community as a dynamic learning experience. From serving food at the local soup kitchen to having an all-night dance-a-thon to collect canned goods for the Salvation Army's food pantry, service learning ignites the spark of humanity that already burns within the emerging young adult. Their reward? The very act itself (Fertman, White, and White 1996).

Matthew J. Harbron

CHAPTER CONCLUSION

Teaching for democracy is teaching for preservation and for hope: the preservation of a society and the hope of a more just and compassionate world. Teaching for democracy, whether it be in Lindsay's classroom government or in Harbron's learning through service to the community, is to lead students in the construction of their own understanding of critical thinking, of problem solving, of respect for diverse opinions and experiences and perspectives. It is, particularly for middle grades students who are at the formative stages of their development of their moral and social identities, teaching for social justice, for advocacy and for action, for tolerance and for respect.

Dewey (1938) held that schools should be authentic forms of an active community, a place where people do indeed work for common aims that demand unity of thought, sympathy of feeling, and commonality of social spirit. Teachers and students engage in common activity as a cooperative enterprise rather than as a dictatorial gesture.

In the spirit of free interchange, of communication of ideas, of shared successes and failures, the community shares a standard of value that prizes individual quality of work as opposed to quantity of work. Schools should not be places of passive, uninformed listening wherein one mind is dependent on another's, but rather they must be communal places that support vigorous learning activity as well as productive ways of interacting. When school is related to life, young adolescents grow in social responsibility, in capacity, and in participation with the community. Knowledge then becomes an actively moving force. And helping others becomes not an act of charity but of allowing individual power and spirit to be set free.

REFERENCES

Barber, B. 1993. "America Skips School." *Harper's* 287, no. 1722 (November): 39–46.

Barkley, W. W. 1989. "Nurturing Adolescent Students." *The Clearing House* 63, no. 9 (September): 43–45.

Barlow, D. 1999. "Learning Service Learning." *The Education Digest* 65 (3): 38–41.

Beane, J. 1993. *A Middle School Curriculum: From Rhetoric to Reality,* 2d ed. Columbus, OH: National Middle School Association.

———. 1997. "Curriculum for What? The Search for Curriculum Purposes for Middle School Students." In Judith Irvin, ed., *What Current Research Says to the Middle Level Practitioner* (203–207). Columbus, OH: National Middle School Association.

———. 1998. "Reclaiming a Democratic Purpose for Education." *Educational Leadership* 56 (2): 8–11.

Bellah, R. 1999. "Freedom, Coercion, and Authority." *Academe* 85 (1): 16–21.

Bennett, P. 1999. "Service Learning: Curriculum, Standards, and the Community." *School Library Journal* 45, no. 2 (February): 58–59.

Brazee, E. 1997. "Curriculum for Whom?" In Judith Irvin, ed., *What Current Research Says to the Middle Level Practitioner* (187–201). Columbus, OH: National Middle School Association.

Burns, L. T. 1998. "Make Sure It's Service Learning, not Just Community Service." *The Education Digest* 64, no. 2 (October): 38–41.

Cairn, Rich, and Susan Cairn. 1999. "Service Learning Makes the Grade." *Educational Leadership* 56, no. 6 (March): 66–68.

Dewey, J. 1938. *Experience and Education.* New York: Touchstone.

———. 1944. *Democracy and Education: An Introduction to the Philosophy of Education.* New York: Free Press.

Erb, T., ed. 2001. *This We Believe . . . and Now We Must Act.* Westerville, OH: National Middle School Association.

Fertman, C., G. White, and L. White. 1996. *Service Learning in the Middle School: Building a Culture of Service.* Columbus, OH: National Middle School Association.

Frost, R., E. Olson, and L. Valiquette. 2000. "The Wolf Pack: Power Shared and Power Earned—Building a Middle School Nation." *The Middle School Journal* 31 (6): 30–36.

Glasser, W. 1992. *The Quality School: Managing Students without Coercion.* New York: HarperPerennial.

Glickman, C. 1990. "Open Accountability for the 90s: Between the Pillars." *Educational Leadership* 47 (7): 38–42.

———. 1991. "Pretending Not to Know What We Know." *Educational Leadership* 48 (8): 4–10.

———. 1998. "Revolution, Education, and the Practice of Democracy." *The Educational Forum* 63 (1): 16–22.

Gutmann, A. 1987. *Democratic Education.* Princeton, NJ: Princeton University Press.

———. 1999. *Democratic Education.* Princeton, NJ: Princeton University Press.

Harbron, M. 2000. "Making a Difference." Master's thesis, Eastern Michigan University.

Hope, W. C. 1999. "Service Learning: A Reform Initiative for Middle Level Curriculum." *The Clearing House* 72, no. 4 (March/April): 236–238.

Hytten, K. 1997. "Cultural Studies of Education: Mapping the Terrain." *Educational Foundations* 11 (4): 39–60.

Jackson, A., and G. Davis. 2000. *Turning Points 2000: Educating Adolescents in the Twenty-First Century.* New York: Teacher's College Press.

Kahne, J., and Westheimer, J. 1996. "In the Service of What? The Politics of Service Learning." *Phi Delta Kappan* (May): 593–599.

Knowles, T., and D. Brown. 2000. *What Every Middle School Teacher Should Know.* Portsmouth, NH: Heinemann.

Kohlberg, L. 1970. "Moral Development and the Education of Adolescents." In R. F. Purnell, ed., *Adolescents and the American High School* (46–72). New York: Holt, Rinehart, and Winston.

Kohn, A. 1996. *Beyond Discipline.* Alexandria, VA: Association for Supervision and Curriculum Development.

Lindsay, A. 2002. *Teen Regime: From Classroom to Community.* Master's thesis, Eastern Michigan University.

McAleavey, S. J. 1996. *Service-Learning Theory and Rationale.* In D. Dorge, ed., *Disciplinary Pathways to Service Learning* (8–14). Mesa, AZ: Campus Compact National Center for Community Colleges.

Meier, D. 1995a. "Central Park East Secondary School: The Hard Part Is Making It Happen." In James Beane and Michael Apple, eds., *Democratic Schools* (113–139). Alexandria, VA: Association for Supervision and Curriculum Development.

———. 1995b. "How Our Schools Could Be." *Phi Delta Kappan* 76 (5): 369–373.

———. 2000. *Will Standards Save Public Education?* Boston: Beacon Press.

National Middle School Association. 1995. *This We Believe: Developmentally Responsive Middle Level Schools.* Columbus, OH: Author.

Nelsen, J., L. Lott, and S. Glenn. 2000. *Positive Discipline in the Classroom.* Roseville, CA: Prima Publishing.

Noddings, N. 1999. "Renewing Democracy in Schools." *Phi Delta Kappan* 80 (8): 579–583.

Patmor, G., and D. McIntyre. 1999. "Involving Students in School Decision Making." *NASSP Bulletin* 83 (607): 74–78.

Riley, D. 2000. "Champions of a Cause." *Teaching PreK–8* 30, no. 5 (February): 6–7.

Shelton, G. G. 1999. "Service Learning: An Avenue to Community Partnerships with Section 8 Family Self-Sufficiency Program." *Journal of Family and Consumer Sciences* 91 (2): 52–55.

Sizer, T. 1985. *Horace's Compromise: The Dilemma of the American High School.* Boston: Houghton Mifflin.

———. 1992. *Horace's School: Redesigning the American High School.* Boston: Houghton Mifflin.

Smith, T. W. 1999. "Miracle at Mound Fort Middle School: Reading, Service Learning, and Character Education." *NASSP Bulletin* 83, no. 609 (October): 52–56.

Soder, R., ed. 1996. *Democracy, Education, and the Schools.* San Francisco: Jossey-Bass Publishers.

Soder, R., J. Goodlad, and T. McMannon, eds. 2001. *Developing Democratic Character in the Young.* San Francisco: Jossey-Bass Publishers.

Stevenson, C. 1998. *Teaching Ten to Fourteen Year Olds,* 2d ed. New York: Longman.

Swick, K. J. 1999. "Service Learning Helps Future Teachers Strengthen Caring Perspectives." *The Clearing House* 73, no. 1 (September/October): 29–32.

Tice, T. N. 1999. "Service Learning." *The Education Digest* 64, no. 6 (February): 38–39.

Varlotta, L. E. 1997. "Confronting Consensus: Investigating the Philosophies that Have Informed Service Learning's Communities." *Educational Theory* 47 (4): 43–76.

Wysocki, B. 1999. "Evaluating Students in a Course on Social Advocacy." *Social Education* 63, no. 6 (October): 346–350.

Web Sites Consulted

http://www.ncss.org
http://www.nmsa.org
http://www.alfiekohn.org

Chapter Seven

❦ Directory of Organizations, Associations, and Institutes

Kathryn Lewis vonEnde

This directory presents a variety of organizations, associations, web sites, conferences, workshops, institutes, and publications for a specific audience. The first section targets resources for middle level educators. Subsequent sections focus on resources for specific subject areas in middle level education; for middle level students; and for coalitions of parents, communities, and educators. Within each section the topics and resources are alphabetized. Because of the frequency with which contact persons change, none are listed. Many of the organizations and associations in this directory have developed coalitions with each other.

RESOURCES FOR MIDDLE GRADES EDUCATORS

American Federation of Teachers (AFT), American Federation of Labor–Congress of Industrial Organizations
555 New Jersey Avenue NW
Washington, DC 20001
(202) 879-4400
online@aft.org
http://www.aft.org

The AFT, the second largest educator organization in the United States, has worked for more than eight decades to support members and their families professionally and personally while promoting public education and public services in the nation and world. The organization provides educators with meetings and conferences, grants and scholarships, public policy stances, annual national conventions, and publications.

Publications: *Inside AFT, American Educator*

Apple Learning Interchange Learning Resources: Middle School Lesson Plans
http://www.ali.apple.com/edres/mslessons/ms-menu.shtml

Apple's Middle School Lesson Plans provide middle level educators with a wide variety of sample instructional materials in a diverse area of disciplines.

Center for Adolescent Studies (CAS)
Indiana University School of Education
Bloomington, IN 47405-1006
(812) 856-8113
http://www.education.indiana.edu/cas

The Center for Adolescent Studies collects and disseminates recent information and encourages research to expand knowledge about all aspects of adolescent transitions. Various programs include annual conferences, publications, lesson plans, and forums for parents, teachers, and students. The center also sponsors the Adolescence Directory On-Line (ADOL), an electronic guide to web sites on adolescent issues (see entry in "Miscellaneous Resources for Middle Level Educators" section).

Publication: *Teacher Talk*

Classroom Connect
8000 Marina Boulevard, Suite 400
Brisbane, CA 94005
(800) 638-1639
(650) 351-5100
(650) 351-5300 (fax)
http://www.classroom.net

As part of Harcourt, Inc., Classroom Connect has received several citations for providing staff development and curriculum materials to increase Internet use in education through a subscription service package.

Make It Happen!
Education Development Center, Inc.
55 Chapel Street
Newton, MA 02458-1060
(617) 969-7100 (ext. 2426)
(617) 969-3440 (fax)
http://www.edc.org/FSC/MIH

Resulting from ten years of research, Make It Happen! approaches middle school learning with interdisciplinary I-Search units integrated with technology to benefit learners with diverse learning abilities.

Publication: *Make It Happen! Manual*

Middle School Partnership
P.O. Box 1331
Mary Street
Skowhegan, ME 04976
(207) 474-2702
http://www.middleschool.com

The Middle School Partnership brings together businesspeople of International Paper with educators to improve the education and lives of middle level students by providing staff development, lesson plans, and general research information for educators in accordance with the recommendations of the Carnegie Institute Reports on Adolescent Development.

Middleweb—Middle Grades Resources
http://www.middleweb.com

Middleweb is an on-line source for a wide variety of issues in middle level education, including professional development, curriculum development, parent partnerships, leadership, assessment and evaluation, and needs of individual students. Subscribers may receive free e-newsletters and participate in discussions about key issues.

National Alliance of Black School Educators (NABSE)
310 Pennsylvania Avenue SE
Washington, DC 20003
(800) 221-2654
(202) 608-6310
(202) 608-6319 (fax)

http://www.nabse.org

The NABSE coalition promotes the education of all students, especially those of African descent; provides a forum for ideas and strategies along with professional development in those areas; and strives to identify leaders and influence public policy for the education of African Americans. An annual conference, the National Education Policy Institute (NEPI), and other local and regional conferences provide further support for educators.

Publication: *NABSE Newsbriefs*

National Education Association (NEA)
1201 16th Street NW
Washington, DC 20036
(202) 833-4000
(202) 822-7974 (fax)
http://www.nea.org

The NEA, the oldest and largest U.S. organization to promote public education nationally and abroad, supports educators through research, publications, public policy stances, local and regional workshops, state affiliates, national conferences, foundations, and grants.

Publications: *NEA Today, Inspired Classrooms Series*

National Indian Education Association (NIEA)
700 North Fairfax Street, Suite 210
Alexandria, VA 22124
(703) 838-2870
(703) 838-1620 (fax)
niea@niea.org
http://www.niea.org

The NIEA assists Native learners in becoming contributing members of society by supporting Native cultures and values. The association provides educational opportunities, resources, member advocacy, public policy support, annual conventions, legislative updates, and various programs and initiatives for indigenous people.

National Middle School Association (NMSA)
4151 Executive Parkway, Suite 300
Westerville, OH 43081
(800) 528-6672

info@NMSA.org
http://www.nmsa.org

The NMSA dedicates its full commitment to the personal and academic needs of young adolescents. Through the annual conference, a variety of staff development opportunities, curriculum development, numerous publications, and research, NMSA strives to support educators in improving the education and lives of middle level students.

Publications: *Middle School Journal, Middle Ground*

National Resource Center for Middle Grades Education
University of South Florida
College of Education EDU 162
4202 East Fowler Avenue
Tampa, FL 33620-5650
(813) 974-3400
http://www.coedu.usf.edu/middlegrades

The National Resource Center for Middle Grades Education strives to support middle level educators and their students in the United States and abroad through a variety of methods: staff development, consultation for evaluation of programs and needs assessments, seminars, development and dissemination of educational materials, and innovative projects.

Web Resources . . . Helpful to Middle School Teachers
Eastchester Middle School
550 White Plains Road
Eastchester, NY 10707
http://www.westnet.com/~rickd/Teachers.html

Web Resources contains extensive lists of sites useful to middle level educators according to academic areas, specific topics, and general middle level organizations and resources.

Young Citizens
875 Sixth Street, Suite 206
New York, NY 10001
(800) 646-4623
(212) 679-2482
(212) 679-7461 (fax)
http://www.nationalhelpers.org

Young Citizens provides resources for educators, youth programs, and community agencies to develop service learning projects through professional development, publications, curriculum materials, and innovative models that are created and piloted by the organization.

Publications: *Reflection: The Key to Service-Learning,* 2d edition; *Reading, Writing, and Reflecting: Helpers Promoting Literacy*

RESOURCES FOR SPECIFIC SUBJECT AREAS IN MIDDLE LEVEL EDUCATION

Children with Exceptionalities

Council for Exceptional Children (CEC)
1110 North Glebe Road, Suite 300
Arlington, VA 22201
(703) 620-3660
(703) 264-9494 (fax)
http://www.cec.sped.org

The CEC, an international organization, supports the improvement of educational outcomes for all individuals with exceptionalities, including the gifted. This organization serves educators and their students through government policy stances, professional development, publications, conferences and workshops, and assistance in finding resources to improve teaching and learning conditions.

Publications: *TEACHING Exceptional Children; About Exceptional Children*

Learning Disabilities Association of America (LDA)
4156 Library Road
Pittsburgh, PA 15234-1349
(412) 341-1515
(412) 344-0224 (fax)
http://www.ldanatl.org

The LDA advocates for students and adults with or affected by learning disabilities through the promotion of public awareness, publications, conferences and workshops, and a variety of interrelated activities with educators and other professionals, families, and government officials.

Publications: *LDA Newsbriefs; Learning Disabilities: A Multidisciplinary Journal; LDA: News from Washington*

National Association for Gifted Children (NAGC)
1707 L Street, Suite 550
Washington, DC 20036
(202) 785-4268
(202) 285-4248 (fax)
http://www.nagc.org

The NAGC forms a coalition of parents, educators, and communities to support the education and personal growth of gifted and talented children through staff development, research, communications, publications, and general advocacy for the children's unique needs.

Publications: *Gifted Child Quarterly; Parenting for High Potential*

National Clearinghouse for English Language Acquisition (NCELA)
George Washington University
2121 K Street NW, Suite 260
Washington, DC 20037
(800) 321-6223
(202) 467-0867
(800) 531-9347 (fax)
askncbe@ncbe.gwu.edu
http://www.ncbe.gwu.edu

The NCELA is funded by the U.S. Department of Education's Office of English Language Acquisition, Language Enhancement, and Academic Achievement for Limited English Proficient Students. Through national conferences, publications, an on-line library and communication system, technical assistance, curriculum and staff development, and databases, the NCELA provides support for English language acquisition.

Publications: *Directions in Language and Education; Idea Book: Dual Language Education; CrossCurrents*

Counseling and Psychology

American Counseling Association (ACA)
5999 Stevenson Avenue
Alexandria, VA 22304
(703) 823-9800
(703) 823-0252 (fax)
http://www.counseling.org

The goal of the ACA, self-described, is to enhance the quality of life in society through its foundations, annual conventions, publications, leadership training, and other support of counseling professionals.

Publications: *Journal of Counseling and Development (JCD); Counseling Today*

American School Counselors Association (ASCA)
801 North Fairfax Street, Suite 310
Alexandria, VA 22314
(800) 306-4722
(703) 683-2722
(703) 683-1619 (fax)
http://www.schoolcounselor.org

The ASCA represents the nation's school counselors and provides support through professional development, research, publications, and public policy stances for the benefit of school counselors, educators, and students.

Publications: *Professional School Counseling; ASCA School Counselor*

National Association of School Psychologists (NASP)
4340 East-West Highway, Suite 402
Bethesda, MD 20814-4411
(301) 657-0270
(310) 657-0275 (fax)
http://www.naspweb.org

The NASP certifies school psychologists in the United States and abroad as it seeks to provide services for the mental health of school children and adolescents. The organization provides a resource library, publications, and informational workshops while also advocating for its members and students through position statements and active lobbying on those positions.

Publications: *Communique; School Psychology Review*

English/Language Arts/Literature/Reading

International Reading Association
800 Barksdale Road
P.O. Box 8139
Newark, DE 19714-8139

(302) 731-1600
(302) 731-1057 (fax)
http://www.reading.org

The International Reading Association promotes and develops high literacy rates for all readers through professional development, national conferences, leadership in the improvement of reading instruction, partnerships, research, dissemination of information, and global literacy development.

Publications: *Reading Today; The Reading Teacher; Journal of Adolescent and Adult Literacy; Reading Research Quarterly*

National Council of Teachers of English (NCTE)
1111 West Kenyon Road
Urbana, IL 61801-1096
(800) 369-6283
(217) 328-9645 (fax)
public_info@ncte.org
http://www.ncte.org

The NCTE provides educators with publications, national conferences, research support, publications, commissions, committees, information about relevant materials, awards, and interest groups to improve the instruction and knowledge of English, literature, and the language arts. The Assembly on Literature for Adolescents (ALAN) of NCTE is a special-interest group with its own foundation, workshop, and awards.

Publications: *Voices from the Middle; Language Arts; School Talk; ALAN Review*

Fine Arts

Association for the Advancement of Arts Education (AAAE)
655 Eden Park Drive, Suite 730
Cincinnati, OH 45202
(513) 721-2223
http://www.aaae.org

The AAAE promotes the integration of the arts into all elements of educational programming, especially through collaboration among educators, students, community leaders, and arts professionals. Staff development opportunities, lesson plans, chat rooms, assessment procedures, incentives and recognition activities, and general information are available from this organization.

K–12 Resources for Music Educators
Mankato Area Public Schools, Music Department
P.O. Box 8741
Mankato, MN 56002-8741
(507) 387-8516
http://www.isd77.k12.mn.us/resources/staffpages/shirk/k12.music.html

K–12 Resources supports music educators in all areas with in-depth information about organizations, lesson plans, bulletin boards, print resources, technology, and other web sites helpful in the teaching of music.

National Art Education Association (NAEA)
1916 Association Drive
Reston, VA 20191-1590
(703) 860-8000
(703) 860-2960 (fax)
naea@dgs.dgsys.com

http://www.naea-reston.org

NAEA promotes art education and provides educators with a variety of services: professional development, national conferences and institutes, awards and recognition, leadership, numerous publications, and other special programs.

Publications: *Middle School Art: Issues of Curriculum and Instruction; NAEA News; Journal of Art Education*

National Association for Music Education (MENC)
1806 Robert Fulton Drive
Reston, VA 20191
(800) 336-3768
(702) 860-4000
mbrserv@menc.org
http://www.menc.org

MENC encourages the study and enjoyment of music through various avenues: development of standards for music education, numerous publications, national and local conferences and workshops, staff development, public relations campaigns and partnerships to advance the cause of music education, and preparation of teacher guides.

Publications: *Journal of Research in Music Education; Music Educators Journal*

Foreign Language

American Council on the Teaching of Foreign Languages (ACTFL)
6 Executive Plaza
Yonkers, NY 10701
(914) 963-8830
(914) 963-1275 (fax)
headquarters@actfl.org
http://www.actfl.org

The ACTFL, the only national organization dedicated to the teaching and learning of all foreign languages at all instructional levels, provides workshops, publications, national conventions and expositions, standards, proficiency tests, grants, and publications to enhance and expand foreign language instruction. The National Standards for Foreign Language Education is a collaborative project of the ACTFL and various other organizations.

Publications: *ACTFL Performance Guidelines for K–12 Learners; Standards for Foreign Language Learning: Executive Summary*

Health, Physical Education, and School Nurses

American Association for Health Education (AAHE)
1900 Association Drive
Reston, VA 20191
(800) 213-7193
(703) 476-3437
(703) 476-6638 (fax)
aahe@aahperd.org
http://www.aahperd.org/aahe/template.cfm

As an association of the American Alliance for Health, Physical Education, Recreation, and Dance, the AAHE supports health educators and other professionals to promote the health of all people. This support is accomplished through special projects, national conventions, professional development, committees, standards and evaluations, and leadership in developing and promoting appropriate legislation and policies.

Publications: *American Journal of Health Education; HE-XTRA*

National Association for Sport and Physical Education (NASPE)
1900 Association Drive
Reston, VA 20191
(800) 213-7193
(703) 476-3410
(703) 476-8316 (fax)
naspe@aahperd.org
http://www.aahperd.org/naspe/template.cfm

The NASPE, an association of the American Alliance for Health, Physical Education, Recreation, and Dance, provides publications, training, conferences, professional development, research, information, policies for legislation, and other services to promote knowledge and awareness of the benefits of sport and physical activity, and especially of the need for physical education in the schools.

Publications: *Journal of Physical Education, Recreation, and Dance (JOPERD); Research Quarterly for Exercise and Sport*

National Association of School Nurses (NASN)
Eastern Office:
P.O. Box 1300
Scarborough, ME 04070-1300
(877) 627-6476
(207) 883-2117
(207) 883-2683 (fax)
Western Office:
1416 Park Street, Suite A
Castle Rock, CO 80104
(866) 627-6767
(303) 663-2329
(303) 663-0403 (fax)
nasn@nasn.org
http://www.nasn.org

The NASN promotes the academic and personal success of students and supports the school nurse with publications, awards, annual conferences, professional development, development of programs, publicity and public awareness, and other issues surrounding the health profession.

Publications: *NASN Newsletter; Journal of School Nursing*

Library/Media Specialists

American Association of School Librarians (AASL) and its affiliate, American Library Association (ALA)
50 East Huron
Chicago, IL 60611
(800) 545-2433
(312) 440-9374 (fax)
membership@ala.org
http://www.ala.org

The American Library Association in conjunction with AASL provides its members with professional development, leadership in policymaking, research, publications, coalitions, and educational programs to promote diversity, continuous learning, equity of access to library materials, intellectual freedom, public education, and twenty-first-century literacy, especially in the use of information technologies.

Publications: *American Libraries; ALSC Newsletter* (Association for Library Service to Children)

Young Adult Library Services Association of the ALA (YALSA)
(See contact material above for the ALA)
http://www.ala.org/yalsa

As a division of the ALA, YALSA provides librarian/media specialists and other educators with professional development, special services and programs, publications, access to information and materials, representation in government and industry, and evaluations of materials of interest to adolescents.

Publications: *YAttitudes; Young Adult Library Services*

Mathematics and Science

Eisenhower Regional Consortium for Mathematics and Science
Mid-Continent Research for Education and Learning (McREL)
2550 South Parker Road, Suite 500
Aurora, CO 80014

(800) 949-6387
(303) 632-5552
(303) 337-3005 (fax)
info@mcrel.org
http://www.mcrel.org

The Eisenhower Consortium assists in the development and reform of mathematics and science education through numerous publications, curriculum development and guides, dissemination of information, policymaking, and collaborative efforts.

Publications: *Changing Schools Newsletters; Noteworthy Series*

Math Forum@Drexel: Ask Dr. Math—Middle School Level
3210 Cherry Street
Philadelphia, PA 19104
(800) 756-7823
(215) 895-1080
(215) 895-2964 (fax)
http://www.mathforum.org/dr/math/drmath/middle.html

The Math Forum, a research and educational enterprise of Drexel University, provides an on-line service to students and teachers as a self-described searchable archive with questions and answers solicited, researched, and categorized. Web site users can submit questions, peruse the math library, and utilize the reference section.

National Council of Teachers of Mathematics (NCTM)
1906 Association Drive
Reston, VA 20191-9988
(703) 620-9840
(703) 476-9027 (fax)
nctm@nctm.org
http://www.nctm.org

The goal of NCTM is to provide a high-quality math education program to all students through publications, dissemination of information, conferences, policymaking, and setting of principles and standards.

Publications: *Mathematics Teaching in the Middle School (MTMS), Journal for Research in Mathematics Education (JRME)*

National Science Teachers Association (NSTA)
1840 Wilson Boulevard

Arlington, VA 22201-3000
(703) 243-7100
http://www.nsta.org

The NSTA provides numerous publications, professional development, position statements, annual conventions, an on-line institute, and an on-line discussion board to assist members in modeling excellence, embracing innovation, and promoting interest and support for science education.

Publications: *NSTA Reports; National Science Education Standards*

Social Studies

National Council for the Social Studies (NCSS)
8555 Sixteenth Street, Suite 500
Silver Spring, MD 20910
(301) 588-1800
(301) 588-2049 (fax)
membership@ncss.org
http://www.socialstudies.org

The NCSS, the largest association for social studies education, promotes all levels and areas of social studies with annual conferences, Internet links, teacher resources, professional development, opportunities abroad, awards and recognition, publications, standards, and a link for the various disciplines in social studies education.

Publications: *Middle Level Learning; Social Education; The Social Studies Professional*

Technology, Career, and Life Skills

American Association of Family and Consumer Sciences (AAFCS)
1555 King Street
Alexandria, VA 22314
(703) 706-4600
(703) 706-4663 (fax)
info@AAFCS.ORG
http://www.aafcs.org

The AAFCS represents family and consumer sciences professionals in various content areas by providing publications and products, training and certification standards, public policy stances, coalitions, and conferences in order to assist society and improve the quality of life.

Publications: *Journal of Family and Consumer Sciences (JFCS); Family and Consumer Sciences Research Journal (FCSRJ)*

Association for Career and Technical Education (ACTE)
1410 King Street
Alexandria, VA 22314
(800) 826-9972
acteonline@acteonline.org
http://www.acteonline.org

The ACTE, dedicated to the preparation of youth and adults for careers, provides the following to its members: annual conventions, awards programs, publications, expositions, business education partnerships, member services, government policy stances, information and teaching materials, and publicity with special occasions such as Career and Technical Education Week.

Publications: *Techniques; Career Tech Update*

International Society for Technology in Education (ISTE)
480 Charnelton Street
Eugene, OR 97401-2626
(800) 336-5191
(541) 302-3778 (fax)
iste@iste.org
http://www.iste.org

The ISTE supports and promotes the appropriate use of technology for K–12 and teacher education through its leadership in providing information and evaluation of innovative research, networking, publications, professional development, relevant projects, and guidance in the incorporation of technology in the schools.

Publications: *Learning and Leading with Technology; Journal of Research on Technology in Education (JRTE)*

Meridian: A Middle School Technologies Journal
North Carolina State University
Raleigh, NC 27695
(919) 515-2011
http://www.ncsu.edu/meridian

An electronic journal for research and practice of computer technology in the middle schools, Meridian presents research findings, articles by educators, book excerpts, honors, and further resources twice a year.

National Centers for Career and Technology Education (NCCTE)

National Dissemination Center for Career and Technical Education
1900 Kenny Road
Columbus, OH 43210-1090
(800) 678-6011
(614) 292-9931
(614) 688-3258 (fax)
ndccte@osu.edu

National Research Center for Career and Technical Education
1954 Buford Avenue
St. Paul, MN 55108-6197
(800) 322-9664
(612) 624-3000
(612) 624-7757 (fax)
nrccte@tc.umn.edu
http://www.nccte.org

The NCCTE consortium partners (five major universities), funded by the Office of Vocational and Adult Education of the U.S. Department of Education, utilize practitioner-driven approaches to direct research, disseminate the results, and plan professional development activities for educators at all levels. Programs and projects, on-line discussion groups, national institutes, technical assistance, and numerous publications are available through the centers.

Publications: *CareerTech Correlations; Highlight Zone: Research@Work*

RESOURCES FOR MIDDLE LEVEL STUDENTS

Aspira Association, Inc.
1444 Eye Street NW
Washington, DC 20005
(202) 835-3600
(202) 835-3613 (fax)
info@aspira.org
http://www.aspira.org

Aspira Association, Inc., leads a movement to develop the full potential of every Puerto Rican, Latino, and non-Latino youth with resources, clubs, leadership training, cultural awareness, opportunities for community action, institutes and convocations, publications, and mentors.

Publications: *Aspira News; Apex Workshops Series*

Boys and Girls Clubs of America
1230 West Peachtree Street NW
Atlanta, GA 30309
(800) 854-2582
(404) 487-5700
(404) 487-5757 (fax)
LmcLemore@BGCA.org
http://www.bgca.org

The Boys and Girls Clubs of America provide young people in every state with twenty-five national programs on topics such as health, careers, and family support; through these programs and the safe environments in the clubs, youths develop personal strengths to become responsible members of society.

Child Welfare League of America (CWLA)
440 First Street NW, Third Floor
Washington, DC 20001-2085
(202) 638-2952
(202) 638-4004 (fax)
http://www.cwla.org

The CWLA promotes legislation and policies to protect children and families through publications, conferences and training, and programs including the National Data Analysis System with child welfare statistics on the Internet.

Publications: *Child Welfare Journal; ChildLine PLUS; Children's Voice Magazine*

Girls and Boys Town
The Village of Boys Town
Boys Town, NE 68010
(800) 448-3000 hotline/admissions
admissions@boystown.org
http://www.girlsandboystown.org

Girls and Boys Town assists troubled children, their parents, and professionals to find ways to extend hope and healing through group homes, counseling, training, publications and videos, and special programs such as "Reading Is FAME" for seventh through twelfth graders.

Publications: *Boundaries: A Guide for Teens; Parenting to Build Character in Your Teens*

Girls Incorporated
120 Wall Street, Third Floor
New York, NY 10005-3902
(800) 374-4475
(212) 509-2000
(212) 509-8708 (fax)
http://www.girlsinc.org

Girls Incorporated defines itself as a national information center/association/clearinghouse to assist girls in such areas as health, education, and leadership through newsletters, meetings and conferences, publications, training and seminars, and technical information.

Publication: *Strong, Smart, and Bold: Empowering Girls for Life*

International Youth Foundation (IYF)
32 South Street, Suite 500
Baltimore, MD 21202
(410) 347-1500
(410) 347-1188 (fax)
youth@IYFNet.org
http://www.iyfnet.org

The IYF develops programs, builds partnerships, and gathers resources to improve the lives of all young people. YouthNet International (YNI) provides the results of research and practice to support programs that work for young people and encourage investment in their futures.

Publications: *What Works in Youth Participation: Case Studies from Around the World; What Works in Education Facing the New Century*

National Beta Club
151 Beta Club Way
Spartanburg, SC 29306-3012
(800) 845-8281
(864) 542-9300 (fax)

http://www.betaclub.org

The National Beta Club, a service organization for students, seeks to recognize personal and academic success and leadership among students through club membership and projects, eighteen state conventions, publications for students and educators, and encouragement to continue education after high school.

Publications: *Beta Journal; Beta Reporter; Beta Parents*

National Dropout Prevention Center/Network
Clemson University
209 Martin Street
Clemson, SC 29631-1555
(864) 656-2599
(864) 656-0136 (fax)
ndpc@clemson.edu
http://www.dropoutprevention.org

The National Dropout Prevention Center/Network provides professional development, fifteen effective strategies, examples of model programs, conferences, grants, resource materials, special projects such as Service Learning, and recent research results about lowering dropout rates among youths.

Publication: *Journal of At-Risk Issues*

National 4-H Council
7100 Connecticut Avenue
Chevy Chase, MD 20815
(301) 961-2853
(301) 961-2894 (fax)
http://www.fourhcouncil.edu
http://www.4-h.org

4-H (Head, Heart, Hands, Health) clubs are administered through the land-grant college system as a youth education branch of the Cooperative Extension Service, a part of the U.S. Department of Agriculture. Youth from ages four to twenty-one learn life skills through camps, conferences, projects, programs, and awards for their efforts.

Tiger Woods Foundation
4281 Katella Avenue, Suite 111
Los Alamitos, CA 90720
(714) 816-1806

(714) 816-1869 (fax)
http://www.twfound.org

The Tiger Woods Foundation provides grants; scholarships; camps, fund-raising events; and contributions to individuals, programs, and organizations to assist young people in reaching their highest personal and academic potential.

RESOURCES FOR COALITIONS OF PARENTS, COMMUNITIES, AND EDUCATORS

Communities in Schools, Inc.
277 South Washington Street, Suite 210
Alexandria, VA 22314
(703) 518-2557
(703) 837-4557 (fax)
Greenfeldm@cisnet.org
http://www.cisnet.org

Communities in Schools builds partnerships among families, schools, communities, organizations, and businesses for the benefit of students through programs for mentoring, tutoring, parent involvement, national conferences, after-school activities, counseling and education, training, and service to the community.

Families and Advocates Partnership for Education (FAPE)
PACER Center, Inc.
8161 Normandale Boulevard
Minneapolis, MN 55437-1044
(888) 248-0822
(952) 838-9000
(952) 838-0199 (fax)
fape@pacer.org
http://www.fape.org

FAPE, a project of the PACER Center, serves as a clearinghouse for information for parents and advocates of children with disabilities, providing awareness and clarification of the Individuals with Disabilities Education Act (IDEA) via publications, workshops, seminars, referrals, research, and technical assistance.

Publications: *Special Education Evaluation; Understanding the Special Education Process*

National Association of Partners in Education, Inc. (NAPE)
901 North Pitt Street, Suite 320
Alexandria, VA 22314-3483
(703) 836-4880
(703) 836-6941 (fax)
napehq@nape.org
http://www.NAPEhq.org

NAPE provides educators at all levels, communities, businesses, and leaders in all areas with manuals, guides, publications, training, public awareness campaigns, research results, and other resources to promote effective coalitions to assist students toward personal and academic success.

Publication: *Keeping Children at the Center*

National Coalition for Parent Involvement in Education (NCPIE)
3929 Old Lee Highway, Suite 91-A
Fairfax, VA 22030-2401
(703) 359-8973
(703) 359-0972 (fax)
ferguson@ncea.com
http://www.ncpie.org

NCPIE builds partnerships among educators, families, communities, and advocacy organizations by serving as a clearinghouse for resources and by providing seminars and conferences, legislative information, projects, and other activities to increase student success and strengthen communities.

National Community Education Association (NCEA)
3929 Old Lee Highway, Suite 91-A
Fairfax, VA 22030-2401
(703) 359-8973
(703) 359-0972 (fax)
jocelyn@ncea.com
http://www.ncea.com

The NCEA promotes the partnerships of schools, parents, and communities to utilize the school facilities beyond the traditional school day for academic and career preparation, recreation, health and social services, and leadership training for people of all ages. The NCEA issues weekly reports on issues of public policy, holds conferences, bestows awards, establishes certification, and otherwise provides support for the establishment of the partnerships.

Publications: *Transforming Schools into Community Learning Centers; Community Schools: Serving Children, Families, and Communities*

National Congress of Parents and Teachers (PTA)
330 North Wabash, Suite 2100
Chicago, IL 60611
(312) 670-6782
(312) 670-6783 (fax)
b_carney@pta.org
http://www.pta.org

The National Congress of Parents and Teachers promotes partnerships and school involvement of parents and the general public to support all students. Publications, awards, press releases, national conferences, media kits, partnership information, and other practical resources are available to parents and educators.

Publications: *Our Children; Building Successful Partnerships*

National Council of La Raza (NCLR)
1111 19th Street NW, Suite 1000
Washington, DC 20036
(202) 785-1670
(202) 776-1792 (fax)
agarza@nclr.org
http://www.nclr.org

NCLR addresses the Hispanic community's needs for improved educational opportunities through the Center for Community Educational Excellence (C2E2), publications, annual conferences, research, and various programs and projects. Public policies and support mechanisms assist in ensuring a quality and equitable education for Hispanics, involving families in the educational process, and developing community-school collaborations to the benefit of society.

Publications: *Moving Up the Economic Ladder; U.S. Latino Children: A Status Report*

**National Information Center for Children and Youth
with Disabilities (NICHCY)**
P.O. Box 1492

Washington, DC 20013
(800) 695-0285
nichcy@aed.org
http://www.nichcy.org

NICHCY, funded by the U.S. Department of Education, supports families, educators, and other professionals with information, referrals, personal responses to questions, publications, and information searches about children and youth with disabilities.

Publications: *News Digest; Transition Summary*

Office of Indian Education Programs (OIEP)
1849 C Street NW
Washington, DC 20240
(202) 208-6123
(202) 208-3312 (fax)
http://www.oiep.bia.edu

The OIEP seeks to provide quality educational programs from birth to adult for Indian students through Family and Child Education (FACE) family literacy programs, guidance and collaboration with schools, technical assistance and training, national conferences, studies and reports, setting of content standards, and public policy stances. The Johnson O'Malley (JOM) programs grant assistance to schools to meet the unique needs of Indian students.

Publications: *OIEP Annual Report, FACE Newsletter*

MISCELLANEOUS RESOURCES FOR MIDDLE LEVEL EDUCATORS

Adolescence Directory On-Line (ADOL)

http://www.education.indiana.edu/cas/adol/adol.html

ADOL, sponsored by the Center for Adolescent Studies at Indiana University (see "Resources for Middle Grades Educators" section), is an electronic guide to web resources for adults and teens interested in conflict and violence, mental health, other health issues, counseling, teen-specific web sites, and teacher resources.

American Association of School Administrators (AASA)
1801 North Moore Street
Arlington, VA 22209-1813
(703) 528-0700
(703) 841-1543 (fax)
http://www.aasa.org

The AASA provides a network for school administrators with publications, conferences, legal support, current information, and public advocacy.

Publications: *AASA Professor; The School Administrator*

American Bar Association (ABA)
Division for Public Education
541 North Fairbanks Court, 15.3
Chicago, IL 60611-3314
(312) 988-5735
(312) 988-5494 (fax)
abapubed@abanet.org
http://www.abanet.org/publiced

The ABA Division for Public Education provides publications, awards, projects, current information about practical law, and career information to assist students and the general public in understanding the law and its importance in society.

Publications: *Insights on Law and Society; Everybody Wins: Mediation in the Schools*

Consortium for School Networking (CoSN)
1555 Connecticut Avenue NW, Suite 200
Washington, DC 20036
(202) 466-6296, ext. 15
(202) 462-9043 (fax)
http://www.cosn.org

The CoSN promotes telecommunications networking to improve learning in all schools by providing leadership with major initiatives, conferences and workshops, information on current issues, and public policy stances.

Council of the Great City Schools
1301 Pennsylvania Avenue NW, Suite 702
Washington, DC 20004
(202) 393-2427
(202) 393-2400 (fax)
http://www.cgcs.org

The Council of the Great City Schools, a coalition of the fifty largest urban areas in the United States, seeks to improve student performance through research and publications, special projects, reports on promising practices and educational trends, conferences, instruction in technology and management, and public relations.

Publications: *Advancing Excellence in Urban Schools; How We Help America's Urban Public Schools*

Institute for Education and Social Policy (IESP)
1640 Roxanna Road NW
Washington, DC 20012
(202) 882-1582
(202) 882-2138 (fax)
henderam@aol.com
http://www.nyu.edu/iesp

The IESP of New York University utilizes research, public policy studies, technical assistance, evaluations, and coalition building to improve urban education, especially in low-income areas and communities of color.

Publications: *NYC SchoolWatch; Charter Schools; Teacher Policies*

National Association of Elementary School Principals (NAESP)
1615 Duke Street
Alexandria, VA 22314-3483
(800) 386-2377
(703) 684-3345
(800) 396-2377 (fax)
naesp@naesp.org
http://www.naesp.org

The NAESP promotes the well-being of children by supporting elementary and middle level principals and other leaders in education with training, publications, meetings and conferences, collaboration with training institutions, and public policy stances.

Publications: *Middle Matters; PRINCIPAL; Communicator*

National Association of Secondary School Principals (NASSP)
1904 Association Drive
Reston, VA 20191-1537
(703) 860-0200
http://www.nassp.org

The NASSP supports middle level and high school principals, assistant principals, and other education leaders by providing training, conferences, representation on public policy, public awareness of relevant interests and issues, sponsorship of student activity associations, and promotion of high standards.

Publications: *Principal Leadership; NASSP Bulletin*

National Rural Education Association (NREA)
820 Van Vleet Oval, Room 227
University of Oklahoma
Norman, OK 73019
(405) 325-7959 (phone/fax)
nrea@cahs.colostate.edu
http://www.nrea.net

The NREA provides educators and communities in rural areas with support through publications, research, leadership training, conventions, coalition building, policy development, forums, public awareness, and leadership nationwide.

Publications: *Rural Educator; NREA News*

National School Boards Foundation (NSBF)
1680 Duke Street
Alexandria, VA 22314
(703) 838-6722
(703) 683-7590 (fax)
info@nsbf.org
http://www.nsbf.org

The NSBF promotes educational improvement with opportunities for school board members to attend conferences, receive training, and study the latest research and publications; in addition, the organization sponsors major initiatives, surveys, and partnerships.

Publications: *Improving School Board Decision Making: The Data Connection; Are We There Yet?*

National School Public Relations Association (NSPRA)
15948 Derwood Road
Rockville, MD 20855
(301) 519-0496
(301) 519-0494 (fax)
http://www.nspra.org

NSPRA promotes improved education in school districts through communication products, research and resource files, training workshops and national professional development, newsletters, networking and coalition opportunities, and auditing services with recommendations for improved communication.

Publications: *Network; PRincipal Communicator*

Chapter Eight

⊷ Selected Print and Nonprint Resources

Pat Williams-Boyd

The resources listed in this chapter are grouped according to topic as well as format. The first section, of books, is grouped according to curriculum, instructional strategies, assessment and evaluation, classroom management, middle grades programs and practices, professional development, developmental student characteristics, diversity, family and community, and teacher preparation and higher education. Although there is a wealth of materials written for middle grades, these have been selected because they are both examples of the topics and are exemplary works. The next sections are of videotapes, web sites, and other resources that are useful and provide best-practice information.

BOOKS

Curriculum—General

Atwell, Nancy. 1987. *In the Middle: Writing, Reading, and Learning with Adolescents.* Portsmouth, NH: Boynton/Cook Publishers.

This is a practical guide for writing and reading workshops with implications for K–12. It is also a classroom-based example of how a teacher who listens to her students can build her instructional practice around adolescent learning.

Beane, James. 1993. *A Middle School Curriculum: From Rhetoric to Reality.* Columbus, OH: National Middle School Association.

In this landmark text, Beane examines the separate-subject view of curriculum and poses general curriculum as a response to the personal and social concerns and developmental needs of young adolescents.

Compton, Mary, and H. Hawn. 1993. *Exploration: The Total Curriculum.* Columbus, OH: National Middle School Association.

The main premise of this thoughtful and practical text is that curriculum must be based on the natural curiosity of young adolescents. It examines exploration in general and in each of the subject-area fields.

Dickinson, Tom, ed. 1993. *Readings in Middle School Curriculum.* Columbus, OH: National Middle School Association.

Dickinson's text challenges the general sense of national curriculum by looking at issues of gender, self and social meaning, curriculum integration, and the core curriculum and seeks a fresh look at curriculum and at middle grades schools.

Hawkins, Mary Louise, and M. Dolores Graham. 1994. *Curriculum Architecture: Creating a Place of Our Own.* Columbus, OH: National Middle School Association.

Hawkins and Graham call for neighborhood schools that will responsively create curriculum based on the community's, the family's, and the student's characteristics, culture, and needs. It encourages active participation of students and teachers in the construction of rich learning experiences.

Kucer, Stephen B., Cecilia Silva, and Esther Delgado-Larocco. 1995. *Curricular Conversations: Themes in Multilingual and Monolingual Classrooms.* New York: Stenhouse Publishers.

This text combines theory and practice of teaching with themes and offers practical teaching strategies, a conceptual framework, and specific ways in which teachers may move from teaching at the lower levels of the learning taxonomy to more thoughtful and engaging higher levels.

McNeil, John. 1999. *Curriculum: The Teacher's Initiative,* 2d ed. Upper Saddle River, NJ: Merrill–Prentice Hall.

McNeil's text is organized around the themes of the purpose of curriculum, the most effective method of instruction, and the kind of organization of knowledge that encourages constructivist meaning.

Mee, Cynthia. 1997. *2,000 Voices: Young Adolescents' Perceptions and Curriculum Implications.* Columbus, OH: National Middle School Association.

Mee's engaging and easily read text presents questions that afford the reader a true snapshot of young adolescents and their view of themselves, their schools, and the world.

Messick, Rosemary, and Karen Reynolds. 1992. *Middle Level Curriculum in Action.* New York: Longman.

Based on the developmental view of students, this text presents a rationale, teaching strategies, and exploratory programs that are effective. It examines the ways in which middle grades schools have worked with at-risk students, and it promotes the kind of teaching that is reflective and enduring.

Perna, Daniel, and James Davis. 2000. *Aligning Standards and Curriculum for Classroom Success.* Arlington Heights, IL: Skylight Professional Development.

Perna and Davis have taken on what many schools see as the daunting task of aligning their classrooms and their curricula with state standards and benchmarks. The text presents practical ideas, suggestions, and examples in each of the general content fields.

Sheppard, Ronnie, and Beverly Stratton. 1993. *Reflections on Becoming: Fifteen Literature-Based Units for the Young Adolescent.* Columbus, OH: National Middle School Association.

This is a wonderfully creative brief text that examines themes relevant to young adolescents and then presents a case study and accompanying literature units for each theme.

Siu-Runyan, Yvonne, and C. Victoria Faircloth. 1995. *Beyond Separate Subjects: Integrative Learning at the Middle Level.* Norwood, MA: Christopher-Gordon Publishers.

Beyond Separate Subjects merges two philosophies about teaching and learning. One examines communication and language skills while the other targets the nature and curriculum needs of young adolescents. The authors' belief that reading and writing connect a school's curriculum permeates the change from the separate-subject approach of junior high schools to the integrated approach of the middle school.

392 MIDDLE GRADES EDUCATION

Curriculum—Literacy

Allen, Janet. 2000. *Yellow Brick Roads: Shared and Guided Paths to Independent Reading 4–12.* New York: Stenhouse Publishers.

This is both a research text and a practical guide with classroom-tested strategies that help teachers assist students who struggle to comprehend reading in literacy as well as in content classes.

Rycik, James, and Judith Irvin. 2001. *What Adolescents Deserve: A Commitment to Students' Literacy Learning.* Washington, DC: International Reading Association.

The authors focus on literacy access for all students, supportive instruction, comprehensive and collaborative programs, and reimagining adolescent literacy learning.

Wood, Karen, and Janis Harmon. 2001. *Strategies for Integrating Reading and Writing in Middle and High School Classrooms.* Columbus, OH: National Middle School Association.

This is a wonderful collection of teaching strategies for actively engaging students in reading and writing.

Wood, Karen, and Thomas Dickinson, eds. 2000. *Promoting Literacy in Grades 4–9: A Handbook for Teachers and Administrators.* New York: Allyn and Bacon.

This is a reference text for teachers who want to promote literacy and a climate of valuing literary skills. The text includes research on the role of the principal, effective literacy programs, and particular strategies for teaching young people.

Curriculum—Integrated and Interdisciplinary

Alexander, Wallace. 1995. *Student-Oriented Curriculum: Asking the Right Questions.* Columbus, OH: National Middle School Association.

Alexander chronicles the willingness of two veteran teachers to jump into writing student-centered integrated curriculum with their students. The text offers examples and insights and shows the results of people committed to each other and to learning.

Beane, James. 1997. *Curriculum Integration: Designing the Core of Democratic Education.* New York: Teachers College Press.

Long an advocate for student involvement in their own learning, Beane makes a defensible argument for conducting the business of school and of learning based on the democratic principles that construct and interpret our society.

Brazee, Edward, and Jody Capelluti. 1995. *Dissolving Boundaries: Toward an Integrative Curriculum.* Columbus, OH: National Middle School Association.

Brazee and Capelluti offer a well-balanced presentation of the integration of theory and practice with regard to curriculum integration and interdisciplinary study. From the planning stages to the development of interdisciplinary units, the text offers insights and reflections that help guide any reader in the ongoing work of curriculum connections.

Clark, Sally, and Donald Clark. 1995. *The Middle Level Principal's Role in Implementing Interdisciplinary Curriculum.* Reston, VA: National Association of Secondary School Principals.

The authors present an overview of and rationale for interdisciplinary curriculum and then examine the role of leadership in the organization, development, and implementation of interdisciplinary curriculum.

Easterday, Kenneth, Morgan Simpson, and Tommy Smith. 1999. *Activities for Junior High School and Middle School Mathematics.* Vol. 2. Reston, VA: National Council of Teachers of Mathematics and the National Middle School Association.

This is a valuable compilation of a variety of kinds of exercises that use math as problem solving, as reasoning, as a connection to other content, as communicating, in relationships, in patterns and functions, in probability, as statistics, as algebra, in measurement, as geometry, and in assessment.

Forte, Imogene, and Sandra Schurr. 1994. *Interdisciplinary Units and Projects for Thematic Instruction for Middle Grade Success.* Nashville, TN: Incentive Publications.

Forte and Schurr indicate that this text is written on the basis of young adolescents' needs for content connection, for thinking-skill development, for instruction based on learning styles, for product assessment, and for the use of thematic organization for lifelong learning. The book offers fully developed learning centers, mini-units, and major interdisciplinary thematic units.

———. 1996. *Integrating Instruction in Language Arts.* Nashville, TN: Incentive Publications.

This text and those for other subjects are integrated texts that provide a wealth of practical examples, instructional strategies for all learners, higher-order thinking-skill and problem-solving activities, and authentic assessment examples that facilitate easy use of curriculum integration.

———. 1996. *Integrating Instruction in Math.* Nashville, TN: Incentive Publications.

Coupled with read-and-relate activities and multiple intelligences, this text provides classroom-based examples of authentic assessments, cooperative learning activities, learning stations, and high-level thinking skills.

———. 1996. *Integrating Instruction in Science.* Nashville, TN: Incentive Publications.

This integrated unit accommodates all interests, abilities, and learning styles through the use of learning stations and multiple intelligences. Practical examples offer the classroom teacher easy access to well-developed curricular connections and engaging activities.

———. 1996. *Integrating Instruction in Social Studies.* Nashville, TN: Incentive Publications.

Like the others in this series, this text offer strategies, activities, tools, techniques, and projects for successful curriculum integration in social studies. It centers around the themes of the Civil War, the power of the constitution, the birth of civil rights, the world in spatial terms, electing a president, early empires, the western movement, women who shaped world history and revolutionary times.

———. 1997. *Health and Wellness.* Nashville, TN: Incentive Publications.

Forte and Schurr provide lessons and activities, projects and topics, problem-solving exercises and assessments, and grouping practices that challenge the skill and personal growth levels of all middle grades students

Jacobs, Heidi. 1997. *Mapping the Big Picture: Integrating Curriculum and Assessment K–12.* Alexandria, VA: Association for Supervision and Curriculum Development.

Jacobs offers twenty sample maps that help teachers visually see the connections across content areas that naturally arise and could lead to integrated units. She suggests a seven-step process in designing the kind of curriculum map that lends itself to interdisciplinary thinking.

Lounsbury, John, ed. 1992. *Connecting the Curriculum through Interdisciplinary Instruction.* Columbus, OH: National Middle School Association.

Lounsbury marries interdisciplinary teaming with interdisciplinary instruction and presents a work that makes practical the theoretical. From how to organize teams to how to evaluate interdisciplinary instruction, the text is as thoughtful as it is useful.

Lown, Fredric. 1997. *Langston Hughes: An Interdisciplinary Biography.* Portland, ME: J. Weston Walch Publishers.

This is an exciting example of an interdisciplinary unit that is based in history and literature and that offers creative activities in global geography, politics and law, music, various genres of writing, and African American history.

Martinello, Marian, and Gillian Cook. 1994. *Interdisciplinary Inquiry in Teaching and Learning.* New York: Macmillan College Publishing Company.

Martinello and Cook approach the study of interdisciplinary inquiry from an open-ended and critical thinking approach. They discuss habits of mind, how to start thinking interdisciplinarily, how to align thematic studies with content standards, and how to develop and find resources for interdisciplinary studies.

Opie, Brenda, and Douglas McAvin. 1995. *Effective Language Arts Techniques for Middle Grades: An Integrated Approach.* Nashville, TN: Incentive Publications.

This skill-based guide provides creative and challenging (and reproducible) activities and exercises for the language arts classroom. Students are motivated through engaging editing and proofreading exercises, writing opportunities, dictionary assignments, vocabulary strategies, and book report suggestions.

Post, Thomas, Alan Humphreys, Arthur Ellis, and L. Joanne Buggey. 1997. *Interdisciplinary Approaches to Curriculum: Themes for Teaching.* Upper Saddle River, NJ: Merrill–Prentice Hall.

Post and his colleagues examine the rationale for interdisciplinary teaching and learning as understood through multiple intelligences theory and cognitive psychology; discuss the pedagogy of interdisciplinary teaching with thematic identification, planning, implementation, and evaluation; and provide creative examples on various themes.

Stevenson, Chris, and Judy Carr. 1993. *Integrated Studies in the Middle Grades: Dancing through Walls.* New York: Teachers College Press.

The text's authors in collaboration with classroom teachers have designed some creative and innovative units about topics that address young adolescent social and personal interests.

Vars, Gordon. 1993. *Interdisciplinary Teaching: Why and How.* Columbus, OH: National Middle School Association.

Based on the theme "Come Fly a Kite!" Vars takes the reader through the interdisciplinary process in planning, implementation, and assessment with attention to skill development and engaging activities as well as to the program components that serve this kind of thinking.

Instructional Strategies—General

Jacobsen, David, Paul Eggen, and Donald Kauchak. 2002. *Methods for Teaching: Promoting Student Learning,* 6th ed. Upper Saddle River, NJ: Merrill–Prentice Hall.

This thoughtful text presents teaching in a three-phase process: planning, implementing, and assessing. This edition increases the focus on constructivist learning theory, on the presence of national standards, and on the importance of integrating technology into the curriculum.

Joyce, Bruce, and Emily Calhoun. 1996. *Creating Learning Experiences: The Role of Instructional Theory and Research.* Alexandria, VA: Association for Supervision and Curriculum Development.

Teachers create learning experiences for their students based on certain models of thinking and instruction. This brief text examines some of those models from inductive thinking to advance organizers, to mnemonics and social as well as processing models.

———. 1998. *Learning to Teach Inductively.* Boston: Allyn and Bacon.

The authors present both a conceptual model and practical examples of how teachers could stimulate their students' natural curiosity, problem-solving abilities, and sense of community.

Reinhartz, Judy, and Don Beach. 1983. *Improving Middle School Instruction: A Research-Based Self-Assessment System.* Washington, DC: National Education Association.

This brief text builds lesson planning and assessment on the developmental characteristics of adolescents and adds a case study as an example of self-assessment.

Skowron, Janice. 2001. *Powerful Lesson Planning Models: The Art of 1000 Decisions.* Arlington Heights, IL: Skylight Publishing.

This compilation of lesson plan templates is based on developing lessons using four different models: basic, integrated, differentiated, and problem based.

Smith, Patricia L., and Tillman Ragan. 1999. *Instructional Design.* New York: John Wiley and Sons.

Smith and Ragan look at the process of instructional design and offer examples and explanations from a full-process perspective: planning, writing, implementing, assessing, and rewriting.

Wiggins, Grant, and Jay McTighe. 1998. *Understanding by Design.* Alexandria, VA: Association for Supervision and Curriculum Development.

Understanding by Design joins the standards-based movement with authentic performance assessments in an exciting and unique way of instructional thinking.

Wood, Karen D. 1994. *Practical Strategies for Improving Instruction.* Columbus, OH: National Middle School Association.

This valuable text offers twenty-four kinds of teaching strategies that improve comprehension and vocabulary development, cooperative learning, and reading and writing assessment and offers guidelines for the thoughtful use of learning through videos, lectures, and field trips.

Instructional Strategies—Using Multiple Intelligences Theory

Armstrong Thomas. 1998. *Awakening Genius in the Classroom.* Alexandria, VA: Association for Supervision and Curriculum Development.

Armstrong challenges the traditional notions of genius and challenges teachers to see every child as a genius on the basis of curiosity, sensitivity, inventiveness, imagination, and joy. He then suggests a variety of activities and helpful resources.

———. 2000. *Multiple Intelligences in the Classroom,* 2d ed. Alexandria, VA: Association for Supervision and Curriculum Development.

This is a practical guide for educators that includes all eight of Howard Gardner's multiple intelligences. Armstrong provides curriculum development, lesson plans, assessments, cognitive skills, career development activities, and technology strategies and activities.

Bellanca, James. 1997. *Active Learning Handbook for the Multiple Intelligences Classroom.* Arlington Heights, IL: Skylight Publishing.

Bellanca offers over 200 active learning activities based on cognitive mediation multiple intelligences theory.

Costa, Arthur, and Bena Kallick. 2000. *Habits of Mind: Discovering and Exploring.* Alexandria, VA: Association for Supervision and Curriculum Development.

Rather than looking at students in the classroom from an abilities perspective, Costa and Kallick identify sixteen kinds of intelligent behavior that can aid students and adults in solving life's problems. They add action to critical thinking in instructional strategy and in habits of work and of mind.

Fogarty, Robin, and Judy Stoehr. 1995. *Integrating Curricula with Multiple Intelligences.* Arlington Heights, IL: Skylight Publishing.

Fogarty and Stoehr build their ten-curriculum integration models on Gardner's multiple intelligences theory and provide an instructive text with interactive lessons and strategies for developing, implementing, and assessing units and making connections across content areas.

George, Paul, Joseph Renzulli, and Sally Reis. 1997. *Dilemmas in Talent Development in the Middle Grades: Two Views.* Columbus, OH: National Middle School Association.

Editor Tom Erb frames an interesting dialogue between two views of working with gifted and talented students: Renzulli and Reis, nationally recognized experts, examine giftedness in middle grades, and George, as a recognized leader in the middle grades movement, examines middle grades groupings of students.

Hoerr, Thomas. 2000. *Becoming a Multiple Intelligences School.* Alexandria, VA: Association for Supervision and Curriculum Development.

Hoerr looks at one school that attempts across a ten-year period to become a rigorous multiple intelligences school. In a very revealing commentary, he contends that the necessary requirements of collegiality and commitment to diversity, standards, and multiculturalism underscore the hard work of change and academic achievement.

Jasmine, Julia. 1996. *Multiple Intelligences Activities (Grades 5–8).* Huntington Beach, CA: Teacher Created Materials.

Jasmine examines how to identify the intelligences in students, how to assess learning, and ways to teach and assess using center-based and project-based instruction as well as infusion of curriculum and teaching as separate subjects.

Jensen, Eric. 1995. *The Learning Brain.* Del Mar, CA: The Brain Store.

Jensen's text is a seminal study in the nature of learning and the capacity of the brain. Some of the aspects he examines are learning, thinking strategies, intelligence and learning, memory and recall, states of attention, music in learning, motivation and rewards, and environments.

Lazear, David. 1999. *Eight Ways of Knowing: Teaching for Multiple Intelligences.* Arlington Heights, IL: Skylight Publishing.

This companion book to Lazear's teaching text, *Eight Ways of Teaching,* provides the initial ways in which teachers can recognize the intelligences in students and help them express their understandings in multiple venues and ways in which teachers can nurture various understandings in students.

———. 1999. *Eight Ways of Teaching: The Artistry of Teaching with Multiple Intelligences.* Arlington Heights, IL: Skylight Publishing.

Lazear presents practical examples and instructional tools in turning the classroom into a multiple intelligences classroom.

Schlemmer, Phil, and Dori Schlemmer. 1999. *Challenging Projects for Creative Minds.* Minneapolis, MN: Free Spirit Press.

The Schlemmers provide twenty creative self-directed enrichment projects and use project-based learning, authentic assessment, and multiple intelligences as their guides. The projects develop critical thinking
and lifelong learning that go beyond the core curriculum.

Sousa, David. 2000. *How the Brain Learns: A Teacher's Guide,* 2d ed. Reston, VA: National Association of Secondary School Principals.

Sousa bases the teaching of thinking skills and learning on a sound understanding of how the mind works. He presents reader-friendly, practical examples using memory and retention and brain-processing skills
to plan daily lessons and provide rich learning experiences.

Instructional Strategies—Critical and Creative Thinking

Balton, Joyce, and Denise Nessel. 2000. *Thinking Strategies for Student
Achievement.* Arlington Heights, IL: Skylight Publishing.

This is a practical guide of examples that help students develop specific
thinking skills. Intended for all learners, the text helps teachers use
questioning as a tool for learning and helps students learn meaningful
relationships between content knowledge and themselves.

Baron, Joan, and Robert Sternberg. 1987. *Teaching Thinking Skills: Theory and Practice.* New York: W. H. Freeman and Company.

Baron and Sternberg bridge the theory of thought and the practical application of thinking and thinking-skill development through ten essays
written by leading educators, philosophers, and psychologists. They focus on creative and critical thinking skill development and on how to
teach and evaluate in order to develop these skills, and they identify
promising programs in critical thinking.

Bergmann, Sherrel, and Gerald Rudman. 1985. *Decision-Making Skills
for Middle School Students.* Washington, DC: National Education Association.

This brief monograph presents sample activities and teaching strategies
for provoking decisionmaking skills in middle grades students.

Blond, Geri. 1991. *Inventions and Extensions: High-Interest, Creative
Thinking Activities.* San Antonio, TX: ECS Learning Systems.

This is a very practical text on famous inventors and their inventions that stimulates students' creative and critical thinking in developing their own inventions.

Burggraf, Frederick. 1998. ***Thinking Connections: Concept Maps for Life Science.*** Pacific Grove, CA: Critical Thinking Books and Software.

Burggraf's text is included here as an example of the kinds of critical-thinking materials the company offers. As do all their texts, this book presents a collection of concept maps and helpful visual organizers.

Chuska, Kenneth. 1995**.** ***Improving Classroom Questions: A Teacher's Guide to Increasing Student Motivation, Participation, and Higher-Level Thinking.*** Bloomington, IN: Phi Delta Kappa.

This practical teacher guide provides an examination of the kinds of questions that motivate students to greater participation and higher-level thinking.

Fisher, Alec. 2001. ***Critical Thinking: An Introduction.*** Cambridge: Cambridge University Press.

Fisher offers creative and challenging thinking maps that help students develop thinking skills, and he poses over 220 questions to check the reader's progress through what he calls the "stimulus material."

Forte, Imogene. 1997. ***Tips, Tools, and Timesavers for Thinking Success.*** Nashville, TN: Incentive Publications.

Forte creatively integrates learning taxonomies and teaching strategies into these practical lessons that answer the questions: "What is this particular taxonomy or strategy? Why should I use it in my classroom? How can I put it to use in my classroom?"

Forte, Imogene, and Sandra Schurr. 1995. ***Using Favorite Picture Books to Stimulate Discussion and Encourage Critical Thinking.*** Nashville, TN: Incentive Publications.

Forte and Schurr encourage collaboration, discussion, critical thinking, and comprehension skills through sixty picture-book-based units.

Freedman, Robin. 1994. ***Open-Ended Questioning: A Handbook for Educators.*** Menlo Park, CA: Addison-Wesley Publishing Company.

Freedman presents thinking strategies and examples that encourage higher-level thinking through open-ended questioning for the mixed-ability classroom.

Neal, Peggy. 1994. *Problem Solving: A Heterogeneous Approach for Integrating Middle School Math Activities.* Topsfield, MA: New England League of Middle Schools.

Based on her firm belief in heterogeneous grouping as opposed to ability grouping, this middle grades math teacher offers a rich variety of examples of thinking skills that challenge all students to problem solve in her math classes.

Picciotto, Madelein. 2000. *Critical Thinking: A Casebook.* Upper Saddle River, NJ: Prentice Hall.

Picciotto presents case studies of fictional college students in order to help her students think critically about diversity and difference, academic integrity, same-sex relationships and public opinion, free speech and college policies, and living and learning on campus.

Scheid, Karen. 1993. *Helping Students Become Strategic Learners: Guidelines for Teaching.* Brookline, MA: Brookline Books.

Scheid bases lesson planning on cognitive theories of instruction and offers teaching strategies and practical examples to help improve reading, writing, and mathematics.

Shermis, S. Samuel. 1992. *Critical Thinking: Helping Students Learn Reflectively.* Bloomington, IN: EDINFO Press.

Shermis's text runs the gamut of looking at critical thinking theoretically and practically. From philosophy to implications for applied inquiry, the text presents a framework in which to understand thinking and classroom examples in order for readers to understand the translation into practice.

Walch, J. Weston. 1991. *Mathematical Thinking Activities for Student Groups.* San Antonio, TX: ECS Learning Systems.

Walch offers teachers fifty engaging and interesting stories through which to teach basic reasoning skills, cause-and-effect relationships, and critical thinking.

Zorfass, Judith. 1998. ***Teaching Middle School Students to Be Active Researchers.*** Alexandria, VA: Association for Supervision and Curriculum Development.

Zorfass provides practical information about inquiry-based, interdisciplinary learning and helping middle grades students become active researchers.

Instructional Strategies—Preparing Students and Schools for Success

Breeden, Terri, and Emalie Egan. 1995. ***Strategies and Activities to Raise Student Achievement.*** Nashville, TN: Incentive Publications.

These exciting activities encourage esteem building while improving test-taking skills. The text examines in easy-to-read format what is necessary for students to excel and how to use strategies and problem-solving techniques to raise their achievement levels.

Danielson, Charlotte. 2002. ***Enhancing Student Achievement: A Framework for School Improvement.*** Alexandria, VA: Association for Supervision and Curriculum Development.

Danielson conceives educational reform through a four-part model: curriculum, team planning, policies, and practices that affect students. These are coupled with the fundamental beliefs and values that school personnel hold. Each chapter ends with a provocative rubric summarizing the chapter's main points.

Forte, Imogene, and Sandra Schurr. 1996. ***Graphic Organizers and Planning Outline for Authentic Instruction and Assessment.*** Nashville, TN: Incentive Publications.

Forte and Schurr present eight kinds of graphic organizers that will help all students organize their learning and their responsibilities: charts, graphs, and grids; cognitive taxonomy outlines; forms for group learning; forms for interdisciplinary teaching; planning forms and outlines; research and study aids; the web; and writing planners and organizers.

Frender, Gloria. 1994. ***Teaching for Learning Success: Practical Strategies and Materials for Everyday Use.*** Nashville, TN: Incentive Press.

Frender presents a collection of creative ideas and ready-to-use forms that address the full range of activities and responsibilities of the classroom teacher. Some of the things included are teacher aids, parent letters, planning guides, content ideas and teaching strategies, games for all content areas, class summary logs, and help with organizing student activities and work.

Graham, Leland, and Darriel Ledbetter. 1996. *Preparing Students to Raise Achievement Scores, Grades 7–8.* Nashville, TN: Incentive Publications.

Intended to help students with their confidence in taking tests, this guide presents activities in a variety of skills: test taking, vocabulary, spelling, reading comprehension, language mechanics and usage, mathematical computation, concepts and applications, and the use of reference materials.

Harris, Douglas, and Judy Carr. 1996. *How to Use Standards in the Classroom.* Alexandria, VA: Association for Supervision and Curriculum Development.

The authors present successful ways of incorporating state and national standards into meaningful units of study for the classroom.

Marzano, Robert, Debra Pickering, and Jane Pollock. 2001. *Classroom Instruction that Works: Research-Based Strategies for Increasing Student Achievement.* Alexandria, VA: Association for Supervision and Curriculum Development.

Marzano, Pickering, and Pollock synthesize effective schools literature and present nine broad teaching strategies that improve student academic achievement. Each of the strategies is portrayed with classroom examples, rubrics, organizers, charts, and various frames of implementation.

Rubinstein, Robert. 1994. *Hints for Teaching Success in Middle School.* Englewood, CO: Teacher Ideas Press.

Presenting practical teaching strategies that suggest new ways of thinking about multicultural awareness and interpersonal communication, the text challenges the classroom teacher to examine the classroom, school practices, staff relations, parent connections, and testing in positive and dynamic ways.

Thompson, Randy, and Dorothy VanderJagt. 2002. *Fire Up! For Learning: Active Learning Projects and Activities to Motivate and Challenge Students.* Nashville, TN: Incentive Publications.

This includes fifty exciting, engaging, interactive, motivational, and student-centered activities for use in any content or advisory class.

Instructional Strategies—Constructivism

Brooks, Jacqueline Grennon, and Martin Brooks. 1999. *The Case for Constructivist Classrooms.* Upper Saddle River, NJ: Merrill–Prentice Hall.

The search for deep understanding is presented here in the case for constructivist teaching, the kind of education in which students construct their own meaning. This brief text is an excellent one-source book that explains constructivism, its guiding principles, and the implications for teachers.

Lambert, Linda, Michelle Collay, Mary Dietz, Karen Kent, and Anna Ershler Richert. 1996. *Who Will Save Our Schools? Teachers as Constructivist Leaders.* Thousand Oaks, CA: Corwin Press.

Lambert and her colleagues present a new look at teachers as constructivist leaders who work in learning communities to help students discover rich meaning and deeper understanding.

Richardson, Virginia, ed. 1997. *Constructivist Teacher Education.* London: Falmer Press.

Constructivism is examined here as a descriptive theory of learning in which individuals make meaning as they connect new ideas with that which they already know. Although not offering any prescriptions for teaching, Richardson offers some thoughtful instructional approaches.

Instructional Strategies—Curricular and Programmatic Planning

Forte, Imogene, and Sandra Schurr. 1993. *The Definitive Middle School Guide: A Handbook for Success.* Nashville, TN: Incentive Publications.

This is a comprehensive resource guide that provides effective schools information in the following categories: interdisciplinary teaming, advisory, cooperative learning, creative and critical thinking skills, assessment, interdisciplinary instruction, and the nuts and bolts of middle grades education.

Schurr, Sandra. 1989. *Dynamite in the Classroom: A How-To Handbook for Teachers.* Columbus, OH: National Middle School Association.

This tools and techniques book begins with an application of the young adolescent developmental characteristics as they appear in the middle grades classroom and follows with differentiating instruction and the application of various taxonomies to learning activities and assessments.

————. 1995. *Prescriptions for Success in Heterogeneous Classrooms.* Columbus, OH: National Middle School Association

This collection of teaching techniques equips the classroom teacher with the tools to creatively challenge all learners.

Instructional Strategies—Using Technology

Burniske, R.W. 2000. *Literacy in the Cyberage: Composing Ourselves Online.* Arlington Heights, IL: Skylight.

Burniske explains how teachers can use technology to enrich their classroom teaching by offering nine interrelated literacies that focus on a given on-line communication skill. The text also examines networked technological and on-line learning environments that teach critical literacy skills.

Churma, Michelle. 1999. *A Guide to Integrating Technology Standards into the Curriculum.* Upper Saddle River, NJ: Merrill–Prentice Hall.

This brief text is designed for methods and computers in education courses. Through a CD-ROM database it contains 275 lesson plans and strategies for the integration of technology into the K–12 curriculum.

Forcier, Richard, and Deon Descy. 2002. *The Computer as an Educational Tool: Productivity and Problem Solving.* Upper Saddle River, NJ: Merrill–Prentice Hall.

This how-to book is also an account of how classroom teachers have successfully infused technology into their classrooms and used technology to solve problems.

Instructional Strategies—
Problem-Based Classrooms

Delisle, Robert. 1997. *How to Use Problem-Based Learning in the Classroom.* Alexandria, VA: Association for Supervision and Curriculum Development.

The key to problem-based learning for the middle grades is its important link to the students' experiences. As students engage in the problem-solving process, they research topics, test hypotheses, and generate final products while the teacher functions as a facilitator or coach.

Fogarty, Robin. 1997. *Problem-Based Learning and Other Curriculum Models for the Multiple Intelligences Classroom.* Arlington Heights, IL: Skylight Publishing.

Fogarty poses six curricular frameworks that actively engage today's students: problem-based learning, case studies, thematic learning, project learning, service learning, and performance learning. Within each framework she offers practical examples and learning activities.

National Research Council. 2000. *Inquiry and the National Science Education Standards: A Guide for Teaching and Learning.* Washington, DC: National Academy Press.

The text provides inquiry-based teaching and learning activities on various science topics. It answers important questions regarding assessment, guidance, and learning structures.

Diversity and Instructional Strategies

Differentiated Instruction

Heacox, Diane. 2002. *Differentiating Instruction in the Regular Classroom: How to Reach and Teach All Learners, Grades 3–12.* Minneapolis, MN: Free Spirit Press.

This how-to book looks at the needs of a mixed-ability classroom and addresses the questions of how to create fair tasks to match student readiness levels, how to met curriculum standards, and how to develop challenging, engaging, and respectful learning experiences.

Kame'enui, Edward, Douglas Carnine, Robert Dixon, Deborah Simmons, and Michael Coyne. 2001. *Effective Teaching Strategies that Ac-*

commodate Diverse Learners. Upper Saddle River, NJ: Merrill–Prentice Hall.

This text combines teacher-directed and student-centered instruction with a focus on higher-order thinking in each of the content areas.

Pauley, Judith, Dianne Bradley, and Joseph Pauley. 2002. *Here's How to Reach Me: Matching Instruction to Personality Types in Your Classroom.* Baltimore, MD: Paul H. Brookes Publishing.

The authors contend that when teachers understand their students' personalities, they can thoughtfully match student-centered instruction to student need.

Renzulli, Joseph S., Jann Heppien, and Thomas Hays. 2000. *The Multiple Menu Model: A Practical Guide for Developing Differentiated Curriculum.* Mansfield Center, CT: Creative Learning Press.

Renzulli's expertise in the area of gifted and talented teaching and learning is focused on differentiated instruction in the heterogeneous classroom.

Silver, Debbie. 2003. *Drumming to the Beat of a Different Marcher: Finding the Rhythm for Teaching a Differentiated Classroom.* Nashville, TN: Incentive Publications.

The book offers practical examples, models, strategies, and teaching tips for the differentiated mixed-ability classroom.

Skowron, Janice. 2001. *How to Differentiate Instruction.* Arlington Heights, IL: Skylight Publishing.

This brief booklet offers an overview of the theory that supports differentiated instruction and then gives some practical decision-driven planning tools.

Tomlinson, Carol Ann. 1999. *The Differentiated Classroom: Responding to the Needs of All Learners.* Alexandria, VA: Association for Supervision and Curriculum Development.

This is the premier text on challenging all students in the mixed-ability classroom. Tomlinson provides actual lessons, units, and daily instruction tools for all teaching levels.

———. 2001. *How to Differentiate Instruction in Mixed-Ability Classrooms,* 2d ed. Alexandria, VA: Association for Supervision and Curriculum Development.

This follow-up to *The Differentiated Classroom* provides extended lessons, additional products, and varied strategies for differentiating instruction in the heterogeneous classroom.

Tomlinson, Carol Ann, and Susan Demirsky Allan. 2000. *Leadership for Differentiating Schools and Classrooms.* Alexandria, VA: Association for Supervision and Curriculum Development.

School leaders who are responsible for change in instruction become the center of this text, which offers a variety of ways in which principals can initiate and support differentiated classrooms.

Diversity and Equity

Allington, Richard. 2001. *What Really Matters for Struggling Readers: Designing Research-Based Programs.* New York: Longman.

Recognized reading expert Dick Allington offers best practices in teaching reading for struggling readers, based on three themes: children need to read, they need access to appropriate books, and they need to develop fluent reading to become proficient readers.

Banks, James, and Cherry McGee Banks, eds. 2003. *Multicultural Education: Issues and Perspectives.* New York: John Wiley and Sons.

James Banks has long been the recognized leader in the field of multicultural education. This landmark text examines the present and future knowledge teachers need to have in order to effectively work in the diverse classroom.

Bigelow, Bill, Brenda Harvey, Stan Karp, and Larry Miller, eds. 2001. *Rethinking Our Classrooms.* **Volume 2:** *Teaching for Equity and Justice*. Milwaukee, WI: Rethinking Schools.

This is a rich collection of curriculum ideas, lesson plans, poetry, resources, and classroom-based activities for teachers committed to social justice and all students' academic achievement.

Bimes-Michalak, Beverly. 1998. *Teaching for Achievement in Urban Middle Schools.* Topeka, KS: Clark Publishing.

Bimes's Writing to Learn Curriculum, now adopted by thirteen urban school districts, encourages collaborative teaching strategies based on high expectations, high support, and high content. This book includes examples and classroom-based strategies that have successfully helped struggling students succeed.

Bullard, Sara. 1996. *Teaching Tolerance: Raising Open-Minded Empathetic Children.* New York: Doubleday.

The author contends that when parents teach their children the equality of all people, then the rising rate of violence by children against children will decrease. This is a very thoughtful guide to fostering the type of open-minded perspective that breeds understanding and harmony.

Cole, Robert. 1995. *Educating Everybody's Children: Diverse Teaching Strategies for Diverse Learners.* Alexandria, VA: Association for Supervision and Curriculum Development.

Coming from ASCD's Urban Middle Grades Network, this text offers an assortment of research-based and classroom-tested instructional strategies for the entire learning community.

Garcia, Ricardo. 1998. *Teaching for Diversity.* Bloomington, IN: Phi Delta Kappa Educational Foundation.

This thoughtful text has a dual focus: how to teach diverse students and how to teach students to deal with diversity.

Haberman, Martin. 1995. *Star Teachers of Children in Poverty.* West Lafayette, IN: Kappa Delta Pi.

Haberman makes a case for the difference between the kinds of challenges teachers in large urban settings confront and the challenges teachers in smaller districts face. Teachers who work in high-poverty, diverse-cultural urban schools can literally make the difference between life and death for their students.

Hale-Benson, Janice. 1982. *Black Children: Their Roots, Culture, and Learning Styles.* Baltimore, MD: The Johns Hopkins University Press.

Although written over two decades ago, this text offers a rich understanding of the effects the black culture plays on a child's intellectual development. Hale-Benson argues for educational reform that would allow black children to develop their cognitive abilities within the culture of their families.

Huber-Brown, Tonya. 1993. *Teaching in the Diverse Classroom: Learner-Centered Activities that Work.* Bloomington, IN: National Educational Service.

Huber-Brown's text is an exciting collection of classroom-tested learning experiences written from a variety of student entry points through both personal and group investigation. Included are references and resources that promote further learning development and lesson construction.

Idola, Lorna, and J. Frederick West. 1993. *Effective Instruction of Difficult-to-Teach Students.* Austin, TX: Pro-Ed.

The text is a useful collection of student-based assessments, instructional strategies, classroom management techniques, and student progress evaluations.

Knapp, Michael. 1995. *Teaching for Meaning in High-Poverty Classrooms.* New York: Teachers College Press.

Knapp and his colleagues argue for the kinds of learning experiences that emphasize meaning and understanding over the more prevalent low-level rote drill and practice. He examines school practices in high-poverty areas and offers both research and practical examples of effective teaching.

Lewis, Anne. 1991. *Gaining Ground: The Highs and Lows of Urban Middle School Reform, 1989–1991.* New York: The Edna McConnell Clark Foundation.

Lewis examines the Baltimore, Louisville, Milwaukee, Oakland, and San Diego school districts and chronicles a kind of systemic change that fosters higher expectations, higher achievement, and more motivated and enthusiastic learners.

———. 1993. *Changing the Odds: Middle School Reform in Progress, 1991–1993.* New York: The Edna McConnell Clark Foundation.

Lewis essentially debunks the notion that disadvantaged youth can't and don't want to learn. With high expectations, high content, and high support, she demonstrates profound rewards are witnessed in the changed lives of students who are again allowed to hope.

———. 1995. *Believing Ourselves: Progress and Struggle in Urban Middle School Reform.* New York: The Edna McConnell Clark Foundation.

Lewis continues to follow middle school reform that is effective to change leadership attitudes, family investment, teacher expectations, and student participation and achievement.

Manning, Lee. 1994. *Celebrating Diversity: Multicultural Education in Middle Level Schools.* Columbus, OH: National Middle School Association.

Manning makes the case for the thoughtful infusion of cultural diversity into the curriculum rather than the add-on perspective of specific ethnic events. He offers practical cultural information and suggests developmentally appropriate ways the classroom teacher may celebrate the diversity of the people of the United States.

McCarthy, Tara. 1994. *Multicultural Myths and Legends.* New York: Scholastic Professional Books.

McCarthy offers seventeen stories with accompanying activities that help build cultural awareness and appreciation for diversity.

Norgaarden, Carol. 1995. *Create A Culture.* Santa Barbara, CA: The Learning Works.

Create A Culture is a collection of creative and motivating activities, reproducible for the classroom, that challenge students to experience a culture from a totally hands-on perspective.

Obidah, Jennifer, and Karen Manheim Teel. 2001. *Because of the Kids: Facing Racial and Cultural Differences in Schools.* New York: Teachers College Press.

Two teachers who work together in an urban school examine the issues of race and culture as they are played out in their classrooms.

Rodriguez, Fred. 1987. *Equity Education: An Imperative for Effective Schools.* Dubuque, IA: Kendall/Hunt.

Although this book was written almost two decades ago, it is still timely in its analysis and examination of the issues of equity and achievement. Rodriguez offers dynamic instructional strategies based on longitudinal research with activities and plans that challenge the classroom teacher to examine her practice.

Shade, Barbara, Cynthia Kelly, and Mary Oberg. 1997. *Creating Culturally Responsive Classrooms.* Washington, DC: American Psychological Association.

This book is a rich collection of motivational ideas, goals, instructional strategies, and self-directed questions, with a glossary and list of suggested readings.

Sleeter, Christine, and Carl Grant. 2003. *Making Choices for Multicultural Education: Five Approaches to Race, Class, and Gender.* New York: John Wiley and Sons.

Sleeter and Grant once again present dynamic and powerful approaches to dealing with diversity in education: teaching the exceptional and culturally different, human relations, single-group studies, multicultural education, and education that is reconstructionist and multicultural.

Williams, Belinda. 1996. *Closing the Achievement Gap: A Vision for Changing Beliefs and Practices.* Alexandria, VA: Association for Supervision and Curriculum Development.

The authors examine historical and contemporary social dynamics, cultural differences, teaching practice, physical and social environments, opportunity-to-learn variables, and the need for change in closing the gap in achievement between urban children and students in other settings.

Winebrenner, Susan. 1996. *Teaching Kids with Learning Difficulties in the Regular Classroom.* Minneapolis, MN: Free Spirit Press.

This book is an exciting collection of classroom-tested strategies for working with students who present unique challenges. Teaching for intervention, for multiple intelligences, for getting parents involved, for appropriate behavior, for improving students' learning success, and for using technology are some of the topics covered.

Cooperative Learning and Inclusion

Bruffee, Kenneth. 1999. *Collaborative Learning: Higher Education, Interdependence, and the Authority of Knowledge.* Baltimore MD: The Johns Hopkins University Press.

Bruffee makes a compelling call for changes in the pedagogical and epistemological teaching and learning of higher education, a call to interdependent, collaborative work.

Cohen, Elizabeth. 1994. *Designing Groupwork: Strategies for the Heterogeneous Classroom,* 2d ed. New York: Teachers College.

Designing Groupwork combines workable theory with practical classroom teaching strategies that can be flexibly used in any educational situation. The text includes skill building for advanced as well as for beginning students and suggests successful ways to work with the mixed-ability classroom.

Developmental Studies Center. 1997. *Blueprints for a Collaborative Classroom.* Oakland, CA: Developmental Studies Center.

A rich intermingling of activities, literature, collaboration, and social justice guides the twenty-five formats that are presented in this text. The blueprints include problem solving, poetry, mind mapping, visual organizers, poetry, graphic arts, and model building, to name a few.

Hertz-Lazarowitz, Rachel, and Norman Miller, eds. 1992. *Interaction in Cooperative Groups: The Theoretical Anatomy of Group Learning.* New York: Cambridge University Press.

The theoretical concepts that underpin cooperative learning and the research that supports its tenets are carefully examined in this text.

Johnson, David, Roger Johnson, and Edythe Johnson Holubec. 1994. *The New Circles of Learning: Cooperation in the Classroom and School.* Alexandria, VA: Association for Supervision and Curriculum Development.

This is the basic primer on cooperative learning. It includes a working definition and a description of the component parts, the qualities of formal and informal cooperative groups, and activities and lessons that are cooperative.

Kagan, Laurie, Miguel Kagan, and Spencer Kagan. 1997. *Cooperative Learning Structures for Teambuilding.* San Clemente, CA: Kagan Cooperative Learning.

The Kagans have presented a compilation of cooperative activities ready for the classroom. They use brainstorming, blind sequencing, formations, line-ups, and pairs-compare activities in addition to various team projects and statements, interviews, and roundtable exercises.

Pool, Harbison, and Jane Page, eds. 1995. *Beyond Tracking: Finding Success in Inclusive Schools.* Bloomington, IN: Phi Delta Kappa Educational Foundation.

The text is a compilation of the best research and practice on the perils of tracking and the power of the heterogeneous classroom in the inclusive school.

Schneidewind, Nancy, and Ellen Davidson. 1998. *Open Minds to Equality: A Sourcebook of Learning Activities to Affirm Diversity and Promote Equity.* New York: Allyn and Bacon.

This is an exciting sourcebook of activities that address all areas of diversity and challenge teachers and students to create a democratic, participatory, and cooperative classroom.

Villa, Richard, and Jacqueline Thousand, eds. 1995. *Creating an Inclusive School.* Alexandria, VA: Association for Supervision and Curriculum Development.

This is a comprehensive text on including children and youth with disabilities in general education classrooms. The expert opinions included in the text present ways in which schools can provide the "least restrictive environments" for all children.

Diversity and Gender

Finders, Margaret. 1997. *Just Girls: Hidden Literacies and Life in Junior High.* New York: Teachers College Columbia.

Finders portrays the lives of adolescent girls as they make sense of their worlds through reading and writing and the power each has to hurt them and to help them.

Gilligan, Carol. 1982. *In A Different Voice: Psychological Theory and Women's Development.* Cambridge: Harvard University Press.

In this landmark text, Gilligan presents a different view of female identity and the psychological and socialized development of moral commitment and place in the world.

Gilligan, Carol, Nona Lyons, and Trudy Hanmer, eds. 1990. *Making Connections: The Relational Worlds of Adolescent Girls at Emma Willard School.* Cambridge: Harvard University Press.

The unique aspect of this text is that it incorporates the voices of young adolescents and women in the process of developing their own sense of self, their relationships with each other and the world, and their sense of morality.

Golombok, Susan, and Robyn Fivush. 1994. *Gender Development.* New York: Cambridge University Press.

Golombok and Fivush examine gender and its formation from a developmental perspective and review theory and practice with regard to cognition, moral development, play and friendships, school and work experiences, hormonal influences, and psychopathology.

Kohl, Herbert. 1967. *36 Children.* New York: Penguin Books.

This is a classic study of a creative teacher's year in Harlem with thirty-six sixth-grade students who daily confront the problems of the urban ghetto.

Leadbeater, Bonnie Ross, and Niobe Way, eds. 1996. *Urban Girls: Resisting Stereotypes, Creating Identities.* New York: New York University Press.

These essays offer groundbreaking thinking regarding the differing development patterns and perspectives of urban adolescent girls and young women. Topics addressed include racism, sexuality, health risks, parent and peer relationships, and human development.

Noddings, Nel. 1984. *Caring: A Feminine Approach to Ethics and Moral Education.* Berkeley: University of California Press.

Noddings builds a view of ethics that contrasts with the masculine view in its principles and tenets. Beginning from the moral attitude or longing for goodness, Noddings draws from both a theoretical perspective and a wealth of experience to create a feminine dialogue that emphasizes giving care and being cared for.

Orenstein, Peggy. 1994. *School Girls: Young Women, Self-Esteem, and the Confidence Gap.* New York: Doubleday.

School Girls is an authentic look at the real lives of girls as seen through their own eyes. Despite the changes in the rights of women, it is still the case that girls experience traditional patterns of low self-image and self-censorship.

Pipher, Mary. 1994. *Reviving Ophelia: Saving the Selves of Adolescent Girls.* New York: Ballantine Books.

Dr. Pipher presents the challenging world of adolescent girls through their own stories of their struggles with eating disorders, depression, addictions, and suicide.

Pollack, William. 2000. *Real Boys' Voices.* New York: Penguin Books.

Pollack portrays contemporary young male adolescents with all of their struggles and passions as told in their own words.

Sadker, Myra, and David Sadker. 1995. *Failing at Fairness: How Our Schools Cheat Girls.* New York: Simon and Schuster.

With two decades of research in hand, the Sadkers irrefutably examine how gender bias makes it impossible for girls to receive an education equal to that of their male counterparts. This is the single most referenced text on gender and adolescents.

Adolescent Psychology

Balk, David. 1995. *Adolescent Development.* Pacific Grove, CA: Brooks/Cole Publishing.

Balk's full examination of adolescent growth and development comes from the refreshing perspective that adolescent behavior is a normal part of the human life span.

Csikszentmihalyi, Mihaly. 1996. *Creativity: Flow and the Psychology of Discovery* and *Invention.* New York: HarperCollins Books.

This is a wonderful text filled with interviews with creative people in all fields of endeavor. The author uses their stories to explain his flow theory of the creative process and how creativity enriches all lives.

Eggen, Paul, and Don Kauchak. 2001. *Educational Psychology: Windows on Classrooms,* 5th ed. Upper Saddle River, NJ: Merrill–Prentice Hall.

This broad examination of adolescent development is unique in that it presents a classroom case at the beginning of each chapter, gives examples of theory in practice, integrates diversity, and integrates technology with an interactive CD-ROM attached to the text.

Elkind, David. 1994. *A Sympathetic Understanding of the Child.* Boston: Allyn and Bacon.

This frequently referenced and highly acclaimed child-centered approach to adolescent development is readable, rich, and powerful in its theory and practical application to the classroom.

Kaplan, Louise. 1984. *Adolescence: The Farewell to Childhood.* New York: Simon and Schuster.

Kaplan brings a vibrancy to the inner and outer worlds of young adolescents and the struggle for adolescent identity that causes the theoretical parts of the text to be readable and rewarding.

Phelan, Patricia, Ann Davidson, and Hanh Yu. 1998. *Adolescents' Worlds: Negotiating Family, Peers, and School.* New York: Teachers College Columbia.

This rich dialogue between researchers and adolescents portrays the struggle young people endure to integrate the worlds of family, school, peers, and communities with themselves.

VanHoose, John, and David Strahan. *Young Adolescent Development and School Practices: Promoting Harmony.* Columbus, OH: National Middle School Association.

This brief monograph examines the developmental characteristics of adolescents and the appropriate school practices that maximize learning.

Adolescent Development—Adolescents at Risk

Csikszentmihalyi, Mihaly, and Reed Larson. 1984. *Being Adolescent: Conflict and Growth in the Teenage Years.* New York: Basic Books.

These two psychologists and researchers gave seventy-five adolescents beepers and randomly asked them to record their thoughts, feelings, responses, and activities. The result is a unique portrait of the daily world of adolescents.

Dryfoos, Joy. 1990. *Adolescents at Risk: Prevalence and Prevention.* New York: Oxford University Press.

Dryfoos's life work with adolescents challenged with multiple layers of peril prepared her to write this powerful text on the problems today's young people face, including delinquency, substance abuse, teen pregnancy, and school failure.

Elkind, David. 1981. *The Hurried Child: Growing Up Too Fast Too Soon.* Reading, MA: Addison-Wesley.

Elkind chronicles the children of the 1980s as children without childhood, children forced to assume adult responsibilities without the necessary adult tools. Though written over two decades ago, Elkind's observations are still poignant today.

———. 1984. *All Grown Up and No Place to Go: Teenagers in Crisis.* Reading, MA: Addison-Wesley Publishing.

Through his own practice, research, and case studies, Elkind contends that today's teens suffer dangerous repercussions because of the daily social pressure put upon them.

———. 1994. *Ties that Stress: The New Family Imbalance.* Cambridge: Harvard University Press.

Elkind examines the changes in the family structure and the toll they are taking on young adolescents.

Erikson, Erik. 1968. *Identity: Youth and Crisis.* New York: W. W. Norton.

Erikson collects two decades of essays and research regarding the connection between individual struggle and the social order.

Humphrey, James. 1998. *Helping Children Manage Stress.* Washington, DC: Child and Family Press.

Humphrey looks at how societal violence and pressure cause stress in the lives of young people, and he presents some helpful and profound ways in which adults can be sensitive to the warning signs and to the causes of stress in lives of children.

Hymowitz, Kay. 2001. *Ready or Not: What Happens When We Treat Children as Small Adults.* San Francisco: Encounter Books.

The author confronts the ways in which society and popular culture have caused young people to be treated as young adults and how this has skewed our contemporary perceptions of childhood.

Lavin, Paul, and Cynthia Park. 1999. *Despair Turned into Rage: Understanding and Helping Abused, Neglected, and Abandoned Youth.* Washington, DC: Child Welfare League of America.

Lavin and Park examine the reasons young people in foster care appear angry toward authority, and they offer intervention strategies as well as interviewing techniques that are helpful to the educator, to the family, and to the student.

Schulenberg, John, Jennifer Maggs, and Klaus Hurrelmann. 1997. *Health Risks and Developmental Transitions during Adolescence.* Cambridge: Cambridge University Press.

This interdisciplinary text brings together health risks and adolescent developmental transitions within multiple contexts and offers practical, planned interventions to ameliorate points of vulnerability.

Assessment

Anfara, Vincent A., and Sandra Stacki. 2002. *Middle School Curriculum, Instruction, and Assessment.* Greenwich, CT: Information Age Publishing.

This second volume of *The Handbook of Research in Middle Level Education* series examines a variety of teaching and learning topics from curriculum integration to character education and the facilitation of talent development

Bellanca, James, Carolyn Chapman, and Elizabeth Swartz. 1994. *Multiple Assessments for Multiple Intelligences.* Arlington Heights, IL: Skylight Publishing.

This text serves as a companion piece to the multiple intelligences instructional texts. It provides examples for performance and product assessments and constructs various graphic organizers and other authentic assessment tools.

Danielson, Charlotte. 1996. *Enhancing Professional Practice: A Framework for Teaching.* Alexandria, VA: Association for Supervision and Curriculum Development.

Danielson uses PRAXIS III: Classroom Performance Assessments criteria to identify the teacher responsibilities and tasks that enhance student learning. She divides teaching into twenty-two components in four domains: planning and preparation, classroom environment, instruction, and professional responsibilities.

Forte, Imogene, and Sandra Schurr. 1997. *Authentic Assessment.* Nashville, TN: Incentive Publishing.

Forte and Schurr create high-interest activities, lessons, and projects to be assessed in a variety of practical and student-centered ways.

Goodwin, A. Lin, ed. 1997. *Assessment for Equity and Inclusion: Embracing All Our Children.* New York: Routledge Press.

Goodwin looks at assessment through the lenses of diversity and equity and offers a critical dialogue regarding the use of standardized tests and the possibilities of innovative teaching and authentic ways of measuring knowledge acquisition.

Lewin, Larry, and Betty Jean Shoemaker. 1998. *Great Performances: Creating Classroom-Based Assessment Tasks.* Alexandria, VA: Association for Supervision and Curriculum Development.

The authors offer a four-step approach to teaching and to the use of assessments that instruct, from large-scale projects to mini daily assignments.

Lustig, Keith. 1996. *Portfolio Assessment: A Handbook for Middle Level Teachers.* Columbus, OH: National Middle School Association.

Lustig offers a thoughtful distinction between grading and evaluation and examines the ways in which portfolios can be designed, implemented, and assessed.

McMillan, James. 1997. *Classroom Assessment: Principles and Practice for Effective Instruction.* Boston: Allyn and Bacon.

This is a thorough examination of the kinds of assessments; of how to create high-quality classroom assessments; and of how to use them in portfolios, performance-based assignments, grading, reporting, assessing all mainstreamed students, and interpreting standardized tests.

Paris, Scott G., and Linda R. Ayres. 1994. *Becoming Reflective Students and Teachers with Portfolios and Authentic Assessments.* Washington, DC: American Psychological Association.

As one of the texts in the *Psychology in the Classroom* series, this book examines the use of portfolios in student-centered classrooms and looks at the characteristics of reflective teachers and how to strengthen the connections between the home and the school.

Schurr, Sandra. 1992. *How to Evaluate Your Middle School.* Columbus, OH: National Middle School Association.

Schurr has assembled a practitioner's guide for the informal evaluation of a middle grades program. She examines the advisory program, interdisciplinary teaming, exploratories, parent involvement, health and physical education, community relationships, and evaluation and reporting.

———. 1999. *Authentic Assessment: Using Product, Performance, and Portfolio Measures from A to Z.* Columbus, OH: National Middle School Association.

Schurr offers twenty-six different creative and motivating ways students can both assess their own learning and demonstrate to their teachers what they have learned.

Stiggins, Richard. 1994. *Student-Centered Classroom Assessment.* New York: Macmillan College Publishing.

Stiggins's philosophy—that the central focus of teaching and learning is students—permeates this thorough presentation of assessment methods, classroom applications, and student interactions.

Weber, Ellen. 1999. *Student Assessment that Works: A Practical Approach.* Needham Heights, MA: Allyn and Bacon.

Weber provides both discussion and examples of authentic and performance-based assessments along with a critique of expanded assessment activities and traditional testing.

Classroom Management

Burden, Paul. 2003. *Classroom Management: Creating a Successful Learning Community.* New York: John Wiley and Sons.

Thoughtfully shaping the interactions within the classroom as a community sparks discussion of how to motivate students, the tools needed to solve problems, and the principles of teaching and learning.

Burke, Kay. 2000. *What to Do with the Kid Who . . . : Developing Cooperation, Self-Discipline, and Responsibility in the Classroom.* Arlington Heights, IL: Skylight.

Burke presents the newest theories and research on classroom management, violence prevention, emotional intelligence, inclusion, and cooperative learning in classroom-ready format.

Cohen, Jonathan, ed. 1999. *Educating Minds and Hearts: Social Emotional Learning and the Passage into Adolescence.* New York: Teachers College Press.

This book synthesizes the current understanding of the emotional social intelligence and the attendant opportunities for learning.

Curwin, Richard, and Allen Mendler. 1999. *Discipline with Dignity.* Upper Saddle River, NJ: Merrill–Prentice Hall.

With the rush of changes in society, in learning, in the family structure, in relationships, and particularly in the middle schooler per se, the need to provide a controlled yet creative atmosphere for children is keen. The authors contend that when students are taught to be critical thinkers and problem solvers, the atmosphere of the classroom becomes one of instruction rather than one of discipline and punishment.

Froyen, Len, and Annette Iverson. 1999. *Schoolwide and Classroom Management: The Reflective Educator-Leader.* Upper Saddle River, NJ: Merrill–Prentice Hall.

The authors present a thorough examination of the foundations and assumptions upon which classroom management is built and the extent to which it affects schoolwide discipline, communication, instruction, student choices, and interrelationships.

Larrivee, Barbara. 1999. *Authentic Classroom Management: Creating a Community of Learners.* Boston: Allyn and Bacon.

Larrivee analyzes the needs of learners and the responsive classroom management styles from the vantage points of the teacher, the student, the classroom, and the general culture.

Shor, Ira. 1996. *When Students Have Power: Negotiating Authority in a Critical Pedagogy.* Chicago: The University of Chicago Press.

Shor presents an engaging and compelling argument for democratic teaching on the basis of his experience with sharing classroom authority with students across one semester.

Stevens, Ronald. 1995. *Safe Schools: A Handbook for Violence Prevention.* Arlington Heights, IL: National Education Service.

This is a very practical text that helps schools examine themselves and their sites, create a specialized program for safety, and address legal and legislative requirements.

Strahan, David. 1997. *Mindful Learning: Teaching Self-Discipline and Academic Achievement.* Durham, NC: Carolina Academic Press.

In a standards-based, test-crazed era, Strahan demonstrates how a teacher can join personal support and instruction enrichment through the bonds of caring. He shares strategies that help students maximize learning and make wise choices regarding their own behavior.

Ullinskey, Nancy. 1994. *Challenges and Choices: Using Creative Stories to Identify and Resolve Middle Grades Issues.* Nashville, TN: Incentive Press.

Ullinskey uses nine original stories to help students identify crucial issues such as personal and community responsibility, drugs, cheating, lying, and obeying rules and to help them make thoughtful choices about the issues they confront in their everyday lives.

Williams, Jeff. 1996. *How to Manage Your Middle School Classroom.* Huntington Beach, CA: Teacher Created Materials.

This how-to book covers all aspects of a teacher's work responsibility. From creating order in the classroom to parental involvement, Williams has created ready-to-use examples that are useful and resourceful.

Higher Education and Leadership

Ames, Nancy, and Edward Miller. 1994. *Changing Middle Schools: How to Make Schools Work for Young Adolescents.* San Francisco: Jossey Bass.

Ames and Miller offer inspirational stories of the teachers who work with and care for young adolescents and in so doing paint the picture of a successful middle school.

Arth, Alfred, John Lounsbury, Kenneth McEwin, and John Swaim. 1995. *Middle Level Teachers: Portraits of Excellence.* Columbus, OH: National Middle School Association and National Association of Secondary School Principals.

Through the use of interviews and case studies, the authors offer rich contextual portraits of outstanding middle grades teachers and the unique qualifications that are necessary for working with young adolescents.

Ayers, William. 2001. *To Teach: The Journey of a Teacher.* New York: Teachers College Press.

Ayers takes the reader on an intellectual, ethical, and emotional journey through the life of a teacher, capturing the complexities of the classroom and the commitment that outstanding teachers make.

Bliss, Traci, and John Mazur. 1998. *Secondary and Middle School Teachers in the Midst of Reform: Common Thread Cases.* Upper Saddle River, NJ: Merrill–Prentice Hall.

This is a valuable case method book on effective school reform as experienced from within and outside of the school.

Borich, Gary. 1990. *Observation Skills for Effective Teaching.* Columbus, OH: Merrill Publishing.

Borich offers the profession one of the most thorough examinations of observation: why, how, and what to observe are clearly analyzed in the service of professional growth.

Butler, Deborah, Mary Davies, and Thomas Dickinson. 1991. *On Site: Preparing Middle Level Teachers through Field Experiences.* Columbus, OH: National Middle School Association.

The authors challenge higher education professionals to offer thoughtful, effective, and integrated pre-service teaching experiences. He offers several models and suggests ways in which effective field experiences can affect the career of a teacher.

Calderhead, James, and Susan Shorrock. 1997. *Understanding Teacher Education.* London: Falmer Press.

This is a thoughtful case study book that portrays the stories of first-year teachers and the ways in which they successfully face the challenges of the classroom.

Carroll, Susan Rovezzi, and David Carroll. 1994. *How Smart Schools Get and Keep Community Support.* Bloomington, IN: National Educational Service.

Schools are addressing more of society's ills than ever before and experiencing more success with higher student challenges, but public opinion and support have been low. This book gives proven ways in which schools can regain community help, commitment, and support.

Clark, Sally N., and Donald C. Clark. 1994. *Restructuring the Middle Level School: Implications for School Leaders.* Albany: State University of New York Press.

This is a valuable text for all middle level teachers, administrators, and leaders who are engaged in the business of restructuring to help young adolescents reach their cognitive, emotional, moral, physical, and social success.

Clarke, John, Karin Hess, Jane Briody Goodman, Stephen Sanborn, Judith Aiken, and Nancy Cornell. 1998. *Real Questions, Real Answers: Focusing Teacher Leadership on School Improvement.* Alexandria, VA: Association for Supervision and Curriculum Development.

This is a manual of sorts for problem-based school development.

Cohen, Kathleen. 2000. *The Schooling Practices that Matter Most.* Alexandria, VA: Association for Supervision and Curriculum Development and the Northwest Regional Educational Laboratory.

Cohen examines both the contextual and instructional attributes of effective schools.

DuFour, Richard, and Robert Eaker. 1998. *Professional Learning Communities at Work: Best Practices for Enhancing Student Achievement.* Bloomington, IN: National Education Service.

Sensitive to the complexities of the organization of school, this book suggests powerful critical concepts about the importance and nature of the strategies necessary for developing communities of professionals committed to and supported for assisting students to achieve academically.

Fogarty, Robin. 2001. *Ten Things New Teachers Need to Succeed.* Arlington Heights, IL: Skylight.

This is a quick and useful guide for the novice teacher.

Gallagher-Polite, Mary, Lela DeToye, John Fritsche, Nanci Grandone, Charlotte Keefe, Jacqueline Kuffel, and Jodie Parker-Hughey. 1996. *Turning Points in Middle Schools: Strategic Transitions for Educators.* Thousand Oaks, CA: Corwin Press.

Through the guise of a fictional middle school, the authors follow the successes and disappointments of a traditional junior high school as it transitions into a middle school. They include instructional practices, group and personal dynamics, components of a successful middle school, and the examination of the change process itself.

George, Patricia. 2002. *No Child Left Behind: Implications for Middle Level Leaders.* Westerville, OH: National Middle School Association.

The federal legislation of No Child Left Behind has powerful implications for every middle school in the country. This brief text examines what the act is, what the requirements are, the opportunities, and the steps middle level leaders must take to ensure that they meet the legislation's requirements.

George, Paul, and William Alexander. 1993. **The Exemplary Middle School.** New York: Holt, Rinehart, and Winston.

This is a basic comprehensive textbook for students in middle grades education. It is thorough and classroom based, and it offers a wealth of resource information following each chapter.

George, Paul, Gordon Lawrence, and Donna Bushnell. 1998. *Handbook for Middle School Teaching.* Reading, MA: Longman.

This is a general middle level text for pre-service or in-service teachers that examines students, middle grades schools, instructional strategies, and professional development. Unique to the book is a collection of activities that follows each conceptual idea.

George, Paul, Chris Stevenson, Julia Thomason, and James Beane. 1992. *The Middle School—And Beyond.* Alexandria, VA: Association for Supervision and Curriculum Development.

The authors focus on how the nation's middle schools are accommodating diversity, addressing developmental student needs, integrating curriculum, emphasizing a supportive learning community, and creating the kinds of learning experiences from which young adolescents may grow and succeed.

Ginsberg, Margery, Joseph Johnson, and Cerylle Moffett. 1997. *Educators Supporting Educators: A Guide to Organizing School Support Teams.* Alexandria, VA: Association for Supervision and Curriculum Development.

The authors provide practical and experiential advice about developing teams that support each other through increased collaboration, through the control of school resources, through federal funding, and through the reconfiguration of the school day.

Glatthorn, Allan. 1997. *Differentiated Supervision.* Alexandria, VA: Association for Supervision and Curriculum Development.

Glatthorn presents a variety of ways educational leaders may evaluate and supervise the teachers in their buildings.

Henderson, James. 1992. *Reflective Teaching: Professional Artistry through Inquiry.* Upper Saddle River, NJ: Merrill–Prentice Hall.

Henderson offers a provocative discussion of how teachers may lead lives of inquiry with their students in democratic classrooms.

Irvin, Judith, ed. 1997. *What Current Research Says to the Middle Level Practitioner.* Columbus, OH: National Middle School Association.

Irvin provides a compilation of the most recent findings in middle-level research. Over forty authors collaborate with the National Middle School Association's Research Committee to provoke ongoing critical study.

Johnson, Susan Moore. 1990. *Teachers at Work: Achieving Success in Our Schools.* New York: Basic Books.

Johnson vividly presents a scathing rebuke of current school reform and how it thwarts the work of dedicated classroom teachers.

Kellough, Richard. 1999. *Surviving Your First Year of Teaching: Guidelines for Success.* Upper Saddle River, NJ: Merrill–Prentice Hall.

This is a brief collection of practical suggestions that will encourage the first-year teacher dealing with all the tedious tasks as well as the major challenges of the profession.

Kellough, Richard, and Noreen Kellough. 2003. *Teaching Young Adolescents: A Guide to Methods and Resources.* Upper Saddle River, NJ: Merrill–Prentice Hall.

This is a solid methods book and workbook for the pre-service middle grades teacher. It examines the why, what, how, and how well of teaching and learning.

Kohn, Alfie. 1998. *What to Look for in a Classroom.* San Francisco: Jossey-Bass Publications.

In this refreshing collection of essays, Kohn critically examines current school practices and offers his perspective of what classrooms ought to look like.

Kowalski, Theodore, Roy Weaver, and Kenneth Henson. 1990. *Case Studies on Teaching.* White Plains, NY: Longman.

First-year teachers present thirty-six cases that run the gamut of the most common experiences first-year teachers confront.

Lemlech, Johanna. 2002. *Curriculum and Instructional Methods for the Elementary and Middle School.* Upper Saddle River, NJ: Merrill–Prentice Hall.

Lemlech's comprehensive basic textbook is unique in its inclusion of portfolio activities at the end of each chapter, technology applications, virtual field trips, authentic assessments, and attention to the national content standards.

Levenson, Stanley. 2002. *How to Get Grants and Gifts for the Public Schools.* Boston: Allyn and Bacon.

Levenson offers exercises in addition to proven strategies that are successful in fund-raising and grant writing.

Lieberman, Ann, and Lynne Miller. 1999. *Teachers—Transforming Their World and Their Work.* Alexandria, VA: Association for Supervision and Curriculum Development.

The authors sensitively examine the phenomenon of teachers who struggle with the personal and institutional processes of change, and they offer both conceptual road maps and practical examples of personal and institutional reform.

Lipsitz, Joan. 1995. *Successful Schools for Young Adolescents.* New Brunswick, NJ: Transaction Publishers.

Lipsitz presents case studies of best-practice middle grades schools.

McEwin, C. Kenneth, and Thomas Dickinson. 1995. *The Professional Preparation of Middle Level Teachers: Profiles of Successful Programs.* Columbus, OH: National Middle School Association.

This is the most complete volume on specialized middle grades teacher preparation, written by two leaders of the middle school movement.

McLaughlin, Maureen, and Mary Ellen Vogt. 1996. *Portfolios in Teacher Education.* Newark, DE: International Reading Association.

For undergraduate and graduate programs that may use portfolios as capstone experiences, this text is an excellent guide. Divided into theory, practice, and promise, it presents a defense for the use of portfolios through the evaluation of a completed portfolio.

Redman, George. 1999. *Teaching in Today's Classrooms: Cases from Middle and Secondary School.* Upper Saddle River, NJ: Merrill–Prentice Hall.

Redman has written this text with the purpose of supplementing methods and foundations courses and student teaching seminars.

Sagor, Richard. 2000. *Guiding School Improvement with Action Research.* Alexandria, VA: Association for Supervision and Curriculum Development.

Sagor takes the reader through the seven-step process of action research: selecting a focus, clarifying theories, identifying research questions, collecting data, analyzing data, reporting results, and taking informed action.

Scales, Peter. 1995. *Connecting Communities and Middle Schools: Strategies for Preparing Middle Level Teachers.* Carrboro, NC: Center for Early Adolescence.

Scales's brief monograph examines young adolescent developmental characteristics and then links them to the community. In so doing he offers a defense for promoting the links between higher education teacher preparation programs and the general community.

———. 1996. *Boxed In and Bored: How Middle Schools Continue to Fail Young Adolescents—And What Good Middle Schools Do Right.* Minneapolis, MN: Search Institute.

In a brief monograph, Scales examines healthy communities, young adolescent developmental characteristics, and how middle schools can "unleash the power" of young adolescent minds.

Scales, Peter, and C. Kenneth McEwin. 1994. *Growing Pains: The Making of America's Middle School Teachers.* Columbus, OH: National Middle School Association and Center for Early Adolescence.

Commissioned by the DeWitt Wallace–Reader's Digest Fund, this is a research study of the higher education preparation of middle grades teachers.

Stevenson, Chris. 2003. *Teaching Ten to Fourteen Year Olds.* Reading, MA: Longman.

If there were a single text to be read about being an effective middle grades educator, it would be this one. Stevenson writes from a rich and successful career in the classroom and at the university level, and every page speaks of students and how people who work with them can maximize success.

Swaim, John, and Greg Stefanich. 1996. *Meeting the Standards: Improving Middle Level Teacher Education.* Columbus, OH: National Middle School Association.

This monograph is an example of the National Middle School Association's commitment to the specialized preparation of middle grades teachers and to their certification and licensure.

Thurston, Cheryl Miller, ed. 1997. *Survival Tips for New Teachers.* Fort Collins, CO: Cottonwood Press.

Classroom teachers offer words of wisdom for new teachers on such subjects as planning and organizing, building rapport with students, communicating with parents, and dealing with classroom discipline.

Villegas, Ana Maria, and Tamara Lucas. 2002. *Educating Culturally Responsive Teachers: A Coherent Approach.* Albany: State University of New York Press.

The authors present a conceptual framework in addition to practical strategies for teacher preparation programs to use in the preparation of students to work with populations that are increasingly diverse—racially, ethnically, and economically.

Waldron, Peter, Tani Collie, and Calvin Davies. 1998. *Telling Stories about School: An Invitation* . . . . Upper Saddle River, NJ: Merrill–Prentice Hall.

Each of the text's chapters is framed by a fundamental question that invites readers to self-reflection and self-critique regarding values, beliefs, and underlying assumptions regarding their educational commitments and practices.

Watson, Charles. 1997. *Middle School Case Studies: Challenges, Perceptions, and Practices.* Upper Saddle River, NJ: Merrill–Prentice Hall.

Through the cases presented, Watson offers students, teachers in training, and teachers furthering their training, as well as parents and the community, a firsthand look at the issues middle schools confront on a regular basis.

Welner, Kevin, and Jeannie Oakes. 2000. *Navigating the Politics of Detracking: Leadership Strategies.* Arlington Heights, IL: Skylight.

The academic merits of detracking students are clear; however, the process is often met with harsh criticism and a lack of understanding. Welner and Oakes offer a single case study of a fictitious school that has detracked, and they offer ways to survive the emotional obstacles and failures and move on to become a successful middle school.

Wheelock, Anne. 1998. *Safe to Be Smart: Building a Culture for Standards-Based Reform in the Middle Grades.* Columbus, OH: National Middle School Association.

Wheelock argues for the standards movement not from a political vantage point but from an educational one. Long in need of more attentive teachers and responsive educational backgrounds, today's schools can well use the standard movement to give credence to aligned practice.

Wiles, Jon, and Joseph Bondi. 2001. *The New American Middle School.* Upper Saddle River, NJ: Merrill–Prentice Hall.

This comprehensive middle grades textbook is rich in examples, perspectives, classroom-tested strategies, and the thoughtful integration of technology and activities. With the exception of the chapter on full-service schools, this is one of the most outstanding general texts written.

Zeichner, Kenneth, and Daniel Liston. 1996. *Reflective Teaching.* Mahwah, NJ: Lawrence Erlbaum.

Much in the vein of John Dewey, the authors stimulate the reader's thinking about the critical importance of reflection for ongoing democratic teaching. The text is a stimulant for rich classroom discussion.

The Family

Burns, Rebecca Crawford. 1993. *Parents and Schools: From Visitors to Partners.* Washington, DC: National Education Association.

For those schools that are looking for ways to make connections with families in the interest of their children's academic success, this book will be valuable. It is practical, based on the experiences of classroom teachers, and easy to use.

Epstein, Joyce. 1997. *School, Family, and Community Partnerships: Your Handbook for Action.* Thousand Oaks, CA: Corwin Press.

Epstein offers a guide through the process of developing, implementing, and sustaining an effective partnership among the school, family, and community.

Henderson, Anne T., and Nancy Berla, eds. 1997. *The Family Is Critical to Student Achievement.* Washington, DC: National Committee for Citizens in Education.

The research findings in this text are grouped by studies that evaluate the effects of programs or interventions and studies that examine family processes or how families interact with their children. The text includes a wealth of references as it responds to the question, "Why have the family involved in the work of the school?"

Loucks, Hazel, and Jan Waggoner. 1998. *Keys to Reengaging Families in the Education of Young Adolescents.* Columbus, OH: National Middle School Association.

Based on the research-supported contention that family involvement is the most critical factor in a child's success in school, this manual examines family engagement in the work of the school in six main areas, as decisionmakers and advocates; as communicators; as learners; as teachers and coaches; as supporters, volunteers, and audiences; and as partners with the community.

Myers, John, and Luetta Monson. 1992. *Involving Families: Middle Level Education.* Columbus, OH: National Middle School Association.

This very broad discussion of how to engage the family in the work of the school will be helpful to teachers, administrators, counselors, and librarians.

Shaheen, Jo Ann, and Carolyn Caselton Spence. 2002. *Take Charge! Advocating for Your Child's Education.* Albany, NY: Delmar Publications.

These two teacher-authors provide a thoughtful framework in which parents and families can become advocates for their children. They examine the school environment and offer resources, guidance, and support for families who desire to help make changes in their children's education.

Middle Grades Programs and Practices

Academic Service Learning

Fertman, Carl, George White, and Louis White. 1996. *Service Learning in the Middle School: Building a Culture of Service.* Columbus, OH: National Middle School Association.

This text presents a wealth of information and guidelines for middle schools to begin academic service learning programs.

Lewis, Barbara. 1995. *The Kids' Guide to Service Projects.* Minneapolis, MN: Free Spirit Publishing.

Lewis shares over 500 service ideas for young people who want to make a difference in their community. Ideas are grouped by animals, community development, crime fighting, the environment, friendship, hunger, literacy, politics and government, safety, and senior citizens.

Totten, Samuel, and Jon Pedersen, eds. 1997. *Social Issues and Service at the Middle Level.* Needham Heights, MA: Allyn and Bacon.

This collection of essays is an in-depth examination of how community service and academic service learning can be successfully implemented in schools in all disciplines.

Advisory

Galassi, John, Suzanne Gulledge, and Nancy Cox. 1998. *Advisory: Definitions, Descriptions, Decisions, Directions.* Columbus, OH: National Middle School Association.

For teachers who want to design or redesign advisory activities that are valuable to young adolescents, this small text is a solid beginning.

Hoversten, Cheryl, Nancy Doda, and John Lounsbury. 1999. *Treasure Chest: A Teacher Advisory Source Book.* Columbus, OH: National Middle School Association.

This is a wonderful collection of 120 classroom-ready activities grouped to facilitate easy selection by the advisory teacher.

James, Michael, and Nancy Spradling. 2001. *From Advisory to Advocacy: Meeting Every Student's Needs.* Columbus, OH: National Middle School Association.

In this brief book, the authors offer a compelling case for student advocates in the school and provide specific activities and ways in which teachers can move from advisors to advocates.

Schrumpf, Fred, Sharon Freiburg, and David Skadden. 1993. *Life Lessons for Young Adolescents: An Advisory Guide for Teachers.* Champaign, IL: Research Press.

This collection of ready-to-use activities is divided into the following sections: building a team, school success, celebrate yourself, communication and conflict resolution, relating to others, and your community.

Scheduling

Williamson, Ronald. 1998. *Scheduling Middle Level Schools: Tools for Improved Student Achievement.* Reston, VA: National Association of Secondary School Principals.

Everything that a middle school would wish to know about effective scheduling—from time as a resource to kinds of schedules—is included in this brief monograph.

Student-Led Conferences

Kinney, Patti, Mary Beth Munroe, and Pam Sessions. 2000. *A School-Wide Approach to Student-Led Conferences: A Practitioner's Guide.* Westerville, OH: National Middle School Association.

This wonderful how-to book presents the power and practices of conducting student-led conferences. From planning, to implementation, to evaluation, the authors present easy-to-use resource information for consideration and implementation.

Teaming

Arnold, John, and Chris Stevenson. 1998. *Teachers' Teaming Handbook: A Middle Level Planning Guide.* Fort Worth, TX: Harcourt Brace College Publishers.

Whether a novice or an expert team approaches this text, the handbook offers useful and readily applicable information regarding team planning, team products, and team "how-tos."

Bailey, Gerald, Tweed Ross, Gwen Bailey, and Dan Lumley. 1998. *101 Tips, Traps, and To-Dos for Creating Teams: A Guidebook for School Leaders.* Bloomington, IN: National Educational Service.

The opening page of this easily used handbook sums up the thrust of the 101 suggestions: guiding groups to become teams, facilitating their becoming high-performance teams, and empowering them to become technology-based teams.

Dickinson, Thomas, and Thomas Erb, eds. 1997. *Teaming in Middle Schools: We Gain More than We Give.* Columbus, OH: National Middle School Association.

This is to date the most comprehensive examination of middle level teaming, which includes its complexities, frustrations, rewards, challenges, and potential. A theoretical analysis of teaming, the twenty-three chapters written by experienced middle grades professionals challenge the middle level educator to new heights in the service of young adolescents.

Hoffman, Connie, and Judy Ness. 1998. *Putting Sense into Consensus: Solving the Puzzle of Making Team Decisions.* Tacoma, WA: Vista Associates.

This is a practical guide that will help every team with decisionmaking and problem solving. It answers the questions of what consensus is, when it should be used, and how it is reached.

Merenbloom, Elliot. 1991. *The Team Process: A Handbook for Teachers.* Columbus, OH: National Middle School Association.

Merenbloom examines effective middle schools and offers activities that will help teams become effective in their leadership and in their work with each other and will aid them with their ongoing growth.

Rottier, Jerry. 1996. *Implementing and Improving Teaming: A Handbook for Middle Level Leaders.* Columbus, OH: National Middle School Association.

Rottier breaks down the interdisciplinary team into pieces that can be evaluated and reassembled in thoughtful, practical, and effective ways.

———. 2002. *Taking Teaming to the Next Level: The Principal's Role.* Westerville, OH: National Middle School Association.

This brief text challenges administrators to renew their commitments to the benefits of teaming, to identify specific actions that will take teams to higher levels, and to analyze the leadership given to teaming.

Schurr, Sandra, and John Lounsbury. 2001. *Revitalizing Teaming to Improve Student Learning.* Westerville, OH: National Middle School Association.

This staff development kit will give middle grades teachers a resource to critically upgrade their team's performance.

Thompson, Randy, and Dorothy VanderJagt. 2001. *Wow What a Team: Essential Components for Successful Teaming.* Nashville, TN: Incentive Publications.

Thompson and VanderJagt look at twelve components that make interdisciplinary teaching teams effective. Each chapter presents a specific strategy for creating high-performance teams and concludes with an activity that guides the implementation process.

Influential Documents

Carnegie Council on Adolescent Development. 1989. *Turning Points: Preparing American Youth for the 21st Century.* New York: Carnegie Corporation.

Carnegie presents its recommendations for the kinds of middle schools that prepare young people for the new century.

———. 1996. *Great Transitions: Preparing Adolescents for a New Century: Abridged Version.* New York: Carnegie Corporation.

The shortened version of the full Carnegie report offers examples of each of the committee's major recommendations.

Erb, Thomas, ed. 2001. *This We Believe . . . And Now We Must Act.* Westerville, OH: National Middle School Association.

These are the national association's follow-up recommendations for middle grades educators and policymakers who are making changes in middle grades education on the basis of research.

Jackson, Anthony, and Gayle Davis. 2000. *Turning Points 2000: Educating Adolescents in the 21st Century.* New York: Teachers College.

The lead author of the Carnegie Council's previous seminal report, Jackson, with Davis, synthesizes the major lessons learned by middle grades teachers and administrators who attempted to implement the Carnegie recommendations across a decade.

National Middle School Association. 1995. *This We Believe.* Columbus, OH: National Middle School Association.

This is the national association's position paper on best-practice developmentally appropriate middle grades education.

JOURNALS AND NEWSLETTERS

Rather than cite specific articles under the respective topics, it is more helpful to note the journals devoted specifically to the research of young adolescent education, development, and growth.

The Family Connection is produced periodically by the National Middle School Association as a service to principals and assistant principals.

The information provided can be copied and inserted into school and parent communications and newsletters.

Middle Ground is published four times a year and is more directly aimed at middle grades classroom teachers. It includes instructional tips and strategies, news to use, tips on integrating technology, and specific projects that successful schools are engaged in.

Middle Matters Online enjoyed its first issue in November 2002. It is a newsletter for middle level educators that shares projects and ideas that can be easily implemented in the classroom.

Middle School Journal is the journal of the National Middle School Association. Edited by middle grades expert Tom Erb, it is printed five times a year and covers a wide variety of practical issues that confront the classroom teacher, administrator, and student as well as the researcher.

Research in Middle Level Education Quarterly, which is published three times a year, presents research data regarding middle grades educational policy, practice, and philosophy.

Target is the National Middle School Association's one-page newsletter that carries a message from the president and news and notes regarding the latest resources, institutes, and workshops.

SELECTED NONPRINT RESOURCES

Web Sites

The Middle Web Index
http://www.middleweb.com
Middle Web offers links to material on middle grades curriculum and instruction; assessment and evaluation; the professional development of teachers, parents, and the public; standards-based school reform; and students and school life.

National Middle School Association (NMSA)
http://www.nmsa.org

NMSA offers a variety of print and nonprint materials on-line and for purchase. The web site carries full press releases, research articles, position papers, calls for research papers, headlines, and hot issues as well as information regarding resources, a full on-line bookstore, and notices of workshops, conferences, and professional development.

Databases

Children's Defense Fund (CDF)
http://www.childrensdefense.org
CDF has a national headquarters in Washington, D.C.; regional offices in California, Colorado, Minnesota, Mississippi, New York, Ohio, South Carolina, Tennessee, and Texas; and an affiliate, Stand for Children, in Washington, D.C. This web site has a CDF listserv; links to similar organizations; publications, news, and reports, all of which can be downloaded free of charge; and a job opportunity databank.

Videotapes

Becoming a Multiple Intelligences School. 2000.

In this fifteen-minute tape, Thomas Hoerr looks at New City School in St. Louis, Missouri, and explains what led him to adapt the curriculum, instruction, and assessment to the theory of multiple intelligences.

Available through: Association for Supervision and Curriculum Development, 1703 N. Beauregard St., Alexandria, VA 22311-1714; (800) 933-2723; email: info@ascd.org; Internet: www.ascd.org (ASCD members $79; nonmembers $95).

Developing the Gifts and Talents of All Students: The Schoolwide Enrichment Model. 1999.

Acclaimed expert in gifted and talented education Joseph Renzulli explains his Schoolwide Enrichment Model. He shares a hands-on approach to three interrelated types of enrichment, specific strategies for modifying and differentiating the curriculum, the high standards and advanced levels of academic challenge that replace the low-level drill and practice methods, and finally a total talent portfolio that focuses on student strengths in academic areas.

Available through: National Professional Resources, Inc.; 25 South Regent Street, Port Chester, NY 10573; (800) 453-7461.

How to Engage Students in Critical Thinking. 2000.

This fifteen-minute videotape presents practical ways of establishing a classroom environment that cultivates critical thinking. The tape addresses how to plan and prepare for critical thinking, how to foster the use of critical thinking in all students, and how to help students reflect and apply their critical thinking skills.

Available through: Association for Supervision and Curriculum Development, 1703 N. Beauregard St., Alexandria, VA 22311-1714; (800) 933-2723; email: info@ascd.org; Internet: www.ascd.org; (ASCD members $79; nonmembers $95).

How to Organize Student Learning Groups. 2000.

This fifteen-minute tape examines different ways of grouping students. Classroom teachers share their experiences in how to use mastery groups to help students learn, how to use cooperative learning, and how to problem solve in groups.

Available through: Association for Supervision and Curriculum Development, 1703 N. Beauregard St., Alexandria, VA 22311-1714; (800) 933-2723; email: info@ascd.org; Internet: www.ascd.org (ASCD members $79; nonmembers $95).

Multiple Intelligences in Action: Tuning in the Learner: MI in the Middle and High School Grades. 1995.

David Lazear presents vignettes of teachers, administrators, students, and parents involved in multiple intelligences (MI) at all levels. He presents an MI classroom in action and offers practical examples on how to create lesson plans, curriculum, and assessments that honor all learning preferences.

Available through: Zephyr Press, P.O. Box 66006, Tucson, AZ 85728-6006; (520) 322-5090.

Problem-Based Learning. 1997.

This two-tape set with a facilitator's guide examines the principles of problem-based learning and the steps necessary in designing problem-based units.

Available through: Association for Supervision and Curriculum Development, 1703 N. Beauregard St., Alexandria, VA 22311-1714; (800) 933-

2723; email: info@ascd.org; Internet: www.ascd.org (ASCD members $396; nonmembers $466).

Video Sets

The following 1997 video sets from the Association for Supervision and Curriculum Development provide a series of taped classroom sessions, interviews with teachers, and examples of instructional strategies appropriate to each of the topics:

At Work in the Differentiated Classroom

This series includes three tapes with a facilitator's guide that takes a deeper look at differentiation, its methods and implementation. The tapes address planning curriculum and instruction, managing the classroom, and teaching for learner success.

(ASCD members $180; nonmembers $210)

Educating Everybody's Children

This is a six-tape series with a facilitator's guide that shows how teachers can set high expectations for all students, honor students' cultural differences, create classroom environments that celebrate diverse learning preferences, and motivate students through the use of a variety of instructional strategies.

(Six twenty- to twenty-five-minute videotapes and two Facilitator's Guides. Entire series $820 for ASCD members, $1,040 for nonmembers; individual tapes $180 ASCD members, $220 nonmembers)

Teaching Students with Learning Disabilities in the Regular Classroom

This two-tape series gives classroom teachers some further working tools and techniques they need to help students with learning disabilities achieve at high levels. The tapes address adjusting for learner needs and using learning strategies.

(ASCD members $495; nonmembers $595)

Inquiry Kits

The following inquiry kits from the Association for Supervision and Curriculum are multimedia presentations of activities, research articles, video clips, and instructional strategies on various topics. The kits are available through: Association for Supervision and Curriculum Development, 1703 N. Beauregard St., Alexandria, VA 22311-1714; (800) 933-2723; e-mail: info@ascd.org; Internet: www.ascd.org.

Assessing Student Performance. 1996.
Developed by Judith Arter, the kit includes video segments that show performance assessments, hands-on assessments for high-quality tasks, and examples of student portfolios, rubrics, and exhibitions. ($189 ASCD members; $220 nonmembers)

Constructivism. 1997.
Developed by Jacqueline Grennon Brooks and Martin Brooks, this is a multimedia kit about why school experiences should provide students with opportunities to build knowledge through searching through their own patterns of learning and problem solving. (ASCD members $189; nonmembers $220)

Differentiating Instruction in the Mixed-Ability Classroom. 1997.
This comprehensive look at the mixed-ability classroom includes detailed instructions for implementing differentiated instruction, video clips of classrooms in which differentiation has been successfully implemented, readings, and activity sheets for staff development. This is the most complete collection of Carol Ann Tomlinson's seminal work on challenging all students in mixed-ability classrooms. (ASCD members $189; nonmembers $220)

Promoting Learning through Student Data. 1999.
Developed by Marian Leibowitz, this multimedia kit of classroom video clips, learning activities, and examples helps teachers learn how data can be turned into meaningful ways to improve practice. The tapes and activities provide methods for identifying and analyzing problems, tools and techniques for interpreting data, and strategies for recording and reporting student progress. (ASCD members $189; nonmembers $220)

Appendix A:

❧ Robert's Rules of Order

ROBERT'S RULES OF ORDER: STUDENTS' ABRIDGED VERSION

Speaking during a Meeting

Any person who wishes to speak during a class meeting must be recognized by the president of the class before speaking. Speaking out of turn may cause you to be out of order and will cost you your opportunity to speak. This rule is not to prevent anyone from talking, but rather to allow more people to be involved.

Making a Motion

When any person in the class wishes to place an item of discussion up for a vote, they must make a motion. There are several reasons to vote in a classroom meeting.

- I move to have the class participate in a Christmas fundraiser to support the Make-a-Wish foundation. (This is used to take action on an item being talked about.)
- I move to amend the motion above to include Hanukkah and Kwanzaa in the holiday fundraiser to support the Make-a-Wish foundation. (This is used to change a motion that has already been made.)
- I move to end discussion. (This is used to stop any discussion of a topic.)
- I move to table this item of discussion. (This is used to move the item being talked about to a later time or later meeting.)

- I move to suspend the rules. (This is used when it might be necessary to have a discussion without the requirement to use motions and wait for the president to call on each person to speak.)
- I move to recess. (This is used to take a break during the meeting for small group discussion, individual activities, or other need for a few minutes. This does not mean it is time to go outside and play.)
- I move to adjourn. (This is used to end a meeting.)

President's Powers

- The president of the class runs the meeting.
- He or she has the power to recognize speakers and to move on to other items on the agenda.
- He or she does NOT have the power to end discussion or to cut off any recognized speaker unless the speaker is speaking inappropriately.
- The president may tell speakers who have not been recognized that they are out of order and that they must stop speaking and sit down.
- The president counts votes after a motion has been made. The president may vote on a motion.
- The president may offer his or her opinion on an issue on the floor, but cannot use his or her power to allow only one side of an issue to be discussed.
- The president brings the meeting to order, keeps the class on the agenda, quiets discussion when needed, and adjourns the meeting after a motion has been made to adjourn.

Appendix B:

☙ Objectives from Curriculum Lessons

Cognitive

Students will:

- become familiar with the philosophy of service learning
- document personal growth
- brainstorm a relevant concern of the group
- use speaking and listening skills
- analyze a realistic problem and solution situation
- use research skills to obtain information on a designated topic
- take notes from the research
- complete a "What I Know/What I Want to Know/What I Learned" diagram
- learn to write survey questions
- graph the information they find
- choose a fiction piece of literature with a theme that corresponds to the chosen concern
- make predictions based on prior knowledge and experiences
- compare and contrast their book to our service learning experience
- write about a meaningful experience that relates to our chosen concern
- experience the writing process
- complete an outline using research materials
- write about their choices of reflection

Affective

Students will:

- interact in a meaningful way

- construct meaning in a thoughtful manner
- be open to others' opinions
- work cooperatively in a team environment
- illustrate positive and negative communication
- reflect about a book in their journal
- establish meaning through personal expression
- select a poem or song that connects thematically with their chosen book
- share their writing
- select reflection pieces and organize them in a meaningful way

Psychomotor

Students will:

- move around the room
- participate in role-playing activities with team members
- conduct a survey
- create and display related artwork
- present material to others
- effectively communicate with an audience using persuasion
- display their portfolios

MICHIGAN CONTENT STANDARDS AND BENCHMARKS ADDRESSED IN THIS CURRICULUM

Language Arts

CS 2: Demonstrate the ability to write clear and grammatically correct sentences, paragraphs, and compositions.

B3: Plan and draft texts, and revise and edit their own writing, and help others revise and edit their own writing, and help others revise and edit their texts in such areas as content, perspective, and effect.

CS 3: Focus on meaning and communciation as they listen, speak, view, read, and write in personal, social, occupational, and civic contexts.

B4: Practice verbal and nonverbal strategies that enhance understanding of spoken messages and promote effective listening behaviors.

CS 4: Use the English language effectively.

B5: Recognize and use levels of discourse appropriate for varied contexts, purposes, and audiences, including ternminology specific to a particular field.

CS 5: Read and analyze a wide variety of classic and contemporary literature and other texts to seek information, ideas, enjoyment, and understanding of their individuality, our common heritage and common humanity, and the rich diversity in our society.

B3: Identify and discuss how the tensions among characters, communities, themes, and issues in literature and other texts are related to one's own experience.

CS 6: Learn to communicate information accurately and demonstrate their expressive abilities by creating oral, written, and visual texts that enlighten and engage an audience.

B2: Demonstrate their ability to use different voices in oral and written communciation to persuage, inform, entertain, and inspire their audiences.

CS 10: Apply knowledge, ideas, and issues drawn from texts to their lives and the lives of others.

B2: Perform the daily functions of a literate individual.

B3: Use oral, written, and visual texts to identify and research issues of importance that confront adolescents, their community, their nation, and the world.

CS 11: Define and investigate important issues and problems using a variety of resources, including technology, to explore and create texts.

B1: Generate questions about important issues that affect them or topics about which they are curious; narrow the questions to a clear focus; and create a thesis or hypothesis.

B3: Organize, analyze, and synthesize information to draw conclusions and implications based on their investigation of an issue or problem.

CS 12: Develop and apply personal, shared, and academic criteria for the enjoyment, appreciation, and for evaluation of their own and others' oral, written, and visual texts.

B4: Create a collection of personal work based on individual, shared, and academic standards, reflecting on the merit of each selection.

Social Studies

Public Discourse and Decisionmaking

CS 1: State an issue clearly as a question of public policy, trace the origins of the issue, analyze various perspectives people bring to the issue, and evaluate possible ways to resolve the issue.

B3: Explain how culture and experience shape positions that people take on an issue.

CS 2: Engage their peers in constructive conversation about matters of public concern by clarifying issues, considering opposing views, applying democratic values, anticipating consequences, and working toward making decisions.

B1: Engage each other in conversations that attempt to clarify and resolve national and international policy issues.

Citizen Involvement

CS 1: Consider the effects of an individual's actions on other people, how one acts in accordance with the rule of law, and how one acts in a virtuous and ethically responsible way as a member of society.

B2: Engage in activities intended to contribute to solving a national or international problem they have studied.

Inquiry

CS 2: Conduct investigations by formulating a clear statement of a question, gathering and organizing information from a variety of sources, analyzing and interpreting information, formulating and testing hypotheses, reporting results both orally and in writing, and making use of appropriate technology.

B2: Gather and analyze information using appropriate information technologies to answer the question posed.

Mathematics

Data Analysis and Statistics

CS 1: Collect and explore data, organize data into a useful form, and develop skill in representing and reading data displayed in different formats.

B1: Collect and explore data through observation, measurements, surveys, sampling techniques, and simulations.

B2: Organize data using tables, charts, graphs, spreadsheets, and databases.

Science

Construct New Scientific and Personal Knowledge

CS 1: Ask questions that help them learn about the world; design and conduct investigations using appropriate methodology and technology; learn from books and other sources of information; communicate their findings using appropriate technology; and reconstruct previously learned knowledge.

B5: Use sources of information to help solve problems.

B6: Write and follow procedures in the form of step-by-step instructions, recipes, formulas, flow diagrams, and sketches.

Arts Education

Theater

CS 1: Apply skills and knowledge to perform in the arts.

B27: Be involved in the process and presentation of a final product or exhibit.

CS 2: Apply skills and knowledge to create in the arts.

B13: Individually and in groups, create characters, environments, and actions that create tensions and suspense.

CS 5: Recognize, analyze, and describe connections among the arts; between the arts and other disciplines; between the arts and everyday life.

B8: Describe ways in which the principles and subject matter of other disciplines are related to music.

B17: Describe ways in which the principles and subject matter of other disciplines taught in the school are interrelated with the visual arts.

Visual Arts

CS 1: Apply skills and knowledge to perform in the arts.

B24: Select materials, techniques, media technology, and processes to achieve desired effects.

B25: Use art materials and tools safely and responsibly to communicate experiences and ideas.

B26: Select and use the visual characteristics and organizational principles of art to communicate ideas.

B27: Be involved in the process and presentation of a final product or exhibit.

> *It is important to note that since the culminating activity will be different for every class of students, additional Michigan Content Standards and Benchmarks could be incorporated (especially those directed toward science).*

MULTIPLE INTELLIGENCES ADDRESSED IN THIS CURRICULUM

Visual/Spatial
Logical/Mathematical
Verbal/Linguistic
Musical/Rhythmic
Bodily/Kinesthetic
Interpersonal/Social
Intrapersonal/Introspective

PRIOR KNOWLEDGE ASSUMPTIONS

Language Arts

1. The writing process
2. Basic grammar rules
3. Paragraph structure including a topic sentence
4. General use of a computer
5. Outlining
6. Speaking and listening techniques
7. Media Center research techniques
8. Appropriate grade reading level
9. Holistic rubric scoring

Math

1. General graphing exercises
2. Figuring percents
3. Use of graphing tools
4. Basic operations
5. Calculator skills
6. Holistic rubric scoring

Social Studies

1. Core democratic values
2. Communication skills
3. Basic investigation skills
4. Internet access capabilities
5. Speaking and listening techniques
6. Holistic rubric scoring

Science

1. Basic investigation skills
2. Reading graphs and tables
3. Following step-by-step instructions
4. Writing skills
5. Holistic rubric scoring

SUMMARY OF CULMINATING ACTIVITY

All of the tasks in this curriculum lead to a culminating activity, the service learning experience that will be the goal the students will focus upon. The activity is devised by the students at the beginning of the class. Therefore, the activity may be different each time the class is taught. The activity must somehow address a problem of the community (whether it be the school community or the town) that is real to the students involved. The activity must include a form of service, yet be connected to curricular activities as well. At the end of the class, students will celebrate their accomplishment with a reception. Invited will be anyone involved with the culminating activity—students, teachers, parents, community members, and organizations

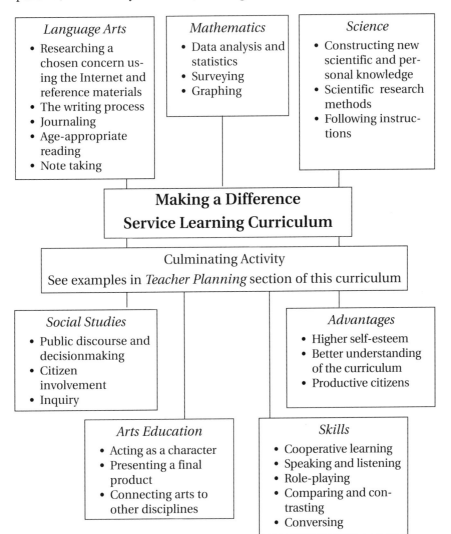

CALENDAR

Week 1	Week 2	Week 3	Week 4	Week 5
Day 1 Pre-Reflection	Day 6 Addressing the Concern	Day 11 Literature 1	Day 16 Research	Day 21 Surveying & Graphing
Day 2 Journaling	Day 7 Role-Playing	Day 12 Research	Day 17 Research	Day 22 Surveying & Graphing
Day 3 Addressing the Concern	Day 8 Role-Playing	Day 13 Research	Day 18 Literature 2	Day 23 Surveying & Graphing
Day 4 Addressing the Concern	Day 9 Literature 1	Day 14 Research	Day 19 Guest Speaker	Day 24 Surveying & Graphing
Day 5 Reflection	Day 10 Reflection	Day 15 Reflection	Day 20 Reflection	Day 25 Reflection

Week 6	Week 7	Week 8	Week 9	Week 10
Day 26 Literature 3	Day 31 Literature 4	Day 36 Speech	Day 41 Speech	Day 46 Portfolio
Day 27 Literature 3	Day 32 Literature 4	Day 37 Speech	Day 42 Culminating Activity	Day 47 Portfolio
Day 28 Plan Activity	Day 33 Literature 4	Day 38 Speech	Day 43 Plan Celebration	Day 48 Portfolio
Day 29 Literature 4	Day 34 Literature 4	Day 39 Speech	Day 44 Rehearse Celebration	Day 49 Celebration
Day 30 Reflection	Day 35 Reflection	Day 40 Reflection	Day 45 Reflection	Day 50 Reflection

❧ Index

⚡ About the Editor

Pat Williams-Boyd is associate professor of education and director of Middle Vision: Associates for Dynamic Middle Level Education at Eastern Michigan University. She has received numerous scholarships, grants, and awards, including teacher of the year, during her twenty-eight years of public school teaching and during her seven years in higher education. Williams-Boyd holds a doctorate in ethnomusicology and a doctorate in curriculum and instruction. Her publications and presentations address issues such as educational leadership, poverty and full-service schools, qualitative research, critical thinking, and excellence in middle grades teaching and learning. She has been an invited speaker throughout the United States and Europe and an invited professional development coach who intensively works with K–12 and particularly middle grades as they embrace best practices on behalf of all students.